GUNBOATS, MUSKETS, AND TORPEDOES

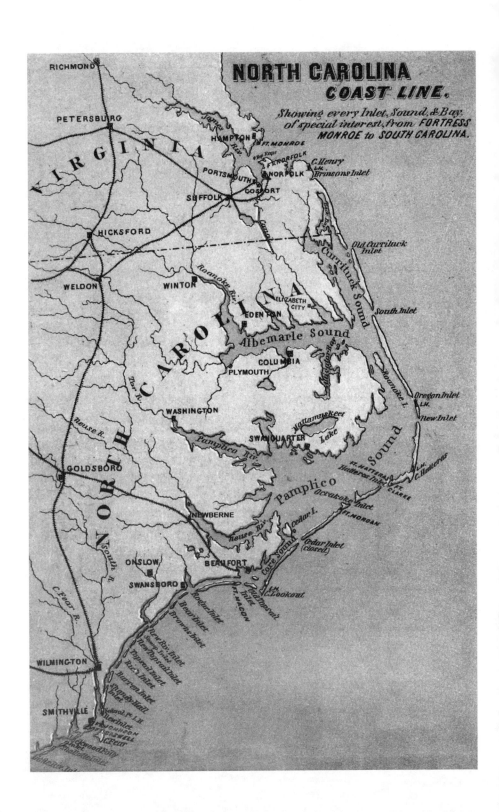

GUNBOATS, MUSKETS, AND TORPEDOES

Coastal North Carolina, 1861-1865

Michael G. Laramie

WESTHOLME
Yardley

Westholme Publishing, LLC
904 Edgewood Road
Yardley, Pennsylvania 19067
Visit our Web site at www.westholmepublishing.com

ISBN: 978-1-59416-336-4
Also available as an eBook.

Printed in the United States of America.

For my Aunt Penny and my Uncle Dan

CONTENTS

Introduction

THE AMERICAN CIVIL WAR OFFERED numerous examples of coastal warfare. Given the nature of this conflict where the North possessed a clear naval superiority over the South, two of the major components of this warfare, blockading and amphibious operations, came to the forefront. These operations were conducted from Virginia to Texas, and along the banks and tributaries of the Mississippi River, often with a devastating effect. The three-hundred-mile seacoast of North Carolina was no exception to this rule, but at the same time, it offered a unique set of challenges and opportunities to both Union and Confederate military planners. The first of these concerned the port of Wilmington. Given the South's dependency on foreign goods and materials to sustain the war effort, Wilmington, along with New Orleans, Mobile, and Charleston, would prove to be one of the most important ports in the Confederacy. The rail lines to South Carolina and Virginia passed through this location, allowing for the quick distribution of war materials and supplies to the Confederate forces in Virginia. The North Carolina port was guarded by a number of natural defenses at the mouth of the Cape Fear River, which restricted all incoming and outgoing traffic to two shallow inlets. The dual approaches to the river aided in its defense by forcing the Union to employ two widely separated fleets to cover these avenues. Coupled with poor weather that battered the blockaders cruising off the cape, and a series of forts, including the formidable Fort Fisher on Federal Point, Wilmington proved an ideal destination for blockade runners, and a source of frustration to the Union.

While the Union Navy struggled to maintain its blockade against Wilmington 150 miles away the interior waters of Pamlico and Albemarle Sounds offered a different opportunity. The sounds, sheltered behind the barrier islands and accessed through the narrow Hatteras Inlet, quickly magnified the state's tidal shoreline from a few hundred miles to a few thousand miles. Fed by several navigable rivers that reached deep into the interior, nearly a third of the state's agricultural products came from this region, and for much of the interior these waterways acted as a transportation hub, particularly the town of Newbern, which was connected to the railroad. It was quickly recognized by both sides that with a single guarded entrance at Hatteras, these inland waterways would offer a safe haven for a fleet of Confederate raiders and blockade runners, as well as a ready-made distribution network for their cargoes and plunder.

The threat was too great to ignore on the part of Union planners, and while simply seizing the Hatteras Inlet would blockade the sounds and deny the Confederates access to the sea, more enticing possibilities presented themselves. Asserting Union naval control over these interior waters would allow for the establishment of a beachhead and the reduction of the principle ports along the sounds. This foothold could then be expanded, and with the major rivers able to support small Union gunboats, the combined force could advance into the interior of North Carolina, opening another front against the Confederacy and threatening the vital north-south railroad line. Rightly suspecting that the enemy was ill-prepared to counter such an amphibious campaign, Federal forces struck in a bold early move that haunted the Confederacy and forced the latter into a series of costly campaigns in an attempt to break the Union stranglehold over the region.

Of course, as the first major conflict of the industrial age there was another important element to this equation—one that would echo through the future and shape conflicts to come. With the advent of steam propulsion, the telegraph, rifled cannon, repeating firearms, ironclads, and naval mines the lessons of littoral warfare were being rewritten in the dawn of the machine age. The methods of old soon faltered and fell to the wayside, and an entirely new set of tenets and principles evolved. The net effect along the coast of North Carolina was to create a fertile ground for the application of new technologies, new ideas, and even the revival of a very old one. The effect was felt ashore as well. At the most basic level the technology had a drastic effect. Men could fire farther and faster than ever before. Repeating pistols and carbines, a few designs of which were experimentally introduced before the conflict, flourished by the end of hostilities and had even led to the next technological step with the introduction of brass-cased cartridges. With rail transportation available, marches were no longer weeks but days or even hours, allowing commanders to quickly shift men and materials to meet an oncoming threat or exploit an enemy weakness. Fortifications changed to meet the challenges imposed by improved artillery, and the telegraph began being employed, which stretched the battlefield even farther.

Yet for all the technological changes, many of which would be harbingers of greater conflicts to come, the real story of this strategic coast is found in the words and actions of the Union and Confederate soldiers and sailors who vied for this region for nearly four years. It is here, where the choices made, whether good or bad, whether misinformed or not made at all, intersected with logistical hurdles, geography, valor, and fear to shape the conflict–a conflict that would ultimately culminate in the capture of one of the world's most powerful forts, the fall of the last major Confederate port, and the birth of a modern naval power.

The USS *Minnesota* as it appeared after the war. Known as a screw frigate, because its boilers ran twin screws at the stern of the vessel instead of paddlewheels, the *Minnesota* had been mothballed in the late 1850s, but was promptly recommissioned at the start of the Civil War. The vessel would prove to be one of the largest and most heavily armed warships employed during the conflict. (*NHHC*)

ONE

Plans and Privateers

NEITHER THE UNION NOR THE CONFEDERATE NAVIES were prepared when hostilities broke out on April 12, 1861, and both soon found themselves scrambling to marshal together their resources and formulate their plans. The Union Navy held a clear advantage over its fledgling opponent in terms of men and material. In all, there were forty-two vessels in the Union fleet, some twenty-six of which were steam powered. Although hardly a formidable force when compared to major European powers of the day, the Union fleet did possess a line of large steam-powered warships that, having been recently decommissioned, were quickly pressed back into service. The USS *Minnesota* was a notable example. Formerly a member of the US East India Squadron, the 3,300-ton 265-foot steam frigate was one of the most heavily armed Union warships of the conflict. By May 1861 it was armed with forty-seven guns, the main battery being thirty-six nine-inch smoothbore cannon protruding from the vessel's sides. This warship would soon not only demonstrate the advances in naval firepower but the deadly effect in which this could be employed when coupled with the maneuvering advantages brought about by steam power.[1]

The Union Navy also held a major advantage over its southern adversary in terms of experience. Over 80 percent of the naval officers on duty when the conflict erupted remained loyal to the Union cause, and the numbers were even higher among the 7,600 sailors and marines that manned and supported the fleet. This was supplemented by retired officers and volunteers from the merchant fleets and maritime communities that called the northern ports home, giving the North a large pool of experienced manpower to draw upon. Another advantage possessed by the Union Navy was its existing organization and logistics. While both would be tested by the challenges ahead, having an established system in place certainly simplified these tasks.[2]

More importantly, even with the loss of Norfolk to the Confederates early in the conflict, the North still possessed a host of ports from Philadelphia to Maine, capable of building ships. There were major dry dock facilities in New York and Boston and iron foundries across the North capable of manufacturing not only the guns needed for these new vessels but the steam engines and basic fixtures required as well. A prominent Boston shipbuilder, Donald McKay, perhaps best captured the North's advantages in this area, saying:

> Our capabilities and facilities for building ships have not in the least suffered by the loss of the seceded States. They never were ship-building States, and as late as 1860 they only built (combined) one full-rigged ship, while the Northern States built one hundred and ten ships of the same description. That is to say, in plain words, all the seceded States combined did not build even one per cent, of the seagoing ships built in the United States.[3]

There were also two other elements working in the Union Navy's favor. First, a plentiful and steady supply of coal was available, and second, the ports along the northern seaboard were open to trade, meaning that war shortages could be addressed through purchases from overseas. With these strategic advantages in place it was not a question of if the Union Navy would succeed in destroying the South's makeshift fleet and maritime commerce, but when.

The initial disparity in strength and the North's industrial might would dictate both navies approach toward the conflict. Given that the resource-starved South would never be able to win a naval arms race to contend for control of North American waters, there would be few if any fleet-level engagements between the belligerents. This left the North in the logical position of blockading Confederate ports. It was a traditional approach that possessed a number of merits. With naval command of southern coastal waters the Union could launch an amphibious assault at any point along this shoreline with little in the way of advance notice. This in turn meant that the South would be forced to employ huge numbers of men to guard a coastline that was simply too vast to defend. The tactic was also exponential in effect. As the Union ports were not at risk, vessels could be continually built to reinforce the blockade. In fact, as time progressed the facilities that constructed these vessels would become more efficient, leading to a steady increase in the number of warships available—all while the South's ability to penetrate the blockade was continually degraded and the number of ports available to them dwindled. Simply put, it was a war of attrition that the South could not hope to win.

While Union leaders agreed that this strategy would lead to victory, the real issue became one of application. The plan called for closing off almost three thousand miles of southern coastline, which was dotted with navigable rivers, bays, and inland waterways. To understand the scope of what would be required, the navy gathered together several prominent shipping merchants and asked their opinion on what would be required to blockade the enemy coast. The verdict was fifty sailing warships. The Union naval planners frowned at the report. First, because they knew the number was far too small, and second, because it was still more vessels than the Union Navy currently possessed. In fact, although the Union navy counted forty-two vessels on its rolls, almost half were sailing vessels which would be of very little help in intercepting and chasing down steamships. To make matters worse, much of the fleet was overseas when the conflict broke out, and it would not be until fall that the bulk of them would return to northern ports.

An aggressive naval construction program was laid out. Resources were gathered along the northern seaboard and orders placed, but as one Union official quickly pointed out, "Neither was there sufficient raw material in the country for the large and sudden demand; the iron, copper, tin, and coal had to be mined and manufactured. Hundreds of steamers, hundreds of locomotives, shops full of tools, tens of thousands of tons of metal were called for instantly, and there was nothing on hand to answer the call."[4]

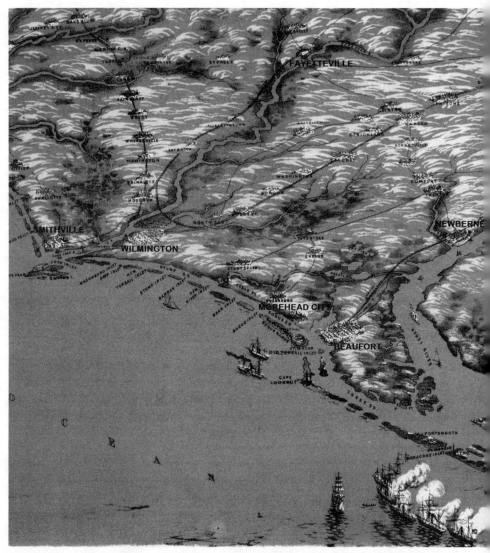

A map of the North Carolina and Virginia coasts from Norfolk to Cape Lookout. Note that the only practical access to the sea from the interior waterways of Albemarle and Pamlico Sounds, and the rivers that feed these waters, was via the narrow Hatteras Inlet or the even shallower Ocracoke Inlet. (*Library of Congress*)

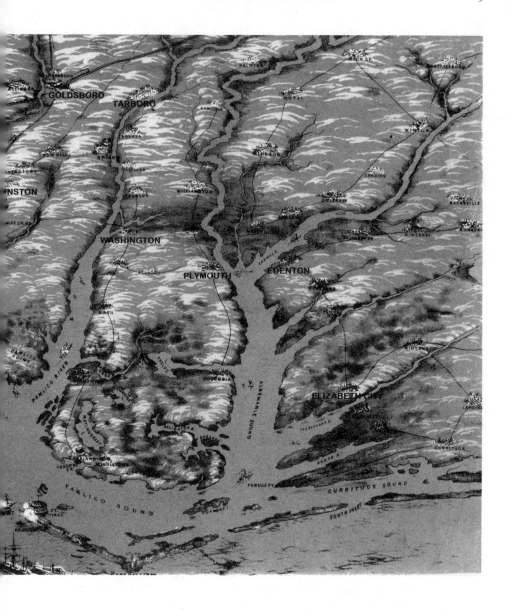

It would take a year for the northern naval yards to respond to the request for warships. In the meantime, the Union Navy had to resort to the same tactics as their opponent and convert merchant ships into warships. At least in this regard they had a large number of established maritime communities to draw upon. The problem, of course, is that commercial vessels were typically not built to withstand the rigors of military service and a good number of the vessels requisitioned were returned to their owners as unsuitable. The program, however, had its merits. Tucked within the harbors of the North was an array of modern steam vessels, some of which could be counted among the fastest in the world and large enough to carry formidable armament. By midsummer a few dozen of these vessels had been converted to warships and were either assigned to escort duties or were committed to blockade operations.[5]

While the challenges before the Union Navy were daunting, they were nothing compared to those before their Confederate counterpart. Beyond what had been captured at Federal naval facilities at Norfolk and points farther south, the Confederate Navy only existed on paper. On April 12, 1861, the South did not possess a single warship nor a single sailor under arms. The basic organization of the Confederate Navy would not exist for several months, meaning that each state was responsible for creating its own navy, which consisted of converting merchantmen into warships. As might be imagined this led to a haphazard effort which was further complicated by deficiencies in manpower, leadership, and the resources required to properly fit out the vessels. Even when the structure of the Confederate Navy was introduced combining the maritime resources of the various Confederate states, the step did little more than define the extent of the existing chaos. While the Union Navy was coming to grips with what it would take to blockade three thousand miles of coastline, the South faced the even more precarious task of defending these shores—a task that most realized could not be done.

As with the Union, the South's initial position dictated that they pursue a traditional path, that of a *guerre de course*, or a commerce raiding war. Unable to face the Union fleet on open waters, privateers and a handful of converted warships would be set loose upon the Northern merchant fleets. Not only would such efforts disrupt the enemy's commerce, but they would also tie down significant portions of their fleet in escort duties and in searching for the raiders. The second element of Southern naval strategy concerned breaking the Union naval blockade. Clearly the major Southern ports had to be held, not only to act as a shelter from which merchant raiders could be launched but to allow for blockade running activities which would be crucial to the overall war effort. In support of this activity a number of warships, and in particular emerging steam-powered ironclads, would be built. These vessels would support the harbor's defenses, challenge the blockaders, and when concentrated, assert temporary command of the local waters so as to allow for the exit and entry of blockade runners and commerce raiders. It was, of course, a doomed philosophy, as all nations who pursued this path would eventually understand, but given the circumstances there was really little choice. While some success might be scored against their stronger opponent it would only delay matters as the Northern fleet grew stronger every month while the South's maritime resources and trade slowly suffocated.[6]

As is customary in this type of naval David versus Goliath scenario, the early initiative was in the hands of the smaller opponent who did not require large amounts of organizational effort and time to put their plan into effect. It only took a few weeks for Southern ports to mount deck guns on commercial steamships and let them loose upon Northern shipping like a school of barracuda. Prominent in this effort were a number of privateers operating out of the waters of Pamlico Sound on North Carolina's Outer Banks. The sandbars and barrier islands of these coastal waters enclosed a 150-mile stretch of sounds, rivers, and inland waterways that reached from Cape Lookout in the south to the Virginia border in the north. These sheltered interior waters were protected by the fact that there were only two practical ways through the Outer Banks, and the deepest of which, the Hatteras channel, was restricted to vessels drawing seven and a half feet of water or less. More importantly, the process of navigating the Hatteras channel into Pamlico Sound was a slow affair, and with a pair of Confederate forts located nearby, a very risky proposition for any ship not flying the right colors. In all, it was a perfect breeding ground not only for mosquitoes but for privateers as well.[7]

One of the first Confederate raiders from this area to find success was the North Carolina naval vessel *Winslow*. Originally a side-

wheeled river steamer named the *Joseph E. Coffee*, the vessel was purchased and refit with a short thirty-two-pound cannon on a pivot
mount amid-ship by the North Carolina Navy in May 1861. Renamed
the *Winslow* and commanded by former US Navy lt. Thomas M.
Crossan, the 207-ton vessel manned by a few dozen sailors was about
to have a big impact on Union naval planning.

On May 12 the *Winslow* claimed its first victim, the brig *Lydia
Frances* which had run aground near Cape Hatteras. The following
month the *Winslow*, now armed with an additional six-pound rifled
cannon, would return to its privateering ways. On June 23 it captured
the 193-ton schooner *Transit* which was returning to New London,
Connecticut, after having delivered supplies and ammunition to Federal troops in the Florida Keys. A little less than a month later the
North Carolina raider captured its fifth vessel, the bark *Linwood*,
which was loaded with close to a hundred thousand bags of coffee.

The *Winslow*'s success ushered in a brief heyday for the Cape Hatteras raiders. The NCN *Gordon* followed quickly in the *Winslow*'s
footsteps. On July 25, 1861, the *Gordon* ran down the brig *William
McGilvery*, and by the end of the week two more prizes were in the
crew's hands. Together the *Winslow*, *Gordon*, and a handful of other
vessels played havoc with Northern commerce near Cape Hatteras
over the course of the summer, taking a dozen more vessels. It was
guerre de course at its finest. True, there were some losses. The raider
York for instance, was beached and burned by its crew after being
chased down by the USS *Union*, but such setbacks were more than
acceptable given the damage inflicted upon the enemy's commerce.[8]

Northern insurance companies soon complained to the secretary
of the navy, Gideon Welles. They pointed to their financial and material losses from the Cape Hatteras privateers and pleaded with the
secretary to take any action "by which this nest of pirates could be
broken up." Welles had also received letters on the subject from Union
naval officers. One from an officer aboard the USS *Cumberland* not
only agreed with the insurance companies but expanded on the point:

> Hatteras Inlet, a little south of Cape Hatteras light, seems their prin-
> cipal rendezvous. Here they have a fortification that protects them
> from assault. A lookout at the lighthouse proclaims the coast clear,
> and a merchantman in sight; they dash out and are back again in a

The sloop-of-war USS *Pawnee*. Launched in 1859 this steam driven warship and a handful of others bore the brunt of the Union's blockade efforts in the early stages of the war. (*NHHC*)

day with their prize. So long as these remain it will be impossible to entirely prevent their depredation, for they do not venture out when men-of-war are in sight; and, in the bad weather of the coming season, cruisers cannot always keep their stations off these inlets without great risk of going ashore.[9]

Another letter that arrived from Lt. Reigart Lowry of the USS *Pawnee* clearly laid out the case for an attack on Cape Hatteras followed by a campaign to seize the interior waterways behind it:

A simple inspection of the maps will convince the naval officer of the great advantages and facilities the enemy will have in possessing this vast internal water navigation unmolested, thereby having an egress and retreat to and from the sea for vessels loaded with provisions and munitions, and an easy harbor from prizes and captured goods taken out of prizes too heavy a draft to cross the inlet, or a safe refuge for privateers from our heavy ships of war. Already are their privateers preying upon our commerce, and from these very waters issue with impunity.[10]

The matter became the focus of a naval committee assembled in June to study the best paths toward implementing a blockade of the southern coastline. Early on the committee's attention had fallen on

Cape Hatteras and the interior waterways lying behind the barrier islands. The committee agreed with reports that the shallow waters and limited access through the Hatteras and Ocracoke Inlets made this area not only ideal for privateers but for blockade runners as well. This latter point, however, was perhaps even more important, as this region of North Carolina was known for its cotton and tobacco production. With easy access to these goods via interior waterways blockade runners could hide in the sheltered waters of Pamlico Sound waiting for an opportunity to run the Union blockade.

While seemingly a perfect haven for privateers and blockade runners the area's primary strength, its limited access via the Hatteras and Ocracoke Inlets, was also its greatest weakness. If an amphibious assault were to seize the Confederate forts that guarded these channels, the Union would successfully damage Confederate naval and commercial operations in one decisive stroke. In addition, it would establish a Northern foothold which could potentially be used as a launching pad into the interior portions of North Carolina, and perhaps even a backdoor to the Confederate facilities at Norfolk, Virginia.[11]

With ample reason to strike coupled with political pressure to do so, by midsummer Union naval planners had begun marshaling together resources for an assault on Cape Hatteras, and on August 14, 1861, orders were sent to Rear Admiral Silas Stringham, commander of the North Atlantic blockading squadron at Hampton Roads, to seize the Cape Hatteras batteries.[12]

TWO

The Great Southern Expedition

THE OPENING WEEKS OF THE CONFLICT brought a great deal of anxiety to military commanders in North Carolina, particularly when it came to the Outer Banks and the waters that it sheltered. The barrier islands that protected the interior waters of Pamlico and Albemarle Sound consisted of a long sandbar ranging from half a mile to three miles in width. Little lived on the windswept islands. Small fields of coarse grass and clusters of dwarf oaks were the only color along their sandy length beyond what items the surf cast upon their shores. Although there were several breaks in the islands only two allowed access to heavy vessels. The first of these, and the most frequently employed, was the Hatteras Inlet a few miles southwest of the cape. The second passage was farther southwest and was known as Orcacoke Inlet. The water here was only a few feet deep, effectively barring access to anything beyond small launches.

The interior waterways behind these protective inlets were vital to the Confederate cause. Several major rivers which originated in the interior of North Carolina such as the Roanoke, Tar, and Neuse emptied into Pamlico or Albemarle Sound, providing for easy transportation to and from the sea. To the north along Albemarle Sound a long canal had been cut from Elizabeth City through the Dismal Swamp which opened a water route to the Confederate naval base at Norfolk. Important towns such as Plymouth and Washington rested on the outlets of the Roanoke and Tar Rivers, and to the southwest on the Neuse River the strategic city of Newbern was connected to the interior through the Atlantic and North Carolina Railroad. This same rail line traveled south from Newbern to the coast and supplied the Confederate ports of Morehead City and Beaufort near Cape Lookout.

For a navy looking to pursue blockade running and commerce raiding the area was nearly perfect. Goods could be moved from the interior by water to the sounds where they would be loaded onto blockade runners. These vessels would in turn clear the inlet and then wait under the guns of a fort built at Cape Hatteras for an opportune moment to dash out to sea past the Union fleet. In the same vein, returning vessels would find an awaiting distribution system for their cargos and safe haven once they entered the shallow waters of Pamlico or Albemarle Sound.

The key to taking advantage of this "double coast" was to secure the two major inlets. At the urging of Brigadier General Walter Gwynn, a well-known railroad engineer and West Point graduate who had been appointed to command the Northern Department of the state's coastal defenses, orders were issued in late June 1861 to fortify the Ocracoke and Hatteras Inlets as well as reinforce Fort Macon, which guarded the entrance to Beaufort and Morehead City. While the orders spelled out building fortifications to secure the Hatteras and Ocracoke Inlets, what wasn't clear was where the troops and resources to do this would come from. The Confederate government donated a score of heavy cannons for Fort Macon and a few sites on the Neuse River but little else.[1]

When it came to the manpower needed to erect the defensive works along the coast, Gwynn appealed to the North Carolina public for help. "We are called on to defend our firesides and families against a stealthily encroaching and unscrupulous foe," the brigadier wrote. "Their obvious aim is to take all they can and to hold all they take. Then let all patriots do what they can to resist and repel such a foe." Citizens and their slaves that answered this call were to bring shovels, picks, and axes. More importantly, they needed to act now; "Delay is dangerous."[2]

Disorganized and short on resources, North Carolina built a small sand fort near the Ocracoke Inlet and then sank a hulk in the main channel to further secure the location. The main effort rightly focused on the Hatteras Inlet. Here two forts were raised. The first, and smaller of the two, was Fort Clark. This octagon-shaped earth fort was positioned at the seaside entrance of the inlet. Armed with seven heavy cannon and garrisoned by a few hundred men it was hardly an imposing structure. The second stronghold, known as Fort Hatteras, was located at the western end of the Hatteras passage. Like Fort Clark, Fort Hatteras was built by raising earth and sand walls, which were braced with wood. A parapet was fashioned and wooden firing platforms laid along the length of the walls. A pair of earth mounds were erected in the center of the fort, and bomb-proof shelters dug into them to provide shelter for the garrison as well as act as the fort's magazine. The remaining portions of the wall, as well as the magazine and bombproof mounds were then covered with blocks of sod. It was a traditional approach that left much to be desired. While such a fort could boast fifteen-foot thick walls the general construction guaranteed that this would not be the case for long. Water was the great enemy of such fortifications and given the storm-swept nature of the Outer Banks it would require a great deal of maintenance to ensure that the walls did not simply erode away.

When it was completed the square structure was approximately 250 feet to a side and had firing platforms built to handle fourteen heavy cannons recently hauled to the location from Newbern. Together with Fort Clark, the two structures provided a crossfire on any enemy vessel attempting to enter the inlet, leading Chief Engineer major W. Bevershaw Thompson to report on July 25, 1861, that "I now consider this inlet secure against any attempt of the enemy to enter it." His garrison, however, was too weak to repel an infantry attack on the landward approaches should the enemy put ashore farther up the island and march on the forts. "If we had three or four more infantry companies here," he wrote, "I should feel quite safe, even in that event."[3]

By the midsummer of 1861 the Hatteras Inlet appeared secured. The two forts which bristled with close to thirty heavy guns were garrisoned and ready. The reality, however, was much different. While earth forts were excellent defensive structures so long as they were maintained against the elements, the garrison, its guns, and its logistics proved the real vulnerabilities behind the position. Illness harkened by the weather and difficult living conditions took hold. Basic supplies never seemed to be keeping up with demand and storms pummeled the twin structures with wind, rain, and surf, further disrupting the supply lines and souring the garrison's mood.

General Gwynn who had been given command over the defenses of the Outer Banks and its interior waterways, faced three major problems. First, he was severely short of men and supplies. While North Carolina had answered the Confederate cause by raising close to two dozen infantry regiments, the bulk of these were immediately dispatched to Virginia, taking with them the best equipment and the most seasoned men. This left Gwynn with only the poorly armed and ill-equipped 7th North Carolina Regiment to guard the length of the barrier islands, Fort Macon, and key locations on Pamlico and Albemarle Sound. This lack of infantry left both Forts Clark and Hatteras vulnerable to an amphibious assault, which given the nature of the terrain, would quickly cut both forts off from relief.[4]

Another problem Gwynn faced concerned the smoothbore guns at Fort Hatteras and Fort Clark. While smoothbore cannons were far less accurate than their rifled counterparts, the real issue was one of range, and just as importantly, the numbers that could be brought to bear. In regard to this last element, it was clear that any attack would be supported by several Union warships, likely large frigate-class warships that carried a score of heavy guns. If even three such vessels were to appear with a landing force, the two strongholds that guarded the passage would quickly find themselves outgunned. Just as importantly, one of the fort's great vulnerabilities was that its guns were mounted *en barbette*, which provided no overhead cover for the gun crews against airbursts and the clouds of shrapnel they produced. Outgunned, and unable to effectively man their guns, an enemy landing seemed certain to succeed under such circumstances.

The last vulnerability with the Hatteras forts concerned logistics. There was nothing on Hatteras Island. Tools, materials, provisions, and even drinking water had to be transported to the fort, typically from Newbern almost a hundred miles away. This in turn meant that it might be several days before a relief force could even reach the forts, and once there they would likely have to run past the enemy's guns to reach the garrisons.

On July 10 the Union warship *Roanoke* conducted a reconnaissance of the Confederate positions at the Hatteras Inlet. The vessel steamed past the forts firing a few shots, which did little beyond alarm the garrison, and then made its way back out to sea. Beyond the flow of blockade runners and privateers towing their prizes, there was little else in the way of activity at Forts Clark and Hatteras. By late August Gwynn only had six hundred troops along the barrier islands, the bulk being at Hatteras Inlet with a few detachments monitoring the other inlets. The general had pleaded for more men, but along with his requests for more and larger cannon, it had been ignored.[5]

While life at the Hatteras forts slipped into the routine, farther north Fort Monroe and Hampton Roads buzzed with activity. Acting on his orders, Admiral Stringham had assembled several warships and troop transports for his expedition against Hatteras. Foremost among these was Stringham's flagship the forty-six-gun USS *Minnesota*. This vessel alone outgunned the Confederate batteries at Hatteras, but to put the matter beyond doubt the admiral assigned the steam frigates *Wabash* (45 guns), *Susquehanna* (17), *Pawnee* (15), *Monticello* (6), and *Harriet Lane* (5) to the expedition along with the sailing frigate *Cumberland* (24). The troops for the expedition consisted of 220 men from the 9th New York, 500 men from the 20th New York, 100 men from the Coast Guard, and 60 artillerymen from the US 2nd Artillery. These were supplemented by the marine detachments from the various warships and placed under the overall command of Major General Benjamin Butler. The transports *Adelaide*, *George Peabody*, and *Fanny* along with a number of schooners and supply vessels were contracted to carry the infantry and the small boats that would be used for landing.[6]

As this was the first major expedition against the Confederates, there was a good deal of excitement and anxiety as the flotilla put out to sea on August 26, 1861. By the following evening Stringham's squadron had dropped anchor just south of Cape Hatteras. Rough surf and heavy swells the next morning called the infantry landings into question, but it was agreed to press forward with the plan. After a quick breakfast, at 6:45 a.m. the order was given to commence land-

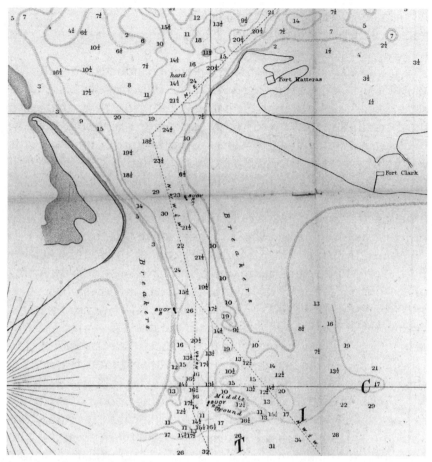

A portion of an 1862 chart of the Hatteras Inlet showing the location of Fort Hatteras and Fort Clark as well as the beginning of the channel into Pamlico Sound. From this point the water level would drop to 7 to 8 feet in depth. Note that the soundings are in feet. (*Library of Congress*)

ing operations. The warships *Pawnee, Monticello,* and *Harriet Lane* stood ready to support the effort with their guns, as the flotilla of whaleboats, surf-boats, and cutters took aboard their blue clad cargo. When this was completed the signal was given, and the first wave of Union troops advanced toward the shore around 10:30 under the cover fire of the nearby warships.

The point selected was about three miles north of Fort Clark. While there was no enemy resistance to contend with the sea proved just as trying an adversary. The flat-bottomed iron surf-boats, one of which was carrying a pair of field pieces, managed to make their way ashore, but with the weather deteriorating and the swells worsening none of the surf-boats could get back off the beach. The smaller vessels suffered far more. A number were swamped forcing their occupants into waist-deep water, while others were unceremoniously flung onto the shore or even capsized in the turbulent surf. Once ashore these vessels, like the surf-boats, were unable to return for the second wave of troops.[7]

As the soaked Union troops gathered themselves and their supplies together along the shoreline, farther south Admiral Stringham's warships were bearing down on Fort Clark. Led by the *Wabash* towing the sailing frigate *Cumberland* and followed by the frigate *Minnesota*, the trio steamed toward the sand fort in line ahead fashion with the *Susquehanna* following in the distance. While tradition called for Stringham to bring his ships to anchor in front of the fort to conduct his bombardment, the admiral chose instead to employ the naval merits of steam power. At 10 a.m. the order was given to commence fire. The port guns on the *Wabash* and the *Cumberland* flashed to life, followed by those on the *Minnesota*, as the vessels steamed past the Confederate fort. The *Susquehanna* soon joined the fray, adding its guns to the barrage. Once past Fort Clark the line wheeled 180 degrees and unleashed their starboard guns on the Confederate position as they steamed past in the opposite direction.

Stringham's vessels repeated these firing passes against the fort for the next few hours, each time changing their course and speed slightly to throw off the enemy gunners' aim. It was an effective tactic, and no doubt it diminished the damage inflicted by the fort's guns, but as it was the Confederate guns were operating at extreme range with their gunners reporting that many of their shots were falling short.[8]

While the Confederate guns were having difficulty finding their mark, the Union cannon were battering the recently erected fortress with explosive rounds, which one Confederate officer characterized as "a flood of shells." For the defenders of Fort Clark their seven-gun battery was simply unable to harm or dissuade the Northern warships. With shells and shrapnel raining down upon the earthworks, and reports of Union troops having landed to the north, Colonel William Martin ordered the fort abandoned. The guns were spiked and the garrison retreated to Fort Hatteras before a white flag was raised over the structure around 1:30 that afternoon.[9]

With a white flag flying over Fort Clark, and no flag flying over Fort Hatteras Stringham ordered the fleet to cease fire. A detachment of marines from the three hundred men who landed in the first wave advanced on Fort Clark and took possession of the structure shortly thereafter. A wind-swept lull fell over the area as the guns which had been thundering away for hours fell silent. A few hours later seeing little in the way of enemy activity, Stringham ordered Commander J.P. Gillis of the *Monticello* to take his vessel through the inlet. A pilot was put on board and the ship eased its way into the main channel. The captain and crew eyed the silent rebel fort half a mile away as the vessel crawled forward in search of deeper water, frequently touching bottom along the way.

The *Monticello* was approaching where the channel turns quickly to starboard when Fort Hatteras came to life. When Martin consolidated his forces at Fort Hatteras he realized that it was senseless and nothing more than a waste of ammunition to fire at the Union fleet which was simply too far way for his guns. Instead the fort would remain quiet in hopes that the Union fleet would creep within range. Now, as he watched the *Monticello* inch its way down the length of the inlet, Martin realized it was time to strike back. A series of flashes and rolling columns of smoke moved down the length of the fort's ramparts as its cannon concentrated on the nearby Union warship.

A pair of shots struck the Union warship sending forth a shower of splinters, and in one case, leaving the deck heaved up in a fractured line that reflected the rounds passage a few feet below. Gillis ordered his men to return fire as he attempted to extract the vessel from the narrow confines. For the next fifty minutes the captain and crew of the *Monticello* fought for their lives. In response to the Confederate guns which repeatedly struck the vessel or showered it with water from a string of near misses, the *Monticello* returned thirty shells which threw columns of sod and sand into the air or burst above the fort in a cloud of shrapnel.

Major Thomas Sparrow of the 10th North Carolina Artillery and his men were approaching Fort Hatteras onboard a flotilla of small boats led by the CSS *Ellis* and had a panoramic view of the duel between the *Monticello* and Fort Hatteras. "Part of the fleet were firing upon Fort Clark, and part upon Fort Hatteras, but the principal engagement seemed to be between Hatteras and the *Monticello*," Sparrow wrote. "We could trace every shot fired at the latter, and see every gun fired by her. Some fell to the right of her, but a number we could see went into her."[10]

Commander Gillis and his men were fortunate in that Stringham was quick to respond, signaling the rest of the fleet to engage. Soon it was difficult to even make out the fort as the clouds of dust and dirt from the explosions mixed with the smoke from the guns to create an artificial fog. In all it helped Gillis extricate the warship, but only after the vessel had been struck half a dozen times including one hit below the waterline. With the *Monticello* now freed Stringham gave the order to cease fire a little after 6 p.m. and the fleet moved off to anchor for the evening.[11]

While Fort Clark had been captured there was still plenty of apprehension on both sides. For Stringham and Butler the greatest concern was for the landing party. The admiral had ordered several of his smaller warships to stay close ashore for the evening to support these troops, but the reality of the situation was that these three hundred men were short on water and powder, most of the latter having been ruined or lost during the landing. If the Confederate garrison was large enough, or as reports were indicating, reinforced, the enemy might launch a night assault on Fort Clark and capture the landing force along with the works.[12]

For Colonel Martin and defenders of Fort Hatteras the situation was far worse. Fort Clark was captured and now occupied by enemy troops. Fort Hatteras had been deluged by shot and shell and there was little they could do in response given the range of the enemy's guns. Had Martin realized the precarious position the Union landing force was in, he might have used his garrison to counterattack, recapture Fort Clark, and deal the enemy expedition a serious blow. But the truth of the matter was that his men were too beleaguered and too rattled after being subject to a daylong artillery barrage to even make the attempt if he had known.

Nightfall brought good news. Close to 250 reinforcements arrived at the fort, and even better for Martin, the CSS *Winslow* pulled ashore not long after carrying Commodore Samuel Barron, the ranking naval officer in the region, and Major William Andrews, the commander of Forts Hatteras and Clark who had been at Newbern when the attack occurred. An exhausted Martin gladly handed command over to Commodore Barron, who, having served in the Federal Navy before the war, was more versed in fortifications and siege craft than either Martin or Andrews. Barron agreed to take command and quickly formulated a plan to attack Fort Clark. Before he left Newbern a regiment of North Carolina volunteers was preparing to embark to relieve the forts. If these troops arrived before daybreak, he would combine them with the garrison and retake the captured post.

The news traveled quickly and the troops inside the fort readied themselves for their comrades' arrival, but when the sun rose on the morning of August 29 no relief force was to be seen. Barron and his officers watched as the Union warships sailed toward the fort and then dropped anchor just out of range. Only a few of the fort's guns could even be brought to bear so the commodore ordered the other crews and the rest of the garrison into the bomb-proof shelters. At 7:40 a.m. the Federal warships, along with a three-gun battery that the landing force had erected overnight, opened fire.[13]

"A hailstorm," is how one Confederate defender recalled the ensuing barrage. A few of the fort's guns returned fire, but seeing their shots fall short, they were only used occasionally for the next few hours, more as a symbol of defiance than anything else. Having zeroed in on the stronghold and finding little in the way of opposition the fleet began a rapid fire on the structure. After a short time, the fort became obscured by dust and smoke, but it didn't matter. The guns were on target and simply needed to be fed. Over three thousand rounds were fired at Fort Hatteras over the next three hours, and according to one witness at the peak of the bombardment an explosive round was striking the structure every other second. For the defenders it was only a matter of time. When a round exploded on the top of a bomb-proof shelter, badly shaking and weakening the structure, and another (which proved to be a dud) plunged through a ventilator shaft into a second bomb-proof shelter, Barron had seen enough. At 11:30 he ordered a white flag raised and requested a parley to discuss surrender terms.

A few hours later Hatteras Inlet was officially in Union hands. It was a serious blow to the Confederacy, the consequences of which would soon ripple throughout the region. For the Union it was a stunning success. In fact, it was perhaps too stunning of a success. Butler's orders were to demolish the Confederate fortifications and withdraw, thus there had been no plan in place to exploit the capture of the enemy posts. This stopped the expedition in its tracks and, in the mind of Commander Stephen Rowan of the USS *Pawnee*, had undermined a golden opportunity. "The complete success of our arms at this place," he wrote the secretary of the navy Gideon Welles, "has produced a perfect panic in the counties on the Sound. Had we an organized force of smaller steamers we could, ere this, have destroyed a great portion of the commerce and been in possession of Roanoke Island, which is the key to Norfolk and Albemarle Sound."[14]

THREE

The Gathering Storm

HE CAPTURE OF THE CONFEDERATE BATTERIES at Hatteras was a badly needed victory for a Union that had seen nothing but setbacks from the start of the conflict. General Butler's original orders were to raze the Confederate defenses, but supported by Commodore Stringham he wisely refrained from doing so. Both men would leave immediately after the battle to press this point with their superiors, and a few days later orders were issued calling for the establishment of a Federal garrison at the forts.

For Fort Hatteras's new commander, Colonel Rush Hawkins of the 9th New York, one of the first orders of business was to secure and destroy the remaining Confederate posts on the barrier islands. News reached Hawkins and Commander Rowan of the *Pawnee* that the Confederates had abandoned the fort at Ocracoke Inlet. A small detachment of marines under Lt. James Maxwell was dispatched on the morning of September 5 to investigate. The force was towed to the site by the steam tugboat *Fanny* and landed before the fort in small boats. After examining the deserted post Maxwell complimented the structure's builders and some of the precautions they had taken. The retreating garrison had burned the gun platforms and carriages, but the cannon themselves, fourteen thirty-two pounders, and four eight-inch shell guns, were still in the fort. Three more eight-inch guns were found on the beach not far away near the fishing town of Portsmouth and were promptly disabled and tossed into the sea. The guns at Fort Ocracoke, however, proved more troublesome. After attempting to knock the trunnions off the guns with sledgehammers and dropping cannonballs on the guns from several heights with no success, Maxwell turned to firing "solid shot from a 64-pounder at them, and in this manner disabled them." When this was complete a small vessel being used as a lighthouse and everything that would burn in the fort was put to the torch before the expedition returned to Fort Hatteras.[1]

With the major inlets secured and news that the shallower inlets to the north had been abandoned, Hawkins and his men turned toward fortifying their position. Much of the fort needed to be rebuilt due to the damage wrought by the Union warships, but just as importantly, platforms had to be erected to allow the bulk of the garrison's guns to face Pamlico Sound instead of the sea. A platform was erected on the beach before the fort for a ten-inch columbiad to be manned by army personnel, and entrenchments dug nearby to support this position. The garrison consisting of some 1,800 men soon sympathized with the former owners as they faced the heat, sand, mosquitos, violent storms, and a complete dependence on supply from the sea for everything including drinking water.

For the Northern warships stationed nearby the next few weeks provided a slew of Confederate prizes. Not knowing that Fort Hatteras had been captured, half a dozen blockade runners fell into Union hands when they appeared before the cape. While this would be the case until word of the fort's capture reached all Confederate ports, a more pressing concern was the need for shallow draft warships to control Pamlico Sound. In addition there were rumors of a Confederate expedition gathering at Roanoke Island aimed at retaking Hatteras Inlet.[2]

In response to these reports in late September Hawkins dispatched Colonel William Brown and six hundred men of the 20th Indiana Regiment to secure Chicamacomico, a location near the northern end of Hatteras Island some forty miles from the Hatteras forts. The shallow draft steamers *Ceres* and *Pallas*, which had passed into Pamlico Sound, were loaded with men and supplies on the morning of Sep-

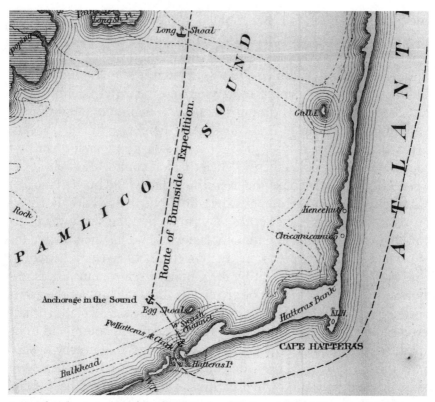

A map showing a portion of Pamlico Sound and Hatteras Island. (*Library of Congress*)

tember 29, and within a few hours had dropped anchor three miles from Chicamacomico, the water being too shallow to proceed any farther. Brown's men were transferred to small boats and sent ashore where they found the location deserted. As the Federal troops dried themselves and set up a defensive perimeter the problem became more one of supplies than the enemy. There had not been room on the two steamships for the regiment's supplies. These were to be brought up the next day by the *Fanny*, but when this vessel failed to appear Brown and his men began to worry.[3]

Only a few hours after Brown's troops made camp, on Roanoke Island Colonel Ambrose R. Wright of the recently arrived 3rd Georgia Volunteers, Colonel Henry Shaw of the 8th North Carolina, and Commodore William F. Lynch, the newly appointed senior Confederate naval officer in the region, listened intently to reports that Fed-

eral troops had landed at Chicamacomico. After hearing the information, the three men agreed that the
commodore should take several of his
small steamers to investigate.[4]

Lynch, a Virginian and former US
naval captain, had been appointed to
his new position with the capture of
Commodore Barron at Fort Hatteras.
He was a well-regarded officer known
for his daring and bravery. His experience with large naval guns, and artillery in general, would prove
invaluable to the Confederate forces
on Roanoke Island and throughout
the area. At the moment, however,
Lynch's primary responsibility lay
with the makeshift Confederate
flotilla that had been formed under
his predecessor.[5]

Commodore William Francis Lynch.
(*NHHC*)

The "Mosquito Fleet," as it became known, was actually born immediately after the declaration of hostilities when the state of North
Carolina purchased and commissioned the small side-wheeled
steamer NCSN *Winslow* to help secure its coastal waters and prey on
enemy commerce. The *Winslow* success prompted several additions
to the fleet. The first were the *Ellis* and *Beaufort*. Both were formerly
screw-driven steam tugs, built to ply the Dismal Swamp Canal from
Albemarle Sound to Norfolk and occasionally the shallow waters of
Pamlico Sound. The two vessels were approximately a hundred feet
in length, seventeen feet in beam, and a hundred tons in displacement, but more importantly both only drew six feet of water. The two
vessels were modified to accept a thirty-two-pound rifled cannon on
a forward pivot mount and a small howitzer astern, and each carried
a compliment of twenty-five to thirty-five men.[6]

Not long after its commission the *Beaufort* became involved in one
of the first naval engagements of the war when it sparred with the
much larger converted merchantman USS *Albatross* on July 22, 1861.
The Federal warship had just left Hampton Roads to patrol the North

Carolina coast when it encountered a pair of Confederate steamers at Oregon Inlet. The first steamer, the *Currituck,* was towing a schooner through the inlet while the second Confederate steamer, the *Beaufort,* lay closer partially obscured by the three-quarters-of-a-mile-wide sand spit known as Bodie's Island. Captain George Prentiss of the *Albatross* ordered his men to their stations and at a range of one and a half miles he opened fire on the *Beaufort* with his forward eight-inch gun. The Beaufort's thirty-two-pound gun returned fire, and for the next half hour the two sides exchanged errant shots. Prentiss finally shifted the *Albatross* farther south giving him a better look at the Confederate gunboat while at the same time preventing his opponent from bringing their forward gun to bear. When geysers of water began sprouting up around the Confederate vessel it became clear to Lt. R.C. Duvall and the crew of the *Beaufort* there was nothing to do at this point but retreat. After a few parting shots the *Albatross* steered out to sea, leaving both sides in the same position of having failed to score a single hit during the engagement. For the crew of the little *Beaufort,* however, it was a defiant victory.[7]

Another senior member of the Mosquito Fleet was the NCSN *Raleigh.* The *Raleigh* was a screw-driven tug some thirty tons smaller than the *Ellis* and *Beaufort.* It initially only had a small cannon or two for protection, which was considered acceptable at the time, as the vessel, like the other elements of the fleet, was employed more as an armed transport than a warship.

This small fleet was transferred over to the Confederate Navy a few months later. Not long after another addition to the fleet came in the form of the iron hulled side-wheeled steamer *Curlew.* Employed before the war as a well-known passenger liner on Albemarle Sound the 240-ton, 135-foot vessel had been commandeered at the start of the conflict and used as a troop transport. The *Curlew* was the largest and fastest ship in the flotilla, able to make twelve knots under full steam. Joining the flotilla around the same time as the *Curlew* was the *Forrest.* The *Forrest* began its life as a screw-propelled canal tug known as the *J.A. Smith.* Purchased in the early summer of 1861 the vessel's name was changed to the *Edwards.* The same basic size as the *Ellis* and *Beaufort,* the *Edwards* was armed in a similar fashion and was ordered to join the Mosquito Fleet in late July 1861. The *Edwards* had not been well maintained, and after a short cruise on the sound, its new Captain James W. Cooke complained that the vessel's boilers were unreliable and needed replacing as did many of the vessel's timbers which were rotting away. The *Edwards* returned to Norfolk in September via the Dismal Canal, and after being refit and renamed the *Forrest*, rejoined the Mosquito Fleet in early October.[8]

While Commodore Lynch had agreed to conduct a reconnaissance of the Union landing at Chicamacomico, there was a problem. Several of his vessels were not armed. The remainder of the day was spent rectifying this oversight, and by the morning of October 1 the *Raleigh*, *Curlew*, and the recently arrived small canal tug *Junaluska* had been modified to take on a thirty-two-pound rifled gun in a forward pivot mount and a small naval howitzer mounted astern. Of course, Lynch now needed men to operate the guns and act as marines. Colonel Wright assisted him in this matter by drafting soldiers out of the 7th North Carolina and 3rd Georgia Regiments, which only partially solved the problem given that most of these men had never fired a cannon before or been on a ship.

Lynch departed Roanoke Island around noon on October 3, his passage barely noticed by the two thousand or so grey-clad troops that toiled away at erecting gun batteries and field entrenchments across the island. When the task force approached Chicamacomico a few hours later cries rang out from the lookouts. As Lynch peered through his field glasses, he could not believe his luck. There a few miles in front of him was a small Federal steamer lying at anchor three miles offshore.

Loaded with supplies for the 20th Indiana the USS *Fanny* had been anchored off of Chicamacomico for three hours waiting for Colonel Brown's men to dispatch small boats. The lookouts and crew onboard the *Fanny* saw the approaching Confederate warships but later claimed that nothing had been done because the vessels identities were uncertain. This last part became more definitive when Lynch's amateur gunners began firing ranging shots as the distance closed to a mile and a half. As it was, the lack of earlier action doomed the Union gunboat and the confusing orders that followed only cemented the vessel's demise. When the first shots splashed nearby the *Fanny* raised anchor and began returning fire with its forward gun. The supplies were ordered to be thrown overboard along with a pair of rifled cannon destined for Brown's troops. Halfway through this operation, however, the order was countermanded. The enemy warship had fired seven or eight shots, and although their aim seemed poor fear was that it would greatly improve as the range closed. After moments of indecision and confusion it was finally agreed to run the gunboat aground and surrender.[9]

It was nothing short of a boon for the Confederate cause in the region and a victory for the Mosquito Fleet. The Union steamer was filled with goods; a pair of rifled cannon, a thousand overcoats, shoes, muskets, powder, shot, and tents. Over $100,000 worth of supplies had fallen into Lynch's hands, almost all of which could be immediately pressed into Confederate service. The *Fanny*'s crew of forty-nine were taken prisoner, and the undamaged steamer was casually pulled off the sandbank while Brown and his men watched helplessly from their vantage point a few miles away. The four vessels then set a course for Roanoke Island and disappeared into the twilight, leaving Brown with a sinking feeling in his stomach.

There was good reason for the colonel's anxiety. He was isolated and without supplies. Lynch was quick to point this out to Colonel Wright when he returned. The two men agreed that, if they acted quickly, they could land troops above and below the Union forces and crush them before any relief could arrive. Commanders and quartermasters were called together and orders passed for the bulk of the Georgia and North Carolina regiments to prepare for the expedition, which would take place the next night on the new moon.[10]

A few hours before midnight on October 4 some 1,500 anxious Confederate troops made their way down to the shore and slowly filtered aboard the awaiting flotilla which consisted of the gunboats *Raleigh*, *Curlew*, *Junaluska*, the newly captured *Fanny*, and the recently arrived transport steamers *Empire* and *Cotton Plant*. Around 1 a.m. the force left Roanoke Island and carefully proceeded down Croatan Sound. The agreed-upon plan called for two landings. The first detachment led by Lynch and Wright would land with seven hundred men above the Union troops, while a second detachment consisting of Colonel Shaw and his North Carolinians onboard the *Empire* would continue another two dozen miles farther south and conduct a landing opposite the Hatteras lighthouse.[11]

As the first rays of light touched the region, they revealed the odd-looking amphibious assault force; a jumbled assortment of converted

Colonel William Brown, left, of the 20th Indiana. (*Author*) Colonel Ambrose Wright, right, of the 3rd Georgia Volunteers. (*Confederate Memorial Literary Society*)

merchantmen gliding over the dark waters to the reassuring rhythm of their engines, their decks stuffed with grey-clad infantry. Towed behind these vessels was an array of small boats and barges that held the rest of the invasion force and their supplies. From shore Brown and his staff watched in disbelief as this flotilla inched its way toward them. About three miles from the shore Lynch's vessels halted when the water became too shallow and began deploying small boats full of troops. The *Cotton Plant* with Colonel Wright and three companies of the 3rd Georgia onboard was able to get a mile closer, giving Brown and his officers a better look at the cannon mounted on several of the small boats that were now approaching their position. As the scope of the enemy force became clear, Brown realized he had seen enough. Isolated, short on supplies, and now threatened with envelopment the colonel ordered a retreat down the island toward the Hatteras Lighthouse. Little did he realize how well his men would take to the task.

What followed next is known as the Chicamacomico Races. As Wright and his men struggled ashore, some wading for a mile and a half in knee-deep water, the 20th Indiana was busy marching to the south having abandoned its encampment and everything that could not be carried. When they came within range the six-inch howitzers on the landing craft opened fire on the retreating bluecoats, hastening their jittery flight. A few men broke formation and began to run. Brown's officers tried to calm the others, but it was too late. Panic ran through the formation like a zipper, and what was a retreat had now become a self-imposed rout.[12]

Wright organized his exhausted men as they came ashore, and when he had gathered together a sufficient number he set off in pursuit. While the colonel managed to capture a number of stragglers and skirmished with the rearguard he could not keep pace with the Federal column which was making excellent time even with the sandy nature of the terrain. Although frustrating, Wright realized that it didn't matter. If things went as planned Shaw's detachment was waiting for the fleeing Yankees near the Cape, meaning that they were now trapped.

Wright was correct. If things had gone as planned there is a good chance that the Confederates would have captured the 20th Indiana, but things did not go as planned. The *Empire* grounded on a sandbar half a dozen miles from the lighthouse, and when Shaw's troops tried to wade ashore, they found their way blocked by a series of deep channels forcing them to abandon the effort.

Brown and most of his men arrived at the Cape Hatteras Lighthouse around dusk with others still filtering in hours later. Here the colonel found not only the normal detachment assigned to protect the lighthouse but five hundred men of the 9th New York sent from Fort Hatteras by Colonel Hawkins. Supplies were landed and distributed from the nearby naval vessels while the Indiana officers struggled to reorganize their units. There were now close to 1,300 Federal troops encamped near the lighthouse, and almost to a man they expected a Confederate attack at sunrise.[13]

Wright and his exhausted men halted for the night at Kinakeet, a dozen miles from the Union lines. It was a cold night on the barren barrier island for the seven hundred or so Confederates, and they too, almost to a man, expected to attack the next morning. At daybreak this quickly changed when Wright was informed that Shaw had not been able to land his troops. The tables had now reversed, and Wright ordered his men back up the island to their boats. The USS *Monticello* spotted the Confederate column at a little after one o'clock and slipped closer to the island to bring its guns to bear. Pacing the enemy retreat the Union warship banged away with round shot, canister, and shell at the grey formation for the rest of the day, but to little effect as Wright and his men returned to their vessels and departed with "every man who started in the pursuit from Chicamacomico, except a member of the Governor Guards, who died from exhaustion."[14]

With the exception of a few dozen Union troops captured by Wright's men, nothing was accomplished on either side. It was truly a race with no winner. The one thing that did come out of the affair was a level of caution on both sides. With the fall storm season upon them and winter close behind both the Confederate and Union forces looked to consolidate their positions which led to a lull in the fighting. Soon the year passed quietly into the next, and although many may have wished otherwise, it would not remain this way for long.

FOUR

Burnside's Expedition

WITH THE APPOINTMENT OF General George McClellan as commander of the Union Army the waters of Pamlico and Albemarle Sound took on more importance. McClellan saw great potential in joint army and navy operations against the Confederate coast. First, it took advantage of Union naval superiority and a current lack of preparedness on the part of Southern forces. Second, it allowed for the rapid concentration of power at key points along the enemy coast. From here, Union forces could move into the interior before the enemy could concentrate against them, cutting telegraph and rail lines which further degraded their opponent's communications and logistical paths. While this approach would be tested on a grand scale with an attempt to seize Richmond that culminated in a Union defeat at the Seven Days Battle, the case of Pamlico and Albemarle Sound was to prove a first test of these principles, albeit, in a far more limited scope than the Peninsular Campaign.

While the opening moves of this approach, the seizure of the Hatteras Inlet, had been successful it would not be until the fall of 1861 that Union planners eyed Roanoke Island at the north end of Pamlico Sound as their next target. Possession of the island would give Federal forces control over Croatan Sound to the west, and thus, access into and out of Albemarle Sound. From here Union forces could control the outlets of several prominent rivers and control access to and from Norfolk through the Dismal Swamp Canal. Capturing the major towns along the sound would crush Confederate production and water transportation in the region as well as allow for staging points from which Union forces could strike into the interior looking to disrupt railway and water traffic. Were these advantages not enough, added to the decision-making process was rumors of Confederate ironclads being built in the area. Should a few of these be completed and successfully launched, Union naval control over the inland waterways would be in jeopardy, and with it, control of the Hatteras Inlet.

In early January Brigadier General Ambrose Burnside and Rear Admiral Lewis Goldsborough were given command of twelve thousand troops and a fleet of 120 vessels, including two dozen shallow draft warships, and ordered to expel the Confederate forces from Roanoke Island and advance into Albemarle Sound. It was a major expedition so early in the war, and one that tested Union logistics, but by January12, 1862, the troops had been embarked and the various elements of the expedition had departed for Cape Hatteras. The timing could not have been worse. The fact that the fleet of transports, supply vessels, and small warships set sail in the stormiest season for one of the most dangerous points on the Atlantic coast perhaps speaks more to the urgency of the operation than the choice of its timing. The bulk of the fleet arrived at the Hatteras Inlet just in time for a powerful several-day-long nor'easter that pounded the Carolina coast and threatened to bring a swift end to the expedition.[1]

To carry the troops and supplies a large number of merchant steamers were contracted throughout the Northern ports, and while the effort worked in general, many of the vessels were simply not up to the task and succumbed to the wind and waves. The canal boat *Grapeshot* carrying hay and oats floundered in the storm and had to be abandoned. The vessel was found driven ashore a dozen miles above the cape the next day. The old steamer *Pocahontas* carrying 113 horses for the artillery was next. The vessel's boiler was damaged followed by the steering gear. As the storm intensified the smokestack came down, and shortly thereafter the vessel went ashore losing much of its precious cargo in the process.

Corporal George Allen of the 4th Rhode Island Regiment gave a harrowing account of the storm onboard the steamer *Eastern Queen*.

> Our own steamer bravely bowed herself to the seas, which running to an enormous height, threatened with each succeeding wave to engulf us all in those awful depths. As she rose on the crest of a mighty wave and poised a moment, we would cast a hasty glance around us and see perhaps fifty sail of vessel, on all sides of us, and then plunging down, down, till it seemed as if we were really going to the bottom, another huge wave would roll up toward us, towering high above our decks, and our vessel would strike it, keel over almost on her beam ends and rise to its crest, and rolling over on the other side plunge down into the trough of the sea to rise again as before. Each time we lifted we could see sometimes a dozen, sometimes more sail of our fleet, who, like us, were rolling over the great seas.[2]

The gunboat *Zouave* was not as lucky as Allen's vessel. It slipped its anchor during the storm and had its bottom torn open in shallow waters before sinking. One of the more valuable transports to fall victim to the tempest was the *City of New York*. A large screw steamer carrying ordinance stores for the expedition, the vessel went aground near the entrance of the inlet early in the storm and over the remainder of the day slowly swung around to present its broadside to the sea. The breakers and heavy winds made it impossible to rescue the crew, so those onboard lashed themselves to the vessel for two days while the nor'easter slowly disassembled the craft. While the crew was eventually saved the cargo, which consisted of 400 barrels of powder, 1,500 rifles, 800 artillery shells, tents, and hand-grenades was a complete loss. On the second night of the storm, "We experienced on that night more discomfort and dread, if possible, than on the preceding one," Burnside wrote. "At times, it seemed as if the waves, which appeared to us mountain high, would engulf us, but then the little vessel would ride them and stagger forward in her course." All in all, the Union fleet was fortunate. A number of transports were grounded on the outer bar over the course of the storm only to have the fleet's tugs pull them to safety during a lull in the weather—an act that no doubt saved many vessels and their crews.[3]

With the damage from the storm tallied and tended to the weather-beaten fleet began the arduous task of navigating the Hat-

Rear Admiral Lewis Goldsborough, left. (*Hampton Roads Naval Museum*) General Ambrose Burnside, right. The two Union commanders would oversee one of the first successful joint operations of the war. (*Library of Congress*)

teras Inlet. Admiral Goldsborough's warships passed through the channel first and there they waited for the next several weeks as Burnside's transports navigated the passage. In most cases the transports had to be lightened to get through the shallow waterway, which meant a good deal of time not only to unload the vessels but to reload them again after their passage. For Goldsborough it was a frustrating delay. Had he not needed Burnside's troops to deal with the Confederate infantry on Roanoke Island he informed the secretary of the navy, he would have immediately sailed for the Confederate forts on the island and pounded them into submission.

As it was, the admiral would have to wait until January 31 for the last of the fleet to enter Pamlico Sound. There was one benefit from the delay, that being the amount of information reaching Goldsborough's fleet. "During our detention at the inlet," the admiral wrote, "we resorted to every means in our power to get accurate information of the enemy's positions and preparations, and we obtained enough to enable us to arrange our program of attack." The information reaching Goldsborough and Burnsides was essentially accurate, placing the enemy strength on the island at some two thousand men and forty to fifty guns. The enemy had constructed three forts along the west shore of Roanoke Island and placed a fourth across the northern portion of Croatan Sound on the mainland. Besides these strong-point reports indicated that perhaps half a dozen small Confederate gunboats would also be encountered, likely near the entrance to Albemarle Sound where they could be covered by the guns of the nearby Confederate forts.[4]

The plan was to land Burnside's troops on the central part of the island at Ashby's Harbor about two miles below the first Confederate fort. While the location certainly offered the best conditions for landing operations, nearby Sandy Point, if occupied by a Confederate battery, would make the entire venture questionable. Fortunately, there had been no signs of enemy defenses or activity in this area. Prior to and during the landing operations, the main elements of the fleet, now some sixteen warships strong, would press north and systematically engage the Confederate forts on Croatan Sound. Caught between the advancing Union army and the guns of the fleet the enemy forces on the island would be placed in a precarious position—one that would hopefully quickly force their surrender.[5]

Confederate forces were busy during the lull in late 1861. The forts at Cape Hatteras had fallen primarily because of lack of preparation on the part of the South, but in looking to change this approach the Confederate command encountered a problem. Unlike their Northern counterparts Southern resources in the area were quite limited. The entire military force along the North Carolina coast was just seven regiments, one battalion, and one light artillery battery. There were a good number of heavy naval guns sent from Norfolk to support this force but only a handful of gunners to operate these. In the Pamlico Sound region, there were far fewer troops to call upon, a pair of regiments at Roanoke Island, another pair at Newbern, and just five companies at Fort Macon. General Richard Gatlin in charge of the North Carolina coast pleaded with Richmond to send him at least twelve regiments, but the best he could get were a number of heavy naval guns that only a few individuals in his command even had an inkling of how to use.

With the loss of the Hatteras forts and the limited number of troops available there were almost too many possibilities to guard. Many saw Newbern as the next logical Union target. Seizing this location would not only isolate Beaufort and Morehead City by cutting the nearby railroad line, but it would bottle up traffic on the Neuse

River as well. Still others pointed to Beaufort near Cape Lookout as the next best location for a Northern expedition. The town was still a functioning seaport and available to raiders and blockade runners, which the Union Navy certainly wished to suppress. In addition, Fort Macon which defended the channel leading to Beaufort mounted only a handful of guns and was ill prepared to handle a siege. Lastly came Roanoke Island. Most Southern commanders recognized the benefits of capturing this position and the peril it would create should it fall. The entire Albemarle Sound and all the townships along the banks of this profitable waterway would be open to Union attack should the Confederates lose control of this location. Just as importantly, by seizing these waters the Union would cut communications to the Confederate naval base at Norfolk and possibly even pose a threat to this stronghold through the Dismal Swamp.[6]

In the end, without reinforcements there was little Gatlin could do but fortify each location as best as possible. At Roanoke Island the 3rd Georgia and 8th North Carolina Regiments along with a number of naval and artillery personnel were set to the task in the fall of 1861. The work proved grueling on the damp windswept island. A shortage of tools forced the garrison to work in three shifts. Earth redoubts were built by shovel and backbreaking labor before the firing platforms were laid down. Limbers had to be built for the heavy guns, but the terrain was such that even after this was accomplished some gun carriages proved so heavy that the horse teams couldn't move the guns into position. The Georgia troops showed an active spirit, but the same could not be said of the North Carolina troops. "The North Carolina troops that are here are in a state of disorganization," Wright confided to General Huger, "and but little can be expected from them."[7]

In the middle of October North Carolina native General D.H. Hill, who had been placed in command of the sector, reported on the condition of the island to the secretary of war:

Roanoke Island is the key of one-third of North Carolina, and whose occupancy by the enemy would enable him to reach the great railroad from Richmond to New Orleans; four additional regiments are absolutely indispensable to the protection of this island. The batteries also need four rifled cannon of heavy caliber. I would most earnestly call the attention of the most Honorable Secretary of War to the importance of this island. Its fall would as be fatal as that of Manassas.[8]

Unable to obtain any cannon or additional men for Roanoke Island, Hill set the troops to work on a series of earth fortifications, the most ambitious of which was a redoubt that stretched from shore to shore near the center of the island. For Richmond the general's report was moot. Hill's assessment might well be correct, but with a possible Union attack on a dozen coastal positions there were no troops to spare whether it was the case or not. The defenders of Roanoke Island would have to make do with what they had on hand, and as for Hill, he was soon assigned to a position in Virginia.

Command of the area now fell upon General Henry Wise, but instead of keeping this command under the control of General Richard Gatlin who oversaw the Department of North Carolina, it was assigned to General Benjamin Huger at Norfolk, Virginia. Huger was a solid military engineer but a dismal commander, being dubbed by one of his colleagues as "a barnacle on the Confederacy," and his fears of a Union assault on the heavily defended Norfolk controlled his thoughts to the point of obsession. Wise toured the ill-defended island and dispatched request after request to Huger for engineers, guns, and men. What he received shocked him. Huger, who commanded fifteen thousand idle troops at Norfolk, dismissed the reports coming from the politically appointed general, and replied that he had no men to spare. He then informed Wise that what he should be looking for was "hard work and coolness among the troops you do have, instead of more men." As if to reinforce this point, Huger then recalled Wise's best unit, the 3rd Georgia, without replacing it.[9]

A frustrated Wise appealed to the governor and carried his complaints to the secretary of war, Judah Benjamin, in Richmond. Benjamin viewed Wise's opinion and actions as those of an unexperienced upstart and dismissed him by saying that he would look into the matter. Good to his word, the secretary carried through with his promise by writing General Huger and throwing the problem back into his lap. The result was a set of orders to Wise telling him to stop bothering his superiors and to focus on the task at hand. At least something came from the efforts. The governor transferred the newly raised 31st North Carolina Regiment to the island to replace the veteran 3rd Georgia, and Huger granted Wise permission to use the

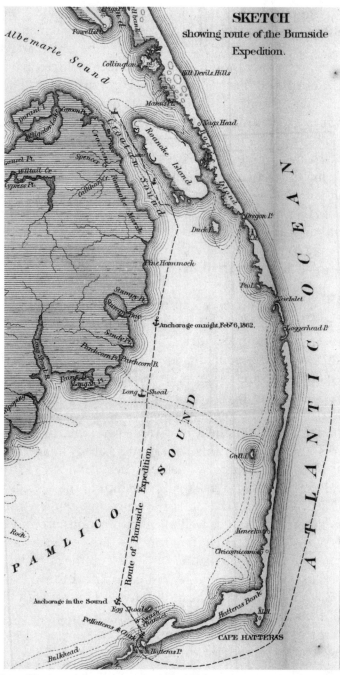

A map of Pamlico Sound from Hatteras inlet to Albemarle Sound showing Burnside's advance against Roanoke Island. (*Library of Congress*)

troops of his own Virginian legion, but efforts to forward the legion to Roanoke Island proceeded so slowly that only 450 men and none of the artillery had reached the island before the Union attacked.

In the intervening months Wise had erected three earthen forts along the northwest shore of the island, Fort Bartow, Fort Blanchard, and Fort Huger. To supplement this Fort Forrest, which was in reality nothing more than a makeshift redoubt made of old vessels filled with earth and braced with timber, was built on the mainland directly across Croatan Sound from Fort Huger. Together these positions could bring thirty-two heavy guns to bear against any Union vessels entering the nearby waters. In keeping with at least some of the elements of Hill's previous plans Wise also erected an eighty-foot-long earthen barricade across the only road that ran the length of the twelve-mile-long island. Here he placed a three-gun battery, the nature of which illustrates the disregard shown by Richmond and Huger toward the defenses of the island. The first piece was a twenty-four-pound howitzer, the next a captured eighteen-pounder from the Mexican-American War, and the last a six-pound gun that had formerly been used to fire salutes. The earth redoubt was flanked on both sides by wooden redoubts several hundred yards long that terminated in thick cypress swamps that the engineers, and even the native islanders, were of the unanimous opinion were "absolutely impenetrable." For the moment at least, it appeared Wise had created a position that would funnel Union troops into a narrow front before his works, and thereby nullify their numerical advantage.[10]

One of the few resources available to the defenders of Roanoke Island was the dozen or so makeshift warships of the Mosquito Fleet. Lynch's little fleet spent the fall of 1861 moving supplies, troops, and guns to Roanoke Island as well as other positions around Pamlico Sound. While Confederate forces continued to entrench at Roanoke Island, Wright and Lynch planned an attack on the rattled defenders of Fort Hatteras, but it would never materialize. Instead Lynch took the *Curlew* and elements of the Mosquito Fleet to spar with Fort Hatteras and some of the vessels in the anchorage in late October, but little came of the effort. More importantly, a few weeks later the *Winslow* struck a submerged wreck and sank. It was a blow to Lynch's little fleet, but fortunately several reinforcements had arrived which lessened the loss.

The first of these, the *Sea Bird*, was another pre-war passenger service side-wheeler taken into the Confederate cause. About the same size as the *Curlew*, the *Sea Bird* displaced almost forty tons less, giving it a shallower draught. With a crew of forty-two men the vessel was fitted out with a thirty-two-pound rifled cannon forward, and a thirty-two-pound cannon aft. When it arrived in Albemarle Sound via the canal in late 1861 Lynch quickly made it the fleet's flagship. The second vessel to arrive was the familiar canal tug *Empire*, which now bore the name *Appomattox*. Originally a member of the Virginia State Navy, the propeller-driven tug was roughly on par with the *Ellis* and *Beaufort* and had been recently armed in like manner before being renamed and dispatched to Lynch's fleet. The last ship to arrive was the 150-ton sailing schooner *Black Warrior*. Formerly the merchantman *M.C. Etheridge*, the *Black Warrior* carried a pair of smoothbore thirty-two-pound cannon, but these were primarily for defensive purposes. The sailing vessel's limited mobility in the shallow waters of the sound forced Lynch to use the craft as a tender rather than in an offensive role.[11]

The Mosquito Fleet and the defenses of Roanoke Island were soon to be tested. On February 5 the Union fleet consisting of nineteen warships and two-dozen army transports and smaller craft, steamed north. Progress was slow as the little fleet, strung out for over a mile, snaked its way toward the southern entrance to Croatan Sound. By sundown the flotilla had arrived off Stumpy Point some ten miles from the inlet. Here they dropped anchor for the evening. The next morning the gunboats *Ceres* and *Putnam* were sent ahead of the main columns. There had been worries that the enemy might have placed a battery of guns on the marshes, small islands in the center of the inlet through which the main navigation channel passed, but nothing was found. Although the way appeared clear, fog and rain hampered the fleet's movements. For a short period of time the weather cleared and the attackers could see the island, the enemy redoubts strung along the island's western coast, and the Mosquito Fleet anchored near the shore between Pork and Weirs Point. It was a momentary glimpse of what was to come for ninety minutes later the weather turned bad enough that the decision was made to drop anchor for the evening a few miles short of the inlet.

The Union troops checked their equipment and spent another restless night aboard the transports, convinced that if they saw the enemy that the enemy also saw them and knew they were coming. In this they were correct. Around 5 p.m. a visitor, the CSS *Appomattox*, appeared before the fleet. The little Confederate steamer quickly turned about and disappeared in the fog before any action was taken, but as it was, Goldsborough had no intentions on firing on the enemy vessel, preferring instead that the Confederates knew the magnitude of what they were up against.[12]

Commodore Lynch who had arrayed his makeshift flotilla behind a hastily constructed barrier of sunken ships and pylons driven into the shallow bottom, lamented the sight and reports of the Union fleet. "To meet these," he wrote to the secretary of the navy, Stephen Mallory,

> I have two old side-wheel steamers, and six propellers—the former possessing some speed; the latter slow in their movements and one of them frequently disabling its shaft; but my greatest difficulty is in the want of men. So great has been the exposure of our crew that a number of them have necessarily been invalided; consequently the complements are very much reduced, some of them one-half. I have sent to Washington, Plymouth, Edenton and Elizabeth City for recruits without success, and an earnest appeal to Commodore Forrest brought me only four. To meet the enemy I have not more than a sufficient number of men to fight half the guns.[13]

Had he been at Roanoke Island Wise would have sympathized with Lynch's assessment, but the general was bedridden with pneumonia at Nags Head and would take no part in the battle. This left command of Roanoke Island to Colonel Henry Shaw of the 8th North Carolina Regiment. Shaw's conduct in the region had already come under suspicion. The former US congressman had been branded a Northern sympathizer at one point, and he was not well liked by his men whose needs he generally ignored. As the hour approached no doubt many of the island's defenders wished for a sudden return of Wise or even better, Colonel Wright and his 3rd Georgia Volunteers.

Although Shaw was not a soldier by trade, he was under no illusions. He had a few field fortifications, some three dozen guns, and perhaps two thousand men with which to repel an attack by two-dozen warships, fifteen regiments of infantry, and two batteries of artillery. In fact, even this was an optimistic appraisal. There was a shortage of explosive shells for most of the island's guns, as well as a shortage of powder and experienced gunners. The troops Shaw had on hand to counter an enemy landing consisted of two raw, ill-equipped North Carolina regiments and portions of two Virginian regiments from Wise's legion, and even this meager resource was slowly being eroded as the damp weather and poor living conditions had put over two hundred men on the sick roll.

When reports of the Union fleet reached Shaw he dispatched two hundred men and a pair of field guns to Ashby Harbor, the most likely landing place for a large body of troops. While the colonel didn't believe he could oppose the landing, this reconnaissance force was to inflict what damage they could before falling back on the line of entrenchments across the main road where the bulk of the infantry would be posted.[14]

It would be here that the Battle for Roanoke Island would be decided, and although the odds looked bleak, good news had reached Shaw. Wise's legion, some four thousand troops and their artillery were on their way, but it would be a few days before the entire unit could converge on the island. Thus, the battle ahead was simply one of delay for the North Carolina commander. If his forts could hold before the Union fleet, and he could hold the enemy at bay before his field works, there was still a chance to turn the tables on the Yankees and push them off the island.

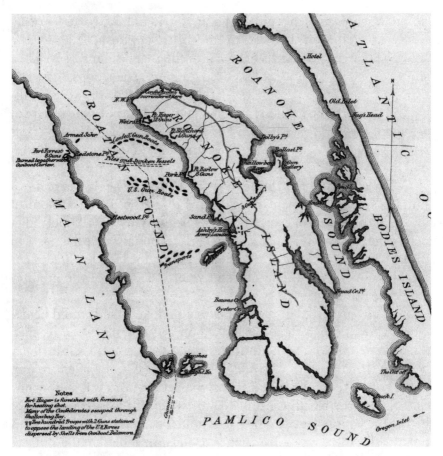

The Battle of Roanoke Island showing the Union landings at Ashby's Harbor, the Confederate gun batteries, the Union warships, and the elements of the Mosquito Fleet arrayed behind a series of barriers sunk across the main channel. (*Library of Congress*)

FIVE

The Battle for Roanoke Island

WINTER SQUALLS AND BROKEN PATCHES OF FOG greeted the Union fleet on the morning of February 7, but by a little after nine o'clock the weather had subsided and the flotilla was once again on the move. Admiral Goldsborough sent the *Ceres* and *Putnam* ahead, as well as the gunboat *Underwriter*. The first two vessels would pass through the marshes to confirm that the channel was clear, while the last vessel was to steam directly for Sandy Point and determine if the Confederates had fortified this key position.

The three warships threaded their way through the narrow channel into the southern portion of Croatan Sound without issue. As they continued north one of the Confederate vessels behind the sunken barrier fired a shot to alert the island's garrison, but it was not necessary. At least three-dozen field glasses watched with interest as one of the vessels broke away and sailed toward Ashby Harbor. A little after 11:00 a.m. the command to fire rang out across the deck of the *Underwriter*. The forward battery responded with a thump and a cloud of blue-white smoke drifted behind the vessel. A dozen pair of binoculars focused on Sandy Point observed the explosive rounds' detonation and strained for any sign of activity. After a few minutes when it was clear that the enemy had not occupied the location, Lt. Jeffers wheeled the vessel about and signaled the fleet "No Battery on Sandy Point."[1]

The news relieved Goldsborough who was convinced that, had the position been protected, "our difficulties would have been materially increased." The information was relayed to the transports who now began moving through the narrow inlet. The Commodore's warships, accompanied by seven armed transports which would cover the landing, advanced in two columns with part of the force positioning itself before the line of Confederate warships and the rest converging on Fort Bartow at Pork Point.

The signal flags "engage the enemy" were run up the Union flagship's mast, and after a ranging shot by one of Fort Bartow's guns fell short, these were later replaced with "close in upon the enemy." While the vessels targeting the fort complied with the command, it was hardly a charge. Once leaving the main channel the water became shallower and the bottom unpredictable. Hence, it became more like the advance of skirmishers who slowly probed the depths for a location that would bring their guns closer to the fort. As it was, almost every ship involved reported striking bottom at least once, and several struck multiple times.[2]

For the defenders of Fort Bartow it was a problematic sight. A little over a mile away over a dozen Union gunboats were slowly creeping their way toward the earthworks, firing ranging shots as they charted out the depths. It soon became clear that only three of the fort's guns could be brought to bear on the enemy. Not that it mattered, as there wasn't enough ammunition to sustain fire with the other five guns in any case. To make matters worse, the three nearby Confederate forts were positioned out of effective cannon range, meaning that Fort Bartow was for all practical purposes on its own. This is not to say that the other forts did not try to support Fort Bartow, on several instances the Confederate guns at Fort Blanchard and Fort Huger did fire upon the Union fleet, but to no effect.

By noon the Union vessels had found the range and at three-quarters of a mile began battering the enemy earthworks with explosive rounds. It would be a long afternoon for the garrison of the fort as shot and shell rained down upon their stronghold. At one o'clock the garrison's flag was knocked down by an explosive round only to be replaced with a smaller ensign on a makeshift pole. Half an hour later the fort's barracks were set ablaze by several explosive rounds, and by two o'clock Lt. J.C. Chapin of the USS *Valley City* reported that "the fire within the fort [was] raging fiercely; the whole fleet pouring an incessant fire of shot and shell into the fort."[3]

Enveloped in smoke and with the fire having spread to several internal structures, the response from the fort's guns slowed to a more deliberate pace. Thus far the poorly equipped Confederate battery had done well. The fire from the fort's guns was reported as high by Union witnesses with a number of vessel's being struck in their upper works, but at the same time the Confederate battery also found some success. Early in the engagement the trio of guns had struck the USS *Louisiana* with one of the few shells the battery possessed and briefly set the gunboat on fire. Shortly before three o'clock the Confederate guns struck the *Hetzel* below the waterline forcing the gunboat to temporarily withdraw, and not long after a thirty-two-pound solid shot tore through the USS *Hunchback* damaging the vessel's engine and leaving the vessel's commander with no choice but to throw out his anchor while repairs were being made. The USS *Commodore Perry* was at the forefront of the Union effort and at several points was able to close to within eight hundred yards of the fort, repeatedly striking the fortifications with over a hundred explosive rounds, but it paid the price for doing so, being hit eight times by thirty-two-pound round shot, one passing through the magazine and two empty powder tanks and another piercing the hull between the wheel and the engine. "Had the enemy fired shell instead of round shot," the commander of the *Commodore Perry* noted in his report, "we must have been destroyed."[4]

As if the enemy artillery was not hazard enough, several of the Union gunboats experienced operation accidents involving their guns. On the *Ceres* a pair of gunners were injured when the thirty-two-pound shell gun prematurely fired due to improper serving of the vent. The extreme case occurred on the *Hetzel* when the eighty-pound rifled cannon burst while firing solid shot, "prostrating every man at the piece and wounding six of them." The force of the breech explosion was powerful enough to fling the forward third of the barrel overboard and another section cartwheeling high in the air until it splashed down along the other side of the ship. The remaining portion of the gun, weighing half a ton, was driven through the deck passing through the magazine and the decking below until it finally came to rest on the keel. The smoldering metal lit the magazine on fire and it was only through the prompt action of the vessel's executive officer Lt. Charles Franklin that the flames were extinguished before the vessel came to an explosive end.[5]

At the north end of the channel a different duel was taking place. Aboard his flagship Commodore Lynch arrayed the elements of his Mosquito Fleet behind the makeshift barricade of pylons and sunken vessels. Together they counted nine ships, one of which, the *Black Warrior*, was a sailing schooner used as a supply ship during the engagement. The remaining eight vessels of the flotilla, the flagship *Seabird, Ellis, Curlew, Appomattox, Beaufort, Fanny, Forrest,* and *Raleigh* could bring nine guns to bear, almost all thirty-two-pound rifled cannon. Lynch faced a number of problems beyond the clear disadvantage in numbers. He lacked experienced gun crews, and as with all the Confederate guns in the region, a shortage of ammunition persisted as well. Fuel was at issue, but perhaps more importantly, the barricade erected across the north channel of Croatan Sound, which the commodore was counting on keeping the Union warships at arm's length, was hardly impervious. Work on this structure had started in early January but proceeded slowly and it was not until a few days before the attack that a true effort had been made to block the channel with sunken vessels and wooden pylons. The haste had left a number of places where a determined enemy could pass, especially on the eastern end, toward Fort Bartow, where a 1,700-yard gap still existed.[6]

The previous evening Lynch had confided to Captain William Parker of the *Beaufort* that he did not believe they would be able to stop the Union attack, given the overwhelming odds and the lack of resources. Parker, and likely every other naval officer in the squadron, agreed. Now as the commodore and his men watched the fleet of Union warships moving into Croatan Sound he became even more convinced of his statement. Lynch had sent the *Appomattox* to Edenton for supplies, reducing his numbers, but it hardly mattered. Nearly a score of warships were arrayed before them, most of which were

The Union gunboat USS *Hetzel*. The 301-ton Baltimore built side-wheeler was originally commissioned as a commercial steamer in 1845, before being purchased for the U.S. Coast Guard a few years later. At the outbreak of the war the *Hetzel* was transferred to the U.S. Navy where it was fitted with an 80-pound rifled cannon on a forward pivot mount, and a 9-inch shell gun aft. The Hetzel would be heavily engaged at Roanoke Island bombarding Fort Bartow and would later serve throughout the inland waters of North Carolina. (*NHHC*)

larger and far more heavily armed than any of his vessels. More importantly, behind these gunboats was a column of transports, too many to count, according to Lt. Commander Simms of the *Appomattox* who had briefly reconnoitered the enemy fleet the day before.

The gun crews of the Mosquito Fleet waited patiently for orders to fire as the Union warships began to diverge with the bulk of the vessels steering for Fort Bartow and the remainder veering toward the Confederate fleet. Not long after the first exchanges of fire between the fort and Goldsborough's fleet a hundred-pound rifled round shrieked through the air terminating in a fountain of water behind the Confederate line. The guns of the Mosquito Fleet replied, and by noon both sides were heavily engaged.[7]

Fifteen minutes later Lynch signaled the fleet to raise anchor and slowly fall back under the guns of Fort Huger and Fort Forest. The idea was to draw the enemy vessels away from Fort Bartow and perhaps even entice an enemy gunboat or two to try to find its way through the barricade. At first, it appeared Lynch might have found some success as the USS *Underwriter* steamed toward the barricade. The gunboat's commander, Lt. Jeffers, noticed as he approached quite close to the obstruction that the four-gun battery at Fort Blanchard could be brought to bear on him. "As it was no part of the plan of attack to force the barricade before the reduction of the forts or their serious injury," Jeffers noted, "I allowed my vessel to drop back with the current to a position where but two guns bore upon her; these only fired at me occasionally." The *Ceres, Stars and Stripes, Hunchback, Morse*, and several other vessels trained at least part of their batteries on the Confederate fleet until it pulled out of range.

While Lynch's fleet was certainly safer positioned north between Fort Huger and Fort Forrest, it was clear that the Union vessels were not interested in forcing the barricade. Soon a few dropped farther south and began to concentrate on Fort Bartow. Seeing that the enticement had failed the Confederate fleet moved back to its original position and began to engage the Union vessels again.[8]

By 2:00 the firing on all sides had become "hot and heavy," Captain Parker of the *Beaufort* recalled. "Our gunners had had no practice with their rifled guns, and our firing was not what it should have been. It was entirely too rapid and not particularly accurate." While the same issues certainly existed on both sides the sheer volume of Union firepower became telling. A half an hour later the Federal gunners scored their biggest success of the day when a solid round struck the *Curlew*'s hurricane deck, passed through the magazine, and blew out one of the iron plates in the bottom of the hull. The ship quickly began taking on water and its captain, Lt. Commander Thomas Hunter, "an excitable fellow" who was known in the region as "Tornado" Hunter, ran up the engines and steered the paddle-wheeler toward Fort Forrest. The vessel soon filled with water, but not before Hunter was able to run it aground in front of the Confederate battery at Redstone Point, completely masking its guns.[9]

A few minutes later CSS *Forrest* became another casualty when a rifled round damaged its propeller and an exploding round near the bridge dangerously wounded the vessel's captain, James Hoole. The crew managed to coax the vessel across the sound and dropped anchor under the guns of Fort Forrest before the machinery gave out, leaving the gunboat out of action.

The rest of the fleet was being battered as well with Lynch noting that a solid-shot round had passed through the side of the *Seabird* without creating any serious damage. The other vessels were also struck, but none reported any significant damage or at least anything that impeded their fighting ability. In fact, Lynch and likely everyone else were impressed that they were still afloat, much less still fighting. Despite the intensity of the fire casualties were light with only half a dozen wounded across the squadron, and there seemed no lack of fighting spirit among the elements of the fleet. They had certainly scored several hits and no doubt some of the damage attributed to the guns of Fort Bartow really came from the Lynch's guns, but now a more pressing problem had come to the forefront: ammunition. Almost every ship in the squadron was down to its last few rounds. Several vessels took the ammunition off the disabled *Curlew* and *Forrest*, but it was nowhere near enough to maintain the fleet's rate of fire.

With signs that the enemy was landing troops near Ashby's Bay and his ammunition exhausted, Lynch ordered the fleet to withdraw a little after four o'clock. The guns and remaining ordinance stores on the *Curlew* were salvaged, and the *Forrest* was taken into tow. Lynch dispatched the *Beaufort* to Fort Huger to notify the commander there that he was departing with the fleet to Elizabeth City to secure ammunition and would return as soon as this was accomplished. While the veteran naval officer felt some remorse in leaving the defenders of the island behind, there was little else he could do. Without ammunition his gunboats were nothing but targets.[10]

A little after two o'clock a launch pulled up alongside the flagship USS *Southfield*. Onboard was General Burnside and several of his staff. The general only had one question for Commodore Goldsborough: was it safe to commence landing his troops? At this point Fort Bartow was covered in smoke, and brief flashes of orange from exploding rounds and the occasional yellow flicker of flames consuming some of its interior structures could be seen. The fire from the Confederate batteries was steady, but the pace was certainly slowing down, and to the north, the enemy fleet was proving no threat having already withdrawn once before recently returning. In all it was enough to inform the general to proceed with landing operations.

At three o'clock the army steamers the *Patuxent* and *Union* left the transports which were anchored a few miles above the marshes.

Loaded with troops the two vessels steered for Ashby Harbor and were soon followed by the steamer *Pilot Boy* which, besides being filled with troops, was also towing a large number of landing boats and a pontoon bridge that was to be employed as a temporary dock at the landing site.[11]

Burnside had put a small reconnaissance team ashore at Ashby Harbor a little after noon. The landing party, seeing no signs of the enemy, were in the process of reembarking when two-dozen muskets opened fire on them from the tree line. The Union troops returned fire, and pulling hard on their oars, made a brisk retreat after suffering a few casualties. The attackers were part of a two-hundred-man observation force under Colonel J.V. Jordan, who had been dispatched to this location the previous evening by Shaw. Jordan was to monitor any signs of an enemy landing and, if possible, ambush the Union forces while they were landing, before withdrawing to the Confederate entrenchments in the center of the island.

Whatever Jordan's intentions, they were soon shattered when the USS *Delaware*, which at the time was to the south of Fort Bartow, ran down the shore to cover the army's landing. Jordan's troops were soon discovered and the *Delaware*, along with the help of the army gunboat *Picket* soon put the Confederate force to flight with a barrage of explosive shells. With nothing to oppose their landing beyond the challenges of the terrain, the operation proceeded like a training exercise. By nightfall Burnside had put six thousand men ashore and was landing more men at the rate of a thousand an hour.

The Union fleet kept up its barrage of Fort Bartow until late afternoon when many of the gunboats reported they were low on ammunition. With the rebel fleet withdrawing and Fort Bartow's response slowing to a crawl, Goldsborough gave the order to cease fire and withdrew back into the main channel for the evening. The commodore's fleet had fired over 2,500 rounds, mostly at Fort Bartow, and while they believed they had seriously injured the fort, the truth of the matter was that they had done very little damage. Navy Lt. Benjamin Loyal, who was in command of the gun crews at Fort Bartow, reported only one man killed and three wounded during the seven-hour bombardment. While the garrison's barracks and a few interior buildings had been set ablaze, there had been no serious damage to the fort and all the guns remained ready for action. That night, as work crews repaired the damage to the earthen parapets, wagon teams arrived from Fort Huger carrying much-needed ammunition. By morning, the fort, in Loyal's opinion, was in the same state as it had been when the engagement started. Given the sustained bombardment it was nothing short of miraculous, and when Goldsborough toured the fortifications after its surrender the commodore could only remark that, "These men must have been made of iron."[12]

Matters were actually far more perilous for the island's defenders. While Fort Bartow and the other forts had held, a more dangerous threat was forming to the south at Ashby's Harbor. Colonel Shaw was at Fort Bartow when reports of an enemy landing first reached him. Shaw sent a messenger to Norfolk to request reinforcements, and braving the shell fire, he and his staff immediately rode off for the entrenchments at the center of the island. Here Shaw found a harried Colonel Jordan who informed him of the size of the enemy force and their approximate location.

At this point there was really little Shaw could do but stand upon the previously erected defensive line which bisected the main north-south road. There was only room for four hundred men in the earthworks to support the battery of three guns, so Shaw stationed the rest of his force, another thousand troops in reserve a few hundred yards behind the works. Three recently arrived companies of Wise's legion led by Captain O. Jennings Wise, positioned themselves in the tangled swamps to either side of the Confederate line. With both flanks covered by impenetrable swamps and a clear field of fire before the defensive works, Shaw felt that the position was not as hopeless as it would appear. The limited front partially neutralized the enemy's superior numbers by funneling their attack to the clear terrain about the road as the rest of the low-lying area in front of the redoubt was covered in a waist-deep swamp. There was also some good news that evening as his men lit fires and bivouacked beneath a cold winter rain. Reports arrived that a thousand men of Wise's legion had landed at Fort Huger and were on their way.[13]

The garrison of Fort Bartow were at their guns at daybreak, but they found little interest from the Union fleet who had been ordered to stand down for fear of striking Burnside's advancing troops. The appearance of several Confederate steamers towing troop ships toward Fort Huger a few hours later triggered another duel between

the Union warships and the fort as the latter tried to cover the Confederate vessels. A repeat of the previous day's action only lasted half
an hour before the Union vessels were ordered to cease fire.

By 7 a.m. three brigades of Union troops, some twelve thousand
men supported by a six-gun naval battery reached the clearing before
Colonel Shaw's redoubt. The naval guns under the command of Midshipman Benjamin Porter of the USS *Hunchback* immediately set up
on the road at the edge of the tree line and responded to the bark of
the Confederate cannons with volleys of shell and cannister which
did "good execution among their reserve in the rear of their battery."[14]

For the Union commanders and their troops, the terrain was a
nightmare. The main north-south road on the causeway before them
was flanked with knee-deep swamps that disappeared into dark cypress woods on either side, saturated with mud from the recent rains.
Foster, who was in command of the battle, reached the edge of the
clearing first with three of the regiments in his brigade. Unable to advance and with the artillery on both sides firing away it was not long
before several thousand muskets added their sound to the proceed-
ings. Soon blue-white clouds of smoke obscured friend from foe, and
while one Union soldier noted that "we could see nothing to shoot
at," it did not stop the barrage, as most felt that if they threw enough
lead in the general direction of the enemy, they were likely to hit
something.

Foster ordered the 25th Massachusetts to advance down the road,
which was the only practical path before them. As the enemy was
aware of this fact as well, advancing down this causeway proved slow
going. Waves of grapeshot and a hail of mini-balls swept the roadway
forcing the Massachusetts troops to crawl forward under the withering fire. Even this modest gain was soon halted and the advance de-
generated into the troops occasionally standing to fire a shot before
hitting the ground again to reload. Alongside these troops were
Porter's guns which had been ordered to advance with the infantry.[15]

After an hour, Foster ordered the 10th Connecticut to relieve the
beleaguered Massachusetts troops on the roadway, but it did little to
break the stalemate. Seeing that something else was called for Foster
ordered the 23rd and 27th Massachusetts of Parke's brigade, which
were on the road behind him, to look for a route through the swamp
on the Confederate left. At about the same time General Jesse Reno

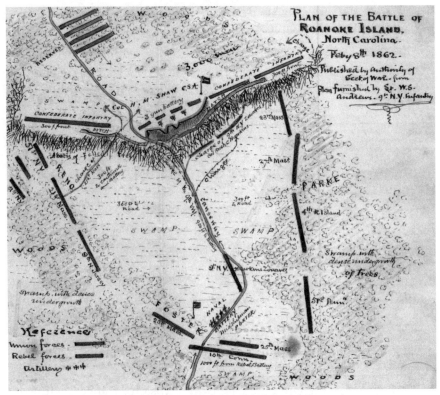

The Battle of Roanoke Island, February 8th, 1862. (*Library of Congress*)

commanding the next brigade in line came to the same conclusion and ordered his men into the swamps on the Confederate right.

It would turn out the swamps that flanked the Confederate line were not impenetrable after all. It was slow going through the muck, thickets, and frigid waist-deep waters, as detailed by Colonel John Kurtz of the 23rd Massachusetts:

> I cannot speak with too much praise of the conduct of the officers and men of my command for their indomitable perseverance in forcing through the swamp. The undergrowth was a thick bush, entwined by a strong brier, which caused it to close immediately upon the disappearance of a man through it. The water and mud all the way was above the knees of the men, several of whom I saw waist-deep in the mire.[16]

Another participant, George Whitman, brother of the famous poet, recounted advancing on the Union left with the 51st New York:

> We worked around on their right flank through a thicket that you would think was impossible for a man to pass through. It was mighty trying to a fellows nerves as the balls was flying around pretty thick cutting the twigs off overhead and knocking the bark off trees all around us, but our regiment behaved finely and pressed on as fast as possible.[17]

After over an hour of feeling their way through the swamp a call went out that some of Reno's men could see the battery. The troops moved to the contact point in small clusters and ragged lines as word spread, and when Reno had amassed enough men, he ordered a charge on the rear of the Confederate redoubt. The timing proved near perfect as a few moments later the 23rd and 27th Massachusetts, having made a similar journey, appeared out of the tree line and opened fire on the battery's left flank. In fear of being enveloped, the earthwork's defenders bolted as yet more blue coats appeared out of the swamp. A number escaped, but Shaw had stationed his reserves too far back to support the redoubt leaving many to fall into enemy hands.[18]

To the front of the Union lines the quick disappearance of gunfire from the Confederate redoubt was seized upon by Colonel Rush Hawkins of the 9th New York. Hawkins asked General Foster for permission to charge the enemy works. Foster, seeing the same thing and clearly understanding from the sound of the current engagement that the flanking maneuver must have succeeded, granted Hawkins' request. Soon the cry of "Zou! Zou! Zou!" rang out as Hawkins' regiment, garbed as French Zouaves, dashed down the causeway. The 10th Connecticut troops were lying prone on the road, having been pinned down by the redoubt's fire, and now feared for their lives as behind them a herd of shouting Zouaves with leveled bayonets threatened to stampede the New Englanders. Fortunately, there were only a few isolated incidents as Hawkins' men swept through the Connecticut ranks and pressed on to the now deserted barricade.[19]

For all intents and purposes the battle was over. Shaw's troops, now infected with fleeing men, moved north under the protection of a small rear guard. The Union troops, their ranks now intermixed and

General John Foster, left. Foster would be in tactical command of the Union army at the Battle of Roanoke Island. U.S. congressman Henry Shaw, right, shortly before the war. (*Library of Congress*)

most having spent over an hour under fire in a wet wooden maze, were in no condition to conduct a pursuit. While the wounded on both sides were tended to and the spoils of war and prisoners tallied, Reno began to reorganize his brigade. An hour later both Reno's and Foster's brigades moved forward. The advance was not pressed, as clear signs of the Confederate defeat in the form of abandoned firearms, wagons, and equipment littered the roadside. At Shallowbag Bay on the east coast of the island Massachusetts troops surprised a number of small Confederate boats looking to escape. A few were successful, but several, including one carrying the mortally wounded Captain O. Jennings Wise of the Virginia Blues, the general's son, were captured.

The Union forces halted around two o'clock for a brief rest and to consolidate their ranks for a final push. Reports were that the Confederate army was at Camp Georgia at the northern end of the island, a little over three miles away. By three o'clock Union skirmishers exchanged fire with the enemy's advanced guard some three-quarters of a mile from Camp Georgia. The engagement was brief and while Reno and Foster organized their men for a bayonet charge a Confederate officer appeared with a white handkerchief flying from the end of his sword.[20]

The envoy, Lt. Colonel Daniel Fowle, 31st North Carolina Regiment, asked to speak with the Union commander, and within a few minutes he found himself before Foster. Fowle asked what terms of surrender he would grant Colonel Shaw's forces, to which Foster replied, "None whatever, sir. Nothing but immediate and unconditional surrender." Fowle then asked for permission to speak with Colonel Shaw which was granted.

For Shaw there was little choice. Although the colonel might not have been the most dynamic commander, at this point even the most foolish one could see that any further resistance was useless. After the loss of the defensive works that barred the main road the outcome seemed clear, and Shaw passed orders on to the Confederate forts to spike their guns and destroy their ammunition. He then retreated to the northern portion of the island and waited until the Federal troops appeared, hoping this interlude would give the garrisons time to accomplish their tasks. Now, as his envoy and one of Foster's officers stood before him, Shaw realized there was only one course of action. He ordered a white flag raised over his tent and agreed to the terms, effectively bringing an end to the battle.[21]

The Confederate defeat at Roanoke was nearly complete. Some 2,500 men surrendered including a detachment of 450 men from Wise's legion who had just landed on the island and found themselves trapped when their boats fled on news of the surrender. Over forty cannon and all the forts along the island's coast, along with their supplies were seized. Losses on both sides were not severe given the number of forces involved. The Union suffered a little under three hundred casualties and the Confederates about half that, which perhaps speaks to the decisive nature of the Union victory and the quick collapse of the Confederate defenses.

Praise was rightfully heaped on Goldsborough, Burnside, and their subordinates. Goldsborough's fleet had neutralized Fort Bartow and the opposing rebel flotilla, allowing a division of infantry and their supplies to be put ashore without interference. The next day Burnside's troops pushed up the island, seized the primary enemy works in a pitched engagement, and collapsed all resistance on the island by late afternoon. Little more could be asked for.[22]

On the Confederate side there were a number of questions that remained. Shaw has traditionally been the scapegoat for the loss of the island, but if so, he had numerous accomplices. General Huger should be counted first among these abettors. His continual disregard for the strategic well-being of Roanoke Island was almost criminal. Certainly, Huger feared an attack on his fifteen-thousand-man garrison at the old federal naval facilities at Norfolk, but the depth of his worries jeopardized not only the security of Albemarle and Pamlico Sound but the backdoor to Norfolk as well. This shortsightedness in the face of numerous reports on Roanoke Island's weak and undermanned defenses by several ranking officers certainly call this Confederate commander's decision-making process into question.

In fact, the entire chain of command up to the Confederate secretary of war deserve some credit for the Union victory. The matter was never taken seriously. The 3rd Georgia, for instance, which had shown itself an excellent regiment, was transferred and replaced with an inexperienced and ill-equipped state regiment although the island was clearly at risk. Furthermore, even when it was agreed to release Wise's legion for duty in the area, only five hundred of these troops had actually been transported to the island weeks after the order was given, and of these only a few companies were actually engaged.

As to this last point, criticism was fairly leveled at Wise. There is little question that Wise should have deployed his troops better and spent more time and effort overseeing the defenses of Roanoke Island, but to guard the northern coast of North Carolina along with Albemarle Sound and Roanoke Island was a tall order for four thousand troops. The lack of supplies, ammunition, and specifically water transportation haunted the Confederate effort. Coupled with Wise's absence at the time of the battle, this left the Confederate troops in the region too scattered, slow to respond, and in the hands of junior officers.

"Enough is known of the surrender at Roanoke Island," Confederate president Jefferson Davis proclaimed a month after the battle, "to make us feel that it was deeply humiliating, however imperfect may have been the preparations for defense." The editor of the *North Carolina Standard* took offense at the statement and responded, "The truth is, Roanoke Island fell because partizan governments made partizan appointments of persons who have proved themselves unfit for their places; and unless we can have less partyism in future, and more regard for merit without regard to party, the Confederate cause itself will be endangered."[23]

SIX

The Destruction of the Mosquito Fleet

WHEN COMMODORE LYNCH ARRIVED at Elizabeth City on the evening of February 7, he found the town in near panic and little in the way of shot and shell to resupply his fleet. After a quick survey Lynch dispatched the *Raleigh* to Norfolk via the Dismal Swamp Canal with orders to return as fast as possible with whatever munitions that could be obtained. In the meantime, the damaged *Forrest* was tended to by work crews, and the limited supplies available distributed to the *Seabird* and the *Appomattox*, which it was agreed would leave for Roanoke Island as soon as possible.

On the morning of February 9 smoke issued from the stacks aboard the *Seabird* and *Appomattox*. Although there had only been enough ammunition for two vessels, Lynch was anxious to return to the island in order to render what assistance he could. The two Confederate gunboats had barely reached the mouth of the Pasquatonk River when a small boat from the island waved down the vessels and informed the commodore of the garrison's surrender. On hearing the news Lynch raced forward in hopes of rescuing the troops stationed at Fort Forrest, but upon sighting a large number of Union warships on the north side of the barricade, he gave the order to return to Elizabeth City.[1]

The commander of the Mosquito Fleet now faced a dire decision. With the absence of the *Raleigh*, the loss of the *Curlew*, and the damage to the *Forrest*, his fleet had been reduced to seven operational vessels. What was worse was that he had little in the way of ammunition and a very limited amount of coal on hand. Even if the *Raleigh* returned before the Federal warships arrived it might not make much difference. The Union fleet was over twice his number and perhaps outgunned his flotilla by eight to one. Their guns were also more powerful, and more importantly, were supported by an ample supply of ammunition that would keep them in action. In truth, there were only two decisions: flight or fight. Lynch considered the first option. There was still time and fuel to withdraw up the Dismal Swamp Canal to Norfolk and save the fleet. Most of the Union vessels were too big and would not be able to follow, and for those that could, it would be an easy matter for Lynch's men to block the canal behind them and thus foil their pursuers.

Ultimately, however, the commodore chose against this option. There was the matter of Elizabeth City's strategic position at the southern end of the Dismal Swamp Canal to consider, but it was the fear that gripped Elizabeth City that had much to do with his decision to stand and fight. Lynch had urged the shaky populace to call out the militia and stand their ground. Under such circumstances, he wrote of his decision, "it would have been unseemly and discouraging" to have deserted them after making such an impassioned request.[2]

The decision made to defend Elizabeth City, Lynch and Captain Parker met with Colonel C. F. Henningsen of the 59th Virginia Volunteers who was in command of the town. At least it was obvious where to defend the river. Just downstream of the town was Cobb Point, which jutted out like a comma from the western side of the river, narrowing the channel to a little over eight hundred yards. A small earth fort had been raised at this location and armed with a battery of four thirty-two-pound smoothbore guns. It was a poorly constructed and neglected structure. The magazine was only partially completed, and the guns, although operational, were mounted in

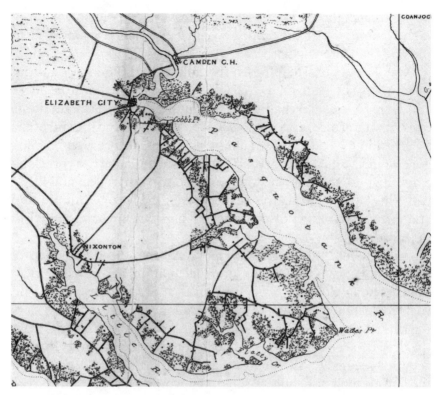

A portion of an 1862 map of North Carolina showing the outlet of the Pasquatonk River, Elizabeth City, and Cobb Point. The entrance to the Dismal Swamp Canal is above Camden. (*Library of Congress*)

such a fashion that only one could fire across the channel while the other three were restricted to firing downstream. Thus, once a vessel steamed past the stronghold there was nothing the garrison could do to hinder its advance.

To support this fort Henningsen's troops, along with the town's questionable militia, amounted to a little over five hundred men, hardly an obstacle given the size of the Union army now occupying Roanoke Island. The colonel did, however, possess several batteries of light guns which Parker noted offered an opportunity to contest the passage of the river near Cobb Point. The captain suggested that the fleet's guns be landed on the eastern bank and used in conjunction with Fort Cobb's battery and Henningsen's light guns on the west bank, to catch the Yankee flotilla in a crossfire. At point-blank range even Henningsen's light cannon would cause significant damage to the wooden Union vessels.[3]

Both Lynch and Henningsen thought the plan too risky and instead it was agreed to array the *Seabird, Ellis, Appomattox, Beaufort,* and *Fanny* across the channel a few hundred yards upstream of the fort with the armed schooner *Black Warrior* anchoring the end of the line close to the eastern shore, almost opposite the fort. Henningsen's guns would be held in reserve. Together with the battery at Fort Cobb a dozen guns were all that stood between the Union fleet and Elizabeth City, and even this was suspect given the lack of ammunition and uncertain abilities of the fort's gunners which Henningsen was to provide.

As night fell and the chill brought forth the seasonal blankets of fog, the lit lanterns of the Mosquito Fleet illuminated an assortment of small boats tied alongside. With the last of the ammunition and coal redistributed among the fleet, these supply boats departed leaving Lynch's crews to their preparations. A few hours before midnight the fleet signaled ready. Now it had become a waiting game. In what certainly seemed to be a depressing pattern Lynch and Parker spent the late evening hours discussing the upcoming battle. Both agreed that the prospects looked bleak and that, unlike the last time they had discussed the matter, this time there was nowhere left to run. An exhausted Parker returned to the *Beaufort* later that evening and the moment he reached his berth found himself fast asleep. "I really believe I did not take off my sword and pistol," he recalled, "and I know I did not remove my cap. I never was so tired in my life."[4]

When the stars and stripes appeared over Fort Bartow late in the afternoon of February 8 it set off a series of rolling cheers, ship's horns, and whistles among the nearby Union fleet. Farther north, at the edge of the Confederate water obstacles, the display was faint but recognizable and elicited a similar response from the crews of the eight warships under the command of Lt. Jeffers of the *Underwriter*. A few hours before Jeffers had been sent forward with orders to penetrate the barricade of sunken vessels and wooden piles and mark a path for the fleet.

The occupants of Fort Forrest on the westside of Croatan Sound responded in a different manner to news of the island's surrender.

Twenty minutes later flames could be seen coming from the Confederate post and not long after billowing clouds of smoke engulfed the *Curlew*, still laying aground in front of the battery. Jeffers' men stopped to watch the spectacle at Redstone Point, speaking among themselves in small groups, occasionally motioning to some perceived feature, when a few moments later they were greeted by a jolt as the charges placed on the steamship erupted in a sonic clap announcing news of the vessel's destruction.[5]

With the excitement over, the Union crews returned to their task. The nautical *cheval-de-frise* did not prove to be impervious, but it did offer plenty of challenges. The primary one, according to Jeffers, being simply finding the main channel in the first place. The *Putnam* had already run aground in pursuing this task and had to be pulled off by tugs. The other vessels stood off a safe distance and sent their longboats forward to take a closer look. One of these small craft from the *Ceres* was successful and reported an opening in the barricade between a line of unfinished piles and a sunken schooner wide enough for the warship to pass through. Not far away the *Lockwood* managed to cut the chain between two sunken vessels and float one away, creating an even larger passage, while the *Valley City* took a different approach to the matter and "made a dash at a row of piles and forced passage between them." By nightfall Jeffers' detachment had marked out several passages, all wide enough for any ship in the fleet to pass through, and now lay at anchor at the north end of Croatan Sound wrapped in a thick mist.[6]

The following morning the lookouts on the *Ceres* were surprised to see a schooner approaching the anchored flotilla. The schooner's captain, carrying a load of coal for what he believed was the Mosquito Fleet lying before him, realized his mistake too late when a shot across his bow brought him to a stop. The schooner captain did not have much to say, but a deserter from the *Fanny* a few hours later was more talkative, giving valuable information regarding the defenses of Elizabeth City and the state of the Confederate fleet anchored there. Rowan was particularly interested in Fort Cobb and was delighted to hear of the fort's limited capabilities, as well as the Confederate fleet's strength and status. With Roanoke Island having surrendered and the water barricade penetrated, the news was enough to convince both Admiral Goldsborough and Commander Rowan to strike.

Signal flags soon ran up the mast of Rowan's flagship the *Delaware*, setting off a flurry of activity. By 3 p.m. the fleet had assembled on the north side of the barricade. It consisted of fourteen warships carrying some fifty-six guns and over five hundred sailors and marines. A few hours later smoke was seen on the horizon as the *Seabird* and *Appomattox* came into view. Rowan gave the signal to chase, but the Confederate steamers quickly reversed course, and by dusk had already entered the river causing the pursuit to be called off. Proceeding slowly into the main channel of the river the Union commander finally gave the order to drop anchor at eight o'clock that evening about ten miles below Cobb Point.

Rowan called together his ship's captains aboard the *Delaware*. It seemed clear, he informed his officers, that the enemy fleet had either run up the canal to Norfolk or lay behind the battery at Cobb Point. He also reminded them that, while they outgunned the enemy, there was a serious shortage of ammunition across the fleet after the recent battle, with most guns having only twenty rounds and some less. To cope with this problem Rowan informed his captains that the fleet would attack the enemy in such a manner that "each vessel as she approached the enemy should run him down and engage him hand to hand." It was to be a cavalry charge, and if need be, a return to cutlass and pistol. No one was to fire until the signal was given, he reiterated. There was a murmur of approval and the nodding of a few heads. With matters settled the commander wished his officers good luck and informed all that the fleet would set out at daylight.

In the morning mists of February 10, 1862, the Union warships ran up their steam, checked their guns, and issued small arms to their crews. The fleet would advance in two columns. The first, led by the *Delaware* and consisting of the *Underwriter*, *Perry*, and *Morse* with the *Ceres* stationed on the column's right flank, would be in advance. The *Louisiana* and the *Hetzel* would lead the remaining column. No one was to engage the battery at Cobb's Point until the fleet had passed the peninsula. At that point the *Valley City* and the *Whitehead* were to turn back and attack the fortification in reverse.[7]

Steaming forward at a few knots the Confederate battle line came into view a little after eight o'clock. As Rowan had anticipated the enemy fleet was arrayed across the river a few hundred yards behind Fort Cobb with the schooner near the eastern bank positioned to create a crossfire with the fort. The *Black Warrior* and the battery at Cobb's Point both fired a few long-range shots at the advancing column, and soon the guns of Lynch's fleet began to slowly supplement this ranging fire.

The guns as Fort Cobb, however, were having problems. Daylight had brought an unanticipated challenge to Commodore Lynch. He had arrived at Fort Cobb early that morning to check on its status. What he found shocked him. The militia assigned to the post had fled, leaving half-a-dozen men behind to operate the guns and a civilian in charge. The position was simply too important to be ignored so the commodore took personal command

Commander Stephen Rowan. Rowan was a career naval officer who had served at the capture of Monterey, San Diego, and Los Angeles during the Mexican-American War. He would eventually reach the rank of Vice-Admiral after the war. (*NHHC*)

and sent a runner to Captain Parker of the *Beaufort* with orders to bring his ammunition and crew to Cobb's Point. Only a skeleton crew was to be left onboard the gunboat and they were to immediately take the vessel up the canal to Norfolk. In the meantime, Lynch had gathered together the handful of militia men and began firing on the Union vessels when they came into view.

The fleet was preparing to engage the advancing Union column when Parker received Lynch's orders. The captain could hardly believe what he was reading. "Where the devil are the men who were in the fort?" he asked the messenger. "All run away," was the response. Parker just shook his head and ordered the crew into the boats along with whatever ammunition they could take. He left the *Beaufort* in the hands of the ship's pilot, its engineer, and two others with orders to escape up the canal or blow the boat up to avoid its capture. Once ashore Parker and his men dashed into Fort Cobb and were able to help man three of the four guns in the battery.[8]

For the next ten minutes both the fort and the Mosquito Fleet increased their rate of fire on Rowan's advancing column, but the Union vessels neither returned fire nor changed their pace. Aboard the Federal fleet the gun crews sat silent as the Confederate rounds shrieked overhead or terminated in a nearby geyser. The fire began to intensify when at three-quarters of a mile from the enemy line Rowan gave the signal, "Dash at the Enemy." The vessels in the fleet began running up their engines and when the *Delaware* fired her forward gun, the rest of the fleet responded with a volley directed at the Confederate gunboats as well as Fort Cobb.

The Union fire quickly found its mark as explosive rounds sent clouds of splinters and jets of steam from the *Seabird* setting the old side-wheeler on fire in several places. The *Fanny* was likewise hit multiple times, as was the *Ellis*. The sudden speed of the Union advance threw off the Confederate gunners. In Fort Cobb Parker's men worked furiously at the guns but found that the poorly constructed mounts made the thirty-two-pound guns difficult to train. Even so, the fort's guns scored one of the few hits on the Union fleet when a shell passed through the *Valley City*'s magazine and exploded in the berth deck. Four men were wounded, the magazine bulkheads staved in exposing the ship's powder, and a fire now threatened to engulf the shattered berth deck. The pumps were manned and the vessel's commander, Lt. Chaplin, raced to the scene to help extinguish the fire "before the ship was blown to atoms." When he arrived he found gunners mate John Davis "seated with commendable coolness on an open barrel of powder as the only means to keep the fire out." The fire was soon suppressed, and the threat to the *Valley City* averted.[9]

Rowan's decision to charge the enemy certainly caught the Confederate vessels off guard. "The enemy seemed to become demoralized at this unexpected move," he would later say of the moment. He was correct. Lynch and several of his captains had been convinced that the Union fleet would halt to neutralize Fort Cobb as they had Fort Bartow on Roanoke Island, but instead they pressed forward, the pillars of thick smoke emanating from their stacks a direct indication of their intent. On the right of the Union advance Captain Charles French of the USS *Whitehead* trained his nine-inch Dahlgren shell gun on the *Black Warrior*. After observing a few hits from the ninety-pound explosive rounds he steered a course directly for the enemy schooner. The crew of the *Black Warrior* had already made up their minds to abandon the sailing ship, and the rapidly approaching gunboat only hastened their decision. The ship was set to the torch and the crew went over the side disappearing into the marshes on the east side of the river. French pulled astride the schooner and attempted to save the supply tender and its cargo of naval goods, but the fire had been set in multiple places and spread too quickly, forcing him to abandon the effort.[10]

The range between the opponents quickly disappeared bringing yet more violence as the gun crews switched from shot and shell to canister and grapeshot. Matters were already desperate aboard the *Seabird*. Battered by a series of nine-inch explosive rounds the two-hundred-ton Confederate flagship was on fire and taking on water faster than its pumps could handle. Matters would soon take a turn for the worse as the *Commodore Perry* approached with a full head of steam. The vessels exchanged rounds of cannister which pelted their wooden hulls in a ripple of dull thuds and churned up the surface of the nearby waters. "The guns of both fleets are sending their huge charges across each other's decks at short range," a gunner on the *Commodore Perry* noted as they closed on the rebel fleet, "belching forth their thunder peals with a noise as if the earth had met its final dissolution."[11]

None of this dissuaded Lt. Flusser of the *Commodore Perry*. Standing next to the helmsman he lined the bow of the five-hundred-foot warship up with the *Seabird*'s broadside and sounded the brace for collision alarm. The Union warship, twice the size of the *Seabird*, slammed into the side of the Confederate steamer, knocking almost everyone on both ships off their feet. There were a few exchanges of musketry and pistol fire, but the *Seabird* was sinking so fast that this quickly came to an end as the crew abandoned ship.[12]

The CSS *Ellis* would suffer a similar fate when the *Ceres*, its decks filled with marines and riflemen, slammed alongside the Confederate gunboat and threw out grappling lines. There was a "huzza" as the Union marines and sailors leapt aboard the captive warship. The crew of the Confederate warship responded with musket, pistol, and cutlass, but were quickly being overwhelmed. When a second Union ship pulled astride the crippled *Ellis* the vessel's wounded commander, Lt. James Cook, "gave the order for the men to save themselves," sending most of the crew over the side.[13]

The *Fanny*, already riddled and taking on water, steered for the western shore. The vessel's captain had decided to run the ship aground and let the crew escape before setting the gunboat afire. The *Fanny*'s gunners and marines continued to fire at the Union warships as they crawled toward land. In doing so they had drawn the attention of several Union vessels who pounded the Confederate gunboat with shell and canister at close range. When it appeared the Yankee gunboats might try and board the *Fanny* the ship shook and shuddered to a stop. A number of fires were lit and the crew abandoned ship with the wounded. A survey party from the USS *Lockwood* boarded the deserted gunboat and captured a few stands of arms, but the fire was found to be too advanced to save the ship. Thus, the former Union warship, "having received ten shots from our squadron, which made daylight through her in as many places," was allowed to burn down to its gunwales.[14]

The unarmed and undermanned *Beaufort* had departed for the canal at the opening of the engagement, and it appeared the *Appomattox* might escape as well. With his forward gun accidentally spiked after firing a dozen rounds, Lt. Charles Simms steered the Confederate gunboat for the Dismal Swamp Canal using his small rear howitzer and musket fire to engage a pursuing Union warship. Lt. Jeffers of the USS *Underwriter* fired at the fleeing Confederate ship with his twelve-pound rifled gun, but the gunboat had a sizable lead on him and soon disappeared around a turn in the river leading Jeffers to call off the chase. For Simms and his men, it seemed nothing short of miraculous that they had escaped the fray. With the Union pursuit having disappeared all aboard were convinced that the *Appomattox* would soon join the *Beaufort* in Norfolk. Unfortunately, the celebratory mood soon faded when the vessel reached the entrance to the canal and was found to be two inches too wide to enter. Groans of disbelief and inventive strings of curses could be heard across the ship, but with little else to do, Simms shook his head and ordered the crew to abandon ship. He then rigged the ship for demolition and blew it up at the entrance to the canal.[15]

The battle was over. Barely thirty minutes had passed since Rowan had given the order to dash at the enemy, and now nothing remained of the Mosquito Fleet. The *Raleigh*, having been sent earlier, and the unarmed *Beaufort*, which also had a head start, were the only sur-

The USS *Commodore Perry*, 1863. This vessel would lead the attack at the Battle of Elizabeth City, and would be responsible for ramming and sinking the Confederate flagship *Seabird*. (*NHHC*)

vivors. The *Ellis* was now in Union hands while the *Black Warrior*, *Fanny*, *Seabird*, and *Appomattox* were either burned or sunk. Lynch ordered the disabled *Forrest* put to the torch, and with Fort Cobb being abandoned, the way to Elizabeth City and the Dismal Swamp Canal was now in Union hands.

While perhaps not a surprising victory, the speed and manner in which it was achieved deserves merit. Rowan's approach in holding his fire until it was most effective, and then closing in on and boarding the enemy, certainly rattled the gunners of the Confederate fleet and ultimately proved decisive. By reducing the battle to a close-range melee Union numbers, regardless of a shortage of ammunition, dictated the outcome. Perhaps just as importantly, it had been accomplished with minimal damage to the fleet and only a dozen or so casualties; a remarkable number given the amount of shot, shell, and musketry fired at such close range.

For Commodore Lynch it was a difficult day. He had worked at the guns of Fort Cobb along with Parker's crew and a few militia troops. At first the makeshift crew had three of the four guns in action, but after a few shots the remaining militia fled and only two guns could be worked. Soon it didn't matter, as the Union fleet sailed past the fort firing shell and shot at the earthworks as they slid by. At that point there was nothing Lynch could do but watch as the Federal warships ran down his fleet and annihilated it. "We in the fort saw this work of destruction going on without being able to prevent it," Captain Parker recalled. "As soon as the vessels passed the fort we could not bring a gun to bear on them, and a shot from them would have taken us in reverse. A few rounds of grape would have killed and wounded all the men in the fort, for the distance was only a few hundred yards."[16]

Mercifully it was over quickly, leaving Lynch visibly stunned. Seeing Lynch's state and the untenable position they were in, Parker took the lead and ordered the guns spiked and the fort evacuated. After the task was nearly completed Lynch finally spoke and half-heartedly objected, but he quickly acquiesced when Parker pointed out that Rowan's fleet would turn its attention on the fort now that the Confederate fleet had been destroyed. Parker would hold no ill feelings toward Lynch's conduct, later saying of the incident that, "As his command had just been destroyed under his eyes, I knew pretty well what his feelings were."[17]

In traditional fashion Lynch and Parker were the last men to leave the fort. As the troops filed out Lynch stopped the civilian he had found in command that morning. The man, a Prussian engineer sent by Richmond to inspect the fort, had stood at his post while the rest of the militia had fled. The commodore thanked the engineer for his service, and perhaps because on a day where so many things had gone wrong for the Southern cause it was important to see something that went right, in his official report he noted that "Mr. Heinrich, the civilian whom we found in charge of the battery, stood by us to the last, and deserves to be gratefully remembered."[18]

SEVEN

The Siege of Newbern

ROWAN ADVANCED ON ELIZABETH CITY after the battle with four vessels. As his force pulled up to the docks, they could see a light artillery battery riding off. Most of the denizens of the town had a similar idea and hastily packed wagons could be seen departing at all angles. At the shipyard he found the CSS *Forrest* up on stocks as well as two other gunboats in various stages of construction. The commander burned these vessels, destroyed or seized the equipment in the shipyard, and then dispatched a shore party to destroy the nearby railroad station. Rowan also sent a few patrols into the city, which was on fire in a number of places and in a general state of panic. After the return of the railroad party, and the capture of a Confederate artillery officer who had been instructed by General Henningsen to put several buildings to the torch, Rowan decided it was best to pull his ships back to Cobb Point to avoid any appearance that the Union fleet had anything to do with firing the town.

The next day, while the fleet attempted to salvage what they could from the enemy vessels, Rowan sent a reconnaissance force to Edenton, which, beyond burning a few public buildings, returned with news that the town was undefended. The following day he dispatched

Lt. Jeffers and several vessels to obstruct the entrance to the Dismal Swamp Canal, which he reported, "was performed with the characteristic zeal and discretion of this officer."[1]

For all practical purposes Albemarle Sound was now a Union lake. There was nothing to oppose Rowan's fleet or the movement of troops to key towns along the major rivers that fed the sound. On February 18 Rowan would use elements of his fleet to carry and support the 9th New York on a raid against the port town of Winston on the Chowan River. After unexpected resistance, the town was abandoned by the Confederates, and contrary to Burnside's policies, it was set to the torch by Colonel Rush Hawkins' angry Zouaves.[2]

Patrols were sent out and other raids planned, but Rowan and his fleet would not spend long in Albemarle Sound. With the northern portion of the inland waterways secured, Burnside turned his attention to the southern portion. Newbern, the second largest town in North Carolina, was the first objective. The town of around six thousand was built at the junction of the Trent and Neuse Rivers. Both rivers were navigable into the interior and were used to bring crops and goods to market. More importantly, Newbern was connected by rail to the port of Morehead City, and traveling inland, to the north-south rail lines between Richmond and Charleston.

The Confederates had fortified the approaches to the town as well as barred access to the Union fleet. Patrols of the area and Union sympathizers reported that a series of batteries had been built along the west bank of the Neuse just downstream of Newbern and that a pair of batteries had been erected in front of the town as well. This was supplemented by a double line of piles and obstacles, which, even though not impenetrable, would force an attacking vessel to come to a near standstill directly in front of the guns of Fort Thompson on the west shore. To make matters worse, there were reports that the Confederates had deployed torpedoes (naval mines) throughout the barrier. As Burnside and his staff discussed the matter with Rowan, who was now ranking naval officer in the region, the path became clear and once again highlighted Burnside's and Rowan's ability to conduct joint operations.[3]

The plan called for Rowan's fleet along with a number of army gunboats to move in advance of the transports and secure the landing site at the mouth of Slocum's Creek, about fifteen miles downriver

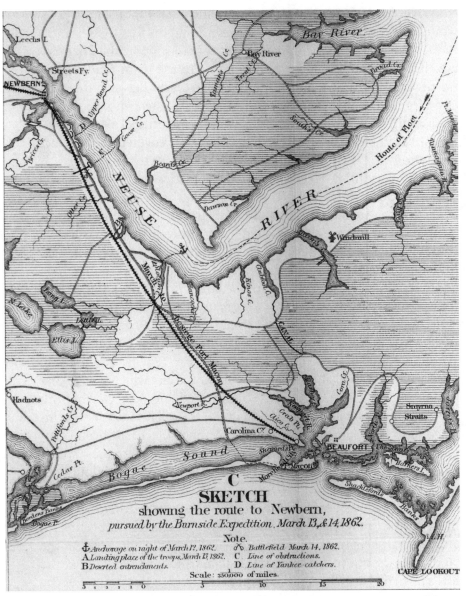

A map of Burnside's expedition against Newbern and Fort Macon. (*Library of Congress*)

from Newbern. Here three brigades, some twelve thousand troops, would be landed and just as with the landing on Roanoke Island a naval howitzer battery would be put ashore to support the infantry's advance. The landing force would march to the main road leading northwest to Newbern and cut the railroad tracks between the latter and Morehead City. Once organized, General Foster, who would lead the assault, would march toward Newbern and attack the shore batteries from behind while Rowan and his fleet covered the advance and pummeled the Confederate earthworks from the river.

With everything agreed upon, the logistics for the operation started in early March. By now ammunition shortages from the earlier actions at Roanoke Island and Elizabeth City had been addressed, and whatever damage that resulted from those encounters as well as some of the smaller interim raids that followed was repaired. On March 5 Burnside's troops were warned to be prepared to march on an hours' notice, but it would still be some time before the fleet of transports and the foul weather were ready to accommodate the general's wishes.[4]

The importance of Newbern was not lost on the Confederacy. When General D.H. Hill toured the area in late 1861 he ordered a set of earthworks raised about ten miles below the city which would later be dubbed the "Croatan Works." This fortified line, protected in front by swampy terrain and reaching inland to the rail line, was never finished although substantial portions of the project had been completed by the time of Burnside's landing. Upstream from these works along the west bank of the river was Fort Dixie, an earth redoubt designed to mount four twenty-four-pound cannon. A half a mile farther upstream was Fort Thompson. It was a solid earthen structure braced with timbers and mounting a dozen guns, but expecting an attack from the river, only four guns could be trained to fire on the landward side of the fort. A set of obstacles and piles lying under the fort's guns had also been placed across the river at this point. For the next two miles above Fort Thompson lay Fort Ellis, Fort Lane, and three redoubts, only one of which had been finished and provided with a pair of guns by the time Burnside's troops appeared. At Newbern two batteries had been raised in front of the town holding a pair of eight-inch columbiads and a pair of thirty-two-pounders. A few gunboats anchored nearby could also be called upon for assistance.[5]

Although powder, shot, and shell was in short supply there were greater problems with the defenses of Newbern. While the river approach toward the town was the principal focus of attention, efforts along the main road and railroad lines on the west bank had been woefully ignored. With too few men to guard the Croatan Works and a series of batteries along the shore that could only train a handful of guns in the landward direction, the entire scheme appeared so vulnerable that one engineer who surveyed the works called them "a disgrace to any engineer." Colonel B. Estvan, a soldier of fortune and veteran of the Crimean War who had signed on to the Confederate cause, completely agreed. Estvan was sent from Raleigh to advise and report on the defenses of Newbern, and what he found amazed him. The forts and batteries were poorly laid out, and the troops as well as their officers showed a lackadaisical attitude toward the entire effort. The Croatan Works were unfinished, not that it mattered since there were nowhere near enough troops to man this position, but more importantly, there were no secondary works being constructed to replace this line and cover the landward approach via the main road and railway line. Even worse, after watching the gunners of Fort Thompson and their dismal performance with a practice target in the river, the colonel concluded that "if General Burnside had only the slightest notion of how matters stood, he would at once make sail for Newbern, and take the place without risking the loss of a man."[6]

In command of Newbern was General L. O'Bryan Branch. Branch, who had served briefly as colonel of the 33th North Carolina Regiment, was from an old and well connected family, which no doubt led to his appointment as general. Although a political appointee like Wise, Branch was not naive and quickly realized that the four thousand ill-equipped troops assigned to him could not possibly man the extensive works below the city. He wrote letter after letter asking for powder and men, but while his superior General Gatlin agreed with him, Gatlin's pleas went unanswered as well.

With too few men to defend the Croatan Works, Branch focused on a second line of defense four miles to the northwest. Fort Thompson would anchor the left end of the Confederate defenses, which would trace the high ground from the river west to the Weathersby Road. This terrain, created by a tributary of Bryce Creek, left the Confederate line in the form of an elongated Z with the right side of the

Confederate line staggered some five hundred yards behind the left. Fortunately for Branch's troops timber abounded. On the right side of the defenses a series of redoubts were built to handle a battery of guns, while on the left side a long wood and earth redoubt was constructed which reached from Fort Thompson west to the edge of a bluff. To reinforce this position even further, more timber was cut, the branches sharpened, and the whole piled in a fifty-yard deep mass of pointed stakes and potential snares. Known as a *cheval-de-frise*, it would slow any infantry attack against the entrenchments down to a crawl exposing the enemy to huge casualties should they attempt to storm the fortifications.[7]

Given the circumstances Branch's defensive arrangements were perhaps the best that could be asked for. He did at least have enough men to cover the majority of the line, and while his flanks appeared strong the section in the center where the Confederate line jogged to the north five hundred yards was suspect. Here, there was an old brickyard with a large brick building cut with loopholes and an earth entrenchment placed before it. This and a handful of troops was all that barred passage through the bluffs on the left and right.

By March 12 Burnside and Rowan were ready. That morning Commander Rowan led his fourteen warships out of the anchorage near Hatteras Inlet and proceeded southwest to the mouth of the Neuse River. Behind Rowan were the transports and supply vessels for the three brigades of Union troops in the landing force. By sundown the entire fleet came to anchor for the night before the mouth of Slocum's Creek, some fifteen miles from Newbern. The next morning Rowan's warships moved forward. At 8:30 the Union gunboats began shelling the landing area and suspected rebel outposts. The troops, having been transferred to small boats, watched the display for an hour as the Union vessels passed by the landing site in line-ahead formation, firing as they did and then wheeled about for another pass in the opposite direction. At 9:30 the naval gunfire shifted inland and the order to land was given.[8]

Although the weather had taken a turn for the worse, the landing proved uneventful as the troops waded ashore in a small inlet which one participant characterized as "a mudhole." By 11:30 no enemy forces had been observed and enough troops were ashore that General Foster, who as at Roanoke Island was in tactical command, began

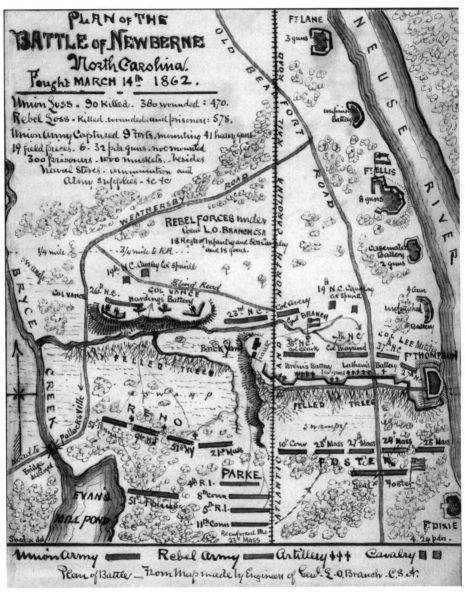

A map of the Battle of Newbern, March 14, 1862. The broken nature of the Confederate line can be seen in this map as well as the location of the forts and batteries along the west bank of the Neuse. Note that the Confederate unit at the brickyard should be the 33rd not 23rd. (*Library of Congress*)

to move inland. Here Union troops encountered signs of abandoned fortifications but no sign of the enemy. With the brigades all ashore and several regiments assembled near the main road, Foster advanced with Reno's troops in the lead. After a few hours' march a captain of the Topographical Engineers along with several of Burnside's and Foster's staff officers entered the lines with news that the Croatan Works were abandoned. Foster ordered the advanced elements of the Union army to occupy the fortifications as a cold rain settled down on the area with patches of fog forming over the bogs and waterways.

By three o'clock Reno's, Parke's, and Foster's brigades had been assembled near the Croatan Works. At this point Burnside ordered the division forward with Reno's brigade advancing down the railroad tracks and Foster's brigade advancing along the Old Beaufort Road with Parke following close behind. The wet soldiers were roused from their temporary shelters by the hoarse calls of their officers and sergeants. The troops formed up, water running off the bills of their caps, and after a series of echoed commands pushed forward. It proved an exhausting march. "We traveled till after sundown over the muddiest road (if road it could be called) that I ever saw," one participant from the 8th Connecticut noted. Another pointed to the cement-like feature of the North Carolina clay when it became saturated and pondered, "whether the mud or the ankle would give way," as he attempted to free himself. Even Burnside agreed, saying, "This was one of the most disagreeable and difficult marches that I witnessed during the war."[9]

Late in the day when the last of Burnside's troops were ashore, Rowan in the *Delaware*, along with the *Commodore Perry*, made a reconnaissance of Fort Dixie. The Confederate battery opened fire on the *Delaware*, and soon the Union vessels and the fort were exchanging fire. Rowan broke off the skirmish at dusk and returned to the landing zone. A thick fog had begun to roll in and the rain intensified as he met with Burnside not long after. The general thanked Rowan for his actions and informed him that he planned to attack the next morning and that the commodore should have his fleet ready to support the advance. Rowan nodded at the news and the two agreed that part of the fleet would support the army's advance with shell fire, while the other elements engaged Fort Dixie and Fort Thompson.[10]

Around 10 p.m. the brigades were halted for the night as scouts returned with news of Confederate entrenchments two miles ahead. As the men pitched their tents in what one participant called a sheet of water and started fires under the wet strands of Spanish moss that hung from the forest like tinsel, the naval howitzer detachment and a pair of gun detachments from two other vessels struggled to get their guns forward in the knee-deep muck. With herculean effort and help from the nearby troops, the last of the cannon came into camp around midnight, just in time for what one witness called "a right smart rain."[11]

General Branch's scouts had kept him apprised of the Union landing and advance. His skirmishers and pickets had fallen back to the line of recently built fortifications extending from Fort Thompson to the Weathersby Road. Along the redoubt on the left of the Confederate line Branch placed nine guns and four regiments of poorly equipped North Carolina troops, the 27th, 37th, 7th, and 35th. The few heavy guns in Fort Thompson that could be trained to the landside were tasked with supporting this position as well. On the bluff anchoring the right-hand side of the Confederate line, Branch placed Colonel Zebulon Vance's 26th North Carolina, one of the general's better units, and supported this position with three cannon and several companies of cavalry.

At the brick building in the vulnerable center of his line Branch strangely posted a battalion of militia under Colonel H.J. Clarke, perhaps his weakest unit having only been in existence for a few weeks. To help deal with any potential attack or breakthrough in this area Branch stationed the 33rd North Carolina a thousand yards to the rear, but the next morning, as if in an acknowledgment that the position was too vulnerable, Branch dispatched a pair of twenty-four-pound guns to the brickyard. Although their crews arrived and were busy digging a redoubt for the guns, the cannons themselves arrived too late to be of help.

Counting the gun crews in the forts and batteries, along with six regular North Carolina regiments, a handful of cavalry, and a few militia units, Branch had perhaps 4,400 men at his disposal. With this force he had to defend the two-mile-long line from Fort Thompson to the Weathersby Road and the west shoreline of the Neuse River against three brigades of Union troops supported by the gunfire of a fleet of

US Navy warships and a battery of naval howitzers. It certainly appeared a daunting task, but his troops were ready for the challenge.[12]

At daylight Burnside ordered the division forward. Foster was to attack the enemy entrenchments extending westward from Fort Thompson, while Reno would launch his brigade at the heights on the enemy's right occupied by the 26th North Carolina. General Parke would move his brigade to the center of the Union line and advance down the railroad tracks behind the other two brigades with the aim of being able to support either Foster or Reno should they require assistance.

"About 6 a.m. we started," a New England soldier in Parke's brigade recalled. "Wet as rats, but due to the southern climate, not cold and our blankets (were) as heavy as eight ought to be." The three brigades of Union troops began their march through pockets of fog that clung to the landscape. Foster's column had marched a little over a mile down the Old Beaufort Road when his skirmishers came into contact with enemy pickets. As the sounds of scattered musketry reverberated through the woods, scouts returned with reports that there was a long wooden redoubt ahead, with a six-hundred-yard wide swamp in front of it and a *cheval-de-frise* at the barricade's base.

Foster and his staff sketched out the Confederate defensive line on their maps and after a brief discussion the general ordered the brigade to deploy from column to line at the edge of the swamp. The 25th Massachusetts moved to take position on the far right of Foster's line followed by the 24th Massachusetts who would form up on their left. The two units had barely reached the edge of the swamp when flashes of musketry and cannon fire erupted from the Confederate redoubt. The naval howitzer battery under the command of Lt. R.S. McCook of the USS *Stars and Stripes*, and a pair of guns from two other vessels in the fleet, took up station in front of the 27th Massachusetts which was the next regiment to fall in line. As McCook's gun crews dragged their howitzers into position and prepared their guns, two more regiments, the 23rd Massachusetts and the 10th Connecticut, moved forward completing Foster's deployment. As the troops moved forward one member of the 10th Connecticut recalled, "a loud, swift whiz went through the air, sounding as if someone had torn a thousand yards of canvas from one end to the other at a single pull." The explosion fell behind the advancing New Englanders, but "a few yards further, and there was another, this time apparently passing but a little above our heads; then another, and still more; some further, and some nearer." The 23rd Massachusetts came under a murderous fire as it moved into position and had barely formed a firing line when a shell burst within its ranks killing its lieutenant colonel, Henry Merritt. As a hail of mini-balls and the occasional burst of grapeshot splattered his ranks the commander of the 10th Connecticut ordered his troops to lie down. "The men were behaving well enough," one witness pointed out, "but they didn't wait to hear the order twice. I never saw a crowd drop quite so suddenly as they did."[13]

The naval howitzers were soon in action adding their low-frequency impulses to the chorus of gunfire that had taken hold down the length of both lines. Soon what was already a hazy morning intermingled with the blue-white smoke to create a veil over the battlefield perforated by a sporadic pattern of broken yellow flashes. It was clear at the moment that Foster had no intentions of advancing against the barricade in front of him. Instead he glanced at his watch and trained his field glasses on the river for his next cue.

At dawn Rowan ordered the fleet underway. The *Delaware* and the *Southfield* crawled forward through patches of fog and began intermittently firing on Fort Dixie. This was joined a few moments later by elements of the fleet stationed farther behind and a few of the vessels anchored near Slocum's Creek. When there was no reply after a few minutes the Union barrage halted and a boat was sent forward to investigate. The fort proved to be abandoned and the stars and stripes were run up the pole to announce its new status.

Rowan's fleet, arrayed in a jagged line across the river, slowly moved forward and began shelling forts Thompson and Ellis. A four-gun battery between the two forts opened fire on the fleet, but it was quickly silenced after having fired only a few shots. The commodore gave the order for the fleet to advance to the first line of obstacles in front of Fort Thompson. With the Union army clearly engaged at the redoubts behind Fort Thompson, Rowan ordered his vessels to focus on the fort, while several vessels fired shells in the "direction of the sound of the enemy's fire in the interior." Although the latter decision, without visual contact or information on the actual position of the Union line, appeared questionable, Rowan later confided in a letter to Admiral Goldsborough that knowing the persuasive effects of a nine-inch shell on enemy troops, "I commenced throwing 5, 10, 15 second shells inshore and not withstanding the risk, I determined to continue till the general sent me word."[14]

Foster's advance had stalled at the Confederate breastworks. As the naval howitzers continued their fire, braving the enemy riflemen and dueling with the Confederate batteries, it became clear from the smoke hanging over Fort Thompson that the Union fleet had engaged the stronghold. The fleet's shell fire was noticeable, even over the steady musketry, flattening trees and sending columns of earth and debris skyward near the fort and along portions of the Confederate line. In fact, it became a little too noticeable. "They had got a low range and their shells were coming dangerously near," one soldier in the 21st Massachusetts noted, "splintering and cutting off the trees, and ploughing great furrows in the ground directly in front of us." Another participant was not so fortunate when a large naval round came tearing through his formation "with a roar such as an ordinary freight train might have made if running at a hundred miles an hour" sweeping away two of his comrades ten feet away. After several such incidents Foster sent a runner to inform General Burnside that the naval gunfire was falling too close to the Union lines.

On the Union left the gullies, ravines, and cypress swamps brought General Reno's advance to a crawl. Fire from the 26th North Carolina regiment and a battery of guns on the high ground before Reno only slowed the advance further. On Reno's right however, the 21st Massachusetts faced the Confederate brick building and its defenses. The two twenty-four-pound guns Branch had promised to reinforce the militia battalion stationed here had just arrived via the railroad and caught Reno's attention. While the cannons were being moved into position the general ordered the commander of the 21st Massachusetts, Lt. Colonel William Clark, to advance and seize the enemy guns.[15]

With sword in hand Clarke rallied several nearby companies, skirted the swamp, and dashed upon the Confederate artillery men who had been busy either unlimbering the cannon or constructing the redoubt. Caught by surprise only a handful of shots were fired as the horses galloped away with their owners following close behind. Clarke had seized the location, but it was not defensible. He quickly began taking scattered fire from the 26th North Carolina on his left and skirmishers from the 35th North Carolina on the high ground to his right. With the enemy already on the run Clarke ordered his men forward against the battalion of militia stationed at the brick-yard. The defending troops, having been in service for only two weeks, bolted at the sight of the charging Union infantry. The con-fused retreat, coupled with the sight of the stars and stripes flying over one of the buildings in the brickyard and cries that the line was outflanked, quickly spread to the troops of the nearby 35th North Carolina who were holding the far right of Branch's wooden redoubt. Branch, who was not far away from the scene, would later write that once the militia retreated the 35th, under Colonel James Sinclair, "very quickly, followed their example, retreating in the utmost dis-order."[16]

Reno could clearly see that the 21st Massachusetts had found the weak spot in the Confederate line. He passed orders for the rest of the brigade to support Clarke's breakthrough, but the dismal terrain and the withering fire from the Confederate units on the high ground before them made this a slow order to execute for most of the troops. Not waiting, Reno and Clarke marshalled together what men they could and pushed forward into the opening left by Colonel Sinclair's retreating regiment, seizing an abandoned battery of Confederate guns and a portion of the Confederate line in the process. The move soon drew Branch's attention and he ordered the 33rd North Carolina to advance on the brickyard to prop up his crumbling center, while several companies of the 7th North Carolina were ordered to change face and push forward to retake the captured battery.

The counterattack worked. Clarke's outnumbered troops soon took flight when the Confederate infantry formations emerged out of a grove of young pine trees. With the Union troops pushed out of the redoubt, the battle now became one for the center of the Confed-erate line. The 21st Massachusetts troops dueled with several com-panies of the 33rd North Carolina near the brick building in some of the hottest action of the day. The Carolinians, led by Major Gaston Lewis, repelled several attacks on their position and twice rallied to counterattack and seize it back. Lt. Colonel Clarke's men had found the key to the Confederate defenses, but they simply did not have enough men to exploit it.

Clarke rode back looking for support and ran into Colonel Isaac Rodman of the 4th Rhode Island and his staff. Rodman, in the vanguard of General Parke's brigade which had been slowly probing forward, was quick to take up Clarke's cause. Sending a runner to inform General Parke of his intentions, he launched the 4th Rhode Island forward in support of the Massachusetts troops. It proved the key point in the battle. The regiment fell upon the same battery that Clarke had seized earlier and in the process caught the overextended 7th North Carolina Regiment in the flank. "It was a grand charge," one member of the 4th Rhode Island recalled.

> Shot and shell, grape and minie-balls greeted their approach, and the men began to drop before the murderous fire; yet never swerving from their onward course, they steadily advanced, loading and firing as fast as possible, till within a hundred yards of the works, when, with a cheer, they charged home, and planting their colors on the ramparts, swarmed over the breast-works. A short, fierce struggle, and the fort was ours, and the beaten and dismayed rebel host fled to the rear, leaving many prisoners in our hands.[17]

Matters were actually worse for the Confederates. When he received Rodman's message Parke ordered two more regiments forward to support the 4th Rhode Island. The 8th Connecticut and the 5th Rhode Island surged forward a few minutes behind Rodman's troops and swarmed over the captured battlements, all but sealing the Confederate army's fate.[18]

His lines cut in two and the prospects of a Union brigade enveloping his forces against the river was enough for Branch to sound the retreat. Many of the Confederate units never received the order. On the Confederate right the 26th North Carolina and the five companies of the 33rd North Carolina posted in the western end of the brickyard, along with several smaller detachments around them, conducted a fighting withdrawal. For the bulk of Branch's troops in the wooden redoubt near the river, the retreat quickly turned to a rout when, upon seeing the Confederate line flanked, General Foster ordered a bayonet charge.

Foster's men, pinned down by fire for several hours, splashed forward as the enemy abandoned their works. Moving over these fortifications a portion of Foster's brigade along with three of McCook's naval howitzers pushed toward the railway station near the brickyard. Here they encountered a large body of enemy troops, or to be more precise, Colonel Clark Avery and the remaining companies of the 33rd North Carolina. After having been forced out of their position they were looking for an escape from the Union advance. With the enemy column only a few hundred yards away McCook ordered the battery to halt and deploy. Within a few minutes the guns were ready for action and McCook gave the order to fire, "but the order could not be executed," McCook wrote in his official report, because of "Acting Master Hammond rashly dashing forward in front of the guns and demanding their surrender." McCook, perhaps as surprised as Avery by the event, then noted that the enemy agreed to Hammond's demand and "complied by throwing down their arms and holding up their hands."[19]

For Rowan and his fleet Fort Thompson provided an easy target, and when an aide from General Burnside arrived warning the fleet that their rounds were falling too close to the Union lines, Rowan adjusted the flotilla's fire back to the fort. As they closed in on the barrier strung across the river in front of the fort the fleet's firepower focused on the earth stronghold, obscuring the structure in smoke, dust, and flashes from exploding rounds.

With the fort not returning fire Rowan looked for a way through the barricade. A shallow shoal divided the river into two channels at this location. Locked stern to stern twenty-four vessels had been sunk in the right-hand channel their rigging still intact protruding like a forest rising from the water. The left-hand channel, which passed in front of Fort Thompson, showed no such obstructions but proved more insidious. Just below the waterline Confederate engineers had placed a submerged *cheval-de-frise* consisting of large iron-tipped wooden stakes that were placed at a forty-five-degree angle pointing downstream. Scattered among these were rumors of some three-dozen infernal machines, or torpedoes, that the enemy had rigged to explode upon contact with a Union vessel.[20]

Looking to press the advantage Rowan signaled the fleet to follow the *Delaware* in line-ahead fashion as he pressed on into the left-hand channel. The ship's pilot warned the commander that his fleet would be blown up, but Rowan informed him that the "risk was to be run" and that he hoped "their machines would not go off." In fact, none of the torpedoes proved an obstacle and although several vessels did strike the iron-tipped stakes, with the *Commodore Perry* signifying the worst of the damage with the broken-off head of one spike stuck in its bottom, none reported any damage serious enough to impede their progress.

As the Union vessels breached the barrier the stars and stripes appeared over Fort Thompson. It was clear that the enemy was retreating, and not long after, Fort Lane exploded with a thunderous clap raining debris down onto the river and surrounding shoreline. Several Union vessels had been firing at this fort and claimed they were responsible. This might be partially true as the fort's commandant, Captain Mayo, had ordered everyone out of the fort and was preparing to fire the magazine when the fort exploded with Mayo still inside. A few minutes later, whether by a well-placed shot or more likely Confederate hands, the magazine of Fort Ellis also erupted, shaking the ground around it and wrapping the structure in a towering column of smoke. At that point Rowan wrote, "the jig was up."[21]

The commodore advanced quickly up the Neuse and navigated a second set of river obstacles without incident. The fleet appeared before Newbern expecting to engage the batteries protecting the city, but they found them abandoned as the Confederate troops and citizen of the town had begun a panicked flight out of the city. The Confederate army was in full retreat and Rowan could see elements of it funneling their way over the great railroad bridge that spanned the Trent River into Newbern. Several Confederate steamboats were caught by surprise and, attempting to escape up the Neuse River, came under fire. One of these, the *Post Boy*, was run ashore by its crew and put to the torch, while the steamer *Albemarle* towing a schooner loaded with commissary stores was captured.

The railroad bridge over the Trent was left open as long as possible, but as Union pickets approached the river it soon became apparent that the bridge had to be destroyed. A fire raft was fashioned from 150 cotton bales and two barrels of turpentine and, after being lit, was set adrift upstream of the structure. As hoped the raft became stuck alongside one of the piers holding up the bridge, and moments later the elegant 750-yard long expanse was wrapped in a sheet of flames. Both the retreating Confederates and their Union counterparts gazed upon the bridge as it burned through the night—a beacon of victory to one and a funeral pyre to the other.[22]

EIGHT

Fort Macon

LITTLE AFTER MIDNIGHT ON MARCH 14 Union troops began to enter Newbern. Several public buildings had been set ablaze, and for those souls that still remained, many fugitives from the surrounding towns and plantations, chaos ruled. Burnside appointed General Foster military governor and directed him to restore order and distribute rations to the displaced populace. This Foster accomplished in short order, leading Burnside to report to the secretary of war that "it is now as quiet as a New England village."[1]

As Foster's brigade moved into the town Reno's brigade took a position along the south bank of the Trent River, from the still burning Trent railroad bridge to the next bridge a few miles upstream. Burnside had assigned a steamer to shuttle troops and supplies across the river to Newbern, but when Reno and his men repaired the damaged bridge above Newbern, the general was able to quickly transport his supplies and artillery over the waterway.

The capture of Newbern had come at the price of nearly five hundred Union casualties. Confederate losses were similar, with Branch reporting 165 killed and wounded and 413 missing. The casualty totals, however, did not reflect the stunning level of the Confederate defeat. Burnside's forces had taken four hundred prisoners and captured nine forts with forty-seven heavy guns, two miles of intrenchments, nineteen field pieces, a thousand stands of small-arms, tents and barracks for ten thousand troops, and a large amount of ammunition, as well as a sizable store of naval goods which were now in Commander Rowan's hands.

More importantly, with the occupation of the town, Burnside was in the position not only to secure all of Pamlico and Albemarle Sounds but to strike into the interior of North Carolina. He had dispatched a regiment of troops a few dozen miles up the Trent River to test Confederate defenses in this direction, while Foster pushed forward repairing the bridges and railway line toward Kinston, where Branch's retreating forces had encamped. In addition, Burnside placed the 24th Massachusetts aboard a dozen transports and sent them under the watchful eye of the *Delaware, Louisiana,* and *Commodore Barney* to seize the town of Washington at the mouth of the Pamlico River. The only obstacle encountered was a series of piles that had been placed in the river as the town proved to be undefended and its inhabitants sympathetic to the Union cause.[2]

As his men consolidated their holdings at Newbern and across Pamlico Sound, Burnside ordered General Parke's brigade as well as several batteries of artillery to lay siege to Fort Macon, which guarded the last Confederate seaport on the Outer Banks. After this, Parke was to advance on Carolina City, Morehead City, and Beaufort, all of which were now cut off from the railroad and their primary supply lines. With Fort Macon and these nearby towns in Union hands, Burnside would have access to a seaport and a direct rail line from this supply depot to Newbern and points along his advance into the interior.[3]

For the garrison of Fort Macon, which was comprised of four companies of the 10th North Carolina, a company of the 14th North Carolina, and an assortment of artillery and naval gunners, some 450 men in all, news of Newbern's capture brought forth the grim reality that they were next. Coupled with this was the equally grim realization that the towns about them were essentially defenseless, and their old-style fort was likely not up to the task.

Completed in 1834 Fort Macon was located on the eastern tip of Bogue Island. A pair of shoals in the main passage between Bogue Is-

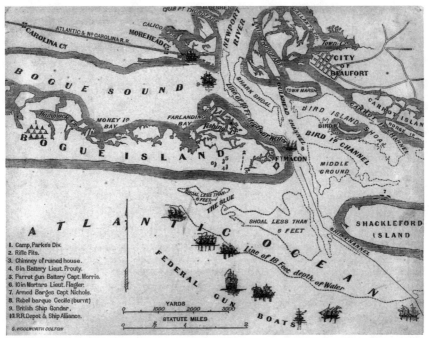

A map of the siege of Fort Macon showing the channel into Bogue Sound as well as the location of Fort Macon and the surrounding towns at the end of the Atlantic & North Carolina Railroad. (*Library of Congress*)

land and Shackleford Island restricted maritime traffic to a narrow channel that passed within six hundred yards of the fort. This made the position particularly strong and easily capable of controlling the main channel to Morehead City with a handful of heavy cannons. The problems with the fort were not so much with its position, but its construction. Started in 1826, the fort was built along the lines of a fortification from the War of 1812 era. The outer wall of the fort was laid out in the shape of a pentagon. A long glacis was placed in front of this wall while behind it was a broad ditch, in the center of which was built the pentagon-shaped masonry fort with an open interior parade ground. In the age of sail this low-lying fort made of stone and earth was deemed sufficiently strong to withstand a naval bombardment, and just as importantly, was capable of withstanding the elements. The fort was garrisoned for brief periods from 1834 to 1849 and several repairs and improvements were made during this time to extend the life of the structure. In September 1849 the fort's last garrison, a company of forty-one men, was transferred to Florida. By 1850 the fort was all but abandoned after being turned over to a custodian, whose job, it appears, was to record the fortification's decay. This caretaker was relieved of this task during the opening days of the conflict, when the weather-beaten structure was occupied by North Carolina troops.[4]

Colonel Moses White, in command of Fort Macon, responded to the news of Newbern's capture by setting his garrison to work digging trenches and filling sandbags to brace the gun positions and parapets. White had already discovered a number of issues with the fort which he could do little about. Although the colonel had mounted forty guns, the structure was designed such that most of its guns faced the sea or Bogue Sound. Without a large garrison to defend the landward approach along Bogue Island, the fort simply did not possess enough guns in this direction to prevent an opponent from moving within range, opening trenches, and erecting siege batteries against the stronghold. This scenario was made worse by the fort's stone construction. The detonation of explosive rounds fired by the enemy would not only pulverize the structure but would create clouds of stone splinters in the process, making it perilous to man the exposed gun positions.

White had hoped to delay Parke and his brigade by burning the railroad bridge over the Newport River, but Union troops managed to secure the nearby Old Beaufort Road bridge and advanced on Carolina City, taking the town without any resistance on the evening of March 22, 1862. Parke ordered two companies to continue on and seize Morehead City, but at the moment, with half of his brigade still marching toward him, he did not feel strong enough to send a detachment onto Beaufort.[5]

The next morning Parke dispatched a pair of officers under a flag of truce to Fort Macon. Here, after the traditional blindfolding and being aimlessly marched about, the two men were brought before Colonel White where they presented him Parke's surrender demand. Parke informed White that he had superior numbers, intimate knowledge of the fort and its defenses, and the means for reducing the fort at his disposal. "Its fall," Parke concluded in the note, "is inevitable." Although Parke offered generous terms, White thanked the officers

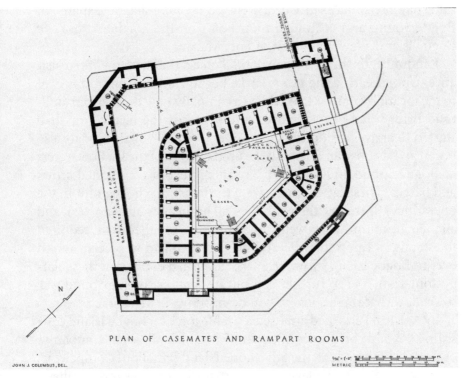

PLAN OF CASEMATES AND RAMPART ROOMS

JOHN J. COLUMBUS, DEL.

A plan of Fort Macon. More reminiscent of a fort from the War of 1812, Fort Macon was a generation out of date when it was besieged by Union forces in the spring of 1862. (*Library of Congress*)

for their efforts and politely refused. Parke shrugged at the response when it was delivered to him a few hours later. He really did not expect White to give up his fort without a shot being fired. It was more a traditional courtesy than anything else. The path before Parke was clear. "We have now but one course to pursue, and that is to invest the place; but with the Newport Bridge destroyed," he informed Burnside, "this will be a slow operation."[6]

He proved correct. Using hand carts brought aboard the transports and whatever else that could be procured, long wagon trains traced the route from Slocum Creek to Carolina City. By March 31 Parke reported that he had invested the fort by occupying the dock facilities at Morehead City and Beaufort, which, when combined with the Union naval blockade off the coast, isolated the stronghold. That same day a reconnaissance party crossed the long shallow expanse of Bogue Sound and grounded their boats on the northern shore of Bogue Island a few miles west of Fort Macon.

Landing at the head of a small tidal creek, the party met no resistance. Upon hearing the news, Parke began transferring troops over to the location in order to establish a camp. By now the Newport railroad bridge had been repaired and some of the heavy guns had started to arrive. In addition, a number of small howitzer boats also began arriving by rail. These Parke used to control the shallow waters of Bogue Sound and to escort his ragtag fleet of confiscated scows and barges. These latter vessels were the logistical choke point in the operation. His troops, their supplies, all his heavy guns, mortars, and all their ammunition, as well as the hundreds of other items required to establish a camp for several thousand men had to be transferred over to Bogue Island by water. Parke never had enough of these flat-bottom craft, and to further complicate matters, Bogue Sound was so shallow that these convoys could only cross at high tide.[7]

By April 10 Parke had amassed a sizable force on Bogue Island consisting of eight companies of the 4th Rhode Island, seven companies of the 8th Connecticut, the 5th Rhode Island Battalion, Company C, First United States Artillery, and Company I, 3rd New York Artillery. Feeling confident enough to press forward, Parke informed the blockading fleet of his intentions and, the next morning, advanced in force. Accompanied by Captain Robert Williamson, of the Topographical Engineers, Captain Lewis Morris, of the Artillery, and Lieutenant D.W. Flagler, of the Ordnance Department, Parke moved to within a few miles of the fort where a small skirmish broke out with a Confederate outpost. The Union troops quickly pushed the handful of enemy pickets back toward the fort after a few rounds were fired at the advancing blue column.

When Parke came within a mile of the fort, shot and shell from Fort Macon began to erupt in fountains of sand near the column. The general ordered his men to take cover and signaled the nearby fleet. Several gunboats responded and soon airbursts could be seen above the fort. Using this as cover Williamson, Morris, and Flagler examined the area and selected several locations for siege batteries, at one point advancing to within eight hundred yards of the structure to complete their survey. Having accomplished this work Parke withdrew out of range. The Union Navy continued shelling the Confederate stronghold for a time, and then abruptly broke off the action.[8]

The next morning Parke returned for good. An advanced guard of five companies was sent forward to push back the Confederate pickets and establish a line of rifle pits within a thousand yards of the fort. Work parties moved in behind these men and began the firing platforms for the siege guns as well as the communications trenches. The guns were then dragged forward on sleds some three and a half miles over rolling sand dunes. The fort fired over seventy rounds at the Union advanced guard and work parties, but it did nothing to hinder the Union efforts and no one was harmed by the bombardment. It now simply became a matter of time. Given that Parke's batteries would be erected under fire, most of the work was done at night. Colonel White's men made a number of small sorties in an attempt to disrupt the advance, and occasionally rained sporadic long range shot and shell upon the Union works, but it accomplished little. "From this date the regular work on the approaches, trenches, batteries, and rifle pits was vigorously pushed forward by all our available force both night and day," Parke penned in his official report. "In spite of the desultory fire kept up by the enemy."[9]

For Colonel White part of the problem was a shortage of ammunition as well as a lack of experienced gunners. Another part of the problem was the nature of the Union batteries. The two Union batteries closest to the fort, some 1,400 yards away, held three thirty-pound rifled Parrott guns and four eight-inch mortars. As mortars did not require a line of sight to the fort in order to fire, their platforms were dug into the opposing bank of a sand dune, out of the defenders' sight. The platforms for the Parrott guns were also dug into the opposing bank of a sand dune, with the top portion of the dune removed to create an embrasure for the guns to fire through. A few hundred yards behind these guns was a third battery consisting of four ten-inch mortars, which, like the earlier battery of eight-inch mortars, were lodged behind a long dune completely obscured from the fort's guns.

While the commander of Fort Macon possessed several dozen cannons, none of these were mortars, meaning that there was little he could do to damage the Union guns. Not that they didn't try, creating deep furrows and explosive clouds of sand on the front side of the dunes, but to no effect. White and his men eventually employed half a dozen old thirty-two-pound carronades angled at a forty-degree elevation to lob explosive rounds at the enemy, but even this effort yielded little success given how concealed the batteries proved to be.

With his guns proving ineffective and his garrison too small to sally out against the enemy, there was little for White and his men to do but wait for the inevitable. Everything had been seen to in preparation for the siege. A merchant ship had been sunk in the main channel next to the fort, the nearby lighthouse disabled, and all of the fort's out-buildings, which might be used as cover for the attackers, had been destroyed. The fort's casemates had been reinforced with iron railroad tracks and the batteries covered in blankets of sandbags.[10]

The wait was clearly eating at the garrison's morale. Nearly a third of the command was on the sick roll, and a number of incidents had occurred leading to several desertions. "The men complained of their fare," White reported, "and seemed to be dissatisfied with being shut up in such a small place." While such feelings might be anticipated given the circumstances, the colonel blamed part of the problem on his officers who "did not act in a proper manner to suppress the difficulty."[11]

By April 23 the matter had come to a head. Parke's batteries were complete and all the ammunition required for a sustained bombardment was in place. Burnside had sent a pair of floating batteries to the area along with the captured USS *Ellis*. These vessels were to drop anchor near the western edge of Shackleford Island and engage the fort with their rifled guns, while the Union fleet shelled it from the sea and Parke's guns bombarded it from the landward side. The matter seemed so much in hand that Burnside, who had arrived on April 22 to oversee the operation, demanded that White surrender the fort the next day. When the fort's commandant refused, Burnside took the unusual step of asking to meet with White the next morning.

At 8 a.m. White's launch pulled ashore on the western tip of Shackleford Island. Standing not far away was Burnside and a number of his officers. The men exchanged greetings before the Union general turned to the matter at hand, and as White recalled, "attempted by persuasion to produce a change in my determination." It was certainly a difficult moment for both men. Honor required that White not surrender the fort without at least making an attempt at defending it,

The commander of Fort Macon Colonel Moses White, left. General John Parke, right, who would lead the effort against Fort Macon. (*Library of Congress*)

and Burnside knew this. The general informed White that he was isolated and outgunned and that the Union batteries would pulverize the old fort. The outcome was not in doubt. One suspects that White believed Burnside, but it did not change his answer; "the fort would be defended as long as possible." As White returned to the fort Burnside cursed the foolish young officer, while at the same time realizing that he would have done the same thing. The West Point graduate and former arms maker shook his head and ordered the bombardment to start at dawn.[12]

At daybreak the garrison of Fort Macon watched as three Union steamships and a sailing bark approached the fort in line-ahead formation. Suddenly one of Parke's Parrott guns shattered the still morning. This was followed by another shot and then a chorus of hollow thumps as the mortars began lobbing their explosive payloads toward the structure. The shriek of incoming rifled rounds and the scattered explosions about the fort as the Union gunner sought to find the range were quickly met by a barrage from the fort's guns.

Lt. Flagler, who was in command of the ten-inch mortar battery, noted that, "At first the enemy's fire was very rapid, principally shells and shrapnel, and the fort was so enveloped in smoke that it was difficult to tell whether our shells were falling within or beyond them." Flagler's gunners continued to experiment with the range until reports arrived from an observer in Beaufort that the rounds were passing over the fort. Lt. Merrick Prouty, in command of the eight-inch mortar battery, faced a similar problem with his initial shots falling short, but after adjusting the powder charges "a good range was obtained in a short time."[13]

Around 9 a.m. the Union warship *Daylight*, followed by the steamer *State of Georgia*, the gunboat *Chippewa*, and the sailing bark *Gemsbok* came to the edge of the shallow shoals near the fort and added their firepower to the bombardment. The *Gemsbok* dropped anchor, while the other three vessels steamed in a large circle firing at the fort as they passed in range. For Commander Samuel Lockwood aboard the *Daylight* there were instantly problems. A stiff wind was blowing onshore, causing the ships to pitch violently in the shallow waters and making the guns "almost unmanageable." Lt. Andrew Bryson of the *Chippewa* agreed, saying that his vessel was rolling so badly that "At times the muzzle of our XI-inch pivot gun was within a very short distance of the water."[14]

While Lockwood's vessels were having difficulty servicing their guns, the gun crews in Fort Macon did not have such a problem. All four Union vessels reported enemy shot and shell falling close by, with the captain of the *State of Georgia* calling it well directed, and Lockwood himself rating it as excellent. Every ship was struck, with most being minor hits in the rigging or, as in the case of the *State of Georgia*, with a round passing through the American flag. The *Gemsbok*, however, received a shot that shattered the main topsail mast, sending it tumbling down onto the deck, and the *Daylight* was struck in the starboard quarter by an eight-inch solid shot that tore through several bulkheads and the deck below before finally coming to rest on the other side of the vessel a few inches above the port engine.

By quarter past ten Lockwood had seen enough and ordered the fleet to move off. The flotilla had fired a little over a hundred rounds at the fort, but the sea and the surf were proving a more difficult enemy. The vessels moved off shore and waited for the weather to subside and would play no further role in the engagement.

Burnside's floating batteries and the *Ellis* also opened fire on Fort Macon from their position across the channel but with little in the way of results. The floating batteries continued a methodical fire during the engagement, but at two miles the range was simply too great for the rifled gun on the *Ellis*, even when the powder charge was increased to questionable levels.[15]

The gunfire from the Union fleet and the floating batteries was helpful, but it was Parke's batteries that pulverized Fort Macon, just as Burnside had said they would. Captain Morris's battery of Parrott guns wreaked havoc on the old fort. The thirty-pound solid rifled rounds slammed into the stronghold's masonry with a shriek, creating an instantaneous cloud of stone and wood debris that left fracture patterns along the fort's walls. In one case a Parrott round cut through a bar of railroad iron before burying itself a foot deep into a stone wall. The Confederate guns proved particularly vulnerable to the rifled gun battery with most of the disabled pieces showing hits from Morris's guns and, in one case, an eight-inch and ten-inch columbiad both being disabled by the same shot.

With the help of an observation team in Beaufort signaling corrections, both Flagler's and Prouty's mortar batteries began to consistently drop their rounds into the confines of the fort. Together with the Morris's Parrott guns the observer in Beaufort noted that "the accuracy of [our] fire astonished ourselves equally with the enemy," and that "after 12 p.m. every shot fired from our batteries fell in or on the fort."[16]

The battering would still continue for several hours. Perhaps as many as six hundred rounds had struck or exploded over the fort. The rate of fire was such that several of the eight- and ten-inch mortars had problems with their platforms, and Morris noted that his Parrott guns were firing so fast that "the vents of all my guns were enlarged, one of them so much so as to render the gun unserviceable." Finally, around 4 p.m., White had seen enough and raised a white flag. By now only a few guns could still respond to the enemy, the fort's walls and structures were shattered, and close to two-dozen guns lay dismounted amidst piles of leaking sandbags.

White asked for surrender terms, but Parke informed him that unconditional surrender was the only option, which White quickly refused. Parke then changed his tone and agreed to a cease-fire until White could meet with General Burnside the next morning. On April 26 the commander of Fort Macon once again found himself standing before General Burnside on Shackleford Island. Burnside was interested in seeing the matter done and offered White and his men their parole for a gallant defense. The twenty-seven-year-old colonel nodded and handed Burnside his sword, officially surrendering Fort Macon.[17]

NINE

The March to
South Mills

EFORE BURNSIDE DEPARTED FOR FORT MACON, he wrote the secretary of war regarding the status of his command. Matters had been greatly simplified when reinforcements poured into the area in the form of eight additional infantry regiments. While the cavalry regiment and two batteries of light artillery the general had requested had not appeared, he was quick to take advantage of the surge in manpower, especially given the rising numbers of men on the sick rolls. A new fort being built above Newbern would be finished in a few days. Mounting thirty guns and capable of holding a thousand men it would be the cornerstone of the town's landward defenses. General Foster was advancing down the railroad line toward Kinston, but obstacles in the form of burned bridges and the general lack of railroad engines and cars, as well as wagons and teams, had brought his effort to a crawl. Burnside was not overly concerned, informing the secretary that "The enemy continues in force at Kinston, but I feel quite sure I can dislodge them after the fall of Fort Macon."[1]

With Parke and three regiments of his brigade investing Fort Macon, another half a regiment at Hatteras Inlet, three regiments at Roanoke Island, and thirteen and a half regiments currently at Newbern, coupled with Commander Rowan's naval superiority over Pamlico and Albemarle Sounds, Burnside had every reason to feel confident. He had secured a Union beachhead along coastal North Carolina, and with a recent influx of manpower he now looked to strike inland.

The focus of his first efforts was to destroy the locks in the Dismal Swamp Canal. Rumors had reached the general that the Confederate naval facility at Norfolk was preparing to send several ironclads down the canal to retake Elizabeth City and assert control over Albemarle Sound. While a sufficient reason in and of itself to launch an expedition, even with operations at Fort Macon still in progress, Burnside informed the secretary of war that there was another purpose behind the effort:

> I sent General Reno up beyond Elizabeth City to destroy the locks in the Dismal Swamp Canal, and to use his discretion as to other operations in the direction of Norfolk, and with a view to creating a diversion in favor of McClellan, and I hope to hear of the successful termination of his expedition within two days.[2]

On the morning of April 17 General Reno ordered the 21st Massachusetts and the 51st Pennsylvania to board a pair of army transports at the town docks. By late afternoon the troops and their equipment had been stowed away, and with a signal from commander Rowan's flagship, the *Philadelphia*, the convoy set out for Roanoke Island. Here they rendezvoused with a brigade of troops under the command of Colonel Hawkins consisting of the 9th and 89th N. Y. and 6th New Hampshire Regiments. Setting out again the next day, by midnight of the eighteenth the entire force was busy with landing operations on the north shore of the Pasquatonk River across the river from Cobb Point.

Hawkins' brigade was ashore by the early hours of April 19, but the second brigade from Newbern was delayed when one of the transports ran aground near the mouth of the Pasquatonk. Reno directed Hawkins to advance toward South Mills and informed the colonel that the second brigade would follow as soon as possible. By 7 a.m. Reno and his men were ashore and marching inland a few hours behind Hawkins. A dozen miles from South Mills, Reno was surprised when he encountered Hawkins and his haggard men. The colonel's

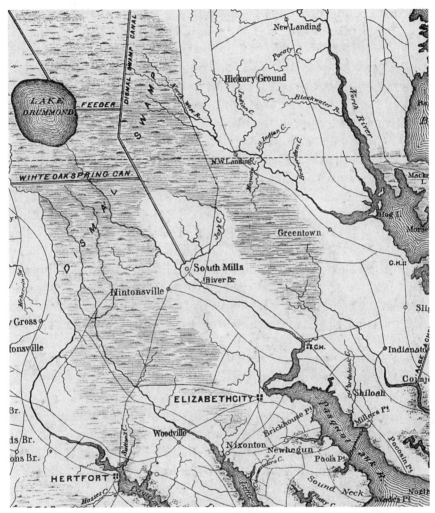

A portion of a contemporary map of the Pasquatonk River showing the Dismal Swamp Canal locks at South Mills, as well as Elizabeth City, and Cobb Point (Brickhouse Point). (*Library of Congress*)

guide had become lost in the darkness and taken the brigade ten miles out of its way.[3]

Reno ordered Hawkins' brigade to follow and pressed forward with the 51st Pennsylvania, the 21st Massachusetts, and a battery of four marine howitzers under Colonel William Howard. The past week had been unusually dry and the oppressive heat from the midday sun cou-

pled with the dust created by a column of several thousand men moving down a narrow dirt road had slowly worn down Reno's advanced
column as well. The woods that flanked the main road finally di-
verged and the head of the Union column entered a large field. The
general was about to call for a halt to rest his troops when the advanced guard of the 51st Pennsylvania noticed what they thought was
a burning farmhouse at the other end of the field, likely put to the
torch when news of Reno's march reached the inhabitants.

Suddenly the discharge of cannon filled the air. The first round,
according to a witness in the 51st Pennsylvania standing near Reno,
"struck in the centre of the road, close in among Co. A boys, and ricocheting over the general's head landed in a field on the left of the
road." This was quickly followed by more solid shot, which skipped
across the landscape in a deadly flight, and the burst above the Union
column that rippled the ground below with a wave of shrapnel. It
soon became apparent that the smoke was coming from a burning
ditch at the other end of the field some six hundred yards away and
that the enemy guns and earthworks had been "skillfully masked" by
the drifting clouds of smoke. Round-shot and canister followed at a
vigorous pace from the Confederate four-gun battery and brought
the Union advance to a halt.[4]

Standing near the busy gun crews was a cluster of grey-clad officers, their field glasses straining to discern the effects of their fire and
the enemy's movements. Prominent among these men was the
bearded Colonel Ambrose Wright. News of a large Union force landing near Elizabeth City had alarmed General Huger in Norfolk. Fearing a Union move toward the port, Huger sent Wright along with the
3rd Georgia, seven companies of North Carolina militia under
Colonel Dennis Ferebee, and a battery of light guns under Captain
William McComas to observe and ascertain the enemy's intentions.
General Albert Blanchard along with the 32nd North Carolina and
the 1st Louisiana would follow to help secure the canal and block any
attempt to use it as a route to Norfolk.[5]

On the morning of April 19 Wright had received news of Reno's
march toward South Wells. He quickly dispatched riders to Blanchard, and riding forward with his staff, he selected the current spot
to challenge the Yankee advance. Assigning two militia companies to
occupy a gun battery across the river, the colonel moved forward with

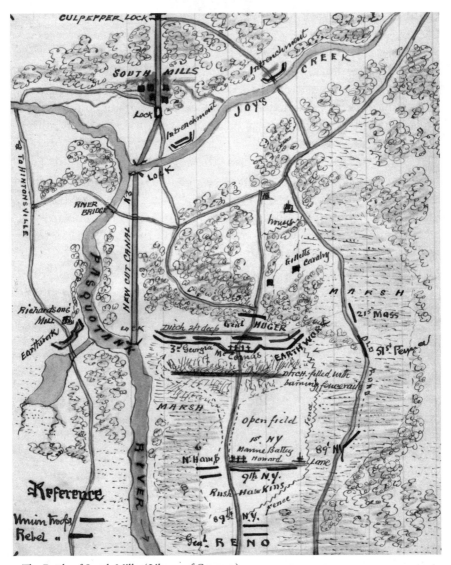

The Battle of South Mills. (*Library of Congress*)

three companies of the 3rd Georgia, five companies of North Carolina militia, and a battery of four six-pound guns under Captain McComas; a little over five hundred men in all. Wright was under no illusion and expected to be badly outnumbered. The engagement was to be an orchestrated delay, a rear-guard action in order to allow Blanchard time to send reinforcements, and an opportunity to gauge the enemy's strength.

Now as he counted the flags of the blue-coated formations arrayed before him, he understood the extent of his handicap. Fortunately for Wright's men the position the colonel had chosen certainly helped make up for their deficiency in manpower. Wright had makeshift for-tifications of fence rails and earth raised, stretching several hundred yards from the Pasquatonk River, across the road where he posted McComas' battery, to the woods at the edge of a marsh on his left. Here, because of the nature of the ground and a road that ran parallel to the east, Wright made a slight turn in the breastworks to help guard his flank. In front of this line was a field some six hundred yards in length flanked on the riverside by bogs and on the landside by dense wet woodlands. To further reinforce his position the colonel utilized a small ditch that ran in front of the earthworks by filling it with tur-pentine-soaked fence rails. The entire line and some nearby dwellings would be put to the torch upon news of the enemy's approach.

Thus far the Georgia colonel was pleased with how events were unfolding. For half an hour the Union column remained halted until a battery of howitzers moved forward and deployed near the road, while a regiment of troops marched up and took a position in the bogs on their left to support them. As the two lines began an artillery duel that would last for several hours Wright and his officers watched as a pair of Union regiments moved into the wood on their left in a clear attempt to outflank the Confederate position.[6]

With Colonel Howard's battery now engaged, Reno sent word to Lt. Colonel Thomas Bell, in command of the 2nd Brigade, to take the 51st Pennsylvania and 21st Massachusetts through the wooded swamp on the enemy's left and turn their flank. When Hawkins' men arrived on the scene Reno sent the 6th New Hampshire to the left of Howard's battery and ordered Hawkins to follow the 2nd Brigade in the flanking maneuver.

For a moment it appeared to both Reno and Wright, who perhaps could see each other through their field glasses, that the matter would be over quickly. Reno was not foolish enough to advance into the Confederate colonel's trap when he could simply outmaneuver his opponent. Wright would soon realize this, bow to the inevitable, and withdraw back to South Wells, likely burning the bridges over the

Pasquatonk River and Joy Creek in the process. Reno would then advance and destroy the locks at Joy Creek and the lower lock on the Pasquatonk River before advancing on South Wells.

What appeared to be a skirmish, however, was soon changed into a battle in part by fatigue, and in greater part by the impatience of Colonel Rush Hawkins. The 51st Pennsylvania and 21st Massachusetts had a difficult time navigating the brambles, tall weeds, and thick groves of trees. Mini-balls ripped through the foliage and the occasional cloud of cannister zipped past like angry hornets, producing a series of knocks when they found wood and a dull thud when they occasionally found their target. Eventually these units found an old road and made slightly better time, arriving mostly intact on the Confederate left a few hundred yards away.[7]

Hawkins, who admitted that only half his men were able to advance due to their grueling morning march, led the 89th New York into the woods on the Union right. The 9th New York, however, and a number of stragglers from the 89th still remained strung out to the right of Howard's battery. The soldiers of the 89th New York would have likely surmounted the quagmire of obstacles before them, just as Bell's brigade had, but exhausted from their previous efforts they now wilted in the low-hanging trees and wet undergrowth. Frustrated with the advance, Hawkins later wrote, "After a short tour of observation I came to the conclusion that it would be impossible to outflank them on the right, the undergrowth and swamp being almost impenetrable."[8]

The colonel ordered the 89th New York to halt and hold its position. He then raced back to the 9th New York, still laying spent from the earlier march. Walking up and down the lines of haggard soldiers he encouraged and scolded his men and then informed them that "A charge through an open field in front of the enemy's position was thought to be the only way in which, they could be dislodged." The exhausted troops responded and the 9th New York formed up its ranks and advanced over the open field toward the Confederate works. With sword in hand Hawkins led his men forward, sending orders for the 89th to follow their lead. Together they would dash upon the works and seize the day just as they had at Roanoke Island.

General Reno could not understand what was happening or who ordered the advance, but like Wright and McComas he realized it was a mistake in motion. Reno had the bugler sound the recall, but it was too late. Beyond a handful of marksmen, and a growing skirmish breaking out on the Confederate far left, the bulk of the troops in the fortifications checked their fire until the waves of Zouaves appeared out of the smoke a few hundred yards away. The Confederate line suddenly erupted into a rolling wave of blue-white smoke. The volley staggered the New Yorkers, thinning their ranks and bringing the advance to a halt until a few bursts of cannister mowed down whole sections "like grain before the sickle," sending the regiment running for cover. Hawkins motioned for the troops to move to the right toward the tree line where the 89th New York was appearing. Many men ignored the order, but for those that obeyed, the arrival of the 89th helped stabilize the situation, although it was clear to all involved that storming the enemy works was not an option.[9]

It turned out there was no reason to storm the Confederate lines. Having navigated the woods, Bell ordered his men forward to the fence line on the Confederate left. From here and in the woods to their right they were able to enfilade the enemy lines. Bell's men watched in surprise as the Zouaves stormed into the smoke and then minutes later returned like a receding tide. With the volume of fire rising on his left flank and the death of Captain McComas having sent his artillery, already down to their last boxes of ammunition, scurrying away in panic with their guns, a little after 4 p.m. Wright ordered a retreat just as Bell ordered the bugler to sound the charge.[10]

The withdrawing Confederates finally offered a clear target to the frustrated Union troops and it's likely that in these last few moments of the engagement Wright suffered the bulk of his casualties, but in general, the retreat was orderly, likely because the victorious Union troops were too spent to take advantage of the moment and offer any kind of pursuit.

Indeed, Reno never considered a pursuit. Instead he ordered the wounded tended to and ordered campfires lit so his men could cook a well-deserved meal and obtain some much-needed rest. Reno's casualties were 127 killed, missing, and wounded with over half of this falling upon the 9th New York. While it proved to be a victory in the sense that the Union held the field at the end of the day, it did not feel like one to the demoralized and exhausted troops. The long march and hard-fought battle with Wright's men had left the general

Brigadier General Jesse Reno, left, and Colonel Rush Hawkins, right. A feud would erupt between the two men after the Battle of South Mills, focusing for the most part on the actions and conduct of Hawkins. (*Library of Congress*)

with a difficult decision. He had only taken supplies for two days in the field, and most regiments were reporting that they were already low on ammunition after the recent engagement. Coupled with the state of his troops, intelligence that Wright would soon be reinforced, and an explicit directive from Burnside not to risk a disaster, at 10 p.m. Reno gave the order for the army to return to its boats. Colonel Hawkins later called the decision into question, to which Reno angrily responded in a letter to Burnside that "In fact, it was his [Hawkins] bad conduct in placing his regiment in a position to get whipped and demoralized that principally induced me to change my first intention, which was to remain on the field and proceed to South Mills in the morning."[11]

Wright briefly fell back on Joy Creek and called in his detachments until he was joined by several companies of the 32nd North Carolina who informed him that Blanchard's brigade was not far away. Late that evening, with his detachments having returned, Wright withdrew to the northwest lock about halfway along the Dismal Swamp Canal and rendezvoused with Blanchard's arriving units later that day.

The colonel reported his total casualties as seventy-three with about a third of this falling on the companies of the 3rd Georgia. Wright had executed a well-thought-out battle plan, and after delaying and inflicting heavy casualties on his opponent who foolishly attempted to storm his position, he conducted an orderly withdrawal to a prepared position on the other side of Joy Creek. While not technically a victory, five hundred men standing up to five thousand for four hours and preventing the latter from achieving their objective was certainly something close. Perhaps Commander Rowan put it best when he quickly summed up the battle by informing Goldsborough that "I regret to inform you that the lock has not been destroyed."[12]

TEN

Wilmington

O NE HUNDRED AND FIFTY MILES to the south of Pamlico Sound sat the most important port along the North Carolina coast, Wilmington. Established in the 1730s as an alternative to the town of Brunswick on the lower Cape Fear River, the town of a few dozen souls was initially referred to as New Town or Newton. In 1739 colonial governor Gabriel Johnston successfully petitioned the North Carolina legislature to change the name of the settlement to Wilmington in honor of the governor's longtime patron, the Earl of Wilmington. The site selected for what would become the most important deep-water port in North Carolina was on the east bank of the Cape Fear River at the confluence of the Northeast Cape Fear River and the Cape Fear River, both of which stretch far into the interior of the state. To the north was Smith's Creek and to the east numerous ponds that had been created over the years via a series of dams. Pine forests circled the landward side of the town and behind these to the east and south lay an arc of marshes and swamps.

The Lower Cape Fear River is six hundred yards wide at Wilmington with the western shore across from the town a long section of tidal marshes cut by ribbons of water from the Cape Fear River. From the town to the confluence of the Brunswick River at the end of the tidal marshes, some three miles downstream, the river remained this width with a channel depth from nine to nine and a half feet at low tide thanks to dredging efforts made before the outbreak of the war. After the entrance of the Brunswick River the Lower Cape Fear began to open up to a mile in width and would remain this way until Old Brunswick after which the river would widen to almost two miles before entering the sea.[1]

In a fashion similar to Cape Hatteras, the mouth of the Cape Fear River was dominated by a series of islands, navigation hazards, and inlets. Federal Point, or Confederate Point as it was renamed by the new government, and the long sand bank known as Zeek's Island formed a narrow water passage known as the New Inlet. This entrance into the Cape Fear River was not originally present when the first denizens of Wilmington settled in the area but was formed when a furious four-day storm pummeled the region in 1761. The main channel through the 1,300-yard expanse opened by the storm was eight to nine feet deep at low tide and twelve to thirteen feet at high tide.

To the west of the New Inlet and farther down river lay a series of shoals that, after passing, led to the Old Inlet; a mile-wide opening between Smith's Island to the east and the edge of Oak Island to the west. A pair of channels passed through this opening to the sea, the easternmost one known as the Bald Head Channel, because it passed close to Bald Head Point on Smith's Island, was the deeper of the two showing eight feet at low tide while the western channel was typically a foot to a foot and a half shallower.

With limited access into and out of the river, tricky shoals and sandbars upon entering the waterway, and a series of islands and peninsulas almost ideally placed to guard these passages, Wilmington was perhaps the best naturally protected port in the Confederacy. This, of course, was helpful but not sufficient. Pamlico Sound had a superb natural defense in the way of the Cape Hatteras Inlet, but failure to act and secure this location had cost the Confederacy dearly. When it came to Wilmington and its approaches via the Lower Cape Fear, the Confederacy would not make the same mistake, although at times they would lose focus and appear to offer the Union an opportunity.[2]

When Brigadier General Richard Gatlin was appointed to command the Department of North Carolina and the coastal defenses of the state on August 20, 1861, he immediately faced a host of problems. Less than a week later a telegram from General Huger at Norfolk arrived warning Gatlin that a Union fleet had departed Hampton Roads and was rumored to be headed for North Carolina waters. There was little Gatlin could do but summon his reserve regiments at Goldsboro and set them to work on the shore batteries below Newbern, but before he could even put this in motion, news arrived that the Confederate forts at Cape Hatteras had fallen and that the Hatteras Inlet was now in Union hands.[3]

Two weeks later the responsibility for the coastal defenses of North Carolina were handed over to Brigadier General Joseph Anderson, a former military and civilian engineer who would report directly to Gatlin. This move was soon followed by a string of reorganizations that would eventually leave General Wise in charge of the Roanoke Island area, General Branch in charge of Newbern and Pamlico Sound, and Anderson in charge of Wilmington and the approaches into the Cape Fear River.

When Anderson arrived at Wilmington, he was well aware of how important the port was to North Carolina and the Confederacy. A major stop on the Atlantic and North Carolina railroad, Wilmington was a town of a little less than ten thousand, almost half of whom were slaves. The ship traffic that cleared the port, however, gave the town the impression of being much larger. Before the start of the conflict the Wilmington docks serviced thirty vessels a day and it was not uncommon to see five hundred or six hundred sailing ships scattered between the town and the Cape Fear approaches. While traffic had certainly dropped, there was still a sizable amount that continued to defy the Union's newly launched blockade. With the Cape Fear Rivers reaching deep into North Carolina and a ferry running northwest to Fayetteville, Wilmington logically become a shipping and transportation hub, but the town's real wealth came from what was known at the time as "naval stores." The nearby pine forests provided lumber in vast amounts, pitch, tar, and turpentine—all products that the wooden ships of the age used in abundance. At Wilmington, pine, not cotton, was king.[4]

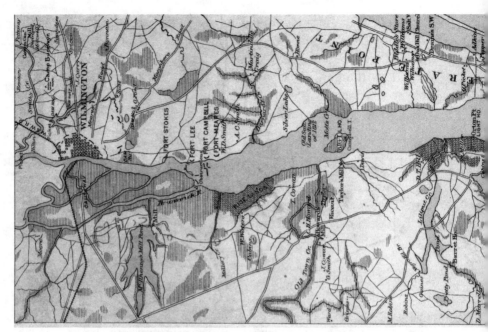

The Lower Cape Fear River from Wilmington to Smith's Island. (*Library of Congress*)

Anderson spent his first weeks at Wilmington touring the defenses in the area. What he found alarmed him. Guarding the southern or river entrance into the Cape Fear were a pair of old forts that had been seized by North Carolina militia a few months before the conflict started. The first of these was Fort Johnston at Smithville on the west bank of the river. The earthwork fort was originally put up during King George's War in the 1740s to guard against Spanish raiders. It had been maintained off and on over the years during times of tension but had been abandoned in the early 1850s. The second stronghold was Fort Caswell. Constructed on the eastern tip of Oak Island in the late 1820s, the fortification was built in a similar manner to Fort Macon; that being a masonry work covered in railroad iron and surrounded by low outer walls. Along the ramparts were sixteen guns almost all of which were trained seaward or on the river. Like Fort Johnston, Fort Caswell had been abandoned in the early 1850s and handed over to the care of a single ordnance officer. On the southern end of Confederate Point work had begun on Fort Fisher. Still in its

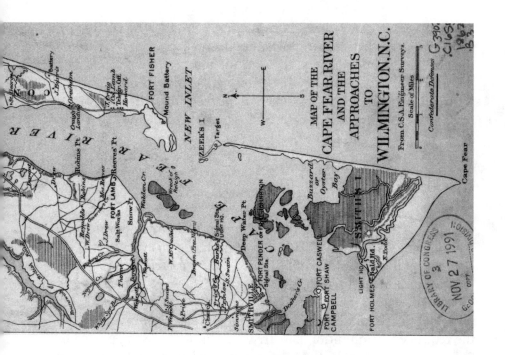

infancy these sprawling earthworks were designed to bar the New Inlet passage and were complemented by a battery across the inlet at Zeek's Island.

A number of positions were noted by the general where defenses were to be later added, but at the moment Anderson was more concerned about having a mobile force of infantry, cavalry, and light guns to patrol both banks of the river and respond to any enemy landings. In addition to this, a sizable force would have to be garrisoned at Wilmington. In all, the general estimated that beyond the garrisons of the forts, four regiments of infantry, three companies of cavalry, and three batteries of six light guns each would be required to defend the region. While it might appear to be a large request on the resource-starved Confederate forces, Anderson reminded Richmond of the strategic position of the region, a point that would not be lost on the enemy as well. He then noted that if the enemy struck quickly and seized the ill-defended area "that by taking this harbor they will command the Cape Fear River, which penetrates the heart of this

State, as well as the railways terminating here, thereby cutting off communication between important points of the country." This left the newly appointed general to conclude that, "I know of no point the seizure of which would give them so great advantage."[5]

Anderson was to be disappointed in the reply. Instead of increasing his forces, he was ordered to dispatch a pair of regiments and a light battery to South Carolina when Port Royal was threatened. By mid-February Anderson was pleading with Richmond once again. He requested that the regiments and guns sent to Port Royal be returned now that the crisis was over. His current strength of 3,500 men fit for duty was simply too small to man the forts, patrol the coast, and cover the approaches to Wilmington. The military engineer pointed out that he had a good deal of confidence in the defensive works being erected, but these would be of little use if he continued to find himself without cannon and arms for his raw troops.[6]

Currently Anderson had 350 men in Fort Caswell and had mounted thirty-four heavy guns along the walls, although not all of the requested ammunition had arrived. This fort was supported by 765 men of the 20th North Carolina stationed at Fort Johnstone. On Zeek's Island he had raised a three-gun battery of heavy guns manned by ninety-nine men. Fort Fisher on the other side of the New Inlet was perhaps Anderson's strongest position. Positions for twenty-five heavy guns had been completed and a garrison of 250 men assigned to man the fort and continue the work. Encamped in the sand dunes nearby were 770 men of the 30th North Carolina and a field battery of four twelve-pound guns. Five ill-equipped cavalry companies, four of which were militia, continually scoured the coastline for signs of enemy movements.

Small detachments and temporary posts were erected along the east and west shores of the river as one moved upstream toward Wilmington. At the town itself a series of trench works were built to the east and south side of the city, in both cases taking advantage of local water features to restrict any attack from this direction. To support these defenses Anderson stationed 933 men of the 28th North Carolina and a battery of six light guns outside the town, even though it was too small of a force to man the length of the entrenchments.

Richmond and even General Robert E. Lee, to whom Anderson had written in frustration, sympathized but could do little to alleviate his plight. Lee agreed that the troops sent to Port Royal should be replaced by additional North Carolina recruits but at the same time acknowledged that arms shortages were delaying these actions and that "the want of arms has prevented my receiving troops that have offered their services." In all, little would change until March 22, when Anderson was ordered to replace Gatlin, officially because of the latter's ill health, and Brigadier General Samuel French was ordered to Wilmington to assume Anderson's old duties. Anderson would not spend long in his new position, and within a few months he would be in command of a brigade during the Peninsula Campaign in Virginia.

French faced similar problems. By April he had three regiments at Wilmington, a handful of cavalry, and twenty companies of artillery and a number independent infantry units manning the fortifications along the Cape Fear River. With a slight increase in numbers and his defensive works improving every day this would seem to be an improvement, but the chronic shortage of arms had left one of his regiments without muskets. In response to French's continued request for arms, Richmond suggested that the new commander consider taking the muskets from the gunners in the forts and issuing them to this regiment. Any deficiencies could be made up by issuing pikes, of which there was found to be an ample supply in inventory.[7]

French would not spend long at Wilmington. A new commander, Brigadier General William H.C. Whiting, was appointed on November 8, 1862. Whiting, first in his class at West Point in 1845, had served in the US Army Corps of Engineers for sixteen years, reaching the rank of captain before resigning his commission to join the Confederate cause. "My first and last request will be for troops the instant they are available," he would state in his first letter to his superior officer, and then to the secretary of war who he wrote shortly thereafter. He pointed out that, "There are now but three great harbors on our coast not in possession of the enemy – Charleston, Mobile, and Wilmington." The latter two, and in particular Wilmington, because of the thirty-mile expanse between the town and the fortifications at the mouth of the river, were difficult to defend without a sufficient number of troops to secure such a large area. "To retain this position 10,000 effective men, with four to six field batteries, is the least force I can recommend as the supporting corps for its defense," Whiting informed the secretary of war. "If this cannot be had we must trust to God in what we have, small as it is, and the blindness of the enemy."[8]

While an accurate assessment of the situation, Whiting would have no better luck than all the former commanders in securing what was considered a sufficient force to guard Wilmington and the Cape Fear River. Instead the general would have to accept that the matter was becoming partially alleviated by the work being done to guard the inlets and the lower part of the river. The New Inlet channel was restricted by placing sunken obstacles on either side in such a manner that the remaining passage could be quickly sealed with a scuttled vessel in the case of an attack. The walls of Fort Fisher grew daily, and by now three dozen heavy guns protruded from its embrasures. The battery at Zeek's Island was doubled, and batteries had been raised along both banks of the river. Works had been planned on Smith Island at Bald Head Point and another battery would be constructed near Fort Caswell to support the old fortification, which now boasted three-dozen heavy naval guns.

General Foster, who had taken over Burnside's command upon the latter's promotion and departure, was well aware of the growing Confederate strength at Cape Fear. Writing the commander in chief of the US Army, Major General Henry Halleck, he painted a closing window of opportunity and a difficult decision.

> At Wilmington and in the defenses at the mouth of the Cape Fear River are about 3,000 men. The extent and strength of the defenses at the mouth of the Cape Fear have been largely increased of late. On Federal Point (Confederate Point), north of New Inlet, a long line of batteries has been erected, inclosing in their limits the light-house and terminating beyond in a large and strong work called Fort Fisher. The number of guns mounted are thirty-six, several of which are of so great caliber as to throw shot farther than any guns carried by the present blockading squadron. The force of the fort is now actively engaged in erecting a large bomb-proof casemate battery of six heavy guns. Across New Inlet is Turk's (Zeek's) Island, on which there is a battery of six guns. At the mouth of the Cape Fear River, Fort Caswell has been strengthened, but to what extent I am unable to say; the sand-hills, however, within range of its guns, have been leveled, so as to afford no shelter.[9]

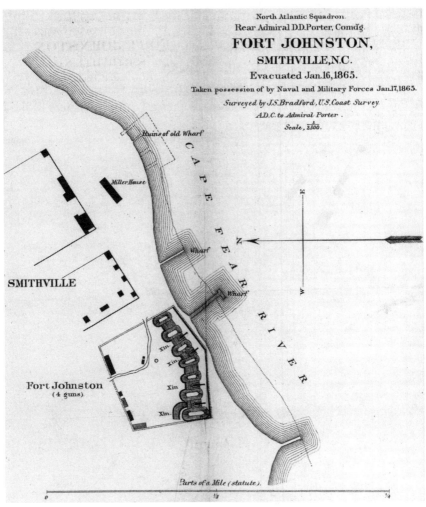

A plan of Fort Johnston at Smithville in 1865. (*Library of Congress*)

Stationed on blockade duty off Cape Fear, Commander William Parker of the USS *Cambridge* watched the Confederate fortifications begin to take shape. The sand walls of Fort Fisher slowly rose higher and extended in length, the line broken in dozens of places by gun platforms which now included a pair of long-range British twelve-pound Whitworth rifles salvaged from the wreck of a French gunboat below Cape Hatteras. "In my opinion," the naval officer proposed to

General Foster, "the present moment is the best time to attack Wilmington and the adjacent forts. The longer the enterprise is delayed the more difficult it will prove to be, as a large number of men are kept at work strengthening the fortifications."[10]

Commander Parker was indeed correct, but with a multitude of troop and naval commitments before them, Union planners looked away, and the moment passed.

ELEVEN

The Blockade of Cape Fear

WHILE THREE OR FOUR BLOCKADING VESSELS constantly cruised a few miles out to sea, there had been very little in the way of direct conflict between the Union Navy and the defenses of Cape Fear. In mid-November 1861 Confederate batteries at the New Inlet briefly exchanged shots with the USS *Monticello*, which quickly steamed out of range, and on the night of December 31, 1861, a pair of small boats from the USS *Mount Vernon* used the hazy conditions to board a deserted light ship near Fort Caswell. The intent was to burn the vessel which helped mark the channel into the river, but when the Union sailors boarded the craft, they found that it was in the processes of being fitted out as a floating eight-gun battery. This brought a little more satisfaction when they set the ship afire and pushed off into the darkness. At first sight of the flames a handful of thirty-two-pound guns from Fort Caswell boomed out blindly into the darkness, but they accomplished nothing more than signal a close to the incident.

Almost a year later, on an early October morning, Confederate gun crews finished setting up a pair of cannons on the beach. For the last week the Confederates had watched the 786-ton screw steamer USS

Maratanza approach to within two-and-a-half miles of the shore and take its normal blockading station. This time, however, the defenders had prepared a surprise and dragged a pair of long-range British Whitworth rifled cannon onto the beach. As the Union warship approached at first light a pair of flashes came from the shoreline. The first round had barely screeched over the warship and erupted in a column of water when the second shot struck the quarter deck and exploded in a whirlwind of metal and wood, leaving two of the crew dead and five others wounded. The captain of the *Maratanza* ran up his engines and stood out to sea, noting in his report that "it is no longer safe to lay within 2 1/2 miles as we have heretofore."[1]

In late November 1862 one of Whiting's northern detachments of cavalry and flying artillery proved even more successful. Lt. William Cushing, now in command of one of the survivors of the Mosquito Fleet, the USS *Ellis*, entered the New River Inlet on the morning of the twenty-third with the intention of launching a raid against Jacksonville, North Carolina. Cushing had only steamed a few miles upstream when he encountered a Confederate schooner loaded with cotton and turpentine. Unarmed, the schooner's crew set the ship ablaze and escaped in their boats to the nearby shore.

By one o'clock Cushing had dropped anchor in front of the town and landed marines to seize the public buildings. There was no resistance and beyond a few dozen guns, some mail, and a pair of schooners in front of the town there was little for Cushing to confiscate. With his prizes in tow the Union commander turned back down the river taking time along the way to throw a few shells into a small enemy encampment along the south bank of the river. A little before dusk the *Ellis* approached the still burning schooner it had encountered earlier that morning. A few minutes later several Confederate cannons opened fire on the vessel. The gunboat was not hit and retaliated with a barrage of shot and shell that chased the attackers away.

Given the low tide and time of day, Cushing's pilots informed him that the ship would not be able to clear the mouth of the river until morning; high water and daylight being "absolutely essential in order to take her out." Cushing agreed and dropped anchor in the river along with his two prizes. The next morning the three vessels pressed forward well aware from the signal fires they had seen burning along the riverbank that the enemy was watching. A few miles from the

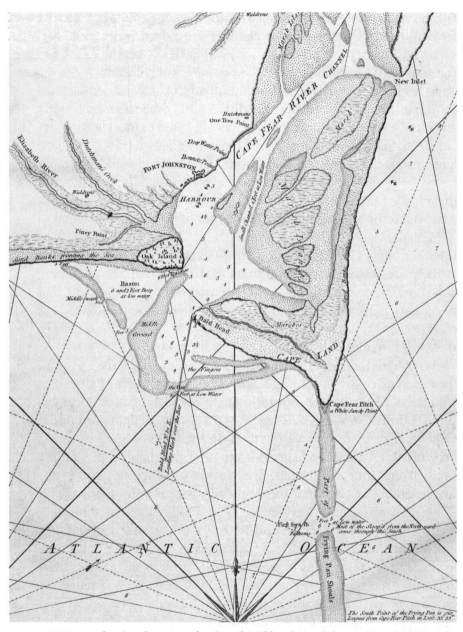

A 1876 map showing the approaches into the Old and New Inlets at Cape Fear. Note the shallow Frying Pan Shoals extending into the ocean from Cape Land (Smith's Island). This navigation hazard essentially divided the blockading force into two parts. (*Library of Congress*)

river's exit Cushing encountered a location where a bluff cut into the river and dominated the main channel a hundred yards away. Not surprisingly, a pair of enemy cannons opened fire on the *Ellis* from this bluff and for the next hour the two sides traded shots.

At length the Confederates withdrew and Cushing pushed forward thinking the matter and the expedition had come to an end, but a few hundred yards downstream he was "destined to meet with an accident that changed the fortune of the day." The two pilots on board had mistakenly identified the channel, and with a shuddering that tested the crew's sea legs, the gunboat came to a halt on a sandbar in the middle of the river. The crew scrambled to lighten the vessel, but it proved to be hard aground in the center of an arc-shaped shoal.

With darkness and low tide approaching, Cushing had his two captured schooners come alongside the *Ellis* and transferred everything to the prize vessels except for a small amount of coal, the pivot gun, and some ammunition. The Union commander was confident that the enemy guns would return in the morning, so he transferred his crew over to the sailing vessels as well and called for six volunteers to stay with him and fight the boat against long odds.

At daylight the schooners moved to the mouth of the river to await the outcome of the upcoming skirmish. Cushing and his half-dozen volunteers did not have to wait long, as a detachment of Southern cavalry under Captain A.F. Newkirk and a battery of light guns under Captain Z.T. Adams soon converged on the location. Adams set up his guns along the shore to create a crossfire and divide the warship's fire between multiple targets. The contest proved one sided as the Confederate guns battered the stranded vessel at point blank range. The engine was shot through letting off a cloud of steam that brought a cheer from the shoreline, and with the vessel hulled in a dozen places, any thought of escape at high tide was impossible. With little in the way of choices Cushing set the *Ellis* afire in several locations and with his crew ran the gauntlet of enemy cannons in a small boat. Once he reached the captured schooners the vessels pressed on over the inlet's sandbar, striking several times in the process before heading out to sea just as Confederate cavalry came galloping down the beach too late to prevent the expedition's escape.[2]

While such incidents continued to occur, the dominant activity in Wilmington at the time had become the blockade and those who defied it. As for the latter, it would take several months before the Confederates attempted to run the Union blockade. When they did it proved an instant success, as three or four vessels could hardly guard the two inlets on Cape Fear River. This stemmed in good part from the nature of the river delta and the Frying Pan Shoals laying offshore that left the two blockading forces connected by an arc some forty miles long. Additionally, the waters along the shore both above and below Cape Fear were shallow but consistent in depth, and just as importantly, the bottom was sandy and free of obstructions. For the light draft blockade runners who had to clear the bar either at the Old or New Inlet, this meant that they could hug the shoreline while the heavier draft Union warships had to stand farther out to sea. The proximity to the British town of Nassau in the Bahamas and even Bermuda, where large amounts of supplies and war materials had been gathered, combined with good seaward approaches and strong defenses in the way of Fort Fisher and Fort Caswell, made Cape Fear one of the favorite destinations for blockade runners.[3]

News of the early successes traveled quickly, and the Union blockade proved so porous that a good deal of the early blockade runners proved to be sailing vessels, many of which were routinely employed in the Wilmington trade at the time. With the enticing financial potential masking many of the risks, a flotilla of these sailing craft, many nothing more than mere fishing vessels, set out into the Atlantic to be battered by storms and chased by Union warships, often finding success. These easy times, however, would soon come to an end when more steam-powered Union warships arrived off Cape Fear. They quickly ran down the schooners, brigs, and small sailing vessels, either sending them back north as prizes or lighting the coast with their funeral pyres.

With starting numbers resembling nothing more than a paper blockade, the Union Navy responded by purchasing and arming almost 150 vessels by the end of 1861. The result was what one would expect if they were to purchase a fleet within the span of a few months. Passenger ships, tugboats, and coastal traders of all models, types, and sizes filled out the Union ranks. Steamships and sailing vessels were purchased, sailors recruited, and captains assigned. In less than a year the number of naval personnel more than doubled and the number of guns that could be brought to bear climbed to just over 2,500. It was a remarkable stop-gap measure enacted while the logistics were put in place to feed the Northern shipyards and create a fleet of five hundred warships.

By early 1862 it became apparent to the Confederacy that guns, powder, and cannon were all desperately needed. Men could be found, but arming and outfitting them proved to be the problem. Many soldiers, dressed in a wide variety of mixed civilian and military garb, brought along their old fowling pieces to at least have some means of defense, and when even this was not possible, they satisfied themselves with large Bowie knives. Ammunition and powder was constantly in demand, as was iron, and arms ranging from pistols to heavy cannon. A steady flow of these critical items, as well as a dozen others, was paramount if Confederate forces were to succeed. It soon became clear that to meet these needs a vast amount of war materials would have to be purchased from Britain and France and then run past the Union blockade into Confederate ports.

Positioned at the outlet of a pair of rivers that reached deep into the interior and a major stop on the Atlantic Railroad, Wilmington would prove an instrumental port in helping the Confederacy establish this crucial logistics chain. In particular, the town would become a lifeline for Lee's army in Virginia; so much so that when Fort Fisher was threatened in January 1865, Lee telegraphed Colonel William Lamb that if Fort Fisher fell, he would have to evacuate Richmond.[4]

The numbers of blockade runners passing through Wilmington and Charleston was eye raising. Through 1861, 1,856 attempts were made to run the blockade with an astounding 97 percent success rate. In fact, the only vessels caught were sailing ships. Certainly, these numbers were swelled by the early participation of coastal sailing vessels in the blockade running effort, but the use of these vessels would rapidly fade away as the increasing number of Union steamships began to sweep the area clear of the slower blockade runners.

The following year proved just as successful. From July 1862 to June 1863, fifty-seven steamers and ninety-one sailing vessels reportedly left Nassau for Confederate ports, many if not most of these having called on the port several times that year. While the Union forces only managed to catch six of the steamers, almost 40 percent of the sailing vessels fell prey to the blockade or the sea. For Wilmington the golden age of blockade running would be from 1863 through 1864

The sleek twin-funneled blockade runner CSS *R.E. Lee*, top. The *R.E. Lee* was captured during its twenty-third attempt to run the blockade on November 9, 1863. The USS *Connecticut*, bottom, one of the more active vessels in the Cape Fear blockade. (*NHHC*)

when just short of four hundred ships arrived, many having made the trip half a dozen times, delivering badly needed military supplies and highly profitable commercial merchandise, the latter of which would become greatly restricted as the Confederate's military deficiencies continued to grow. Part of this success was due to the lessons being learned, which in turn led to a shift in the types of vessels being employed by the blockade runners.[5]

Speed and stealth were everything to a blockade runner. Shallow draft steamships, usually in the range of four hundred to six hundred tons, so as to clear the inlet sandbars, became the craft of choice. Long and narrow, these sidewheelers, often equipped with telescopic funnels and masts, sat low in the water and were capable of twelve to fourteen knots. They were painted light grey to merge with the water and further mask their presence. In fact, even the smoke from their stacks was of concern especially when the United States government halted exports of anthracite coal, which burned cleaner and produced far less smoke than the bituminous coal that many blockade runners were forced to use.

Thomas Taylor, who served on several blockade runners that ran into and out of Wilmington, gave a quick account of such a vessel when he remarked on the newly built *Banshee No. 2* on which he would later serve. "She was a great improvement on the first *Banshee*, having a sea speed of 15 1/2 knots, which was considered very fast in those days," he recalled. "Her length was 252 feet, beam 31 feet, depth 11 feet, her registered tonnage 439 tons, and her crew consisted of fifty-three men in all." While these sleek and maneuverable vessels were well suited to match the Union sentinels patrolling off Cape Fear, there was a cost for such specialization. "As a rule, the blockade runners were ships very slightly built, of light draft and totally unfit to brave the storms of the Atlantic," one prominent captain in the trade noted. This factor would lead to the loss of a number of vessels, "Yet the worse the weather, the better it was liked," this same blockade runner noted, "since a rough sea greatly reduced the danger from the enemy's guns."[6]

As for the blockade runners themselves, the vast majority were not Confederate Navy but contractors, albeit often backed by the resources of Southern investors and foreign companies. Textile firms in Great Britain and France were struck hard by the sudden turn in the Southern cotton market. This led to unemployment in both of these industrial countries and something of a sympathetic ear to the Southern cause if for no other reason than to restore their economic prominence. Others quickly saw an opportunity in the situation. The Bahamas and Bermuda were but a two- to three-day voyage from the Carolina coast for a reasonably fast steamship, and, both being British possessions, were neutral ports. Munitions and commercial goods could be brought to these islands and from there run into Charleston, or more often Wilmington because of the advantages the approach to this port offered.

It is important to note that blockade runners were never armed. While the vessels might run from Union warships and come under fire, by being unarmed and flying no flag or neutral flags, they could not be considered warships by international law. If caught, the Union Navy would certainly seize the vessels for violating the blockade, but their crews were a more delicate matter. They were not prisoners of war, nor combatants, but considered criminals more along the line of smugglers. Looking to use a carrot as opposed to a stick approach, at first many were admonished and released given that they were foreigners, but this soon changed into internment for the duration of the conflict.

A host of British companies, employing a good number of Royal Navy officers on leaves of absence and using assumed names, invested in the speculative commerce. Large amounts of capital were required for the ships and crews, and disaster could await any attempt either by the hand of the sea or the guns of the Union Navy, but the profits were spectacular. It was claimed that, after one or two successful runs into Wilmington or Charleston, an investor could afford to lose a vessel and still come out a wealthy man.

One of the more successful blockade runners was Captain Mike Usina. Usina's activities so infuriated the US consul at Nassau that he secretly purchased the captain's portrait from a local photographer and had it distributed to blockading captains throughout the Union fleet. Usina had a unique perspective on those who participated in the risky venture, claiming that,

> The men who ran the blockade had to be men who could stand fire without returning it. It was a business in which every man took his life in his hands, and he so understood it. An ordinarily brave man had no business on a blockade runner. He who made a success of it was obliged to have the cunning of a fox, the patience of Job, and the bravery of a Spartan warrior.[7]

There were numerous examples to support Usina's assessment. Captain Steele of the *Banshee* once found himself at sunrise alongside the USS *Niphon*. Somewhat surprised at his good luck, and hoping to take the blockade runner intact for the sizable prize money it would bring, the warship's captain called upon Steele to surrender. Steele jumped up onto the paddle-box and shouted back at the Union captain "that he didn't have time to stop, because he was in a hurry." The two men bantered for a few moments while the *Banshee*'s engine room stoked the ship's boiler. When the *Niphon*'s captain saw the *Banshee* pulling away he fired a shot that brought down one of the steamer's short masts. He then raked the ship with cannister in an attempt to get it to halt, but Steele had ordered his men to lie down, and the blockade runner, using its superior speed, escaped. In another instance, when Captain Usina found himself being illuminated at night by Union ships firing off rockets, he devised a counter to the scheme by firing off his own rockets in random directions whenever a Union vessel launched one.

There were also similarities in the various blockade runner's actions and appearance. All had to exercise stealth to slip past the Union watchdogs, and all swore by the flat slate grey paint that covered their vessels. There are numerous Union accounts as to the effectiveness of the paint scheme, particularly in low-light conditions. So important was this camouflage that anyone up on deck had to wear similar colored clothing or they would instantly stand out against the background, potentially giving away the location of the ship.[8]

Captain Usina recalled the combination of these elements at play, and the absolute need for stealth.

> Moonlit nights, as a rule, were nights of rest, few ships venturing to run the gauntlet when the moon was bright. No lights were used at sea. Everything was in total silence and darkness. To speak above a whisper or to strike a match would subject the offender to immediate punishment. Orders were passed along the deck in whispers, canvas curtains were dropped to the water's edge around the paddles to deaden the noise, and men exposed to view on deck were dressed in sheets, moving about like so many phantoms on a phantom ship.[9]

The blockaders side of the equation was more complicated and by far more frustrating. When the blockade of Wilmington was first officially put into effect on July 20, 1861, a single Union warship, the USS *Daylight*, was the sole vessel assigned to the task. More Union ships would follow but not in numbers that would make any significant impact on the commerce going in and out of Wilmington. With the Union Navy involved in several campaigns and a long coastline to monitor, resources were scarce for the first year of the blockade.

Many times, no more than three or four vessels monitored both the New Inlet and Old Inlet. To make matters worse many of the converted Union warships were of questionable ability, primarily lacking in speed. With these limited numbers and an approach to the blockade that at first called for anchoring in a fixed location, it is no wonder why the blockade runners were so successful in the first year of the conflict. While the blockader's tactics were questionable, and would soon change, the root cause was simple; there were not enough ships.[10]

Even with only a handful of vessels patrolling the weather-beaten approaches to Cape Fear there were several notable successes. One of these was the destruction of the blockade runner *Modern Greece* in late June 1862. The 753-ton, 210-foot screw-propelled seagoing freighter was built in Stockton, England, in 1859 and was originally employed in the Baltic lumber trade. Pressing the *Modern Greece* into service as a Wilmington blockade runner was an odd decision and likely points to a miscommunication somewhere in the process given that the vessel drew seventeen feet of water, which was far too much to clear either the Old or New Inlet bar even at high tide.

Carrying a thousand tons of gunpowder, crates of rifles, a battery of six twelve-pound Whitworth rifled cannon, British guns renowned for their accuracy and range, as well as a sizable amount of civilian goods, the *Modern Greece* departed Falmouth, England, in late April bound for Wilmington. By the early hours of June 27, 1862, the freighter was steaming south on a moonless night, hugging the northeast shore above Fort Fisher. As the first rays of light touched Cape Fear the vessel found itself in perfect position a few miles from the New Inlet and the protection of Fort Fisher's guns.

Unfortunately for the crew of the *Modern Greece*, while the setup to enter the New Inlet appeared perfect (other than the unbeknownst fact that the vessel could not clear the sandbar), the approach was interrupted by a pair of Union warships lying a few miles off Federal Point. Commander William Parker of the USS *Cambridge*, the northernmost of the two Federal warships, spotted the blockade runner moving along the coast at 4:15 that morning. Parker and his men had almost missed the English-built ship, which was now within two miles of the inlet and making its final approach. "The atmosphere was hazy and the color of the vessel slate," Parker later reported, "while her stern was towards us, rendering the ship indistinct."[11]

Parker ran up the *Cambridge*'s engines and steered for the intruder while the signal lamps notified the nearby USS *Stars and Stripes* of his contact. As the range quickly closed, the *Cambridge*'s forward eight-inch gun barked away, causing the freighter to unfurl an English flag but not alter its current course. By now the gunners on the *Cambridge* had found the range and soon the fountains of water erupting about the blockade runner became intermixed with hits on the grey freighter.

With smoke still belching out its stacks and the British flag flying, the *Modern Greece* took an abrupt turn away from the New Inlet and ran aground on Federal Point about a half mile above Fort Fisher. The crew quickly took to their boats, leaving the cargo ship to its fate. As the *Stars and Stripes* approached and added its rifled gun to the chorus, a third and unlikely participant, Fort Fisher, began firing on the freighter as well. While the Union vessels were looking to destroy the blockade runner and the goods in it, the Confederate batteries were firing round-shot with the intention of piercing the vessel's hull so as "to wet the powder and prevent an explosion."[12]

The Union warships continued to fire on the stranded cargo ship until the guns of Fort Fisher chased them away. The *Cambridge* and *Stars and Stripes* returned and fired on the vessel and the Confederate salvage crews off and on throughout the day, but their efforts were hampered by a number of long-range guns at the fort. While the *Modern Greece* had been struck a dozen times and was clearly filled with water, the Confederate crews that swarmed over the wreck were able to save much of the cargo, perhaps the most important rescue being four of the Whitworth guns and a good deal of their ammunition. Colonel William Lamb, who had taken over command of Fort Fisher, was delighted by the news that several of the long-range guns had been recovered from the wreck. Lamb would use these guns in October to damage the USS *Maratanza* when it approached too close. "With these guns," Lamb later wrote, "we made the US blockading fleet remove their anchorage from two and a half miles to five miles from the fort. So many vessels were saved with these guns that they soon had a reputation throughout the South."[13]

On September 4, 1862, Rear Admiral Samuel Lee replaced Goldsborough as commander of the North Atlantic Blockading Squadron. Lee, who had commanded a sloop of war in the East Indies before the conflict and the USS *Oneida* during the New Orleans campaign, was quickly brought to reality regarding his new assignment when he found that he had only eight vessels monitoring the twin inlets of Cape Fear. As if this was not enough, a few days later this flotilla was reduced to seven when the *Victoria* was sent home for repairs. Lee pleaded with the navy for a pair of warships to help, noting that of his seven vessels only three were armed well enough to be called warships.

"Our forces here are too small," Commander J.F. Armstrong of the USS *State of Georgia* complained to his superiors.

> One vessel is of necessity constantly away for coal, and as the vessels do not carry the same amount of coal or for the same number of days, it is almost impossible to have only one absent at a time. There should be a force sufficient to allow one vessel to be absent from each side, without reference to vessels on the other. This will require a force of at least ten vessels, and that number is believed to be requisite to maintain the blockade.[14]

While Lee waited for more vessels, he also changed tactics. The steamer *Kate* which had slipped past the blockade into Wilmington on August 6 had escaped on the night of the twenty-seventh. Goldsborough had conducted the blockade by anchoring the fleet in a line about five miles from each inlet, with an average spacing of a few miles between the vessels. Lee's suspicions were that such a static arrangement had led to the positions of the warships being transmitted to the *Kate* before it made a dash out of the New Inlet. To prevent this in the future, the admiral ordered that "The steamers should, between evening and morning twilight, shift their day berths and maintain positions just as near the bar as is safe and practicable."[15]

At first it appeared that the tactic worked, as several blockade runners were captured, but this was more a statistical blip than a long-term pattern. With lookouts only able to discern large objects at five hundred yards at night it was a large patch of ocean to patrol, especially for only a half a dozen or so vessels. In all, it made 1862 and the dreary, storm-strewn early parts of 1863 frustrating duty for the blockaders.

By August of 1863 Lee's position had barely improved. While his numbers around Cape Fear had increased to almost a score, it was a paper illusion. Beyond the fact that several of his ships were supply tenders, the remaining warships suffered from a host of issues. Some, like the *Chocura* and *Victoria* were too slow for the duty to begin with, and almost all needed serious repairs after being continuously battered by the sea and wind off Cape Fear. The *State of Georgia* had been sent back to Hampton Roads for an engine overhaul, and the *Mount Vernon*, ten months on station, was in need of one as well. The *Sacramento*, one of Lee's faster ships, needed new valves for its engines as did the *Ossipee*. This, when combined with the need for coal which persistently reduced the force on station by two or three warships as the vessels made the round trip to Beaufort, left Lee with too few ships to cover both the Old and New Inlets. "I beg leave respectfully and earnestly to represent to the department," Lee wrote Secretary Welles, "that it is generally felt by the officers here that the blockade of this, the most difficult port to close on the coast of the United States, is exposed and inefficient from the want of many more and suitable vessels."[16]

While Lee would see an increase in his numbers allowing him to form two lines across the inlets, essentially creating a higher probability of contact and a more tortuous path for the blockade runner, it was more policy changes and increased vigilance that seemed to pay off in the short term. The move of sending warships to the coast above and below Cape Fear, where most of the blockade runners would first make landfall before following the shoreline to the Old or New Inlets, was perhaps the most productive element of this approach. When coupled with more patrol vessels it netted Lee's forces seven ships in September, and although only another seven would be taken by year's end among these were two of the most renowned blockade runners, the *R. E. Lee* and the *Banshee*.

The *R.E. Lee* had run the blockade twenty-one times under Captain John Wilkinson, but in November Wilkinson turned command of the vessel over to a new captain, who after arguing with his pilot, found himself a few miles off Bogue Inlet at daylight. Unfortunately for the well-known blockade runner, the USS *James Adger* was on its way to Beaufort for coal when it sighted the *R.E. Lee*. A brief chase ensued and after a few close cannon rounds shrieked overhead the Confederate vessel surrendered a few miles west of Cape Lookout. The *Banshee* on its ninth voyage was spotted early on the morning of

November 20 near Cape Lookout by the army transport *Fulton*, and not long after by the USS *Grand Gulf*. An hour-long chase ensued where the *Fulton* finally managed to close the range and score several hits on the blockade runner, bringing it to a halt.[17]

Rear Admiral Samuel Lee. Lee would command the North Atlantic Blocking Fleet for almost two years before being replaced by Rear Admiral David Porter. While Lee achieved a number of major successes during this period, he also found himself frustrated by a lack of resources and an improving class of Confederate blockade runners. (*NHHC*)

Beyond the effect that the loss of such vessels and experienced crews had on the Confederate blockade-running effort, their captures also meant that Lee and his captains were better understanding and executing the task before them. One of the captures in late October particularly pleased the rear admiral. Tucked away in some papers in the captain's cabin of the *Venus* was a list of seventy-five vessels employed in blockade running in 1863. Of the list thirty-three had been captured or destroyed with many of the others having quit the trade and returned to England. Even better was that several of these captured blockade runners, such as the *Calypso*, would be converted to gunboats and added to the Union fleet.

The following year would see the Union numbers about Cape Fear surge, and while the blockade runners were still delivering supplies to Wilmington, their losses began to increase as well, particularly among many veterans of the trade. By late February 1864 Lee's efforts seemed to be paying off, leading him to inform the assistant secretary of the navy, Gustavus Fox, that "since the blockade was strengthened last fall the number is 23 steamers lost to the trade." There was also another trend Lee noted, instead of surrendering, the blockade runners "now take to the beach" whenever they encountered a Union warship, whether it be day or night.[18]

By July 1864 Lee had twenty-five ships on hand, nineteen of them lying off the Cape Fear Inlets, and in a change in tactics, another six patrolling farther out to sea looking to interdict the enemy vessels as they made their initial approach to the North Carolina coast from Bermuda and the Bahamas. Perhaps just as important as numbers, counted among these vessels were a growing number of fast gunboats like the *Nansemond* and a handful of converted blockade runners. The fleet was steadily growing, and all signs appeared to be that the blockade was taking effect, but the Confederacy had seen the trend as well and pushed the English to build Clyde steamers to better performance marks. This in turn led to a number of orders being placed in early 1864, and by late spring these improved vessels were running into Wilmington, once again challenging the blockade.

By October 1864 Wilmington was the last major port open to Confederate blockade runners. While the blockade of Cape Fear was improving as additional vessels were committed to the task, for Union planners it was finally time to deal with the problem in a more direct manner—via an amphibious assault on Fort Fisher. Success would deal a crushing blow to the Confederacy's logistics and its fighting ability, while failure would likely prolong the war. Admiral Lee was replaced by Rear Admiral David Porter, and the focus of the North Atlantic Blockading Squadron shifted from the blockade to the seizure of Fort Fisher, and ultimately, Wilmington.[19]

A remarkable point in regards to the tenacity of the Confederate blockade-running effort during this late phase of the conflict, from October 26, 1864, to the end of the war in April 1865, is that when the Union blockade was at its height in terms of ships and manpower, 4,316 tons of meat, 753 ton of lead, 967 tons of saltpeter, 546,000 pairs of shoes, 316,000 blankets, 260 tons of coffee, 69,000 rifles, 97 crates of revolvers, 2,639 packages of medicine, and 43 cannon were still delivered to Confederate ports. It should be pointed out that both Wilmington and Charleston would fall to the Union in early 1865, meaning that the bulk of these supplies were delivered in three months between November 1864 and January 1865.

While surprising numbers in terms of delivered materials, it was in fact nowhere near what was required to maintain Confederate arms in the field. Perhaps just as importantly, eighty-four vessels are reported to have been involved in running the blockade during this period with thirty-seven being captured or destroyed, and several others being lost, but their cargoes recovered. It was clear that the

Union blockade was taking a toll on Southern logistics. The prolonged effort had not only forced a decline in the number of ships even capable of attempting to run the blockade but had also begun catching the perpetrators in greater numbers, many of which soon found guns mounted on their decks and US colors flying from their staffs. Fast Union cruisers patrolled farther out to sea, while three layers of vessels arranged in progressively larger radii now encircled the Cape Fear delta. Matters were even taken to the waters of Bermuda and the Bahamas where aggressive Union commanders provoked a diplomatic response from the British government and the threat of Royal Navy intervention to maintain Britain's maritime rights. The last months of the war bear out the collapse of the blockade-running effort. Of the twenty-nine vessels attempting to run the Union blockade along the Carolina coast in early 1865, fifteen would be captured, destroyed, or run aground. It was a loss rate that foreshadowed the demise of the blockade runners. Although actually bringing the practice to an end would have taken a good deal of time, the loss of Wilmington and Charleston accelerated this process and formalized the result.[20]

While one could argue that the blockade runners had not been stopped, nor the Union blockade shown to be particularly effective, much less impervious, the bottom line was simple: if not enough supplies were reaching the Confederate Army then it was slowly being strangled. Unfortunately, the Union Navy did not clarify its expectations when they enacted the naval blockade, leaving many with the impression that full compliance was the goal. Under such unrealistic definitions, the naval blockade, along with almost every other blockade in history, was a failure. Clearly, however, perfection was not required. All that was required was to reach a threshold such that the deficiencies in supplies was continually sapping the strength and degrading the ability of the Confederacy to maintain its armies in the field.[21]

Marcus Price in his excellent article on blockade running along the Carolina coast gives the aggregate success rate for blockade runners, both sail and steam, at 84 percent for the entire war. In 1864 alone when the upgraded Clyde steamers came on the scene the success rate was 83 percent, leading one to correctly believe that the blockade was only effective in preventing about 16 percent of all attempts to run goods into Wilmington. However, this statistic is not as important as the level of participation. That is to say, the real question in viewing the effectiveness of the blockade on the Carolina ports, and Wilmington in particular, comes down to not just how successful the blockade runners were in penetrating the Union screen but the actual amount of goods that were delivered.

First, as Price points out, the moment the blockade was announced the visits to Wilmington and Charleston dropped by 50 percent. Other estimates place this initial drop slightly higher, but in either case it was clear that many foreign ships had no desire to be involved in the conflict and simply stopped calling on the southern ports. "The blockade was the North's most potent weapon, the one that made it impossible for the industrially impoverished South to win," Price pointed out. "Its effectiveness lay not so much in the ships and cargoes captured as in the ships and cargoes its mere existence kept away from Southern ports."[22]

For this reason alone, the blockade was worth the effort, but the question remains as to how well the blockade actually performed once it was established? In 1861, the first year of the blockade, 274 vessels were employed in the Confederate trade, and by 1864 this number had declined to 112. All things being equal, the total number of attempts is directly related to the total number of vessels involved, meaning that although the blockade-running success rate remained nearly constant by 1864 the actual number of successful attempts, and thereby the actual amount of goods delivered, had declined to about half of what it was in 1861. The trade in 1861, however, as mentioned earlier, was half of what it was before the blockade, implying that by the end of 1864 75 percent of the shipping traffic that entered the Carolina ports the day the war started was being stopped.[23]

This, of course, begs the question: Was the decline in trade enough to have made the blockade a success? Did it interfere enough with the supply lines of the Army of Northern Virginia to make a difference? Perhaps the easiest way to view this question is to look into a pair of twenty-round cartridge boxes, one Union and one Confederate. When the Union soldier reaches into his box, he finds twenty rounds, when the Confederate soldier reaches into his box, he finds five. Certainly, the blockade made a difference, but it was never a singular solution. It was just one component in the weakening and ultimate defeat of the Confederacy.

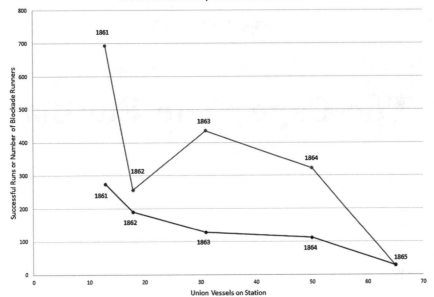

The Blockade of Cape Fear and Charleston

A graph showing the blockade of the Carolina coast. The top light grey line shows the number of successful voyages by Confederate blockade runners vs. the number of Union ships
on station at Wilmington and Charleston. The dramatic decline in 1862 was no doubt due
to the Union warships being successful in apprehending the slower moving sailing vessels
involved in the trade. Note that the steady decline in blockade running efforts from 1863 to
1865 coincides with a steady increase in the number of Union warships on blockade duty.
The lower (darker) line shows the number of blockade runners involved in the trade compared to the number of Union vessels on blockade duty. The decrease in the number of ships
involved in the blockade running trade was not only a function of vessels captured, but a
direct result of additional requirements being placed on runners by the increased Union
naval presence. This requirement further reduced the number of vessels involved, and thus,
the actual tonnage reaching Wilmington and Charleston. (*Author*)

TWELVE

The Cape Fear Flotilla

NOT LONG AFTER GENERAL ANDERSON ARRIVED at Wilmington, he wrote a letter to the secretary of war in Richmond regarding a pair of vessels at the port. The first was the screw tug *Uncle Ben*. This shallow draft workhorse had already been purchased by the government and was waiting for a rifled gun from Norfolk to be commissioned. The other was the steamer *Mariner*. Anderson recommended that the navy buy the latter vessel, and like the *Uncle Ben*, equip it with a forward mounted gun. Placed under the command of a pair of energetic young officers, they would "be of great service here, cruising at and near the mouth of the river," the general informed the secretary. While Anderson wasn't foolish enough to believe that the duo were powerful enough to act as a deterrent to the Union fleet, the craft would be of good use in warding off small boats entering the river in search of information or sabotage. "They could also daily visit the various forts, carrying supplies, and exert a good moral effect."[1]

The *Uncle Ben* received its rifled cannon and by late fall of 1861 was operating on the Cape Fear River flying a Confederate banner. As the general had requested, the navy did buy the 135-ton screw-driven *Mariner*, and after mounting a pair of twelve-pound howitzers and a rifled gun on the vessel, it began operating on the Cape Fear River by late December. While these gunboats provided some security against small craft and raiders trying to slip through the inlet at night, most of their duties concerned supplying and communicating with the various forts along the river.

While both wooden gunboats would prove useful, they were too weak to take on elements of the blockading fleet. This meant that they could not escort blockade runners or cope with a major warship that managed to run the guns of Fort Caswell or Fort Fisher and entered the river. Secretary of the Navy Stephen Mallory had foreseen this problem, and just a few weeks after the opening of the conflict the secretary informed the War Department that, "I regard the possession of an iron-armored ship as a matter of the first necessity. Such a vessel at this time could traverse the entire coast of the United States, prevent all blockades, and encounter, with a fair prospect of success, their entire navy." Unable to compete with the Union ship for ship it was the only path open to the Confederacy if they wished to secure their ports and challenge the blockaders.

In keeping with this approach in June 1862 Mallory awarded contracts to build a pair of Richmond-class ironclads on the lower Cape Fear River. The first contract went to Beery & Brother of Wilmington, North Carolina, at the Eagles Island shipyard across the river from the town. The project started in a promising manner until an outbreak of yellow fever decimated the workforce and brought construction to a halt. In early January 1863 Wilmington's new commandant, General Whiting, informed his superiors that the gunboats were not near completion, although one had its wooden casemate finished. Fearing a Union plan to run a number of ironclads past the guns of Fort Caswell or Fort Fisher, Whiting noted that the warships "would be invaluable, if ready."[2]

Whiting would have to wait only to be disappointed. The first of the vessels, the *North Carolina*, would not be launched until June 1863. While the vessel was based on the design used by the CSS *Richmond* and CSS *Palmetto State*, shoddy workmanship and the use of the *Uncle Ben*'s engine created major problems. The undersized engine strained to propel the armored warship, and it was soon determined that two to three knots were the best that could be hoped for under the circumstances. In addition, the ship ended up drawing twelve to thirteen feet of water, which made navigating the shallow waters of the Cape Fear River problematic, and on more than one occasion the craft found itself sitting on the bottom when the tide went out.

It was soon decided to tow the *North Carolina* to a position near Smithville and use it as a floating battery. Problems soon arose with the vessel. The untreated wood used to construct the hull combined with the lack of a cooper bottom made the vessel a target for shipworms and barnacles in the salty waters near the mouth of the river. Leaks began appearing, and within short order it became a daily struggle to ward off the premature decay of the ship. On occasions the ironclad was towed back to Eagles Island in an attempt to rid it of parasites, but it proved to be of little help. "I'm getting tired of this old ship," one crew member wrote after the warship became grounded during one of these trips. "I want to get on some ship that can get along without [being] towed everywhere she goes." It finally reached a point that the ship's pumps ran constantly in a losing battle against the sea. The vessel was moored in shallow waters near Smithville during the summer of 1864, but in early September it finally lost its struggle with the sea and sank up to its casemate. "The old North Carolina is no more," the vessel's chief engineer noted in his journal, hardly surprised by the event. The crew salvaged what it could and left the wreck to the elements.[3]

The *North Carolina*'s twin, the *Raleigh*, fared much better. This contract went to J. L. Cassidy & Sons at their shipyard in Wilmington. It is difficult to picture two identical designs being built with such different results. First, it was clear that more care and oversight went into the *Raleigh*'s structure. Second, the *Raleigh* was equipped with a much better engine than the *North Carolina*, with reports from a ship's carpenter that worked on the vessel that the *Raleigh*'s engine was newly made at Richmond. While this did not give spectacular performance, it was sufficient to navigate the river, and once clear of the bar, the nearby sea as well.

By spring the armor plates made at the Tredegar Iron works in Richmond had been fitted to the vessel's wooden casemate. Although the craft had firing ports for eight guns only four were carried; a pair of 6.4-inch Brooke rifles on swivel mounts in the bow and stern and

A drawing of the CSS *Richmond*, the flagship of the Richmond class ironclads. Built along the same plans, the *Raleigh* would have appeared nearly identical. (*NHHC*)

a pair of smoothbore guns on each side. The crew had also been assembled at this point totaling 217 sailors, gunners, officers, and marines in all. Command of the vessel had been given to Lt. John Pembroke Jones after the original commander, Lt. John Wilkinson, was transferred to Richmond. Jones, who was in command of the gunboat CSS *Nasemond* when he received the news, was a good choice. A member of the first naval academy class and a veteran of the Mexican-American War, he had previously served as the executive officer on the ironclad *Virginia* and had commanded the ironclad *Georgia* before being assigned to the James River Squadron.[4]

By late April 1864 the ironclad was finished. There were still dozens of minor tasks needed to finish out the warship, but after a few short voyages along the river, the ship's engineer and its captain were pleased with the results. With the vessel now commissioned, and flying the broad pennant of Commodore Lynch, it was agreed to use the new warship to test the Union blockade.

At 7:30 p.m. on May 6, the *Raleigh* raised steam and began to move down the Cape Fear River. A pair of recently built wooden gunboats, the *Yadkin* and the *Equator*, followed not far behind as did a number of blockade runners who had been waiting for an opportunity to run out of the river. Led by the dark low-lying ironclad the procession of

Confederate vessels drew the attention of the lookouts at the various forts and outposts along the way. It did not take long before word spread and others began mounting the parapets and walls to catch a glimpse of the warships. After all, it was not common to see three Confederate warships together, much less led by an ironclad.

As the *Raleigh* approached Fort Fisher red, green, and white lanterns began flashing out a series of signals. Around 8:30 the warship cleared the New Inlet sandbar and steered directly for the nearest blockading vessel, the USS *Britannia*, while the two wooden gunboats took up station two miles outside the bar under the guns of Fort Fisher.

Lt. Samuel Huse, commanding the *Britannia*, had been monitoring the ironclad's progress. When the enemy vessel cleared the inlet, he ordered a series of rockets fired to warn the fleet. The gunboat's thirty-pound Parrott gun opened fire shortly thereafter with no effect. Seeing the ironclad bearing down on him Huse turned about and dashed for open waters, zig-zagging to throw off the enemy gunners while firing away with his aft twenty-four-pound howitzer. While such an action certainly hampered the enemy gunners' aim, it also had the effect of allowing the slower ironclad to close the range. Thus far the *Raleigh*'s gun crews had been patient, but when the range closed to within six hundred yards the order to fire rang out and the forward Brooke rifle flashed in the failing light. The first shot destroyed the *Britannia*'s binnacle lamp, while the next, a few moments later, sailed just over the starboard paddle-box "sounding very like a 100-pound Parrott shot when it tumbles," Huse noted in his report.[5]

Huse changed course again, this time steering toward the shallow waters along the shore. To his relief the ironclad did not follow, turning instead toward open water to the southeast. By now the blockade runners that had followed the *Raleigh* had cleared the inlet and disappeared into the failing light leaving the warship behind. Both the crews of the USS *Nansemond* and the USS *Howquah* sprang to action when the sight of several rockets lit up the twilight. This was followed by flashes of gunfire, leading the captains of both ships to presume that the *Britannia* had encountered a blockade runner. The vessels steamed to the northeast to investigate, but beyond encountering each other, they found nothing and returned to their positions outside of the inlet.

By now Jones had found nothing as well. With night having taken hold he ordered the ironclad to stop. There seemed little sense in steaming about blindly in the darkness on the off chance of finding a target. With the blockade runners accompanying him having escaped and the only Union warship he encountered having fled, the mission appeared a success. All that remained was to wait for daylight and return to the New Inlet.

It was to turn out that Jones did not have to look for the enemy; they found him. A few minutes before midnight the lookouts on the *Nansemond* reported a ship lying motionless to the southeast. Ensign J.H. Porter steamed toward what he thought was a blockade runner waiting for first light to run into Cape Fear. He signaled the craft, which had now started moving, and was answered with an incorrect response. Porter turned to starboard to avoid the craft, which a little over five hundred yards away was crossing the *Nansemond*'s bow, and signaled twice more. When the ship failed the third challenge Porter opened fire with his aft twenty-four-pound howitzer.

Jones was surprised by the unexpected visitor, but it did not take long for the ironclad to raise steam to meet the threat. When the first shot from the *Nansemond* passed overhead the gun crews on the *Raleigh* responded with a shot of their own which also proved high. A few more errant shots rang out as the much faster *Nansemond* turned away and soon disappeared into the darkness.[6]

It was an uneasy night for both sides. Beyond the normal blockade runners that drifted in the darkness like specters, by now several of the Union fleet realized that a Confederate ironclad was lurking nearby. Aboard the *Raleigh*, which had given up its futile search pattern and now drifted near the blockaders' number-one buoy, it had proven a tense night as well. Commodore Lynch, Captain Jones, and the ship's watch stared into the darkness for hours. At 2:30 a.m. a rocket screeched across the sky to the northeast, but nothing followed. Perhaps in frustration Captain Jones issued orders to fire at any lights, thinking that they would be enemy warships signaling one another. Not long after, the crew was jolted by the discharge of one of the Brooke rifles onboard. What was worse was that the gun captain, Marine Lt. Henry Doak, had mistakenly launched a round toward a light source at Fort Fisher. Doak was quickly arrested, but Jones ordered him released, realizing that he had issued a foolish order.

At first light the *Raleigh*'s crew prepared themselves for their return voyage, which they expected would include an encounter or two with the nearby Union fleet. They were not mistaken. At 4:25 a.m. the USS *Howquah* sighted the Confederate ironclad about eight miles from the New Inlet. The gunboats *Yadkin* and *Equator* were farther toward shore while a third vessel, a larger steamship, likely the arriving blockade runner *Annie*, whose captain noted that they had quietly passed the ironclad that evening, was positioned between the two. With the enemy ironclad a mile and a quarter away and turning toward the Union warship, the *Howquah*'s captain, J.W. Balch, ordered all hands to quarters and gave the order to fire.

The *Howqauh*'s thirty-pound Parrott gun sent up columns of water that rained down on the armored vessel. The *Raleigh*'s bow gun responded, but the round exploded short of its mark. For the next hour the two vessels exchanged shots, the occasional bright blue spark from a ricochet informing the Union crew that their round had found its mark, but to little avail. At 5:20 a.m. the USS *Mount Vernon*, the first of several Union vessels converging on the scene, opened fire with its hundred-pound Parrott gun and a nine-inch shell gun, but the rounds fell short. The USS *Kansas* opened fire a few minutes later, but they too were still out of range.

Aboard the *Raleigh* Jones and Lynch faced a decision. There were over half-a-dozen Union warships closing in, and while neither of the men felt the enemy vessels were a serious threat, it was approaching 6:00 a.m. and high tide was an hour away. If the ironclad turned back now it would arrive at New Inlet just in time for the high-water mark through the passage. Even if they wished to continue the engagement, they would eventually have to withdraw under the guns of Fort Fisher and await the next high tide. With the ironclad's maiden voyage already deemed a success it seemed foolish to both officers to tempt fate, and the order was given to return to New Inlet. Before it left, however, a parting shot from the newly built ironclad punched through the *Howquah*'s smokestack with a hollow thump, leaving a two-foot hole in its wake.[7]

Making six or seven knots the ironclad soon came within range of Fort Fisher's guns, effectively ending any Union pursuit. Flying a Confederate flag off its stern and Lynch's red pennant off its bow, the victorious *Raleigh* rendezvoused with the *Yadkin* and the *Equator* and cleared the New Inlet bar to a nine-gun salute and the distant cheers of the fort's garrison.

It was a hazy morning and, as one witness claimed, the ship's pilot was either careless or reckless. Whatever the case, as the *Raleigh* turned upriver the vessel shuddered down its length several times before coming to an abrupt halt throwing the crew and their equipment about in the process. Jones shouted orders to reverse the engines, but it had no effect; the *Raleigh* was stuck fast on a shifting sandbar known as "the Rip." Efforts were made to lighten the ship and tow it off the bank, but neither proved successful. Without the buoyant force acting on the vessel's hull to counteract the mass of its armored casemate, when the tide fell later that afternoon, "the weight of the iron upon (the *Raleigh*'s) shield just crushed her decks in," snapping the hull in two.

It was a devastating loss, especially when coupled with the ills and woes encountered with its sister ship the *North Carolina*. Some of the armor, guns, and supplies on board were recovered, but it was not an easy operation given the shifting bottom and strong currents at the location. A court of inquiry exonerated Jones. The warship's thirteen-foot draft when combined with the tricky river channels appeared to be at fault here, as the court came to the conclusion that "her commanding officer was justified in going back into the harbor when he did."[8]

For the defenders of Cape Fear it was shocking how quickly the tables had turned. The ironclad, perhaps one of the best built specimens of the war, now slowly disappeared beneath the sand and waves as small crews raced against time to salvage what they could from the wreck. A little over a month later one observer noted the *Raleigh*'s sorry state saying that "She was very much sunken at the stern, lifting her bow considerably. Her sides had been stripped of their armor, the smokestack prostrated, and altogether she had the appearance of a monstrous turtle stranded and forlorn." When the *North Carolina* sank at anchor a few months later General Whiting informed Richmond that "The two ironclads, the *Raleigh* and the *North Carolina*, on which we relied to defend the rips, or inner bars, are both gone. We have here no naval forces afloat, and one is greatly needed."[9]

While Whiting's point was clear, it was not exactly true. A third ironclad, the CSS *Wilmington* was started at the Eagles Island shipyard after the loss of the *Raleigh*. This vessel was 229-feet long with a

41-foot beam but only drew 9.5 feet of water. A sleek, low-lying vessel, the *Wilmington* was never completed due to material and labor shortages and was burned by the Confederates in February 1865 when Union forces threatened Wilmington.

There were also several wooden gunboats at Whiting's disposal and a floating battery built to help secure the waterway, but while this handful of vessels might be viewed as a squadron on paper, it is quite likely that the entire Cape Fear squadron could have been defeated by a single Union warship riding quietly off the coast.[10]

The dismal performance of the Cape Fear defense squadron aside, in the summer and fall of 1864 a pair of naval vessels were put into service at Wilmington with offense in mind. The first of these was the commerce cruiser *Tallahassee*. Formerly known as the blockade runner *Atlanta*, the British-built twin-screw steamer could easily make fourteen knots and had been involved in running the Wilmington blockade on several occasions. Purchased by the Confederate Navy and modified to carry a thirty-two-pound rifled cannon mounted forward, and two smaller guns mounted aft, command of the converted warship and its 110-man crew was given to Commodore John Taylor Wood, a former professor at the US Naval Academy and the architect of a pair of raids that had captured three Union gunboats on the James and Neuse Rivers.

When Whiting heard of plans to convert two blockade runners into merchant raiders, he launched a series of letters at Navy Secretary Mallory about the foolishness of wasting the ships on such a task, especially when after the loss of the *Raleigh* and *North Carolina* the two vessels were needed for the defense of Cape Fear. Any benefits that were to be gained from such raiding were outweighed by the real possibility of an attack and the need to be prepared for this. Mallory understood the general's point, and just as importantly, the two agreed on the urgent need for more supplies to reach Wilmington. As such he informed a persistent Whiting that, "A cruise by the *Chickamauga* and *Tallahassee* against northern coasts and commerce would at once withdraw a fleet of fast steamers from the blockading force off Wilmington in pursuit of them, and this result alone would render such a cruise expedient."[11]

The *Tallahassee* ran out of Wilmington on the evening of August 7, 1864, destined for one of the most successful commercial raiding

A photograph of the CSS *Tallahassee* in Nova Scotia, August 1864. (*NHHC*)

cruises of the conflict. The steamer, moving at near full speed through the twilight, encountered the blockader USS *Quaker City* just after sunset. The commander of the *Quaker City*, Lt. Silas Casey, at first thought the vessel was the USS *Gettysburg* which was stationed nearby, but after repeatedly challenging the vessel with signal lights, he concluded that it must be a blockade runner and ordered the gun crews to open fire. The hundred-pound and thirty-pound Parrott guns on the warship flared to life sending thunderclaps racing over the surrounding waters, but Casey was unable to tell if they had any effect, reporting that, "The shells exploded quite close to him, so as to render him distinctly visible, but he continued on at full speed and was soon lost in the darkness."[12]

Wood spent the next day in a series of short chases and in one instance was fired upon by a Union gunboat, but in each case, he managed to lose his pursuers. Free of the blockaders, on the ninth Wood steered north for the target-rich shipping routes into and out of New York and New England. Some eighty miles from the former, the *Tallahassee* made its first capture, the schooner *Sarah A. Boyce*. Within a few days four more vessels had fallen prey to the commerce raider. Wood put a prize crew aboard one of the vessels, the *James Funk*, and converted it to a tender, which itself captured three additional vessels. At this point Wood considered what would have been one of the most daring naval exploits of the war. The commodore laid out a course for New York where he planned to descend upon the Brooklyn Naval

Yard, cause as much damage as possible, and then escape back into the ocean via Hell Gate. The plan, however, was abandoned when he was forced to put his growing number of prisoners on the captured schooner *Carroll* and send it into a nearby port. The alarm was sounded with the *Carroll's* arrival and soon half a dozen Union warships began making their way toward the Confederate raider's last known position.

Moving off to the east Wood made two more captures, one of which he burned along with the *Funk*, which was no longer of use, and the other he sent away loaded with the captured crews. The days that followed proved anxious for the northeastern maritime community and incredibly profitable for the *Tallahassee*. By the end of the following week the Confederate warship had taken seventeen more vessels as its course cut through the profitable fishing waters of Nova Scotia and New England. After seizing four more ships Wood dropped anchor at Halifax on August 18 looking for coal. The British authorities gave Wood just enough coal to return to Wilmington and then informed the commodore that he had to leave the harbor as soon as possible.[13]

Wood departed Halifax the next day and steered south for Wilmington. He captured and burned the brig *Rowan* a few days later, and by the evening of August 25 the cruiser was approaching the New Inlet looking to run into the passage at dawn. The *Tallahassee's* return, however, was to be much like its departure. A little after 9:30 p.m. Wood was about eight miles to the northeast of Fort Fisher slowly making his way toward the shore. Suddenly the USS *Monticello* appeared out of the darkness five hundred yards away. The Union warship signaled a challenge to the *Tallahassee* and, after it was ignored twice, fired a hail of grapeshot at the Confederate ship from its nine-inch gun. To the surprise of the *Monticello's* commander, the enemy vessel shifted course and fired on the Union warship, the thirty-two-pound shell passing overhead and exploding a short distance beyond. The *Monticello* responded with its thirty-pound Parrott gun and nine-inch shell gun while the *Tallahassee* fired a cloud of grapeshot that struck just astern. As the two vessels began to separate a battery just above Fort Fisher added its guns to the fray. The *Monticello* fired away at the Confederate vessel and launched a series of rockets to warn its fellow blockaders, but within a few minutes the

Tallahassee had disappeared into the murk.

Neither side suffered much in the way of damage, but the *Tallahassee* was not finished. An hour later the lookouts on the USS *Britannia* reported an unidentified steamer running close to the shore and headed for Fort Fisher. Lt. Huse turned the Union warship to port to pursue the intruder, and when it was in range, he began firing on the unidentified vessel, at one point illuminating the Confederate warship with a bursting shell directly over its decks. The *Tallahassee* responded, and a running duel of flashes, shrieking solid shot, and exploding

Lt. John T. Wood. Wood would command the *Tallahassee* in late 1864 and during a single cruise capture or destroy 33 Union vessels. (*NHHC*)

shells echoed across the waters. By now several other blockaders had converged on the area, some even close enough to fire a round or two, but like the *Britannia* they quickly turned toward open sea when the guns at Fort Fisher began dropping explosive rounds into the waters around them.

The next morning the *Tallahassee* passed through the New Inlet passage to the salute of Fort Fisher. Although the voyage was brief, just short of three weeks, the tally was impressive. The cruiser had burned sixteen ships, scuttled ten, and ransomed five which carried the captured crews for a total of thirty-one vessels, or more than one a day. Close to 5,500 tons of enemy shipping had been destroyed and another six hundred tons had been bonded for almost fifty thousand dollars.[14]

Wood would be reassigned, and command of the ship was given to Lt. William Ward. After a refit and a name change to the *Olustee*, Ward dashed through the blockade on the night of October 29, 1864, and found some success off the coast of Delaware, capturing seven vessels. Not long after he found himself involved in a long chase with several Union warships near Cape Charles, New Jersey. While the *Olustee* would make good its escape, the next day, a few dozen miles off Cape Fear, Ward was surprised by three captured blockade runners now armed and flying the Stars and Stripes, as well as the gunboat USS *Montgomery*. Ward at first turned seaward and then reversed his course and dashed through the Union vessels toward Wilmington. Trading shots with the Union warships the old *Tallahassee* pushed through the cannon fire, outdistanced its pursuers, and crossed safely over the bar into the Cape Fear River.

It was to be the last cruise for the *Olustee*. The guns were removed and the ship was converted back to a blockade runner named *Chameleon*. Under the command of Lt. John Wilkinson, the *Chameleon* successfully ran the Wilmington blockade on Christmas Eve 1864, never to return. The vessel was seized in Bermuda by British authorities but then released when its falsified papers appeared to show that it was not the *Tallahassee*. While fortunate in this escape, it made little difference. Captain Wilkinson attempted to return to Wilmington with supplies in January 1865 but abandoned the effort upon hearing news of Fort Fisher's capture. He would then try to enter Charleston, but the Union patrols had all but closed down the approaches. With few options before him Wilkinson sailed for Nassau, and there, upon hearing news of Charleston's fall, he set a course for England, dropping anchor at Liverpool on April 6. The old *Tallahassee* was immediately seized by British authorities and would eventually be returned to the United States government the following year.[15]

The second cruiser launched at Wilmington in the fall of 1864 was the *Chickamauga*. Like the *Tallahassee* the *Chickamauga* began its career as a blockade runner. Known as the *Edith* before its conversion, the 175-foot twin-screw vessel had made a pair of successful voyages into and out of Wilmington at its time of purchase. Three rifled guns were fitted to the deck, and a crew of 120 sailors, gunners, and marines placed aboard under the command of Lt. John Wilkinson.

By early October the vessel and its crew were ready for their first cruise, but the moon and the tides were against running out until later in the month. On the evening of the twenty-eighth the warship slipped out into the Atlantic through the New Inlet. The Confederate cruiser was briefly pursued and a dozen shots fired at it, but by the next evening it had lost the trailing Union warship and the following morning set a course for Long Island.

The cruiser CSS *Chickamauga*. A blockade runner, a merchant raider, and finally a Cape Fear gunboat, the *Chickamauga* and its crew were active in the final defense of Cape Fear and Wilmington. (*NHHC*)

The following day the cruiser and its crew made their first capture, the small bark *Mark L. Potter*, which after taking onboard the vessel's crew of thirteen, Wilkinson set afire. Over the next two days the *Chickamauga* seized five ships near the eastern edge of Long Island. While a boon, it was also clear from newspapers found onboard the prizes that the Union Navy had launched a search for the raider.

Wilkinson would capture the bark *Speedwell* the next day and send it on its way along with the recently captured crews for a bond of $18,000. With his coal low and a large Union naval presence about to sweep the area, Wilkinson set course for Bermuda on November 6. By the eighth the *Chickamauga* rested at anchor near St. George. Much to Wilkinson's dismay over sixty-five of the crew deserted over the next few days. When he organized a shore party to arrest these men, the British authorities intervened and prevented their return.

On the afternoon of the fifteenth the *Chickamauga* departed for Wilmington, unable to obtain enough coal to continue its cruise. At dawn on November 19 the Confederate cruiser found itself inside the blockade and just within the range of Fort Fisher's guns. The tide was not right, but fortunately a layer of fog blanketed the cape and surrounding waters. Around 7 a.m. the veil began to lift, and not long after a Union gunboat approached and opened fire. The *Chickamauga* returned fire which soon brought three more enemy gunboats. The two sides exchanged fire and when Fort Fisher joined this chorus the Union warships fell back. Half an hour later five warships returned, but by this point the Confederate cruiser had already bolted for the New Inlet. The Union warships briefly gave chase but broke off when the salvos from the fort guns began landing a little too close.

Like the *Tallahassee*, the *Chickamauga*'s career as a merchant raider was to be short. The defense of Wilmington and Cape Fear, along with significant material and manpower shortages, ended any thoughts of another patrol. In addition to this, General Whiting had expressed his opinion on several occasions that the two commerce raiders be reserved for the defense of Cape Fear. While the *Tallahassee* would ultimately end up as a blockade runner, Whiting would have his way with the *Chickamauga*. Converted to a gunboat and tasked with patrolling the river, transporting troops and supplies, and standing picket duty at the inlets, the former cruiser would be involved in the last battles for Fort Fisher and Wilmington.[16]

THIRTEEN

The Road to Goldsboro

WITH BURNSIDE'S PROMOTION and departure in the summer of 1862 command of the region fell upon General Foster who had been in tactical command for most of the major engagements during Burnside's campaign. For the moment the major waterways were secure, and the defenses of Newbern were slowly being reworked and strengthened. As much as Foster would have liked to have maintained the initiative and advance on the defeated Confederate troops at Kinston, the simple fact was that most of the general's reinforcements and a good portion of his supplies were being diverted to the Union Army's efforts in Virginia.

Unable to strike in large numbers, Confederate forces in the area launched several raids on the Union positions along the interior waterways. One of the larger of these expeditions occurred on September 6, 1862. Around 4:30 a.m. Major Stephen D. Pool of the 10th North Carolina led five companies of infantry, a company of artillery, and a detachment of cavalry, some six hundred men in all, in a surprise attack on the Union-held town of Washington on the Pamlico River. The Confederate plan had unwittingly coincided with a portion of the Union garrison being ordered to the nearby town of Plymouth. The garrison's commander, Lt. Colonel Edward Potter, had departed with five companies of New York cavalry and a battery of guns just an hour before the assault.[1]

Had Pool launched the attack only a handful of hours later it is quite possible that the town would have fallen. Aided by a thick fog the initial Confederate advance achieved the sought-after element of surprise and overran the Union pickets. Led by cavalry troops, the force stormed into the town and laid siege to the artillery barracks there. Caught off guard the Massachusetts, New York, and North Carolina loyalist infantry companies scrambled to the assistance of the artillery troops in a haphazard fashion, but they were soon bogged down in house-to-house fighting.

When the Confederate advance reached the docks half an hour later they began peppering the two Union army gunboats there, the *Louisiana* and *Picket*, with rifle fire. Having already manned their guns at the first sounds of gunfire that morning, the order to fire rang out across the decks of both vessels. The batteries on both ships bellowed out, but the concussion from the *Picket*'s forward gun had yet to fade when it was masked by a tremendous explosion that ripped the craft apart, killing twenty of the crew including the vessel's commander. After being startled by the concussion and falling debris, the Confederate troops began cheering and claiming victory, but it would prove premature.

While the Union infantry struggled against the unexpected blow, Colonel Potter had barely cleared the outskirts of the town when the sound of gunfire brought his column to a halt. Potter quickly wheeled, passed orders to his troops, and launched them into the town at a gallop, assigning each company a major street to be cleared. The charging Union cavalry soon found the enemy and the matter quickly devolved into a confused affair of cavalry duels, skirmishing, and the blast of Potter's field guns, which sent grapeshot ricocheting its way down the town's streets. "The night was intensely dark," one witness recalled, "and between the darkness, fog, and dust it was impossible in many cases to distinguish friend from foe at half a dozen paces."[2]

While the sudden Union attack had halted Pool's men, it had not dislodged them. Seeing he needed additional firepower Potter sent a runner to the *Louisiana*, which responded with a torrential fire "throwing her shells with great precision, and clearing the streets."

Together the assault sent the Confederate troops back toward the edge of town where they reformed into two columns under the falling rounds from the *Louisiana*. With a cheer that could be heard over the artillery fire, the grey columns advanced. One was aimed at separating the Union troops from the *Louisiana*, while the other moved against the Union center.

After several hours of house-to-house fighting, charges and countercharges, Pool sounded the recall and retreated eight miles to Tranter's Creek carrying four captured cannons with him. Potter sent cavalry in pursuit, but they gave up after several miles, likely in no hurry to resume the engagement.[3]

Smaller skirmishes also occupied both Commodore Rowan and General Foster's troops as both sides probed each other for weaknesses and information. In late October Foster received the reinforcements he had been waiting for, albeit ones that appeared to have a minimal amount of training. Armed with these new troops, rumors of three enemy regiments currently near Taraboro, and the desire to take the offensive, Foster organized a five-thousand-man expedition and set out in search of the Confederate forces. It proved a grueling two-week march, and except for a pair of minor skirmishes, little came of the expedition.[4]

On November 7, 1862, Foster's former superior, General Ambrose Burnside, was made commander of the Army of the Potomac. A few weeks later Foster received orders from Burnside to make a demonstration in support of the latter's plan to cross the Rappahannock River at Fredericksburg. For Foster the target was obvious, Goldsboro. Located on the north side of the Neuse River some sixty miles from Newbern the town was a junction of two prominent railroads: the Atlantic and North Carolina, and the Wilmington and Weldon lines. The latter line, connecting to points north and south, was a logistical artery for the Confederate forces in Virginia, making the destruction of the railroad bridge at Goldsboro the primary goal of the expedition.

While a number of Foster's regiments had yet to see battle, the force the general had assembled was impressive. Four brigades of infantry, forty guns of various sizes, and a cavalry regiment. A little under twelve thousand men filed out of Newbern on December 11, 1862, to the music of their regimental bands. The army marched via

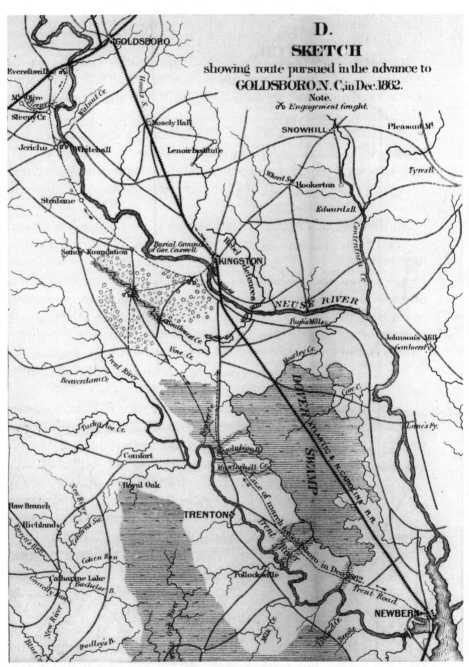

A map of Foster's expedition against Goldsboro, December 1862. Note that Kingston should be Kinston. (*Library of Congress*)

the Trent River road which skirted the Dover Swamp, while the gunboat contingent under the command of Commander Alexander Murray of the USS *Hetzel* began to move up the Neuse to rendezvous with Foster at Kinston, the general's first target.

Foster's column skirmished with Confederate scouts and was halted while the bridge at Beaver Creek was rebuilt, but he did not encounter any serious resistance until it arrived at Southwest Creek a little over half a dozen miles from Kinston. The bridge over the creek had been destroyed, and a regiment of Confederate troops backed by three guns occupied the north bank. Given the disparity of numbers the position would not prove much of an obstacle. The 85th Pennsylvania was ordered to cross half a mile downstream while a battery of guns was deployed, under the cover fire of which the 9th New Jersey would wade across the creek near the broken remains of the bridge. The defenders put up a stiff resistance, but when the Pennsylvanian troops appeared on their left and the 23rd Massachusetts began crossing to support the New Jersey troops, the Confederates abandoned their position.[5]

That evening the sound of distant cannon fire reached the Union troops encamped near Southwest Creek. Most realized that it was the Union fleet moving up the river to challenge the Confederate batteries along the Neuse. This flotilla under the direction of Commander Murray consisted of four navy gunboats and five shallow draft army gunboats. Murray reassigned some naval personnel to assist with the army vessels, which were in reality simply hastily armed transports. He also placed bales of hay and cotton along all the vessels' superstructures and sides to help protect against small arms fire.

The naval expedition went wrong almost from the beginning. The larger Union vessels, like the *Delaware*, kept striking bottom as the flotilla snaked its way up the river. The water was low for the time of year, further complicating the task. The navy warships could only get a dozen miles or so above Newbern, and even then, Murray noted, the *Seymour, Lockwood,* and *Shawsheen* ended up so hard aground that they "will not be gotten off until the wind changes." Proceeding on with four of the army gunboats, by late afternoon on December 13 Murray had approached within two miles of Kinston. Stationed in the lead ship, the *Allison*, Murray guided the little fleet around a bend in the river and suddenly found himself before a ten-gun battery on the north shore. The channel was so narrow that there was not room to turn the vessels around, which meant that the line of ships had to reverse their engines and back down the river. To cover this operation Murray ordered the *Allison* forward and began to engage the Confederate guns. While the commander was pleased with the fire the little gunboat was able to lay down, the shore batteries found little difficulty in finding the range, scoring three hits on the stern-wheeler in a short period of time. Even so, the ploy worked and Murray's ships moved back downriver in the fading light, but with the water levels so low, and unable to bring his more heavily armed vessels to bear, the commander saw no purpose in proceeding any farther and ordered the flotilla to return to Newbern the next morning.[6]

The action with the Union fleet was one of the few things that had gone right for Brigadier General Nathan Evans whose brigade was located at Kinston. While the general and his troops had delayed the Yankee column at Southwest Creek, the enemy's numbers were such that little more could be hoped for out of the engagement. With some 2,200 men at his disposal and only a few dozen guns there were only two possible decisions to make at this point: fight or burn the Neuse bridge and fall back. The general chose to fight, but in the end, it really boiled down to how long he could delay the Union forces and when to burn the bridge.

Evans arranged his troops at the edge of a clearing that extended from the junction of the Trenton-Goldsboro road to the junction of the Newbern road at the south end of the Kinston bridge. High ground in the form of a gentle ridge dominated most of this line and "formed a natural breastwork." In front of this was a three-hundred-yard wide swamp consisting of hanging trees and foot-deep bogs that transitioned into a forest before being interrupted by another cleared field some four hundred yards away. Evans assigned the 17th and 23rd South Carolina Regiments to the ridge. Skirmishers were deployed at the fence that marked the boundary of the swamp which stretched between the Trenton and Newbern roads, and a battery of four North Carolina guns under Captain Joseph Starr was stationed near the three-way intersection of the Goldsboro, Trenton, and Kinston roads. A small church behind the ridge and a small house on the Confederate left were the only structures on the battlefield other than the bridge and the bridge house. Here, near this latter location, the gen-

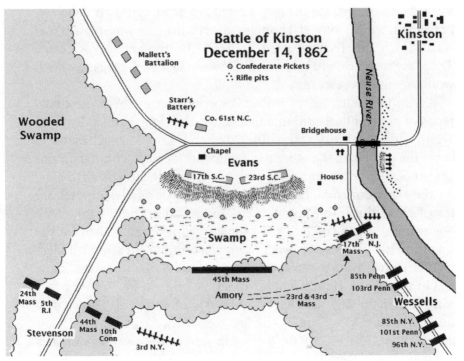

The opening stages of the Battle of Kinston, December 14, 1862. (*Author*)

eral stationed another battery of guns, while along the north bank of the river rifle pits had been dug and an earth redoubt armed with cannon constructed just below the bridge. At daylight on December 14 Evans dispatched his scouts and not long after received good news. The first train from Goldsboro had brought a company of the 61st North Carolina and a battalion of North Carolina troops under Lt. Colonel Peter Mallett. Evans had already received news that Foster was on the march, and after some confusion, he dispatched the two North Carolina units to reinforce the right of his line and cover Starr's battery as well as the intersection.[7]

Early on the morning of December 14 Foster's column advanced down the Trenton road toward Kinston. Tactical command fell to senior brigade commander Brigadier General Henry Wessells, whose unit was on loan from its division in Virginia. Foster's plan of attack was not complex, in part because he commanded a ten to one advantage in men and guns, and in part because the terrain would not allow for it. Wessells ordered his own brigade to advance down the New-bern road, while Colonel Thomas Amory's brigade would push forward down the Trenton road, followed by the artillery, Colonel Thomas Stevenson's brigade, and Colonel H.C. Lee's brigade, which would remain in reserve.

As Amory's skirmishers probed the woods before them, three batteries of guns unlimbered in a field along the right-hand side of the Trenton road. Amory tasked the 23rd and 43rd Massachusetts to cover the guns with the other two regiments located behind their positions. Soon a request to aid the 9th New Jersey Regiment, advancing on the Newbern road, had the Massachusetts brigade commander transferring the 17th Massachusetts to the Union right flank. With Stevenson's brigade arriving and the gun batteries now firing at the town and its defenses, the order was given for the 23rd and 45th Massachusetts to advance into the swamp before the Confederate lines.

On the Union right, General Wessells' brigade was moving forward led by the 9th New Jersey and a trio of batteries. These guns, under Captain Morrison of the 3rd New York Artillery, were soon engaged with the enemy on the south side of the river, as well as a Confederate battery on the other side of the Neuse. Exposed and with the 9th New Jersey engaged with the Confederates before them, the position looked questionable until the 17th Massachusetts arrived to shore it up.[8]

Stevenson's brigade had moved into position and was arrayed in two lines on either side of the Trenton road in front of the Union batteries. The latter thundered away in support of Amory and Wessells' brigades, but it was not helping. The 45th Massachusetts, attempting to navigate through the swamp, had come to a halt under a relentless fire from the Confederate redoubt. "The balls would whistle and hum over our heads, and every now and then a shell would explode and cover us with mud, and too often with blood," one soldier recalled. Seeing the regiment's plight, Wessells ordered Stevenson's 10th Connecticut, 5th Rhode Island, and 44th Massachusetts to advance in support. The remaining regiments were to follow once Colonel Lee's 3rd brigade arrived to relieve them.[9]

On the Newbern road the fighting was fierce. A blue-white cloud had formed over the area from the cannon fire and the hundreds of rounds of musket balls that tore through the vegetation, rippling in thuds against the trees and leaving a trail of falling branches in their wake. Taking fire from the front and from across the river, Morrison's guns were forced to shift positions, but their efforts were beginning to tell. One of the targets was the Confederate battery across the river. Several shells had burst above the enemy redoubt slowing the fire from this position, and to the front it appeared that the enemy was giving way as well.

This last part had two components to it. Wessells' brigade of Pennsylvania and New York troops had moved into position near Morrison's guns. Leaving a pair of regiments to protect the guns, the remaining troops began pushing into the swamp to the right of the beleaguered 45th Massachusetts. "The swamp with its thick undergrowth was next to impassable," the commander of the 92nd New York recalled, "but the men floundered through the bog-holes, sometimes up to their middle, delivering their fire as they advanced." While the weight of four Union regiments began to press against the Confederate left flank, things were no better in the center and Confederate right. Skirmishers in the woods near the junction of the Trenton and Goldsboro roads were encountering a large number of Union troops filtering their way forward in an attempt to outflank General Evans' position. More importantly, the 45th Massachusetts, which had borne much of the brunt of the fighting so far, was suddenly aided by the 10th Connecticut, which advanced rapidly through the swamp to the left.[10]

With several regiments stacked up behind these vanguards, the 10th Connecticut and 45th Massachusetts pushed the Confederate line back. Having fallen back to a second position the South Carolina troops poured a volley into the emerging blue formations, but it did not impede their progress. Soon formations began to emerge on the Confederate left, causing the grey line, desperately short on ammunition, to buckle as it fell back along the main road to Kinston.

This was a temporary situation as Wessells' advance toward the Kinston bridge on the Confederate left threatened to cut off the defenders. The retreat was sounded, and a rush commenced toward the bridge. Unfortunately, for many of Evans' troops, it was too late. To make matters worse, the bridge, which had been rigged for destruction by "pouring spirits of turpentine on cotton" placed strategically throughout the structure, was set aflame before many of the retreating troops had crossed. Short on ammunition and with Starr's battery having already disengaged and packed up for want of ammunition, Colonel Peter Mallett stationed on the Confederate right with a battalion of North Carolina troops marched his men toward the bridge "but on approaching it found it on fire and crowded with men endeavoring to cross. A panic ensued. The enemy pressed upon us from two directions at double-quick in large force and the bridge the only means of escape. The greater portion of my command succeeded in crossing, while the other was driven back by the flames."[11]

Mallet's men were not alone and in all close to four hundred Confederate troops were forced to surrender when their escape path was blocked. The 9th New Jersey and 17th Massachusetts, along with several other regiments on the Union right, took possession of the south end of the bridge, and for the next twenty minutes an artillery and gunfire duel ranged across the river with the Confederate batteries and rifle pits on the other side. By now Evans had seen enough and ordered his troops to withdraw to the other side of town. With the enemy fire fading away, Wessel gave orders to save the bridge which was accomplished fairly quickly. He then ordered the 9th New Jersey, 17th Massachusetts, and the 85th New York to cross and establish a foothold on the opposite bank.

For all practical purposes the Battle of Kinston was over. Evans, reinforced by the 47th North Carolina, reformed his troops in line of battle outside the town. While several Union field officers wanted to pursue, Foster introduced a delay by formally asking Evans if he wished to surrender. The Confederate general scoffed at the idea, but the tactic had given Foster time to move some of his guns forward, which upon Evans' answer began shelling the Confederate's position. With this, Evans finally gave the order to withdraw and fell back half a dozen miles to Falling Creek where he expected to meet reinforcements.

The battle which had raged all morning cost Foster 160 casualties, and while Evans' men suffered only 125 casualties, another four hundred along with several guns were captured. Foster occupied the town which produced five hundred stands of arms and a large supply of commissary and quartermaster stores. He also dispatched a detachment to seize the abandoned Confederate battery below the town, which had caused the navy so many difficulties, but such measures were momentary. The general had accomplished his task of pushing aside the Confederate force at Kinston, which he could not leave at his rear, and now was anxious to press forward before the enemy could rally its defenses to oppose him.[12]

Having left a detachment at Kinston, Foster's column was on the move again the next morning. Following the south bank of the river his troops made seventeen miles before encamping for the evening some three and a half miles from Whitehall. While the troops pitched their tents and cooked a hot meal, three companies of the 3rd New York cavalry under Major Jeptha Garrard and a battery of guns under Captain Edwin Jenney of the 3rd New York artillery galloped down the road toward Whitehall. Foster was hoping to take this small village and the nearby bridge by surprise, allowing his column to pass unimpeded the next morning.

When the Union troops arrived, they were surprised to see the Whitehall Bridge enveloped in flames, with locals informing them that a regiment of Virginia troops had just crossed over to the northern bank. On the opposite shore near the bridge Garrard spotted one of the objects of his reconnaissance—the partially built ironclad *Neuse* still on the stocks. The Union commander called for volunteers to swim across the river and put the vessel to the torch. A trooper named Butler came forward and swam across the river, but as he was trying to light a torch from the burning bridge he was fired upon by Confederate sentries and chased back into the river. With a battery of Confederate guns on the north bank and perhaps two regiments of troops to support these, a firestorm soon broke out, sending ball and shot across the water after the cavalry trooper. It did not prove enough, as Garrard's men pulled Butler ashore, exhausted but otherwise unharmed.

With his first idea having failed, Major Garrard turned to Captain Jenney and his guns. To help in this endeavor Garrard ordered his men to illuminate the riverbank by igniting bales of hay and cotton soaked in turpentine. Combined with the blazing structure of the nearby bridge it appeared the entire river had been set on fire as flashes of musketry could be seen coming from both banks. Although somewhat unusual, the effort proved effective as Jenney's twenty-pound Parrott guns launched canister, shell, and shot at the vessel no more than a few hundred yards away. Screeching over the floodlit waters the rounds brought forth clouds of splinters and the sight of freshly fractured wood with each impact. After ten rounds Garrard signaled Jenney to cease fire. The vessel was riddled and the stocks on which it was mounted on the verge of collapse. Satisfied, Garrard and his detachment returned to the main encampment with news of their efforts.[13]

The following morning Garrard was one of the first men out of camp. Foster had ordered the major to take five companies of cavalry and a detachment of light artillery to Mt. Olive, a town on the Wilmington-Weldon railway fourteen miles south of Goldsboro. Here Garrard was to do whatever damage he could to the rail line, before rejoining the main column. As Garrard and his men rode through Whitehall a Confederate battery and a number of sharpshooters across the river opened fire on them. Garrard's light artillery dismounted, unlimbered their guns, and returned fire until the 17th Massachusetts and the lead elements of the main column arrived fifteen minutes later. Sending Garrard on his mission, the Massachusetts troops took up the fight.

When news of the skirmish reached Foster, the general decided "to make a strong feint," as if he was planning to rebuild the bridge and cross the army to the north shore. Amory's brigade and the 9th New Jersey lined the shores near the smoldering bridge and engaged the Confederates while a dozen cannons were moved into position. A little over an hour after the skirmish started, a ripple of bright flashes came from the south shore followed by a wave of concussions as over thirty guns added their say to the engagement. By noon it was over. The Confederate batteries on the north shore had been silenced, most of the Confederate sharpshooters had been chased off, and just for good measure, a few dozen additional rounds had been launched at the fractured *Neuse*.

With the shooting over, Foster's men reformed and pushed forward along the river for the remainder of the day, pitching camp that evening eight miles from Goldsboro. Garrard's detachment returned that evening having burned the Goshen Swamp bridge, destroyed several miles of track around Mt. Olive, and even shot up a Confederate mail train that was in the area. Foster was delighted by the report. Planning to attack the railway bridge near Goldsboro the following morning, he dispatched Garrard along with four companies of cavalry and a pair of light guns to make a reconnaissance of the nearby Thompson's Bridge over the Neuse, and Major Fitz Simmons with two companies to raid Dudley Station and Everettsville.[14]

Major General G.W. Smith arrived at Goldsboro at 3 p.m. on December 15 and was met by Governor Vance, former commander of the 26th North Carolina Regiment. Smith was quickly briefed on Evans' action at the Kinston bridge and his retreat west along the river to Falling Creek. Reports placed Foster's strength at thirty thousand, up ten thousand from Evans' first estimate, and three times the actual strength. Smith likely suspected as much, and from prior reports he had a reasonable idea of Foster's strength at Newbern before the expedition. Even with this better estimate of ten to twelve thousand, it was clear that the forces in the local area were insufficient to stop the Union column. The general telegraphed the secretary of war, James Seddon, urgently requesting reinforcements. The response was quick and decisive. One regiment was being sent from Blackwater, one from Petersburg, and six from Richmond along with three batteries of guns. In all close to five thousand men would be arriving at Goldsboro by rail.

The next day brought more anxiety for Smith and Vance, who without their staff or any troops in the town improvised "the best means we could for obtaining information from the south side of the river." What they found out did nothing to alleviate their fears. The battalion that had been posted to guard the south end of the Goldsboro Bridge had been decimated at Kinston. "There were no troops there whatever," Smith informed the secretary of war. Nor were there any troops at the small country bridge half a mile above the Goldsboro Bridge. At least some positive reports were arriving from Evans. An attempt by Union cavalry to seize the Whitehall Bridge had been repelled and the bridge destroyed before the enemy could capture it. The next morning the main Union column engaged the Confederate forces on the north shore of the Neuse at Whitehall. It appeared that the enemy troops wished to force a crossing here and perhaps rebuild the burned bridge, but after a stout defense by the troops stationed there, the enemy broke off and marched north.[15]

On the evening of December 16 and the morning of the seventeenth the troops' situation changed. Several regiments had arrived, as well as Colonel Poole's artillery battalion which had marched to

Goldsboro after abandoning the Confederate gun battery below Kinston. Poole and his men dug rifle pits and raised a two-gun battery on the north shore between the railroad bridge and the country bridge. Another gun was positioned on the north bank near the county bridge as well. General Thomas Clingman, who arrived with three regiments of his command the day before, was stationed on the south side of the river along with a pair of two-gun batteries. Clingman soon realized how difficult his position was. He had three regiments, an artillery battalion, and a handful of cannon, perhaps 1,700 men in all, to defend two bridges against a force nearly six times his size. With no better option before him he stationed the 52nd North Carolina in front of the railroad bridge with a pair of guns, the 8th North Carolina with a pair of guns in the field in front of the county bridge, and Colonel William Allen with the 51st North Carolina on the old county road between the two.

General Evans and his brigade arrived that morning giving Smith hope that he might be able to organize a meaningful defense. General Clingman was sent for, and when he arrived in Goldsboro, Smith informed him that he was placing his brigade under Evans' command. Once Evans' men, who were still disembarking at the railway station, reached the county bridge the two brigades would move east in search of the enemy. The conversation had barely finished when a dispatch rider appeared with news that the enemy was three miles from the Goldsboro bridge. Evans sent Clingman back with orders to hold the Yankee advance while he brought up his brigade.[16]

The Union column started forward again at dawn on December 17. The 17th Massachusetts and the 9th New Jersey, under Colonel Heckman, took the lead, followed by Colonel Lee's 3rd Brigade, Wessel's brigade, Stevenson's brigade, and Amory's brigade operating as reserves. By mid-morning Heckman's advance guard was emerging out of the woods about three-quarters of a mile south of the bridge. Scouts had reported enemy troops in the woods on the other side of the railroad track that now lay before them. Heckman detached two companies to watch the enemy, and in skirmish formation began moving up the tracks toward the Goldsboro Bridge. The formation had not traveled far before it came under fire from both infantry near the bridge and artillery on the other side of the river. Using the raised

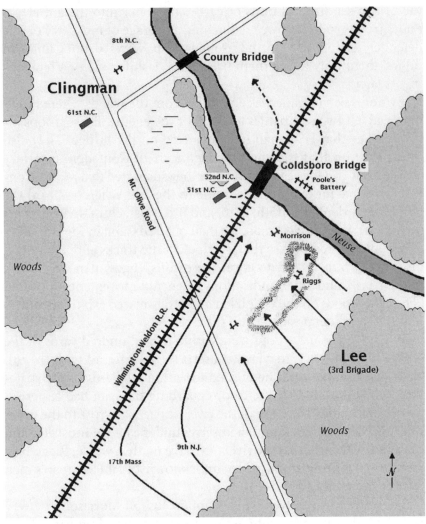

The opening phases of the Battle of Goldsboro Bridge, December 17, 1862. (*Author*)

tracks as partial shelter from the artillery Heckman's troops returned fire and continued to push forward.

Clingman raced back across the county bridge and dispatched Colonel Allen and his regiment to support the troops at the Goldsboro Bridge. Allen had barely taken position to the right of the 52nd North Carolina when Union artillery rounds began to erupt around the bridge sending columns of earth and water into the air. Heck-man's troops soon followed, launching a barrage of musketry on the defenders as well. The North Carolina troops wavered, but Clingman rallied them only to see them break and dash for safety a few moments later.[17]

By now Lee's brigade was emerging from the woods where Heck-man had left two companies to monitor the enemy. These troops informed Lee that Heckman had advanced on the bridge. They also informed him that they had repelled a small Confederate cavalry charge a few minutes earlier, and that they suspected that a large Confederate force lurked in the tree line to the left. When he heard the news, Lee ordered the 25th, 27th, and 3rd Massachusetts Regiments forward to support Heckman. He then ordered Captain Riggs' battery to set up on a nearby rise that overlooked the tracks and positioned his other two regiments to cover these guns. Riggs' men were quick in their task, and when indications of enemy movements appeared before the woods on the Union left a few well-placed explosive rounds sent the Confederates back into the trees.

When Heckman's troops were within a few hundred yards of the bridge he sent the 17th Massachusetts to the left and with the 9th New Jersey on the right he pushed to within ten yards of the structure. While the Confederate troops guarding the span had either retreated west along the bank of the river or dashed across to the other side, the Union forces found themselves under a hail of musketry and cannon fire from across the river. To make matters worse, Riggs' battery was now firing at the bridge unbeknownst that Heckman's men were at the southern end.

The issue was resolved when Captain Joseph Morrison's battery rode forward and went into action about two hundred yards from the river. While Morrison's men split their fire between the Confederate positions across the river and the bridge, Heckman called for a volunteer to put the structure to the torch. Several volunteered and several were halted in the attempt. Finally, Lee's aide-de-camp, Lt. George Graham and another volunteered and moved into position to make a dash for the bridge.[18]

Across the river Lt. Colonel Poole was warning his men of just such an event. "Thinking they had dislodged us, the enemy sent forward 2 men to effect the destruction of the bridge by fire. I cautioned my men of the approach of the [two] men, and as soon as they broke cover for the bridge fire was opened upon them. One fell back wounded, the other succeeded in reaching the projecting brick-work, where he was enabled to complete his work." Poole's men poured a withering fire on Graham's location and even shifted their firing positions to obtain a better angle, but it was to no avail. The bridge had already been rigged for demolition, making the lieutenant's task that much easier. "His work proved successful," Poole noted, "and in less than ten minutes the entire southern and eastern faces of the bridge were in flames." The fire, which soon spread, was aided by the Union artillery which blew large pieces off the structure with every hit. Several more batteries raced to Heckman's support, and soon the bridge was damaged beyond repair.[19]

With the railroad bridge destroyed the defense of the county bridge became paramount, and shortly thereafter Poole and his men were ordered to drag their guns over to the county bridge and position them on either side of the span. Here Poole met Clingman, whose command had reassembled on the north side of the bridge. Clingman had been reinforced by the fourth regiment in his brigade, the recently arrived 61st North Carolina under Colonel William Devane. Together with the other three regiments now lining the shore near the bridge, and the opportune arrival of Poole's men, the brigadier waited for what he believed was the next Union target.

In fact, the Union did not seem to know that another bridge existed, for if they had, they certainly would have destroyed this as well. The cannon on both sides had ceased and beyond the occasional musket discharge, the battle appeared over. The Confederate defenders at the county bridge began to breathe a sigh of relief. That is, until Evans met with Clingman again and revived the earlier plan to advance against the Union line. The general ordered Clingman to move his brigade toward the railroad tracks. Evans' brigade was now near the county bridge and would follow as quickly as possible.

Clingman led his brigade over the bridge and then split it into two parts. The first section consisted of Marshall's and Allen's regiments who had previously been stationed at the bridge. They were to move along the riverbank, and when they reached the bridge, form ranks on the other side of the railroad berm where they would be partially sheltered from artillery fire. Once they heard the fire from Clingman's attack, the two regiments were to cross the railroad and fall on the enemy's right. The second section consisted of the 8th and 61st North Carolina along with two of Fuller's guns. Clingman would personally lead this detachment along the country road toward its intersection with the railroad. Here he would form a line of battle and attack the Union left. With Evans' brigade close behind, the combined weight of eight regiments would fall upon the Union line, giving the Confederates their first chance during the campaign to strike under nearly equal conditions.[20]

The timing of the late afternoon counterattack was close to perfect. With the mission completed, Stevenson's and Wessells' brigades had arrived on the scene only to be marshalled back into columns and sent back the way they came. Lee's brigade was the last to depart. With the railroad bridge enveloped in a shifting column of black smoke several of Lee's regiments had already formed up and started back, when a detachment of New York cavalry patrolling near the bridge reported an enemy formation moving toward the brigade's position. Caught off guard, Lee ordered the 5th Massachusetts to cover Morrison's battery, which, escorted by the cavalry detachment, was being unlimbered on a hill near the bridge. He then ordered Capt. James Belger's battery forward to support them. The other regiments were recalled and deployed into line of battle as they reappeared out of the woods.

Clingman had yet to deploy his detachment and Evans' men were still crossing the county bridge when, to his surprise, Marshall's and Allen's regiments surged over the railroad tracks. Yelling and cheering, they advanced over nearly a thousand yards of open ground toward Lee's right flank. The Massachusetts troops held themselves ready to deliver a volley into the advancing grey line, but it proved unnecessary. It was too little, too late. Firing cannister and shells, Morrison and Belger's guns riddled the advancing line, slowing its progress until it broke and dashed back for the railroad tracks and the safety of the woods beyond. Fuller's battery, which was now only one gun, as the other had been lost in a ditch, was with Clingman on the Confederate right and opened fire to cover the retreat. This set off a brief artillery duel, but little came of it. Darkness was less than half an hour away, and even with Evans' brigade now in line with Clingman's detachment near the rail line it was too late to do anything. Lee was thinking along similar lines. With little else to be accomplished and

Brigadier General Thomas Clingman, left, who would command the brigade defending the Goldsboro Bridge. (*Library of Congress*) Thomas J.C. Amory, right, colonel of the 17th Massachusetts and commander of Foster's 1st Brigade during the Goldsboro expedition. (*Memorial History of the Seventeenth Regiment, Massachusetts Volunteer Infantry*)

one of the creeks along the return route reportedly rising, he gave the order to withdraw at nightfall, and along with the New York cavalry, acted as Foster's rear guard for the uneventful march back to Newbern.[21]

For the Union, Foster's campaign was a success, albeit a limited one. He had accomplished his goals. The Wilmington-Welden line had been disrupted by torn-up tracks and the Goldsboro Bridge destroyed, but the county bridge a short distance above the Goldsboro Bridge had been left intact. This meant that a train could stop, transfer its goods across the river on wagons via the county bridge to an awaiting train on the other side, and send them on their way. While hardly a preferred method, it was nonetheless sufficient until the bridge was rebuilt. On a positive note Union troops had defeated the enemy in three successive engagements and had even managed to destroy a partially built Confederate ironclad in the process. More importantly, the venture had created a distraction, further stretching Confederate manpower and logistics during Burnside's Fredericksburg Campaign. Although Foster's effort was successful and would cause some discomfort to the South's supply lines, it would be relegated to the back pages of the news which displayed numerous stories regarding Burnside's defeat at Fredericksburg.

For the South the campaign was a reminder of how vulnerable even the interior of North Carolina was to raids from the Union beachhead along Pamlico and Albemarle Sounds. Sizable portions of the North Carolina harvest were located within easy reach of these Union-held waterways, and far more were within reach of a coordinated raid like the one that just occurred at Goldsboro. The threat to transportation and agricultural products could not be ignored. It was clear that something would have to be done.

FOURTEEN

Guns and Bread

O NE OF THE FIRST CHANGES THAT CAME to the area was one of command. Robert E. Lee would appoint General James Longstreet to oversee the defenses of Virginia and North Carolina. Longstreet in turn selected well-known North Carolina general Daniel H. Hill to assume command of the North Carolina front. Hill was neither new to the region nor unfamiliar with the problems caused by the Union stranglehold over the sounds and waterways along the coast. The general had toured the area in the fall of 1861 making a number of suggestions in the process. Some of these ideas were finalized, although many were not, and some, like the "Croatan Works" below New Berne, were simply never completed. Known for his aggressive approach to problems, Hill detailed the issues and challenges to be faced in a long letter to Longstreet and the secretary of war in late February 1863.

First, Wilmington and the Cape Fear Inlets were at risk. Fort Caswell at the Old Inlet was a small brick fort from the era of Fort Macon, and like the latter, was ill-suited against bombardment by rifled guns. General Whiting was busy building casemates for the fort's guns and raising the parapet on the harbor side so a Union ironclad could not sail past the fort's guns and bombard the structure from the reverse side. And this they might do, Hill suggested in his letter, for even if the work on the fort's defects was completed, the guns were "so light that vessels might run past with but little risk." What was needed was heavy ten-inch and eleven-inch guns to effectively guard the passage. As for a landward attack on Wilmington, Hill found the land defenses to the east and south of the city insufficient to repel an attack and so slight as to wonder what the troops stationed there had been doing for the last two years. "I feel concerned about Wilmington," the general penned. "The Yankees seem to have become alarmed at the magnitude of the task before them at Charleston and may first try their hand at Wilmington."[1]

Second, although Hill had four brigades under his command "Evans, Pettigrew, Daniel, and the wonderfully inefficient brigade of Robertson," an additional brigade would allow him to go on the offensive. The surplus manpower would let him "bring out a vast quantity of bacon, pork, and corn from the counties on the coast," as well as provide protection for the farmers loyal to the Confederacy and encourage them to cultivate another crop. "To sum up the whole matter," Hill wrote,

> We need more heavy guns at Wilmington; we need another brigade of infantry to harass the Yankees, to detain their troops from Charleston, to protect the planting interest in the rich counties of the east, and to bring out supplies and conscripts; we need an efficient brigade of cavalry to keep the Yankees close shut up in their fortifications.[2]

It was a convincing letter from someone who knew the region, its people, and his profession. Longstreet applauded the ideas, which he thought were along the lines of his own thinking. As such, he informed Hill, he would order Whiting to release one of the brigades at Wilmington. The general estimated that this would put Hill's strength at fourteen thousand men or so. "With this force," Longstreet pointed out, "I think you could cut the railroad behind New Berne and probably force the enemy out to fight."[3]

Hill planned just such an operation for early March. The intent of the expedition was to secure as much of the produce in the area between the Neuse River and Albemarle Sound as possible. To cover this logistical venture Hill originally planned to make a feint on Newbern followed by an attack on the smaller Union garrison at Washington. A demonstration in front of Plymouth was also added to hold the garrison there in place while foraging operations were conducted. Poor weather and organizational issues plagued the operation, causing Hill to drop the attack on Washington, and the slow release of Richard Garnett's brigade at Wilmington further hampered matters. There was also a matter of artillery and, in particular, of obtaining a number of Whitworth rifled guns, which because of their striking power and accuracy would be useful in dealing with the Union warships anchored at Newbern.

General Daniel H. Hill, known as D.H. Hill to distinguish him from another Confederate general, A.P. Hill. A graduate of the U.S. Military Academy and a veteran of the Mexican-American War where he was twice promoted for gallantry, Hill would resign his commission to become a mathematics professor. When the Civil War broke out, he was the superintendent of the North Carolina Military Institute in Charlotte. (*Library of Congress*)

The fact that neither Garnett nor the desired Whitworth guns would arrive in time for the attack did not deter Hill. In its final form Hill planned a three-pronged assault on Newbern. Daniel's brigade would approach the town from the Trent Road while the general's questionable cavalry brigade under Robertson would approach along the southern bank of the Trent River, stopping to tear up the railroad tracks between Beaufort and Newbern as they advanced. The last and most important element of the attack Hill entrusted to Brigadier General John Pettigrew and artillery commander Major John Haskell. Haskell would take the bulk of the expedition's artillery and, along with Pettigrew's brigade, would march from Kinston along the north bank of the Neuse to take up a position from which to besiege Fort Anderson located across the river from Newbern. With this fort in Confederate hands the besiegers could not only shell Newbern but would be in a position to challenge the nearby Union flotilla for control of the river.[4]

While the entire exercise was a diversion, it appears that Hill had promoted the operation as an attempt to seize the town. It is difficult to imagine that Hill, a veteran of half a dozen campaigns in northern Virginia, believed that he was going to seize the Union stronghold with three brigades, one of which was problematic in his mind. It seems more likely that his promotion was done for two reasons. First, in case Northern agents got wind of the plan, and second, because Hill was willing to escalate the venture if Fort Anderson fell and the Union warships protecting it and Newbern could be neutralized. This last point was driven home to Pettigrew and Haskell; Fort Anderson and the Union warships had to be neutralized for the attack to proceed.

There was no lack of effort by Haskell or Pettigrew's men in the early stages of the expedition. Orders arrived at Goldsboro on Monday, March 9, for both detachments to be in position before Fort Anderson on Thursday. The march of almost sixty miles over back roads evolved into a soggy nightmare as heavy rains on Tuesday and Wednesday turned the country roads to quagmires and swelled the creeks and brooks along the way. Along with eleven other guns, Haskell had a battery of four twenty-pound Parrott guns, which, heavier than his other pieces, tested the small bridges in the area. At Palmetto Creek a skeptical Haskell sent his other artillery pieces across the bridge before ordering his Parrott gun battery to cross. "The first gun of which crushed in the bridge and was drawn out by hand with great difficulty." It took three hours to repair the bridge and move the other guns across. A few hours later "the artillery was stopped by the brigade wagon train, which had stalled in the middle of a stream." The wagons were removed and part of the artillery crossed, but the operation came to a halt when the swollen creek proved impassible and a temporary bridge had to be erected. With the roads obliterated and the creeks before them still rising it soon became clear to all involved that they would be late for their rendezvous at Fort Anderson.[5]

On early Friday morning, Hill began the operation by ordering Daniel's and Robertson's brigades forward. Around eight miles from Newbern, Daniel's men encountered a set of earthworks at Deep Gully. A naturally strong position, the post was held by five companies of Union troops supported by a pair of cannons. The garrison was

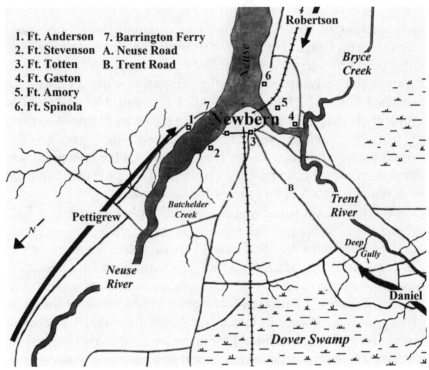

1. Ft. Anderson 7. Barrington Ferry
2. Ft. Stevenson A. Neuse Road
3. Ft. Totten   B. Trent Road
4. Ft. Gaston
5. Ft. Amory
6. Ft. Spinola

A map of Hill's planned attack on Newbern in March 1863. (*Author*)

equipped to handle small patrols, not surprise attacks from a brigade of Confederate infantry. The position fell quickly and much of the garrison was captured. Those that managed to escape spread the news, which quickly reached General Foster. Foster was skeptical about reports of an all-out attack. A large-scale infantry attack against his well-manned and well-supplied defenses was unlikely to succeed and would result in crushing casualties to the enemy even if it did obtain some measure of success. The general sent reinforcements to the area, but suspicious as to the enemy's real intentions he ordered them to "retire slowly, and fight if they were pressed." The next morning Foster's suspicions were confirmed when Pettigrew's brigade appeared in front of Fort Anderson.[6]

An hour before dawn on Saturday, March 14, Pettigrew ordered the 26th North Carolina forward. Arranged in skirmish formation the regiment swept down the wooded road to the fort, seizing a num-

ber of enemy pickets before bursting upon a cleared field. As Pettigrew and his staff arrived, they found the Union fort lay four hundred
yards away on a slight rise. It was hardly an impressive structure, but
it did pose a problem. "It was flanked by a swamp of 3 or 4 miles on
the right and a swampy creek on the left, so that it could only be approached in front." The brigadier shook his head. The onslaught of
rain and the delays it imposed had upset his plans. "I hoped to carry
the work by moonlight on Friday morning with the bayonet, which
I preferred," Pettigrew wrote of the incident, "as the enemy in New
Berne then would not know the result and I might thus be enabled
to intrench the guns before the gunboats attacked."[7]

Now, however, it was daylight, and with only one path by which
to storm the fort the general realized that he might lose as many as a
hundred men in the assault. Haskell's artillery, after leaving a pair of
rifled guns at Pettiford's Ferry a mile upstream from Fort Anderson,
was now entering the clearing and would be unlimbering their guns
in a few minutes. If Pettigrew had stormed the fort under the cover
of his guns there is a good chance Fort Anderson would have been in
his hands in less than an hour. From here he would have been able to
use his batteries to challenge the Union gunboats on the river—one
of the keys to seizing Newbern.

Instead, the general decided to overwhelm the fort's defenders with
cannon fire in hopes of securing a quick surrender. Haskell arranged
his fourteen guns in three batteries before the fort and at 5:45 a.m.
the order to fire was echoed down the line. Shell and case-shot
screeched toward the earth fort while its 250 defenders crouched behind the parapets. As explosions and smoke enveloped the structure
Haskell ordered his battery of twenty-pound Parrott guns to focus
on a pair of ships anchored on the other side of the river. Soon the
guns at Pettiford's landing joined in catching the Union vessels in a
crossfire.

While Fort Anderson did not respond with its guns, the USS
Hunchback and a nearby armed schooner quickly beat to quarters
and began returning fire as fountains of water erupted around them.
The schooner was soon hit and began taking on water, leaving the
Hunchback to engage both Confederate positions with its hundred-
pound Parrott gun and nine-inch shell gun. The Parrott gun broke
after a dozen shots, leaving the entire defense of Fort Anderson in the

hands of the warship's nine-inch gun crew and its small ship's howitzer.

While Haskell was convinced that his rifled guns had scored some hits on the two vessels in the river, he deemed it "impossible, with the very inferior ammunition with which they were supplied, to shoot accurately enough to strike any vital part unless by chance." As to the fort, his guns were striking the structure with every shot, but it did not appear to be having any effect.

The Confederate batteries had been firing for thirty minutes when they suddenly fell silent and a Confederate officer waving a white flag approached the fort. The officer was brought before the fort's commandant, Lt. Colonel Hiram Anderson, where he delivered an official summons to surrender the fort. Although he already knew the answer, Anderson wisely asked for a brief cease-fire to consult with General Foster in Newbern. Although several on Pettigrew's staff were against the cease-fire, the general granted the request which brought the fighting to a halt. While the brief lull appeared to change little, as Anderson declined and the bombardment was resumed, it had given the other elements of Commander Murray's fleet time to move forward in support of the fort.

Pettigrew and Haskell had placed great hopes in a battery of twenty-pound Parrott guns brought along specifically to deal with the Union gunboats. They were soon to be disappointed. One of the guns broke its axle after repeated firings, and as several of Murray's gunboats began dropping shells onto the battlefield, another of Haskell's Parrott guns failed in a thunderous clap. The accidental explosion was such that Commander Murray onboard the recently arrived *Hetzel* was convinced that he had scored a direct hit on the piece with his nine-inch gun. With the *Hetzel*, *Ceres*, *Shawsheen*, and the revenue cutter *Algiers* now involved alongside the *Hunchback*, which after having been struck twice had inadvertently run aground, the tide of the battle began to shift. Pettigrew continued dueling with the Union warships and firing on the fort for another hour and a half before passing the order to withdraw. It was clear that his artillery was not enough to reduce the fort or disable the Union warships. Frustrated at the chain of events, Pettigrew penned a note to Hill that, "The absence of the Whitworth ruined us. The 20-pounder Parrotts are worse than useless . . . I hope never to see them again."[8]

There was little for Hill to do at this point but retreat. The fiery general complained about not receiving the Whitworth rifles on time, about the failure of Robertson's troops to cut the Newbern-Morehead City rail line, and in particular, he had a number of choice words for Whiting who he believed had "spoiled everything" by delaying Garnett's brigade. In the end, however, while Hill was lamenting on what could have been, and while Foster was busy informing Washington that the Confederate attack was "ineffective and weak, inflicting no damage and accomplishing no object," both missed the point that Southern quartermasters had found time to accomplish the expedition's primary goal by procuring and transporting close to fifty thousand pounds of produce from the area.[9]

Hill would next set his sights on Washington two weeks later. The town had been included in his initial plans against Newbern, but the project was dropped for a shortage of troops and logistical reasons. This time the general had three full brigades at his disposal with the arrival of Garnett's Virginia brigade. When he informed Longstreet of his intentions in late March, the general immediately approved of the plan and offered to move Ransom's brigade from Wilmington to Goldsboro in support of the effort. "I do not expect you to take Washington, of course," Longstreet informed Hill, "if it is found to be more difficult than you anticipated. Exercise your own good judgment in the matter. The important question is to draw in all of the meat rations that can be had." To support this goal, he authorized Hill to secure whatever wagons he could lay his hands on "at liberal rates of transportation so as to haul in supplies for our armies."[10]

Hill laid siege to the Federal garrison at Washington, North Carolina, on April 1st. The general used Garnett's brigade to besiege the town, while Pettigrew and Daniel's brigades were stationed south of the Tar River to intercept any relief column sent from Newbern but still close enough to move in support of Garnett's forces should a Union relief force arrive by water. While Hill's siege immediately commanded Foster's attention and the focus of the Union forces at Newbern, there was never a serious threat that Hill would capture the town, or if he did, that he would be able to hold it. The Union garrison of 1,200 was quickly reinforced, and after an attempt to lift the siege failed, Foster, who was in Washington, left to personally take charge of an expedition to relieve the beleaguered town. Confederate troops attempted to block the river and laid down a line of obstructions in an attempt to bar passage to the Union gunboats, but it did not work and these vessels were active throughout the twenty-day siege firing at enemy earthworks and troop formations on a daily basis. The large guns carried by these small warships, firing projectiles five times the weight of a normal field artillery round, had proven decisive on several occasions and proved a sufficient deterrent on this occasion as well. Although Foster had been able to get additional reinforcements into the town creating a stalemate, ultimately the Union flotilla and the lack of a method to wrest control of the local waters from them meant that no Confederate siege or occupation would last long.[11]

In this case it no longer mattered. With the foraging operations complete and word of another Union relief column forming at New-bern, Hill lifted the siege and moved off. For Hill and the Confederates, it was a victory in the sense that the supplies obtained were worth the diversion. Hill in his typical style pumped up the victory, but for the last few months the general had been provided with troops and supplies that put him on par with the Union forces in the area, and at times he had even commanded local superiority, something that had not been the case from the opening days of the conflict. Yet beyond the foraging operations little had come from the surge in manpower. With Lee preparing to move north into Pennsylvania and looking for all the troops that could be mustered, the numerical advantage along Pamlico and Albemarle Sounds would once again swing back in favor of the Union.[12]

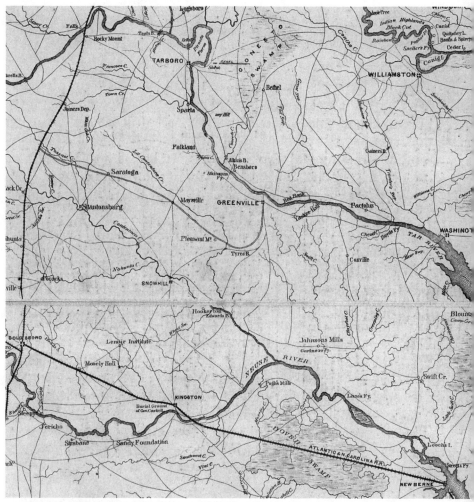

A portion of an 1862 map of North Carolina showing the area between the Tar and Neuse Rivers from Newbern and Washington in the east to the railroad bridges at Goldboro and Rocky Mount in the west. (*Library of Congress*)

FIFTEEN

The Last Battle of Newbern

THE SECOND HALF OF 1863 along Pamlico and Albemarle Sounds consisted of raids, counterraids, small expeditions, and scouts. Much of the reason for this was that the campaigns in Virginia and Pennsylvania had stretched the resources of both sides to the point that neither was looking to launch a major effort in the area. July proved a particularly busy month for these type of Union forays out of Newbern. During the early morning hours of July 3, elements of the 3rd and 12th New York Cavalry, a company from the North Carolina Union Volunteers, and a section of horse artillery from the 3rd New York Artillery, about 650 men in all, set out on an expedition to disrupt the Wilmington-Weldon Railroad at Warsaw. Led by Lt. Colonel George W. Lewis, the detachment worked its way through enemy territory skirmishing with pickets and surprising and routing a Confederate cavalry company at Kenansville on the afternoon of the fourth. By eight o'clock the next morning Lewis and his troops galloped into Warsaw. Here they tore up the tracks for several miles and twisted the rails to make them unusable. Several warehouses filled with foodstuffs were put to the torch, and the telegraph poles for a mile in either direction were cut down. Informed that there was a large Confederate cavalry detachment in the area, Lewis wisely returned immediately, arriving back at Newbern on the seventh having accomplished his task and not having lost a single man in the venture.[1]

A few weeks later another expedition was departing Newbern. This one under Brigadier General Edward Potter was aimed at destroying the Tarboro Bridge and the Rocky Mount railroad bridge over the Tar River. A pair of Massachusetts regiments and a detachment of New York troops under Colonel James Jourdan and a 650-man cavalry detachment under Colonel Lewis crossed the Neuse on July 18 and moved to Swift Creek. Here the force divided. Potter ordered Colonel Jourdan to make a feint toward Kinston and then return to Newbern, while he and Lewis' cavalry advanced on Greenville on the south bank of the Tar River. The column entered Greenville on the afternoon of July 19. The town was surrounded by entrenchments, but there was no one to man the defenses beyond a few sick soldiers who fled at first sight of the Union column. Here Potter divided his command again. The general ordered Major Ferris Jacobs to take his 3rd New York cavalry companies and advance directly on the Rocky Mount Bridge, while the main column moved on Tarboro. At 3 a.m. the following morning Jacobs' men rode out, heading west, while a few hours later Potter's detachment pushed forward, reaching their objective around eight o'clock.

The cavalry quickly formed up on the outskirts of Tarboro and Potter ordered the bugler to sound the charge. The dozen or so Confederate troops manning the defenses fired a few erratic shots and bolted across the bridge or vanished into the countryside. With the town in his hands and his engineers busy rigging the nearby bridge for destruction, Potter rode down to the waterfront where he found the partially completed ironclad CSS *Tarboro*. "I found an iron-clad on the stocks and two steamboats on the river," he noted in his report. "The iron-clad was of the Merrimac model, and her frame was very heavy and solid. All were burned, together with some railroad cars, 100 bales of cotton, quartermaster's, subsistence, and ordnance stores." At 5 p.m. Potter gave the order to fire the bridge, and with his task complete the detachment began its return trip.

The general rendezvoused with Jacobs' detachment later in the day. Jacobs and his men had been as successful as the Tarboro detachment.

Riding into Rocky Mount the Union troops made quick work of the facility. The 350-foot railroad bridge and the supporting 400-foot span of trestle work was put to the torch. So too was the nearby 350-foot county bridge, a large cotton mill, a small factory, a machine-shop, the telegraph office, and three train cars filled with wagons. Reunited, Potter's force made its way back to Newbern, and after a series of skirmishes with their Confederate counterparts, entered the town on July 24.[2]

The next day yet another expedition departed Newbern. This one was aimed at Winston on the Chowan River. A small force of infantry and cavalry had arrived before this town on army transports, and after landing, skirmished with a Confederate detachment before seizing a bridge along the road to Weldon. While the raid was not as successful in capturing and destroying enemy supplies as the others, in part because "everything in that line had been removed by the enemy," it still managed to further degrade the enemy's communication and transportation lines.[3]

There would be more raids by both sides throughout the year. Although the limited size and scope of these operations meant that, regardless of the outcome of any individual skirmish, overall, it did little to break the stalemate that had fallen over the area. As an aggregate, however, those conducted by the Union were starting to have an effect. Confederate forces, stretched thin to begin with, were having a difficult time responding to the incursions. Writing after the destruction of the Rocky Mount railroad bridge in late July, the superintendent of the Wilmington and Weldon Railroad pointed out that, "since January and before (with few days of exception), no troops have been held at Tarboro, a very important depot of Government supplies, that 20 mounted and armed men could have destroyed by a raid from Washington at any time." Just as importantly, the farmers and populace in the area were being worn down by the excursions, and the local militia was exhausted from being constantly called out.

A field officer in the Third North Carolina Cavalry wrote in the fall of 1863 that, "The condition of eastern North Carolina grew hourly more deplorable. Frequent incursions of the enemy resulted in the destruction of property of all kinds. Especially were horses and mules objects of plunder." This was particularly true around the towns of Newbern, Washington, and Plymouth where a ring of commercial and agricultural devastation brought on by frequent Union foraging parties radiated for dozens of miles. Most farms within this radius had been burned or abandoned, and the prosperous fields of a few years' prior were now left to waste. There was yet more. Rogue bands, deserters, and robbers patrolled the swamps and nearby farmlands. The "Buffaloes," as they were called, pillaged and burned with little regard to national allegiance. "Gangs of a dozen men, infested the swamps and made night hideous with their horrid visitations," the Confederate cavalry officer noted, and were this not enough, there was always the possibility as a local farmer or tradesman that Union troops would brand you a sympathizer, seize your produce, and burn down your home. In all, it had a serious impact on local agriculture, which in turn had an effect on the Army of Northern Virginia's supply lines.[4]

In September steps were taken to strengthen Confederate defenses along the Union's Pamlico and Albemarle beachheads. General D.H. Hill had previously been transferred to Richmond and his position filled by Brigadier General Matt W. Ransom. In late September Ransom was replaced by Major General George Pickett. At first it appeared that the North Carolina defenses would receive a major boost as Pickett's entire division would be accompanying him, but in fact one of the reasons for assigning the division to North Carolina was to allow it to be rebuilt. The unit was at less than half strength, and its morale shattered after its disastrous charge at Gettysburg. For the first few months Pickett was content with maintaining the current level of affairs as his unit recruited and expanded. At one point he even pushed back when an attempt was made to transfer the division back to Virginia. "In time I will be able to get the division together and in fighting trim," Pickett informed his superiors. "It most emphatically is not so now."[5]

As winter set in and the year turned, supply problems were beginning to come to the forefront. In the early days of January 1864 Lee pleaded for supplies. "I regret very much to learn that the supply of beef for the Army is so nearly exhausted," he wrote to the commissary general in Richmond. "I have endeavored since first taking command to collect for its use all the provisions I could, and am still making every effort in my power to gather subsistence in front of our line of operations." Were these matters not enough, transportation was just as important. Commissary general of the Confederate Army, Colonel

L.B. Northrop, was having problems moving foodstuffs north because of the railroad. "The (rail) road is now barely able to furnish limited transportation," Lee complained to the secretary of war. "If this is diminished it will be impossible for me to keep the army in its present position." To Northrop, Lee was more direct. "I agree with you that every effort should be made to accumulate subsistence in Richmond. The necessities of this army and the uncertainty of depending upon our railroads render this apparent."[6]

One of Lee's subordinates, who the general had taken a liking to, was Brigadier General Robert Hoke of North Carolina. Hoke had discussed similar issues with Lee concerning coastal North Carolina. He proposed a plan to free up more agricultural product in the area and eliminate the primary source of the raids against the Wilmington-Weldon railroad lines by capturing Newbern. Hoke outlined the idea to the general. The timing was good. The Union had withdrawn troops from the garrison at Newbern, and there had not been a major attack on the town in a year, meaning the pickets would be lax. Manpower was available. Pickett's recovering division gave the Confederates a sizable force with which to accomplish the task. Hoke then presented one of the primary issues with attacking Newbern—the Union gunboats. These vessels acted like floating artillery and were an important part of the defender's arsenal. A method would have to be devised to neutralize these vessels or the expedition would be in trouble. Lastly, and just as importantly, the capture of Newbern would allow for a base of operations for the new ironclad CSS *Neuse* and a number of smaller wooden gunboats, which, along with the CSS *Albemarle* being completed on the Roanoke River, would challenge for control of the interior waters of the sounds.

Lee was sold on the idea and started his January 2, 1864, letter to Jefferson Davis, "The time is at hand when, if an attempt can be made to capture the enemy's forces at New Berne, it should be done. I can now spare troops for the purpose, which will not be the case as spring approaches." He covered the points laid out by Hoke and even suggested a way to deal with the Union gunboats guarding the town. "The gun-boats are small and indifferent, and do not keep up a head of steam. A bold party could descend the Neuse in boats at night, capture the gun-boats, and drive the enemy by their aid from the works on that side of the river, while a force should attack them in front."[7]

Richmond agreed and the matter was quickly settled. Lee had suggested two brigades to conduct the operation, and when asked to suggest a commander, he nominated Hoke. While Richmond likely agreed that the bright and daring brigadier could do the job, given the size of the operation, command rightly fell to Major General Pickett. Hoke's brigade would take part, but overall command would rest with Pickett.

It is not clear if Pickett knew of General Lee's initial choice or not, but to his credit he adopted the major provisions of Hoke's plan. The main component of the attack would consist of General Seth Barton's brigade, General James Kemper's brigade, three regiments from Ransom's brigade, fourteen guns, and six hundred cavalry. This force would leave Kinston, and after crossing the Trent River above Newbern, would push through the Union pickets at Bryce Creek and attack Forts Gaston, Amory, and Spinola from the landside. With these three Union strongholds taken, the Confederate force would then continue its advance across the great railroad bridge into Newbern.

To the north Colonel James Dearing would lead three regiments of infantry, several companies of cavalry, and a battery of three guns against Fort Anderson, which had eluded capture from a large Confederate force the previous year. If possible, he was to secure Barrington Ferry as well. A third attack would be led by Hoke with Pickett accompanying him. Hoke's brigade, with elements of Clingman's and Corse's brigades and ten pieces of artillery, would attack the city from the north hoping to surprise a series of fortifications the Union troops had strung across Batchelder Creek. Even if this wasn't possible, Hoke was to create a diversion and pin down as many Union troops as possible while Barton, Dearing, and Wood secured their objectives, which would leave the town cut off and vulnerable to bombardment. The last element of the plan involved General James Martin's brigade at Wilmington. Martin was to make a feint toward Morehead City in hopes of delaying any Union reinforcements that might be sent north to Newbern.

These three attacks would be launched simultaneously, but the last element of the attack, the naval action Lee had proposed in his letter to Jefferson Davis, would go after the first three had been launched. The idea was the genesis of one of the great commando raids of the conflict. The attack on the town would act as cover for several Con-

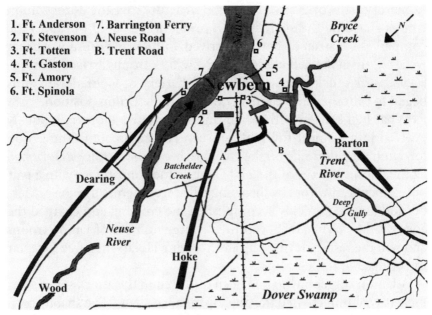

1. Ft. Anderson 7. Barrington Ferry
2. Ft. Stevenson A. Neuse Road
3. Ft. Totten B. Trent Road
4. Ft. Gaston
5. Ft. Amory
6. Ft. Spinola

A sketch of the planned Confederate operations against Newbern, February 1864. (*Author*)

federate boat crews under the leadership of Commander John Taylor Wood. These men would navigate their small launches alongside the Union gunboats, and in the confusion, board them in traditional naval fashion: with cutlass and pistol.[8]

It was agreed that the attack would be launched by all three parties on Monday morning, February 1. On the night of January 30 all seemed on track. Hoke and his men were encamped along the Neuse road five miles from Kinston, Barton was encamped fifteen miles from Kinston, and both Dearing and Martin were moving forward. From here, however, things would go awry.

On the evening of January 31 Hoke and his men halted at Stephen's Forks a few miles from the Union lines at the Batchelder Creek. At one o'clock the next morning Hoke and his men moved forward. An encounter with some Union pickets in the drifting fog alarmed the guard by the bridge over Batchelder Creek, and it was destroyed before the Confederates could reach it. Upon hearing the gunfire Colonel P.J. Claassen, in command of the outposts on the creek, ordered three companies of the 132nd New York to the bridge.

A pair of earthworks raised near the structure gave the dozen Union troops guarding the span enough protection to hold out until the companies Claassen dispatched arrived. But it was close, and a cheer went out from the defenders as the New York troops arrived. This jubilance was quickly drowned when a battery of Confederate guns began to rain shell and cannister down on the Union position.

What had started with a handful of scattered shots had quickly evolved into a smart firefight between Hoke's men and the Union forces on the other side on the creek. To break the deadlock Hoke had Colonel John Mercer of the 21st Georgia move upstream with a pair of regiments and cross by throwing felled trees across the creek. Mercer and his men quickly accomplished the crossing and charged the enemy's flank. The attack captured a large number of Union troops and sent the rest scurrying for safety, leaving Hoke's men free to repair the bridge.[9]

A Union surgeon who had been captured in the attack watched as Pickett's column crossed the quickly mended span. "The shabby condition of the Confederates surprised me," he noted. "No two were dressed alike. One fourth were dressed, in part, in captured U.S. clothing, and nearly all the remainder in butternut homespun, evidently cut by a woman tailor; they were without overcoats, and hundreds of them barefooted, and this in mid-winter." Even their weapons were rusty according to the Union officer, and "They seemed half starved, and at once commenced searching for food, quickly devouring my hospital supplies."[10]

By the time this was completed a small force of Union artillery and infantry had formed up in a field to the south of the crossing. When several enemy regiments approached them in line of battle it soon became apparent to the Union troops that this was not a raid. After firing a volley and discharging their cannons they wisely retreated. Hoke was not interested in this force and detached a few men to see them along their way. Instead, the brigadier raced for the train station where it crossed the Neuse Road. Hoke was convinced that the Yankee garrison had dispatched reinforcements to the creek by rail at first notice of the attack. If he hurried, he might be able to cut them off.

The Union troops had seen this as well and, returning, passed though the station into Newbern just a few minutes before Hoke's men arrived. Here the general halted. Clingman was ordered to take

Brigadier General Robert Hoke, left. An able leader praised for his conduct and gallantry on multiple occasions, Hoke would rise to the rank of major general. After the war he would become a businessman and the director of the North Carolina Railroad. The commander of Union forces at Newbern, Brigadier General Innis Palmer, right. An old cavalry officer who had served with distinction in the Mexican-American War, Palmer would command a division in the final campaigns in North Carolina. (*Library of Congress*)

his troops and move south to cut the Trent Road in order to prevent the Union troops at the nearby Deep Gully post from reentering the town. With Corse's men and the artillery now with him, Hoke advanced to within three-quarters of a mile of the city's northern defenses and dug in. Here he conferred with Pickett, and it was agreed to wait for the sound of Barton's guns at the south end of the railroad bridge over the Trent before pressing forward.[11]

In fact, there would be no sound of gunfire from the south. Barton and his command had crossed the Trent River, but when they arrived before Bryce Creek, they found the stream much wider and deeper than they had been told and a single heavily guarded bridge the only way to cross the span. To make matters worse, when Barton conducted a personal reconnaissance of the area, he noted several large forts mounting over two-dozen guns. With no other crossing but the bridge nearby, Barton decided to invest the position by allowing his skirmishers to fire on Union forces across the river, and his artillery at the nearby Union forts. It was a futile gesture that did nothing but alarm the enemy. Barton then ordered his cavalry to cut the Beaufort-Newbern rail line, but this was not accomplished either. Dearing also was having difficulties, and after a look at the Union forces at Fort Anderson he too deemed it impractical to attack.[12]

By Monday evening the entire venture seemed stalled, but in fact it was not. Commander Wood and his band of 285 Confederate sailors and marines had assembled at Kinston on Sunday, January 31. Here they loaded themselves into fourteen small boats and pushed out onto the Neuse River. According to one participant it would have been difficult to imagine that a battle raged at the end of their journey. "Not a sign of life was visible, save occasionally when a flock of wild ducks, startled at the approach of the boats, rose from the banks, and then poising themselves for a moment overhead, flew on swift wing to the shelter of the woodland or the morass. No other sound was heard to break the stillness save the constant, steady splash of the oars and the ceaseless surge of the river."[13]

By nightfall the broken clouds and shadows, combined with the winding nature of the river, was making navigation treacherous. Around 11 p.m. Wood found the flotilla was above Newbern. He directed his boats to put ashore on a small grassy island near the shore. Here he briefed his men on Pickett's attack and their mission to seize the Union gunboats in support of this. The raiding party stayed under shelter and listened to Hoke's attack throughout the day. When evening fell Wood ordered everyone into the boats. Arranged in two divisions with Wood commanding the first and Lt. B.P. Loyall commanding the second, the two columns slowly moved down the river as bands of rain shuffled across the waterway. When they neared their target, Wood called the boats together to issue some last-minute instructions and say a prayer. Midshipman J. Thomas Scharf vividly remembered the scene:

> It was a strange and ghostly sight, the men resting on their oars with heads uncovered, the commander also bareheaded, standing erect in the stern of his boat; the black waters rippling beneath; the dense overhanging clouds pouring down sheets of rain, and in the blackness beyond an unseen bell tolling as if from some phantom cathedral.[14]

Yet it was not a cathedral bell that rang out but the watch bell on the nearby USS *Underwriter*. The gunboat had been asked earlier in the day to move to the north end of the city, just in line with Fort Stevenson, to provide gunfire support if needed. The gunboat *Com-*

modore Hull was to have accompanied the *Underwriter*, but it ran aground shortly after leaving Newbern. A third gunboat, the USS *Lockwood*, was at Newbern when the attack began. The commander of the *Lockwood*, however, responding to reports of gun and artillery fire near Bryce's Creek, moved the gunboat into the Trent River to be of assistance if needed.

Onboard the *Underwriter*, anchored some fifty yards offshore of Fort Stevenson, the watch had just rung out four bells for two o'clock. Wood and his men took to their oars and cautiously pushed forward through the patches of fog. Five bells had just rung out when a lookout on the *Underwriter*, now only a hundred yards away, shouted out a challenge. Wood and his men said nothing as they closed in on the 350-foot warship. Several more challenges followed in quick succession before Wood bellowed out, "Give way! Give way strong!"

The response fooled no one, but the gunboat's crew had been slow to come to quarters. By the time the bow gun was manned it was too late, the Confederate boats were below its maximum depression. A number of sailors on the *Underwriter* responded with rifle and pistol fire, the flashes of which illuminated the deck of the vessel. The Confederates responded in kind, briefly lighting up their dark vessels, and Midshipman Scharf fired his boat's howitzer at the warship striking the pilothouse with the explosive round.[15]

By now Wood's boats were astride the *Underwriter*. The plan had been to simultaneously board from bow and stern, but most of the Confederate vessels chose the former. "When the boats struck the sides of the *Underwriter*," Scharf recalled, "grapnels were thrown on board, and the Confederates were soon scrambling, with cutlass and pistol in hand, to the deck with a rush and a wild cheer that rung across the waters." The crew of the Union warship, however, had no intentions of giving up so easily. For close to fifteen minutes the two sides battled on the gunboat's rainswept deck with pistol, cutlass, and musket. Finally, numbers and surprise told, and the warship's crew who had not been disabled or captured were driven below decks into the wardroom, where they surrendered.

With the gunboat now under his control Wood sought to move it, but to no avail. The vessel had no steam, and attempts to tow it away were fruitless. The anchor had been slipped and the ship had now drawn the attention of Fort Stevenson. Correctly deducing from the

firing on the vessel what was occurring the fort fired a shell at the
Underwriter which exploded on the deck. It was all Wood needed to
convince him it was time to go. As Fort Anderson and Fort Stevenson
began a scattered fire on the captured vessel, Wood ordered the ship
put to the torch and his men back to their boats. Now ablaze, the
slowly drifting gunboat and patches of fog brought an eerie illumi-
nation to the waterway as Wood and his men escaped. They had destroyed a Union gunboat, captured twenty-six of its crew, and killed
a number of others, including the warship's captain. Confederate
losses had been high as well, with six killed and twenty-two wounded
out of the one hundred or so actually engaged.[16]

The second morning of the battle started with a thunderclap and
a towering sheet of smoke and flames as the magazine on the *Underwriter* exploded just before dawn, finishing the vessel. Hoke and his
forces held their line outside the city throughout the day, occasionally
testing the enemy defenses with brief exchanges of artillery fire. The
fate of the Confederate effort, however, appeared sealed when Barton
informed General Pickett that he would not advance given the circumstances. As Hoke and Pickett watched the Union troop trains arrive at Newbern it also became clear that Barton had not cut the
railroad line either.

For General Innis N. Palmer in command of the 3,500 Union
troops in Newbern, February 2 was a day of patience. Colonel Anderson reported that there was an enemy force near Fort Anderson
but that it had not made any move toward the fort. There was also
some sporadic firing near the south end of the Newbern railroad
bridge, but the enemy had not attempted to close the approach to the
city. This left the only Confederate force to reckon with positioned
before the teeth of the town's defenses with any element of surprise
long since gone. It did not seem likely that the enemy would attack,
so it simply became a matter of waiting. Palmer could afford to wait.
Waiting meant he grew stronger. The trains still appeared to be running, bringing men and materials, and even now a dozen warships
were converging on the town.[17]

While neither Pickett or Palmer knew it at the time, the railroad
line to Morehead City was in fact cut, but not by Barton's troops but
by Brigadier General J.G. Martin and his brigade from Wilmington.
What was designed as a diversion was one of the most successful parts

of the operation. Martin's advance from Wilmington was a miserable march of repairing broken bridges and torrential downpours. The latter may have been of some help masking the brigade's movement for when Martin came upon the Union pickets on the road to Newport Barracks around noon on February 2, they scattered after a quick Confederate charge. The brigade advanced on the barracks and found a Union infantry formation on a hill a few miles from the post. Opening fire on the enemy with his artillery, Martin arranged three regiments before the blue line and ordered a charge. The badly outnumbered Union troops let loose a volley and then broke for the barracks, stopping only long enough to set fire to the railroad and county bridges over the Newport River and their own post before continuing their northern trek.

Martin put out the fires on the railroad bridge, but later that evening he changed his mind and ordered it burned. The general now held Newport Barracks and had severed the Newbern-Morehead City rail line. A fire was seen in Morehead City that evening as the Union troops, fearing an assault, burned their supplies and retreated. Martin now considered moving on the abandoned port town, but a dispatch reached him the afternoon of February 3 that changed any thoughts he had on such matters. The message was from General Barton and it simply read, "Fall back. All the troops are withdrawn. I do not know what it means." Martin received a second message confirming the first not long after, which only added that the troops were being pulled back from Newbern. With little else to be done Martin ordered his column to prepare to march, and at eight o'clock the next morning, he started back to Wilmington.[18]

By February 3 Hoke and Pickett had seen enough, and the order was given to withdraw to Kinston. General Palmer watched the Confederate troops file off in the early morning hours. He didn't do anything to interrupt them, but he did send out cavalry patrols to monitor their progress. In his official report Palmer listed his losses as 13 killed, 23 wounded, and 357 captured, with the bulk of this coming when the troops at Batchelder Creek were outflanked by Mercer's men. He never believed the town to be in jeopardy at any point and questioned the enemy's tactics. The general also noted in his report, several times in fact, his use of the telegraph during the battle. "At no time, I suspect, during the present war has the utility of the military telegraph and the signal corps been more fully demonstrated than during this late attack," he wrote. "The attack had scarcely commenced at the outposts when the telegraph had not only informed me of all that was going on in front, but the whole line of posts to Morehead was placed on its guard."[19]

Pickett estimated Confederate casualties at forty-five killed and wounded. As for the battle itself, clearly Barton and Dearing failed to carry through with their elements of the attack, and with the element of surprise lost, there was little else to do but abandon the effort. "Had I have had the whole force in hand I have but little doubt that we could have gone in easily, taking the place by surprise," Pickett later lamented on the incident. Many, including Pickett, would point to Barton's role in the fiasco, and Barton himself demanded an inquiry after hearing these comments. Hoke, who perhaps had the best reason to complain, simply stated that, in regard to Barton's decision not to attack, "Being junior officer it does not become me to speak my thoughts of this move." Whatever the case, it would prove to be the last opportunity for the Confederacy to retake Newbern and reestablish itself on Pamlico Sound.[20]

SIXTEEN

The Siege of Plymouth and the CSS *Albemarle*

WHILE THE NEWBERN EXPEDITION had proven to be a failure, it was not the last campaign on Pamlico Sound for Brigadier General Robert Hoke. With Pickett's transfer back to Virginia, Hoke assumed the latter's role as military commander of North Carolina in April 1864. The new commander eyed Plymouth as the next target. First, given its much smaller garrison it would prove easier to reduce than Newbern. Second, seizing Plymouth would open up the western end of Albemarle Sound to the Confederates. Even better, word was that the ironclad *Albemarle* would be complete by the time of the expedition and would sail down the Roanoke River to support the operation.

Hoke had a sizable force at his disposal including his own brigade, Kemper's, and Ransom's. This would be supported by elements of a cavalry regiment and four batteries of guns: two from Virginia, one from Mississippi, and one from the 10th North Carolina Artillery. In all it was a force of some 6,500 men. The problem, however, had become one of timing. Hoke wanted the *Albemarle* to participate in the attack, but General Lee, facing indications that the Union Army would commence a spring offensive against Richmond, had asked for the return of Hoke's brigade in the next few weeks. Ironclad or not, Hoke had to act while he still had the manpower. He marshaled his forces at Tarboro the second week of April, and on the morning of April 15 set out for Plymouth.[1]

Even Hoke's superior numbers might not prove enough to capture the Union-held town located near the mouth of the Roanoke River. A little under three thousand men, commanded by veteran Brigadier General Wessells, garrisoned the post which acted as a local strong-hold for Union activities in the region. To the east of the town along the south bank of the Roanoke River, the garrison had constructed Fort Grey. Located across the river from Tarbor Island and armed with several heavy guns, the fort commanded the channel and the rows of obstructions placed across the waterway. The town itself was contained on three sides by the Roanoke and a pair of creeks, Welch's Creek to the west and Conaby Creek to the east. On the far east side of the town a small corridor existed between Conaby Creek and the Roanoke River. About a mile and a half wide, the Columbia Road tra-versed this land which was partially branched by a series of canals and wooded marshes that extended along the north side of creek.

Stretched along the south and west side of the town was a series of earthworks dominated by the six-gun Fort William in the center of the southern wall. Fort Wessel, armed with several cannon, had been built to the southwest to further break up an enemy attack in that direction. The eastern side of the town, where the Columbia Road entered, did not have a wall. Instead Fort Comfort and Conaway's Redoubt had been raised, along with several other field fortifications to guard this approach. In addition, a two-hundred-pound Parrott gun had also been placed along the shore near this point to cover the water approaches to the town.

There was one other element for Hoke to deal with, the Union flotilla. Currently four US gunboats, the *Miami, Southfield, White-head*, and *Ceres* were lying at anchor not far from town, along with the armed army transport *Bombshell*. Between them these ships mounted a dozen guns, and during an attack they would act as mobile batteries, quickly shifting to the most threatened point to bring their heavy hundred-pound rifles and nine-inch shells guns to bear.[2]

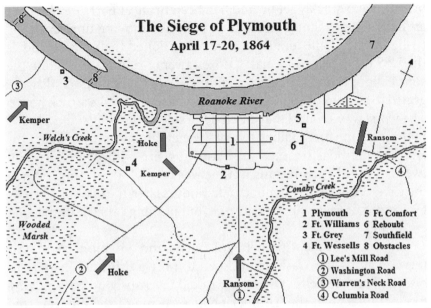

The siege of Plymouth, North Carolina. The map shows Hoke's advance and the position of the Confederate forces shortly before Ransom's final attack. The capture of Plymouth combined with the commissioning of the ironclad *Albemarle* would pose a serious threat to Union control over Albemarle Sound. (*Author*)

By late Sunday, April 17, Hoke's men had routed a Union cavalry patrol and the outer Union pickets some five miles from the town. Here Hoke detached Kemper's brigade, Dearing's cavalry, and a pair of batteries with orders to take the road to Warren's Neck and besiege Fort Grey. With skirmishers from the 1st Virginia thrown forward, Hoke's and Ransom's brigades took a wide loop to the right to avoid a destroyed bridge over Welch's Creek and crossed farther upstream. From here the force split with Hoke's men pressing forward down the Washington Road on the city's west side, while Ransom and his men moved forward along Lee's Mill Road toward Fort Williams. The bugles flared and drums rattled along the Union line announcing the Confederate's presence, but after a volley from the Union artillery only a handful of shots were fired as Hoke's and Ransom's troops came to a halt at dusk a few miles from the city.

With an easier path before them, Kemper's brigade had reached Fort Grey by late afternoon. The batteries that had accompanied the brigade were quickly set up and had been firing at Fort Grey for over an hour when a small gunboat was spotted moving upriver in the twilight. The Confederate gunners repositioned their pieces, and as the USS *Ceres* passed by, half a dozen twenty-pound guns along the south shore erupted one after another. The *Ceres*'s launch disintegrated in a cloud of splinters as the first of several shots struck home. The worst was a round that entered the side of the ship and exploded in the machine room killing two of the crew and wounding eight others. The gunboat steamed on, returning fire with two of its own twenty-pound Parrott guns until it was finally out of range. When the *Ceres* returned to Plymouth a few hours later, the two sides briefly exchanged fire again in the darkness, but nothing came of the passing encounter.

In front of Hoke, Colonel Paul Faison and 250 pioneers moved forward along the Washington Road to raise a three-gun battery to besiege Fort Wessells. The crew worked feverously under a waxing moon. Other than the hammering and sawing of the pioneers, the occasional shot from a nervous sentry, and the steam whistles from the civilian ships at the city docks carrying away the town's women and children, it was a peaceful evening.[3]

As daylight revealed the enemy works near Fort Wessells, both this position and the Union guns along the west side of the town opened fire on the newly raised battery. The Confederate guns along the line replied and by afternoon the newly raised battery had quieted the guns at Fort Wessells. Firing also took hold to the west, as Kemper's brigade and the batteries that accompanied him started a long bombardment of Fort Grey. The fort responded with a pair of thirty-two-pound cannon, but it's big hundred-pound Parrott gun was mounted to cover the nearby river and could not easily be brought to bear on the attackers.

The Union gunboats were also engaged off and on throughout the day in what would turn out to be primarily artillery duels. Both the *Miami* and *Southfield* fired on enemy positions and in several cases on the new batteries erected by Colonel Faison. Ammunition became a concern as Lt. Commander Charles W. Flusser, who was in command of the flotilla, had given a large amount to the army, but in the end, it did not hinder any gunboat operations. While none of the navy vessels were damaged in the fighting, the army transport *Bombshell* was not so lucky. The Confederate gunners targeted the little vessel, and after finding the range struck it several times, one of which was below the waterline. The gunboat's commander quickly turned the vessel toward Plymouth, but the damage was mortal and the vessel sank alongside the wharf.[4]

Late that afternoon Hoke summoned his senior commanders and informed them that his brigade would attack Fort Wessells a little after seven o'clock. To support this Hoke gave Ransom fourteen guns under the command of Lt. Colonel Branch and ordered his brigade to make a demonstration on the central part of the town's defenses. A little after five o'clock Ransom's brigade formed up in line of battle between the Washington and Lee's Mill Roads. A cloud of skirmishers was thrown out in front of the brigade, and Branch's guns were dispersed along the front of the line a little over a mile from the Union fortifications.

At six the drums rolled out the signal to advance. Branch's guns raced forward at a gallop and then halted a few hundred yards away. Here they unlimbered and, to the calls of their officers, were soon firing replies to the Union artillery as the Confederate pickets skirmished with their counterparts. A few moments later a call echoed down the grey line, and the brigade shuffled forward under the light of exploding shells and the rising moon. When they had almost reached Branch's guns they were immediately ordered to lie down. For a time there was nothing but the flashing of guns and the eruption of nearby rounds, as the attackers crawled about for better cover. Suddenly a call rang out and the artillery limbered up their guns, mounted their steeds, and galloped forward another hundred yards before dismounting and putting their guns back into action. "It is now that we learn that our demonstration is to march behind these batteries," one participant wrote, "and receive the fire of the enemy from more than twenty pieces of artillery, besides two-gun boats, throwing every grade of shell from the 200-pound [Parrott] gun to the 12-pound Napoleon."[5]

For three long hours Ransom's brigade and Branch's guns engaged the Union gunners. By now the Confederate skirmishers had forced their counterparts back into the Union lines, but it was the Union artillery that was the real danger, particularly Flusser's flotilla. "The gunboats in the river also took part in shelling our batteries and line," one Confederate soldier recalled. "One shell from a gunboat came over the town, struck the ground about one hundred and fifty yards in front of the Eighth [N.C.], ricocheted, and the next time struck the ground in the line of the regiment and exploded, killing and wounding fifteen men of Company H."[6]

It was a difficult night for the men of Ransom's brigade. The clear sky and nearly full moon illuminated the landscape before the fort making it more difficult to find cover. The line advanced three-quarters of a mile, to within eight hundred yards of Fort Williams, before being ordered to halt. Here the troops stayed for some time, lying on the ground or crouching low as their own guns thundered away at the fort, which responded in kind with shell and grapeshot. Finally, a little after 9 p.m. the recall was sounded and the entire line fell back in increments to its starting position.

If the diversion didn't work, it certainly helped. With the Union guns focused on Ransom's advance, Hoke pounded Fort Wessells with artillery and then threw his brigade at the stronghold. Led by Colonel Mercer of the 21st Georgia the Confederate troops appeared out of the wooded swamp near Welch Creek and dashed upon the fort. The garrison responded with musket fire, but it was insufficient to halt the charging numbers. The fort was soon enveloped, and the attackers began firing through the loopholes into the compound, but the defenders' stout stockade along with the liberal use of hand grenades pushed back the attackers.

The Confederates rallied and returned, and were again repulsed, this time dragging the mortally wounded Colonel Mercer back with them. At this point Hoke had two more batteries raised a few hundred yards away from the structure, creating a crossfire. Now all three gun positions rained shot and shell down upon the earthwork. Rounds exploded on the parapet throwing dirt and sandbags through the air, and large sections were carved out of the earth walls. Shells exploded overhead sending metal shards flying through the compound, and an explosive round struck the slate roof and stone chimney of a small building inside the fort, scouring the compound with a burst of stone fragments. The fort's commander Captain Nelson Chaplin was struck down in the barrage, which left the garrison rattled when the firing suddenly stopped.

Hoke ordered a cease-fire to demand the fort's surrender. With their casualties mounting and their ammunition almost exhausted, Fort Wessells surrendered around 11 p.m., bringing a lull to the fighting. Hoke had achieved his objective for the day, and now as he and his army looked to get some rest, the question became whether reports that the *Albemarle* would make its appearance were true.[7]

At the wharfs along Plymouth's waterfront civilians and wounded were still being evacuated on a handful of transports. A strange fear, or perhaps in some cases fascination, had begun to take hold as reports of the Confederate ironclad placed it only a dozen miles from the town. Helping to oversee the loading of the transports, Commander Flusser quieted those who

Lt. Commander Charles Flusser. Flusser, who was in command of the Union warships at Plymouth during the opening days of the siege, would engage the ironclad CSS *Albemarle* in the early morning hours of April 19, 1864. (*NHHC*)

had made the iron warship out to be more than it was, and when confronted by several women convinced that the Confederate vessel would destroy the Union fleet, Flusser ushered them along, calmly assuring them that "The Navy will do its duty. We shall sink, destroy, or capture it, or find our graves in the Roanoke."[8]

The *Albemarle* and speculation about the ironclad was nothing new for Flusser and most veterans of the region. In mid-1863 intelligence began to reach Union naval officers that an armored battery was being constructed by Confederate forces on the upper Roanoke River. This battery would be towed into position and, no doubt, was intended to be used as part of an attack on the Union-held town of Plymouth at the western end of Albemarle Sound.

As Union officers would soon discover it was not an armored battery but an ironclad that was being constructed on the Roanoke River. The vessel destined to be the CSS *Albemarle* was actually the final manifestation of a contract originally placed in January 1862 and modified a few months after the fall of Roanoke Island for the construction of an ironclad gunboat. The loss of Albemarle Sound and the towns along the shores of this waterway almost ended the project, but assisted by Commander James W. Cooke of the Confederate Navy, the venture was finally restarted at Edward's Ferry on the Roanoke River.

Cooke, who had fought the CSS *Ellis* to the bitter end at Elizabeth City, would prove instrumental in the effort. "When aroused to action," one witness recalled, "Cooke was one of the most industrious and indefatigable officers in the navy." There seems ample evidence to support this claim. While the contractors could build out the vessel's frame, iron was desperately needed to complete the project. Cooke responded by making it his personal quest to fulfill this requirement. He scoured the countryside for bolts, broken tools, and scrap pieces, and his efforts about the ironworks at Wilmington and Richmond became local yore, earning him the nickname the "Ironmonger Captain."[9]

To the astonishment of all, Cooke succeeded, and by the spring of 1864 the ironclad began to take on its final form. Based on a design issued by John L. Dixon, the 155-foot twin propeller craft carried a heavy submerged ram on her prow and sat with her board nearly at the waterline. The armored casemate was constructed with two layers of two inches of iron plate secured to heavy oak beams. Inside, arrangements were made for a pair of 6.4-inch Brooke rifled cannon. Mounted fore and aft, both guns were arranged on a pivot mount and could be adjusted to fire from three fixed firing ports along the bow or stern. The rest of the ironclad's machinery and assemblies were procured through whatever means were possible. The propellers and shafts came from Charlottesville, while the boilers were captured products, and like many of the vessel's components, custom fitted for the task. Built with greenwood and simple tools in a cornfield at the edge of the river, "The entire construction was one of shreds and patches," one participant noted. "The engine was adapted from incongruous material, ingeniously dove-tailed and put together with a determined will that mastered doubt, but not without some natural anxiety as to derangements that might occur from so heterogeneous a combination."[10]

Given that the *Albemarle*'s completion coincided with Hoke's plan to retake Plymouth, Cooke was directed to take his newly launched ironclad downriver and attack the Union warships supporting the town's defense. With his vessel still undergoing final touches and only twenty experienced sailors in his crew of a little over a hundred, Cooke gave the order to cast off on the morning of April 17, and accompanied by the small steam tender *Cotton Plant*, began his trek downriver. Heavy and underpowered like most ironclads of the day, the craft proved easier to handle by drifting downstream stern first. By 10 p.m. the following evening the

Commander James W. Cooke. Cooke would oversee the construction of the *Albemarle* and would command the vessel during several engagements against Union forces. (*NHHC*)

ironclad dropped anchor three miles above Plymouth. Although only having traveled a few dozen miles it had proved a trying trip. The finicky boilers and the couplers to the main shaft had broken, requiring a six-hour stop to repair the damage, and the ship had no sooner gotten underway when the rudder broke, leading to another four-hour repair job.

Having received no word from the army, Cooke dispatched a small boat to scout downriver and ascertain whether or not the ironclad could clear the sunken obstacles the Union forces had placed across the river. Around 1 a.m. the boat returned with both good news and bad news. The water was high enough for the *Albemarle* to clear the obstructions in the main channel, but a pair of Union gun positions lay downriver, one at Warren's Neck and one in the town. Cooke was aware of the latter. Both positions were rumored to be anchored by two-hundred-pound Parrott guns, which the commander realized would test the limits of his ironclad's sheath.

As it turned out, it would not matter. Cooke weighed anchor at 2:30 a.m. and under the cloak of darkness slowly proceeded down the river. The ship cleared the first battery of Union guns with only a few probing shots being launched in their direction, while the battery in the town did not respond at all even through the river was only two hundred yards wide at this point. Sliding past the town along the north bank of the river Cooke and a number of lookouts scanned the dark waters ahead for signs of activity.[11]

The Confederate vessel's movements had not gone unnoticed. On the evening of April 18, the *Whitehead* sat at anchor a few hundred yards downstream of the barrier of sunken vessels the Union forces had erected. It had been a busy day. Although Confederate forces had been repulsed, it seemed only a matter of time to Ensign G.W. Barret, in command of the *Whitehead*, before the *Albemarle* would come downriver to support this effort. He was not to be disappointed. A little after 8 p.m. a pair of vessels were seen approaching the sunken barrier. Barret quietly slipped his cable and drifted downstream watching the enemy vessels' movements. When it became clear that they had crossed the barrier, he turned the *Whitehead* and dashed east. Escape, however, was not so easy. Southern troops had recently set up a three-gun battery downriver which had pelted the gunboat *Ceres* the day before when it arrived carrying orders from Lt. Commander Flusser. With the *Albemarle* behind him and enemy guns before him, Ensign Barret elected to avoid both by running the *Whitehead* into the shallow twisting waters of the Upper Thoroughfare, a narrow passage that linked the Roanoke and Cashie Rivers.

The Union gunboat raised steam and entered the murky side river, but the strong current pushed at the vessel and it soon ran aground on the east bank. A rope was secured to the other bank and, motivated by fear of the *Albemarle*'s appearance at any moment, the vessel was freed. Now committed to his escape route Barret faced another problem. To limit movement down this waterway a series of wooden poles or piles had been driven into the riverbed creating a barrier across the channel. There was little choice now but to attempt to thread the *Whitehead* through one of the intervals between these pilings. All held their breath, as at first it looked close but possible. Soon however the slow rhythm of the paddlewheel was replaced by a grinding noise and then a jolt that tested everyone's balance as the gunboat came to a halt wedged between two pilings. Barret ordered the engines stopped and silence maintained. A few moments later the rebel vessels passed down the river in full view. After giving the ironclad a few moments

The "double-ender" sidewheel gunboat USS *Miami*. Commissioned in early 1862 the 208-foot Union gunboat carried a crew of 134, and was armed with four 24 lb. cannon, a 100 lb. Parrot Rifle, and a 9-inch Dahlgren smoothbore cannon. These shallow draft gunboats earned their "double-ender" title because of the similar bow and stern shapes which allowed them to travel at high speeds both forwards and backwards. (*NHHC*)

to move out of sight, Barret restarted the *Whitehead*'s engines and forced the vessel through the obstructions, allowing him to make his escape but seriously damaging the gunboat in the process.[12]

After crossing into the Cashie River, Barret set course for Plymouth and pulled aside the *Miami* and the *Southfield* a little after midnight. He informed Commander Flusser that the ram was near Warren's Point and that another smaller steamer was accompanying it. After shelling Confederate positions near Plymouth all day, both the *Miami* and the *Southfield* had anchored below the town for the evening. Flusser had fully expected the *Albemarle*'s arrival and had devised a plan to deal with the ironclad. He would chain the six-gun 730-ton *Miami* and four-gun 760-ton *Southfield* together and ensnare the Confederate vessel between the two. At that point the gunboats' hundred-pound rifled cannons would pound the iron beast into submission at point-blank range. It was a bold plan and soon to be tested.

With Barret's report Flusser ordered the flotilla to general quarters and, in keeping with his earlier plan, ordered a chain run between the two large gunboats. All was quiet until a little after 3 a.m. when the *Ceres*, which had been busy taking on coal at the town's docks, came into sight. Passing alongside the *Miami* Captain Foster relayed the news that the Confederate ironclad was a few minutes behind him.[13]

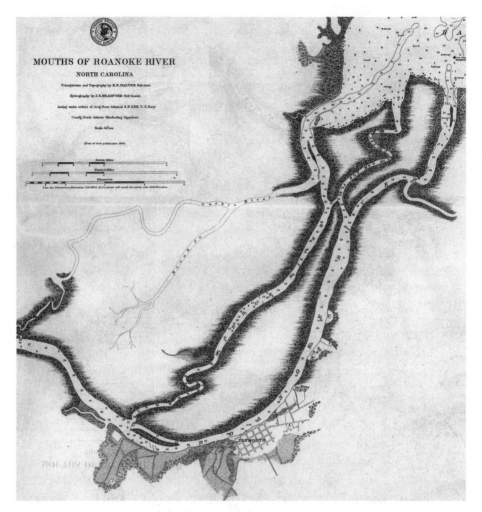

MOUTHS OF ROANOKE RIVER

NORTH CAROLINA

A map of the outlet of the Roanoke River showing the Cashie and Middle Rivers as well as the location of Plymouth. (*Library of Congress*)

Flusser responded by ordering the *Ceres* and the *Whitehead* to take up a position fifty yards downstream. He then gave the command for both the *Miami* and the *Southfield* to raise full steam and advance. The cables were cast off to the sound of bells ringing throughout both ships, and within moments both warships were moving forward with a hundred-foot chain loosely strung between the two at water level both fore and aft.

Within a few minutes both sides became aware of each other. As the distance rapidly closed, the forward guns on all three vessels ignited, sending geysers of water up around the combatants and the occasional spark and dull clang when a round found the ironclad's armored shell. The initial advantage lay with the *Albemarle* simply because of its position along the north bank of the river, which placed it outside of the chain strung between the two Union warships. Within a few minutes of sighting the enemy Cooke ordered the rudder to starboard and the ironclad, its front gun barking defiantly at the enemy warships, shifted, cutting a diagonal path across the front of the oncoming Union warships. The *Albemarle*'s course would first bring it into contact with the starboard bow of the *Miami*, but at the last moment the Union vessel turned toward the attacker. Consequently, the ram landed a glancing blow on the port bow of the *Miami* "gouging two planks nearly through for 10 feet."[14]

The collision not only destroyed the forward chain stretched between the *Miami* and the *Southfield*, but it deflected the *Albemarle*'s path to the right, aligning the craft with the *Southfield*'s exposed starboard bow. Within a few seconds the sound of cannon was obscured by the sound of snapping timbers as the ram struck the gunboat so hard that the ironclad's prow was buried ten feet into its side.

With the *Albemarle* wedged between the two Union warships it soon became the focus of a point-blank barrage from both vessels. The hundred-pound Parrott rifles and the nine-inch Dahlgrens on both Union warships battered the ironclad at less than a pistol shot, lighting the confusion with huge blue sparks and sending the unmistakable ring of a metal on metal echoing across the water. On board the *Miami* Commander Flusser personally directed the nine-inch Dahlgren gun crew. Having been used earlier in the day to shell Confederate attacks on Plymouth, the ammunition readily available was not solid shot but explosive rounds set with a fused delay. Shouting encouragement to the gun crew Flusser had already fired two of these rounds into the ironclad's side with no effect. When the crew rammed home the third round Flusser yanked on the lanyard discharging the cannon in a column of flame and burst of blue-white smoke. The 230mm explosive round leapt forward, deflected upward off the Confederate vessel's armored casemate, and then exploded, spraying the Dahlgren gun crew with shrapnel. When the smoke cleared Flusser, struck several times, lay dead with the gun's lanyard still in his hand, while half a dozen others were wounded in one fashion or another.

Onboard the *Southfield* Lt. Charles French quickly realized that his ship was doomed when reports reached him that the boiler room had been pierced and was now flooding. As the *Southfield*'s and *Miami*'s guns banged away at the Confederate ram with no apparent effect, French gave the order to abandon ship. Some of the crew managed to get to the lifeboats and were later picked up by the *Whitehead* and *Ceres*, while others, including French, were able to jump to the *Miami* when her stern drifted near the *Southfield*. It appears, however, that many of the stricken vessel's complement, especially the gun crews, either did not receive the command or refused to abandon their posts until all hope was extinguished.[15]

The *Southfield* was finished. Captain Cooke realized it the moment his vessel drove its armored prow into the Union gunboat's side. The *Albemarle*'s forward gun and a fusillade of musketry from the other gun ports only added to the doomed warship's misery. The problem, however, was that the Union vessel's rapid sinking was now threatening to take the *Albemarle* with it. Cooke ordered the engines reversed but found himself unable to extricate the vessel. To make matters worse the weight of the crippled *Southfield* "so depressed the forward deck of the *Albemarle* as to cause the water to run into the forward port." Fortunately for the crew of the ironclad the crippled Union gunboat shifted as it sank, freeing the Confederate ram and sending a cheer throughout the ship.

The *Miami*, now commanded by Lt. French, had cut the stern cable between the two Union warships and slipped downstream to obtain a better firing position with his Parrott gun. For the next few minutes the warship fired a dozen rounds of eighty-pound solid shot at the armored beast without making an impression, the projectiles fracturing and ricocheting upon impact. Once the *Albemarle* began to back away from the *Southfield*, which had already begun to settle in the shallow waters with a hiss, French was forced to make a difficult decision. "As far as we discovered," he wrote in his official report, "our shots fell harmlessly on the ironclad sides of the ram. The fatal effect of her prow had been fully demonstrated on the ill-fated *Southfield*, and under these circumstances I reluctantly concluded to withdraw from the river, being fully convinced that had we closed with this vessel it would have resulted in her loss."[16]

The Confederate ironclad CSS *Albemarle*. (*NHHC*)

The *Albemarle*, now realigned with the river, fired a number of rounds at the retreating gunboat, but beyond a glancing shot that did little in the way of damage, the *Miami*, along with the *Whitehead* and *Ceres*, which had monitored the engagement from a position downriver, quickly outdistanced the ram and withdrew to the waters of Albemarle Sound.

It was a crushing defeat for the Union forces. Beyond the loss of the *Southfield* and the casualties on this vessel and the *Miami*, including the squadron's commander, Northern forces had lost control of the Roanoke River, which now left Plymouth surrounded. "The garrison at Plymouth must be captured, as things are now," one participant wrote of the defeat. French, an acting volunteer lieutenant, seems to have raised an eyebrow or two with his precipitous retreat, but once accounts of the engagement circulated all doubt concerning his conduct was cast aside. In Albemarle Sound, he informed his superiors, he had no fear of the ram. His vessels were faster and, with ample room to maneuver, the threat from the *Albemarle*'s prow was minimal. As for retaking the confines of the Roanoke River, however, Lt. French was clear: "I am fully of the opinion that nothing but an iron ram can contend with her in the river."[17]

For Cooke and his men, it was only half a victory. The next morning the Confederate attack on Plymouth resumed. The *Albemarle* spent the day engaging the Union batteries that protected the town, while over by the recently captured Fort Wessells, Hoke was discussing his plans with his officers. Although Fort Grey had not fallen, it was neutralized enough to allow Hoke to move Kemper's brigade over by his own brigade on the western side of the town. Here he had planned to storm the enemy works, but after a thorough reconnaissance of the fortifications he decided against the attack

With the assault called off Hoke looked to the eastern edge of the town for an opportunity and soon found that the *Albemarle* had provided him with one. The defenses on the eastern side of the town were not as elaborate as the rest of the fortifications. While this was due in part to the terrain, it had never posed a problem because the Union gunboats routinely anchored on this side of town and, in the event of an attack, would sweep this area clear with their large shell guns and howitzers. Now, however, the Union warships were gone, compliments of the *Albemarle*. Recognizing this opportunity, Hoke ordered Ransom's brigade along with Dearing's cavalry and several batteries of guns to make a sweeping movement to his right, cross Conaby Creek, and occupy the Columbia Road. The next morning the rest of the army would create a diversion while Ransom's men stormed the town's eastern defenses.

Ransom and his men arrived at the Columbia Road around midnight. The brigade was about a mile from the nearest Union defenses with its right flank resting on the river and its left extending past the road to the edge of a wooded marsh. Here they rested until morning. Union artillery thumped away at Ransom and his men, but it did little other than disturb their sleep. Morning was announced by the call of the brigade and regimental officers as the troops were roused from their sleep and formed into line of battle. When everything was ready, Ransom ordered a flare fired just as the moon began to set.[18]

As Ransom's men moved forward, Hoke ordered the batteries on the left side of the Confederate line to fire and at the same time signaled for both his and Kemper's brigades to launch their feint attack. With its hatches open to improve circulation inside the vessel, the *Albemarle* on Ransom's right opened fire at first light. The ironclad slowly traveled upriver in pace with the Confederate advance, its forward gun methodically firing away.

Fort Comfort was quickly seized in an infantry attack by the 35th North Carolina, and a nearby Union battery erected on the Columbia

A IX-inch Dahlgren smoothbore cannon on the aft pivot mount of the USS *Miami*. The shape of these guns was the result of basic stress analysis that would lead not only to an incredibly safe gun, but the nickname "soda bottles" as well. Able to fire everything from solid shot to canister, Dalhgren's of different sizes were employed by both sides throughout the conflict. (*NHHC*)

Road was captured shortly thereafter by the 24th North Carolina. Together these twin victories unhinged the Union left. With three thousand Confederate troops pouring into the town there was little to do but surrender or seek refuge in Fort Williams. With the rest of the town in Confederate hands Hoke ordered all batteries as well as the *Albemarle* to concentrate their fire on Fort Williams where the last of the garrison had sought refuge. For the next hour, hundreds of rounds exploded on or above the stronghold without one being fired in return. Hoke ordered the barrage halted a little after eleven o'clock to demand General Wessells' surrender. Just to make matters clear, he informed the Union commander that "if he provokes a useless sacrifice of life in requiring an assault, not a man in the garrison will be spared." With no other options before him, Wessells lowered the Stars and Stripes and surrendered Plymouth.[19]

The victory was now complete. Cooke marveled at the spoils: "Immense quantities of commissary and other stores were captured, and free access afforded to two of the richest counties in the state," he informed the Confederate secretary of the navy. Just as importantly, at least from Cooke's perspective, he "captured a large quantity of anthracite coal, probably 200 tons." In the end, Cooke, who had spent so much time and effort in seeing to the ironclad's construction, was quick to shift any accolades that fell upon him onto his officers and crew. "In truth sir," he concluded in his official report, "I can take no credit to myself for the success of the Albemarle in her engagements, for, with such efficient and energetic officers, failure was almost impossible."[20]

The spoils from the victory were in fact larger than Cooke realized. Wessells' entire command, over 2,800 men, had surrendered. With them came thousands of muskets, tons of powder and shot, and thirty pieces of cannon, including a two-hundred-pound Parrott gun. The victory had cost Hoke some 125 killed and another 450 wounded, in what was the largest Union defeat along the waterways of Pamlico and Albemarle Sounds. Just as importantly, the *Albemarle* now had a base from which to operate, and news arrived that the CSS *Neuse* was moving downriver looking to run past Newbern and perhaps link up with the *Albemarle*.

Given the effect that one ironclad had on the outcome of the siege of Plymouth, the idea of two ironclads operating together in Pamlico or Albemarle Sounds set off a near panic among Union garrisons along the waterways. General Palmer in Newbern, who had fended off an attack by Hoke not long ago, expressed concern at news of Plymouth's capture, but amidst the ironclad frenzy he was confident in the navy's ability to handle the armored vessel. "The mouth of the Roanoke River will be held by our gunboats, and I am of the opinion that the rebel ram, which has been the principal cause of the fall of Plymouth, will not be able to get out into the sounds."[21]

General Palmer would prove to be wrong.

SEVENTEEN

The Battle of Albemarle Sound

HE *ALBEMARLE* SPENT the next few weeks at Plymouth. Damage from the battle was minor, "only nine bars (plates) of iron being broken," but the ship had been rushed into battle and a number of matters needed to be resolved before engaging the enemy again. By early May these matters had been addressed and the ram was ready for action. A few days later, on May 4, 1864, Cooke received orders to escort the recently captured (and refloated) gunboat *Bombshell* and the steamer *Cotton Plant*, which were carrying a detachment of Confederate sharpshooters, to the Alligator River at the southeastern end of Albemarle Sound. By the following afternoon the troops and provisions had been loaded, and the three vessels began slowly steaming down the Roanoke River. Captain Cooke fully expected to encounter a few of the Union gunboats that he had chased out of the Roanoke River, as his recent success before Plymouth had sent a ripple of anxiety through the Union Navy.

There were a host of opinions on how to deal with the Confederate ironclad. Taking Lt. French's comments to heart the assistant secretary of the navy, Gustavus Fox, wrote the officer in charge of building the Union ironclad *Tecumseh*, asking if it was possible to build camels (flotation devices) so that the warship could clear the sandbar in Croatan Sound and challenge its Confederate counterpart. Secretary of the Navy Gideon Welles suggested ramming the *Albemarle*, while Rear Admiral Lee, in command of the North Atlantic Blocking Squadron at Newport News, pushed forward an approach of positioning a gunboat at point-blank range on either side of the ram and, with the much taller Union gunboats' guns depressed, maintain a constant fire against the ironclad's top "so as to drive her roof in." Like Flusser, Lee believed that by closing and restricting the ironclad's maneuvering room his warships would negate the Confederate vessel's ability to ram, while at the same time providing the gunboats with an opportunity to truly test the ironclad's construction. "The great point is to get and hold position on each side of the ram," Lee emphasized. "She will then have no use of her ram, and must yield to out batteries. Her plating will loosen and bolts fly like canister, and the concussion will knock down and demoralize her crew."[1]

The end recipient of this advice was Captain Melancton Smith, who Lee appointed to command the Union flotilla gathering in Albemarle Sound. Smith, who until this point had been captain of the Union ironclad *Onondaga*, was recommended by the secretary of the navy and Lee agreed with the selection. In his orders Lee made it clear to Smith that his mission was not to establish a blockade but that he was being sent for the express "purpose of attacking, at all hazards, the rebel ram there in the best manner to assure its destruction." The *Miami*, *Ceres*, and *Whitehead*, Admiral Lee informed Smith, were currently on station near the mouth of the Roanoke River keeping an eye on the Confederate ram and investigating reports of a dozen small enemy gunboats gathering in the Cashie River. Lee would add three more powerful vessels to this force. The *Wyalusing*, and Smith's new flagship the *Mattabesett*, would be detached from the Atlantic Blocking Squadron, while the gunboat *Sassacus* had already been dispatched the night before. At nearly twice the displacement of the *Miami* and nearly twice the speed, the three *Sassacus* class gunboats also carried far more firepower, with of a pair of hundred-pound Parrott rifled guns, four nine-inch Dahlgren guns, and several smaller cannon. In the open waters of the sound, and at over three times the reported speed of the ram, these tall side-wheelers had little to fear from the Confederate vessel's iron prow. More importantly, given the

A *Sassacus* class "double ender" side-wheeled gunboat. Built at the Portsmouth Naval Yard in Maine, three of these 975-ton gunboats would be involved in the Battle of Albemarle Sound. (*NHHC*)

total weight of shot these warships could bring to bear, it seemed certain that they would batter their armored enemy into submission.

After running into a gale, which exposed a number of construction problems, Smith arrived at Hatteras Inlet with the *Mattabesett* and *Wyalusing* on April 26. Here he was informed that the *Sassacus* had crossed into the sound the night before. After waiting for the next high tide to enter Pamlico Sound, Smith steamed north through Croatan Sound to investigate rumors that the *Albemarle* had escaped into the Alligator River. Finding no sign of activity, the *Mattabesett* and *Wyalusing* turned west and rendezvoused with the gathering fleet.

Smith had no sooner dropped anchor than reports began reaching him that the *Albemarle* was planning to lead three Confederate steamers loaded with troops in an attack on Roanoke Island. After stationing several of the smaller gunboats to watch the outlet of the Roanoke River, Smith laid out his general plan on how to engage the enemy ironclad. The fleet would advance in two columns with the larger *Mattabesett, Sassacus, Wyalusing,* and *Whitehead* being in the first column and the *Miami, Ceres, Commodore Hull,* and *Isaac Seymour* forming the second column. The warships would pass by the Confederate ram, fire their broadsides, and then turn to make another firing pass on the opposite side of the ironclad. Smith also suggested fouling the Confederate vessel's propellers with lines dragged from behind the Union ships, possibly ramming the enemy, and having the *Miami*, which had been rigged with a spar torpedo, "endeavor to explode her torpedo at any moment she may have the advantage." In the end, however, he was realistic about such plans, making it clear to his captains that "specific orders cannot be given for the attack, as the maneuvering of the ram cannot be anticipated, and the only orders considered necessary are to sink, destroy, or capture by some or all of the methods suggested."[2]

The new Union commander of Albemarle Sound would only have to wait a few days to test his ideas. Around one o'clock on the afternoon of May 5, 1864, the *Miami*, *Ceres*, *Commodore Hull*, and the army steamer *Trumpeter* were busy laying mines near the mouth of the Roanoke River when lookouts reported the Confederate ironclad and a pair of troop transports moving downriver. Lt. French of the *Miami* dispatched the *Trumpeter* to warn Captain Smith, and for the next few hours the three Union gunboats maintained their distance, slowly giving way before the east-moving enemy column.

Since entering Albemarle Sound Cooke had watched the three Union gunboats. Their actions did not surprise the ironclad's captain and crew, who did not expect a fight after demonstrating their clear superiority over these vessels a few weeks before. Around three o'clock the situation changed as Cooke and his officers eyed several columns of smoke to the east. When the source of this smoke came into sight a little after 4 p.m. Cooke frowned. Four enemy gunboats, three of them a more powerful class than had previously been encountered, were bearing down on them. As the enemy gunboats that had shadowed his track turned to form a second column behind the first, Cooke realized that the coming engagement would be no place for the transport *Cotton Plant* and tiny gunboat *Bombshell*. The *Albemarle* gave signals for both to return to Plymouth. The *Cotton Plant* replied and dashed for the outlet of the Roanoke River, but some confusion on the *Bombshell* led to a misinterpretation of the signals and the gunboat maintained its position a few hundred yards behind the ram.

The *Miami* and the other picket ships passed Smith's first division consisting of the *Mattabesett, Sassacus, Wyalusing,* and *Whitehead* in line-ahead formation and formed a second line. The Union commander gave the order to engage and signaled the warships in the first division to pass alongside the ram's starboard side. A few minutes later at 4:40 p.m. the *Albemarle* officially began the battle with a shot from its forward battery that screeched across the water and struck the *Mattabesett*'s forward launch, exploding in a burst of wooden splinters that wounded several men manning the forward hundred-pound rifle. The *Albemarle* fired another shot that struck the flagship's upper works, upon which the forward guns of both Union lines commenced firing.[3]

Captain Melancton Smith. Smith, a senior U.S. Navy officer with over thirty years of experience, would inherit the task of neutralizing the *Albemarle*. After the war Smith would be appointed commandant of the U.S. Naval Shipyard in Brooklyn, New York. (*NHHC*)

While it was clear from the flashes appearing on the enemy's armored hull and the sound of ricocheting rounds echoing across the waters that the Union gunners' aim was true, onboard the *Mattabesett* it was also clear that the Confederate warship was turning to starboard in an attempt to bring its ram to bear. To avoid the threat Commander John Febiger shifted the flagship's path to port, which in turn shifted the track of the entire first column. The maneuver had neutralized the *Albemarle*'s primary weapon, but in doing so the Union gunboats passed along the ram's starboard side at a distance of 150 yards, "a greater distance than was our intention."

The *Mattabesett* unleashed at broadside upon the ironclad and, when clear of the enemy's stern, swung starboard to round the Confederate vessel. The maneuver brought the Union warship within point-blank range of the *Bombshell*, which bravely fired its forward gun at the oncoming line of big "double-enders." The *Mattabesett* emptied its starboard howitzers and forward hundred-pound rifle into the recently captured Confederate gunship sending clouds of debris into the air when the rounds found their mark. It was to get no better for the riddled *Bombshell*. The next Union ship in line, the *Sassacus*, fired another broadside into the vessel which shook the converted river steamer from stem to stern. Having seen enough, the captain of the *Bombshell* hauled down his colors and surrendered.

As the *Wyalusing* emptied its guns on the slowly turning Confederate ram the *Sassacus* and *Mattabesett* continued their circular path around the ironclad. Both vessels maintained their fire on the *Albemarle*, but matters were becoming confused as the smaller Union vessels of the second column entered the fray to the south. This, coupled with the position of the first division on the opposite side of the enemy vessel, created a friendly fire problem. The *Sassacus*, *Mattabesett*, and *Wyalusing* slowed to a halt to prevent being caught in the crossfire as the ironclad completed its 180-degree turn and was now on a heading back to Plymouth.[4]

Onboard the *Albemarle* the Union guns had shaken the vessel. The opening volley from the *Mattabesett* sent a series of concussions ringing through the armored casemate, and "the splinters flew about" as one shot penetrated the armor, only stopping after fracturing the lower supporting oak beam. The exposed smokestack had been shot through, and the smoke from the engines now mixed with that of the guns within the steel confines. The *Bombshell* had been captured, and the aft Brooke rifle was nearly knocked off its mounts when almost two feet of the gun's muzzle was blown off by a well-aimed shot from the *Mattabesett*. As the Union shells rained down upon the *Albemarle* the outnumbered ram made her opponents pay for approaching so close. With the exception of the *Whitehead*, which being slower did not come into action until later in the engagement, each of Smith's large double-enders had already been shot through by the ironclad's hundred-pound guns, including a few strikes from the damaged Brooke rifle, which the gun crew continued using.

Sitting much lower in the water than his adversaries Cooke was unable to open the upper ventilation hatch for fear of an enemy attack on this vulnerability, and as such, the smoke and heat were becoming oppressive. Repeated hits to the smokestack had also upset the airflow through boiler fires causing the engines to lose steam. Cooke swung the ironclad back toward the Roanoke River. There was

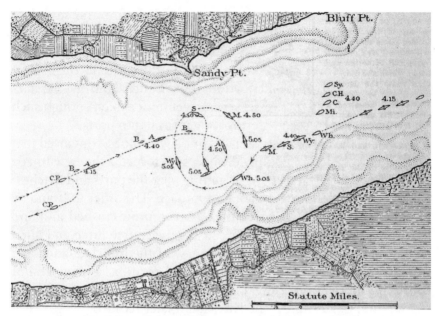

A chart of the opening stages of the Battle of Albemarle Sound, May 5, 1864. A: *Albemarle*; B: *Bombshell*; CP: *Cotton Plant*; M: *Mattabesett*; S: *Sassacus*; Wy: *Wyalusing*; Mi: *Miami*; C: *Ceres*; Wh: *Whitehead*; CH *Commodore Hull*. The vessel marked Sy, not identified by name on the original chart, is the 133-ton converted merchantman USS *Isaac Seymour*. (*Battles and Leaders of the Civil War*)

a lull in the Union fire as the ironclad finished its right-hand turn and reversed its heading back toward Plymouth. Suddenly there were shouts from the wheelhouse and aft gun port as the *Sassacus*, now laying some four hundred yards off the ram's starboard beam, began accelerating toward the Confederate vessel.

Seeing an opportunity when the Confederate vessel swung around, Lt. Commander F.A. Roe ordered maximum revolutions on the wheel, and upon aligning *Sassacus'* bow with the ironclad, now bore down on the enemy's starboard side. The Union warship lurched forward, its wheels tearing at the water. There was little the *Albemarle* could do given the intervening distance other than fire a hundred-pound shot from the aft gun through the Union warships starboard bow right before impact. The prow of the 750-ton double-ender struck the aft starboard side of the ironclad slightly behind the casemate and lifted up out of the water onto the aft deck of the ram. With the other Union vessels having checked their fire, the sound of stressed and splintering wood echoed across the water as did the *Sassacus*'s guns, which a few moments later fired point blank into the *Albemarle*'s armored sides. Roe poured on the steam as the bow of his vessel perched on the aft portion of the ironclad pushed the starboard side of the enemy vessel several feet underwater, enough such that water could be seen entering the ram's aft gun ports.[5]

Onboard the *Albemarle* there was initially panic as, convinced that the Union warship was equipped with a spar torpedo, the crew "made preparations to get overboard by getting near the ports and hatches" when the Union gunboat began its approach. The order to "stand by to repel boarders" rang out, as the *Sassacus*' prow crashed into and over the ram's starboard quarter, causing the ship to lurch and pitch to starboard. The impact jarred the crew of the ironclad, knocking Cooke off his perch in the pilothouse and creating "a good deal of confusion" in the smoke-filled casemate. "Most of the men left their stations and ran around," one participant later recalled.

In retrospect the *Albemarle* had been fortunate. The damage to the ship was confined to the loss of a handful of iron plates at the water's edge as the blow was deflected upward by the ironclad's sloping sides. More importantly, although Commander Roe had ordered full revolutions and estimated his speed at eleven knots before impact, it was clear to other observers that this was not the case. Captain Smith, watching from the *Mattabesett*, estimated that the gunboat, which had accelerated from a stop, was going no more than six knots when it collided with the Confederate warship, which explains the relatively minor damage suffered by the ironclad.

Of more pressing concern for the *Albemarle*'s crew was that the weight of the Union warship's prow was allowing water to enter the gun ports, and to make matters worse, the ram could not bring its guns to bear on the *Sassacus*, leaving the latter free to launch a series of point-blank volleys against the *Albemarle*'s iron casemate. The Union warship's forward hundred-pound Parrott rifle, depressed as far as possible, fired at the ram's aft gun port a few yards away. The solid shot round damaged the sill holding the armored gun shield but in doing so broke in pieces, several of which landed back on the deck of the *Sassacus*. The Union gunboat's aft battery and nine-inch Dahlgren guns hammered the ironclad's side and forward gun ports, but to little avail as the solid shot from these guns fractured against the armored casemate and "flew into the air with a bound leaving no more of an impression than a pea would have done."[6]

With his guns unable to harm the *Albemarle*, Roe did not back away from the ram but instead ran up the *Sassacus'* engines. "At one time I thought she (the *Albemarle*) was going down," Roe wrote of the incident. "I kept the engine going, pushing, as I had hoped, deeper and deeper into her, and also hoping it might be possible for some one of the boats to get up on the opposite side of me and perhaps enable us to sink her." While the *Sassacus* did not carry a spar torpedo, little did the crew of the *Albemarle* realize that, to the southeast, the *Miami* did. More importantly Lt. French saw just the opportunity that Commander Roe had hoped for and dashed toward the ironclad's port side. After a few minutes the unstable equilibrium between the *Sassucus* and *Albemarle* gave way and the Union vessel began sliding off the aft portion of the ironclad with a long shriek as its spinning starboard sidewheel dragged across the ironclad's stern chewing up the ram's launch in the process.

The sudden shift caused the Confederate warship to swing its bow in such a fashion that both of the ram's hundred-pound guns could now be brought to bear. With their ears ringing and throats burning on fumes from the riddled smokestack, the *Albemarle's* gunners were not going to miss their opportunity. The broken aft Brooke rifle fired a round at the Union warship at such close range that the burning embers from the powder charge landed on the gunboat's deck and "blackened the bows of the *Sassacus*." The solid shot struck the *Sassacus'* starboard bow and passed diagonally through the ship, creating a geyser when it impacted the water a hundred yards away. A shot from the ram's forward gun followed in quick succession and proved nearly fatal. The round struck the Union warship four feet above the waterline on the starboard side and tore a path through the hull, the dispensary, and the starboard coal bunker before piercing the starboard boiler and tearing way the steam lines for the port boiler. At this point the shot still had enough energy to fracture an oak spar, which deflected the round into the forward wardroom where it came to rest.

The high-pressure boiler exploded, enveloping the *Sassacus* in a scalding fog. "In a moment the steam filled every portion of the ship,"

Roe reported, "from the hurricane deck to the fire room, killing some, stifling some, and rendering all movement for a time impossible." To many it appeared the warship was doomed, and the signal books were thrown overboard in anticipation of being boarded. The Union warship quickly lost all power and, still wrapped in a blanket of steam, began to drift away from the *Albemarle* and out of the fight.

With the *Sassacus* now disengaged from the ram, the Union warships, who had held their fire for fear of striking the gunboat, once again launched a barrage upon the slow-moving ironclad. The timing and the dangers imposed by the uncoordinated gunfire undermined the *Miami's* torpedo attack on the *Albemarle*, forcing French to turn the ship away and satisfy himself with adding his guns to the chorus of cannon focused on the Confederate warship. As the ram slowly steamed back toward Plymouth, the only visible effects of the ongoing barrage consisted of the ironclad's colors being shot away. It soon became clear that, with Union vessels on all sides of the ironclad firing indiscriminately at the retreating warship, the situation had become more dangerous for friend than foe. To complicate matters, several of the warships, Smith noted, appeared "to be ignorant of all signals, as they answered them without obeying them."[7]

Having seen enough, Smith ordered the flotilla to reorganize into a line and for the next several hours the Union warships made firing passes on the retreating *Albemarle*. This did not come without some risk, as the *Mattabesett* discovered, when a rifled shot passed through the vessel's port side just behind the wheel-cover and narrowly missed the engine room as it tore through the ship. The *Miami* aborted another torpedo attack when her equipment malfunctioned, and later in the engagement the little gunboat *Commodore Hull* crossed the ironclad's bow towing a floating net "for the purpose of fouling his propeller," but nothing came of the effort.

For Cooke and his men, the suffocating heat and acrid fumes sapped their strength and will. The ram's steering lines had been damaged, and a number of iron plates knocked loose on the bow at the waterline were complicating efforts to control the craft. More importantly, the *Albemarle* was having difficulty maintaining steam. "The smokestack was riddled to such an extent as to render it useless," Cooke wrote of the ironclad's plight. "And so great was my extremity at one time that I was forced to tear down the bulkheads, throw in all my bacon, lard, and other combustible matter, to produce steam sufficient to bring me back to the river." Darkness was now the ram's ally and as it set in, Smith called off the attack, leaving the Confederate warship free to proceed unmolested up the Roanoke River. In the opinion of one crew member, the failing light saved the vessel as "She could not have held out an hour longer."[8]

Once again, the uneven contest of wood versus iron demonstrated the latter's clear advantages even when the numbers were lopsided. The six Union vessels engaged had brought an overwhelming superiority in firepower to the battle, but after striking the *Albemarle* with no less than fifty rounds, many at point-blank range, it showed to be of little use. Nor had the *Sassacus'* ramming of the Confederate warship achieved any significant results, and while Smith and his men could claim victory in that the ram had returned to Plymouth, it had done so under its own power and could hardly be said to have been defeated. The ironclad had also fought well. Only the *Whitehead* and the *Commodore Hull* had not been damaged by the enemy's guns, and the devastation and casualties wrought on the *Sassacus* convinced Smith that "side-wheeled steamers cannot be laid alongside of the *Albemarle.*" In the end, while Smith was sure he could contest the open waters of the sound, he had no intentions of entering the Roanoke River in pursuit of the iron titan and viewed any action along these lines as an invitation to disaster.

For Cooke the battle was a defiant defeat. The *Bombshell* and thirty-seven of its crew were needlessly captured through a miscommunication, and the mission to deliver troops and supplies to the Alligator River was a complete failure. It was true that the ram had taken on six warships, three of which were much stronger than those previously encountered, and had not only survived being rammed and struck by over fifty shots but in return crippled one of the larger Union vessels and damaged three others. It was also true that the ironclad had returned under its own power with only three wounded onboard. Such points, however, fail to tell the complete story. While the *Albemarle*'s crew had not been threatened by the hail of enemy shot, the same could not be said of the ship's guns, one of which was badly damaged, and more importantly the vessel's smokestack. The former item was perhaps a case of bad luck, but the vulnerability of the ram's smokestack and the negative effects the loss of this component had on the vessel's ability to make steam, and hence maneuver, was one of the few weaknesses in the warship's design.

With the ironclad anchored at Plymouth, the Union fleet returned to its blockade duties, minus the *Sassacus*, which was so badly damaged that it had to be sent north for repairs. The USS *Commodore Barney* replaced the *Sassacus*, but even with this addition, Smith was having difficulties maintaining his fleet's operational strength. To make matters worse, Admiral Lee had asked him about the possibility of withdrawing the *Mattabesett* and *Wyalusing*, two of his most heavily armed ships. "There is a large nominal naval force under my command, but very few efficient vessels," Smith replied to Admiral Lee.

> The *Hetzel* and *Lockwood* are reported to me as worthless; the *Louisiana* and *Tacony* are repairing boilers; the *Whitehead* may at any moment lose her rudder and cannot be trusted for any duty unless accompanied by another vessel; the *Mattabesett* is obliged to work by hand after reversing engine; the *Wyalusing* can use but one of her rudders, and the *Miami* requires very extensive repairs on boiler, engine, and engine frames.[9]

With his patched-together force Smith was confident that he could control the sound and deal with the *Albemarle*, but he worried that the enemy would raise and equip the *Southfield*. If this should happen, Smith would have a pair of powerful vessels to contend with, and under such circumstances, he informed Lee, it is "my duty to ask for two vessels capable of ramming in addition to my force."[10]

Ultimately it would not matter. The *Albemarle* made a brief appearance at the mouth of the Roanoke on May 24 but soon returned to Plymouth. Here the ironclad would lay idle for the next several months. The *Southfield* was never raised. Instead, a cannon was installed on the wreck, which was now employed as a guard post. The ironclad's inactivity could be traced to the construction of another Confederate ironclad at Whitehall on the Neuse River some seventy-five miles to the south. While it seemed clear to Cooke and others that one ironclad would have difficulty contending with the Union squadron assigned to the area, two would offer a chance to combine their forces and perhaps challenge for control of the Albemarle and Pamlico Sounds. Thus, the *Albemarle* sat tied to a riverside dock awaiting news of the CSS *Neuse*'s completion.

Smith was aware of the work being done on the second ironclad, and not wishing to deal with both armored vessels at the same time, plans were drawn up to sink the *Albemarle* at dock with torpedoes (mines). On the evening of May 25, a five-man detachment carrying two one hundred-pound torpedoes ascended the Roanoke River in a small boat. Pulling ashore before reaching the Confederate guard posts, the detachment set course through the swamps along the north bank of the river carrying their torpedoes on stretchers as they navigated the mire. A few hundred yards above Plymouth, two of the party crossed the river with the torpedoes. Here the devices were strapped together, and after guide-

Lt. William Cushing. A bold young officer who had already run afoul of his superiors for stopping and searching a British merchant vessel that he thought was aiding the enemy, Cushing would demonstrate the value of the torpedo boat and its ability to sink the strongest of vessels. (*NHHC*)

lines were fastened to them, they were set adrift in the river current. The plan had been to guide the explosives alongside the *Albemarle* and then detonate them, but one of the guidelines became entangled on a nearby schooner and the party was discovered. Shouts and flashes of musketry convinced the Union force to abandon the effort. The guidelines were cut, and the detachment retreated into the swamps, all eventually making good their escape. Captain Smith commended the effort, but the news was disappointing. Shallow draft ironclads were being commissioned by the navy, but it would be months before these vessels would be ready. Smith mined the outlet of the Roanoke River, but beyond this, there was little else he could do but maintain his blockade.[11]

Late June and early July would bring a number of changes to the Union squadron in Pamlico and Albemarle Sounds. Captain Smith was transferred to the North Atlantic Blocking Squadron where he was given command of the fleet's fifth division. Commander John Bankhead replaced Smith, and over the next few weeks the new commander was delighted by the arrival of the double-enders USS *Chicopee* and USS *Shamrock*, which significantly increased his flotilla's firepower. July would also bring the genesis of a plan that would ultimately bring an end to the *Albemarle*. In mid-July Admiral Lee received a letter from Lt. William Cushing, a brash young officer in command of the USS *Monticello* stationed with the North Atlantic Blocking Squadron. Cushing's letter to the admiral was short and to the point.

> Sir: Deeming the capture or destruction of the rebel ram *Albemarle* feasible, I beg leave to state that I am acquainted with the waters held by her, and am willing to undertake the task. If furnished with three low-pressure tugs, one or more fitted with torpedoes, and all armed with light howitzers, it might be effected.[12]

Lee passed the plan on to the secretary of the navy who ordered Cushing's torpedo boats to be built. The vessels, inspired by the successful Confederate "David" class torpedo boats, were forty-five-foot wooden steam launches, mounting a small twelve-pound howitzer forward and equipped with a long spar torpedo that could be deployed on the starboard bow. Two vessels were ready by September 20 and set sail for Hampton Roads. Only Picket Boat No. 1 would succeed in making the tumultuous journey with Boat No. 2 being wrecked near Great Wicomico Bay, Virginia, and burned by its crew to prevent its capture. In mid-October Cushing reported to Admiral David Porter, the former commander of the Western Flotilla and now the newly appointed commander of the North Atlantic Blocking Squadron. Porter ordered Cushing to make an attack on the *Albemarle* but wrote to the new commander of the flotilla in Albemarle Sound, William Macomb, "I have no great confidence in his success, but you will afford him all the assistance in your power."[13]

Sailing to the mouth of the Roanoke River, Cushing selected the night of October 26 to launch his attack. The scattered rains and patches of fog no doubt aided Cushing and his crew of fourteen as they crawled up the Roanoke River towing a small rowboat behind Picket Boat No. 1. It was known that the enemy had stationed a picket on the wreck of the *Southfield*. The plan was to slip by this post unnoticed if possible, but if discovered the rowboat would be used to seize this Confederate position while the torpedo boat made its attack

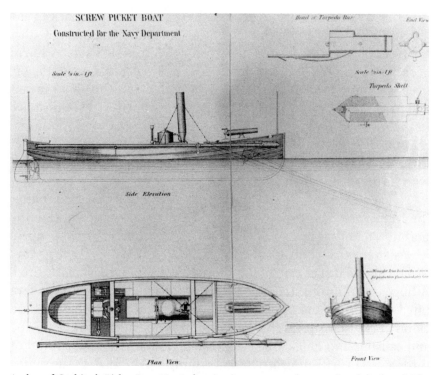

A plan of Cushing's Picket Boat No. 1 showing its spar torpedo stowed and deployed. The complexity of the torpedo was such that several different lines and lanyards had to be manipulated to maneuver the spar under the enemy vessel, arm the explosive, and detonate the warhead. (*NHHC*)

on the *Albemarle*. Aided by the weather and a number of inattentive sentries the plan worked better than expected. Cushing's vessel glided by the *Southfield* a little before 3 a.m. and it was not until they were within thirty yards of the *Albemarle* that a sentry on the ironclad challenged them.

Within seconds the threat was recognized, and flashes of musket fire came from sentries posted around the ram. The rowboat was cast off and a blast of canister from shore tore through the air rippling against the torpedo boat's side in a series of dull thuds and the occasional metallic ring when it pierced the smokestack. The Union vessel fired back with its forward gun as Cushing scanned the scene. The Confederate ironclad was moored to the wharf with its portside protected by a log-boom stationed some thirty feet from its side. Quickly reaching a decision Cushing ordered the pilot to circle back to increase the distance between the two vessels, and then turning with a full head of steam he steered directly for the ironclad's side. A storm of shot and canister focused on the accelerating craft. One of the officers standing next to Cushing fell wounded and Cushing himself had his clothes torn by musket balls in several places as the distance to the ironclad rapidly closed. The sound of the engines, shouting, cannon fire, and musketry all but drowned out the noise of Picket Boat No. 1 slamming into the floating boom and grinding to a halt with its bow hanging over the barricade.

The action at this point was frantic. A cold rain began to spatter the crews' faces as the spar was run out and maneuvered beneath the port quarter of the ram as a firing port on the ironclad began to open. It was a race that concluded with Cushing yanking on the torpedo's firing lanyard just as one of the Brooke rifles on the *Albemarle* fired. A huge column of water suddenly shot into the air. The shockwave lifted the stern of the ironclad and bow of the torpedo boat just as a cloud of canister ripped through Cushing's boat, disabling its engine and causing it to quickly fill with water. No more than a handful of yards away, the enemy called upon Cushing and his men to surrender, and when the Union commander refused, they intensified their barrage. Surrounded and with his crippled ship sinking beneath his feet, Cushing ordered his crew to save themselves and, along with several others, dove into the river. Most were later captured with only Cushing and one other sailor managing to escape.

Those who chose to stay quickly surrendered and, along with their captors, watched by flickering torchlight as the Confederate ironclad struggled with its wound. A six-foot-wide hole had been blown out of its bottom. Lt. Alexander Warley, who now commanded the *Albemarle*, ordered the pumps manned, but "The water gained on us so fast that all exertions were fruitless, and the vessel went down in a few moments, merely leaving her shield and smokestack out (of the water)."[14]

The vessel that had taken away Union control of the Roanoke River, threatened the Union position on Albemarle Sound, and required the constant attention of a dozen Federal warships, was no more. Able to withstand ramming and a hail of hundred-pound rifled cannon rounds, the Southern ironclad had been sunk by a handful

A picture of the sunken *Albemarle* awash to its gun ports and stripped of its iron plates. (*NHHC*)

of daring men using a new type of weapon, the torpedo boat. Admiral Porter who initially doubted the enterprise, heaped praise upon Cushing and his crew, calling the entire venture "a heroic enterprise seldom equaled." More importantly, Porter spelled out in his report, "To say nothing of the moral effect of this gallant affair, the loss of this vessel to the rebels cannot be estimated. It leaves open to us all the Albemarle Sound and tributaries, and gives us a number of vessels for employment elsewhere."[15]

On the Confederate side it was clear that they had been taken by surprise. The outer sentries had failed to sound the alarm, and by the time the skeleton crew on the ram realized the threat there was little they could do to prevent the vessel's destruction. Badly damaged and with neither the resources nor the time to raise and repair the *Albemarle*, it was stripped of its iron skin and guns. When the Confederate army later abandoned Plymouth, a charge was set off inside the vessel that wrecked the interior and blew the roof off the casemate, guaranteeing that the ship would never be used again. Although only afloat for a little over six months, the presence of this single vessel had altered the balance of power in the region. The ironclad had swept the Union Navy from the Roanoke River, was partially responsible for the capture of Plymouth, and had challenged for control of Albemarle Sound. While not successful in achieving this last aim the ram did tie down a disproportionate number of enemy vessels and resources to deal with its presence.

With the chaos created by the ironclad, and the Union's inability to stop the vessel even with vastly superior numbers, one is left to ponder the original Confederate plan to launch ironclads down the Roanoke, Neuse, and Tar Rivers. Although the CSS *Tarboro* was destroyed on the stocks and the CSS *Neuse* was lost in an accident, it is not hard to imagine how the three vessels working in tandem under an aggressive leader could have seriously threatened Union naval control of Albemarle and Pamlico Sounds. In the end, however, much like with the other Confederate ironclads and merchant raiders, Union numbers and a display of gallantry eventually secured the day.[16]

EIGHTEEN

The Descent of the Armada

B Y THE FALL OF 1864 the defenses of Cape Fear had evolved from old Fort Caswell and a few field guns mounted in the dunes on Federal Point to a well-laid-out network of defensive positions. Fort Caswell, located on the western side of the Old Inlet, had been improved and many of its guns were now casemated via a wooden shield covered in railroad track iron. To cover some of the fort's deficiencies, a small battery, known as Battery Shaw, was erected to the west to discourage any Union landing parties, and a few hundred yards past this a sixteen-gun battery was constructed. The new structure, named Fort Campbell, was built like the other sand forts throughout the area. Sand and earth from nearby sources was used to form large earth mounds along one side of a wide ditch. In the case of Fort Campbell these traverses were spaced a few dozen yards apart and were twenty to thirty feet in diameter. The space between the mounds was then filled in such that the slope on both sides was approximately forty-five degrees and matched the traverses. The top portion of this connecting section, which typically was much lower than the flanking mounds, so as to provide partial cover to the gun crews, would then be leveled and gun platforms constructed to mount cannon. The parapet over which these guns fired was either fashioned out of gabions, in which case a half a dozen rows of these contained within a wooden framework stretched between the mounds to form this makeshift wall, or was cut out of the earth during the leveling process and then braced with wood. On the backside of the large earth mounds, tunnels were dug into the base and braced with wood beams and planking, to serve as magazines and bombproof shelters for the garrison.

Another battery known as Fort Holmes was raised across the Old Inlet at Bald Head Point on Smith's Island. While the main channel passed very close to the heavy guns of Fort Caswell, Whiting found that he really had no choice but to fortify this position; otherwise, if the enemy landed and seized Smith Island, they could bombard Fort Caswell into submission from Bald Head Point. At Smithville, another sand stronghold, Fort Johnston, was built to cover the town's waterfront and the northern portion of the Old Inlet. Farther north along the west shore of the river, the three-gun Fort Lamb was erected at Reeve's Point, while a little over three miles farther upriver lay Fort Anderson and beyond that Wilmington.

At the New Inlet a few guns were placed on Zeek's Island to act as a deterrent along the southern portion of the channel and to discourage small enemy raiding parties, while on the northern side of the channel lay Federal Point and the lynchpin of the Cape Fear defenses: Fort Fisher. Originally built as a small redoubt to hold a handful of field guns, the fort was given the name Fisher in honor of North Carolina colonel Charles Fisher who had been killed at Manassas. While a key position, it was not until the arrival of Lt. Colonel William Lamb in 1862 that work began in earnest on one of the world's largest and most powerful sand forts.[1]

Lamb, who received a law degree from the College of William and Mary, was a local politician and the coeditor of a Norfolk newspaper before the war. While Lamb's military experience was limited to the command of a local militia company before the conflict, in the fall of 1861 he was commissioned a major and assigned to General Anderson's staff in Wilmington. Anderson placed Lamb in charge of Fort St. Phillip, which would later be renamed Fort Anderson. The following spring Lamb was made colonel of the 36th North Carolina, and in early July he took command of Fort Fisher with his regiment.

The lawyer-turned-newspaper editor-turned-politician was an unlikely candidate for military engineer, but with Whiting's guidance this is certainly what he became. Given that the fortifications had to be at the southern end of Federal Point in order to dominate the New Inlet, both Lamb and Whiting had to consider the probability of a Union landing on the peninsula above the fort. To deal with this threat Lamb laid out the landside of Fort Fisher to essentially bisect Federal Point. On the left-hand side of the fort the sand wall terminated on the Wilmington Road a few hundred feet from the Cape Fear River. A swamp dominated this area and a small bridge was built over a portion of these wetlands for the road. A wooden palisade and a single cannon defended the small strip of land on the southern side of the road fronted by the swamp. On the northern side of the road sixteen large mounds or traverses, fifty feet across and thirty-two feet tall, were laid out across the peninsula, terminating six hundred feet short of the ocean. Twenty-foot tall and twenty-five-foot thick walls were then fashioned between these earthworks, and to reduce enfilading fire the traverses at either end, "exceeding in size any known to the engineers," extended a dozen feet in front of the curtain wall and towered another dozen feet above the gun platforms. Arrangements were made for nineteen cannons along the wall, all firing in *barbette* because there was no iron to build bomb-proof casemates for the guns. These pieces ranged from a 4.5-inch rifle to a pair of ten-inch columbiads at the endpoints. In addition, three mortars were stationed behind the wall to assist the cannon in repelling a land attack. The magazines and bombproof shelters were dug into the base of the traverses, with every other mound acting as a magazine, and behind the eastern end of the land wall, near where the bastion would be built to connect it to the seaside fortifications, several large traverses were erected which acted as additional bombproof shelters and the fort's magazine.

To slow down the fort's great enemy, erosion, the faces of the traverses were braced with wood or covered with sod. In front of the wall a shallow ditch was dug, and like the other forts in the area, a palisade fence and covered way was constructed. Near the center of this outer line a redoubt was raised to allow the defenders to sweep the walls with small arms and cannon fire, and a sally port was provided to allow troops to exit or retire into the fort. Were this not enough to

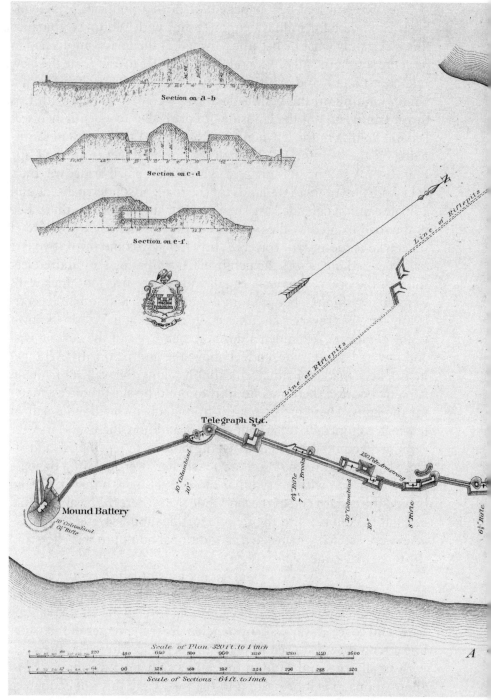

Reaching from the Cape Fear River to the Atlantic Ocean, Fort Fisher was the key to the Confederate defenses at Cape Fear. (*Library of Congress*)

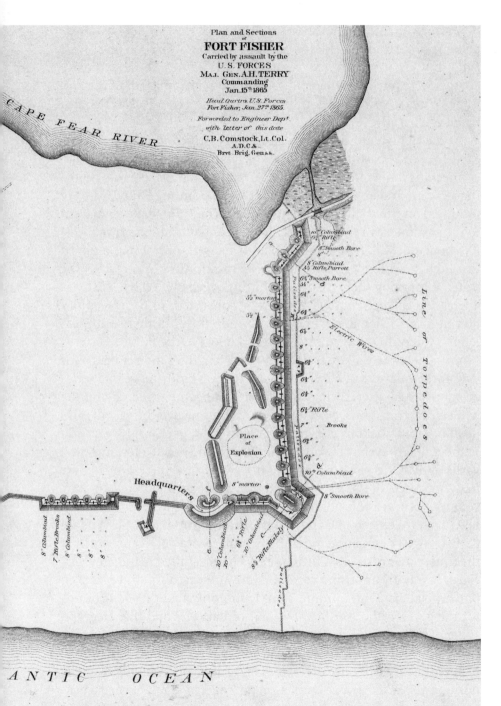

Plan and Sections
of
FORT FISHER
Carried by assault by the
U.S. FORCES
MAJ. GEN. A.H. TERRY
Commanding
Jan. 15th 1865

Head Qurtrs U.S. Forces
Fort Fisher, Jan. 27th 1865.

Forwarded to Engineer Dep't
with letter of this date.

C.B. Comstock, Lt. Col.
A.D.C. &
Brvt. Brig. Gen. A.A.

CAPE FEAR RIVER

Headquarters

Place
of
Explosion

Line or Torpedoes

Electric Wires

10" Columbiad
6½" Rifle
8" Smooth Bore
8"
8" Columbiad
4½ Rifle, Parrott
6½" Smooth Bore
6¼"
6¼"
6½"
6¾"
8"
6¼"
6¼"
6¼"
6¾" Rifle
Brooks
6¾"
6¼"
6¼"
10" Columbiad
8" Smooth Bore

5½" mortar

5½"

8" mortar

8" Columbiad
7" Rifle Brooks
8" Columbiad
8"
8"
8"

10" Columbiad
10"
6½" Rifle
10" Columbiad
8½" Rifle Blakely

ANTIC OCEAN

Engraved in the Engineer Bureau, War Dep't

discourage an infantry attack, Fort Fisher had yet another nasty surprise in store: a minefield. It was referred to as a torpedo line at the
time, but its function was essentially the same. These explosive
charges were buried in the sand six hundred yards in front of the palisade. Wires were run back to the fort and the explosives were detonated electrically.[2]

At the right-hand edge of the landside fortifications a three-hun-
dred-foot wide bastion centered about a large traverse was erected to
connect the land and seaside walls. An eight-inch Blakely rifle pointing seaward and an eight-inch smoothbore pointing landward were
mounted on the resulting U-shaped platform. Immediately adjacent
to the bastion was a traverse and the first elements of the seawall. Unlike the land wall, here the gun platforms were only a half a dozen
feet high so as to allow the gun crews to skip their shot across the
water, improving their chances of hitting an enemy vessel. Next was
a crescent-shaped battery that was converted into a hospital/
bombproof shelter, and some three hundred feet farther south was
Lamb's thirty-foot tall command post known as the Pulpit.

From here the wall extended down the length of the peninsula for
over three-quarters of a mile. This stretch was really more of a series
of connected batteries than the dense arrangement seen along the
landside fortifications. A six-foot-tall wall connected the various gun
positions and was only constructed to provide cover for the garrison
in the unlikely event of a Union landing on the beach a few hundred
yards away. One of Lamb's more prized batteries was a little over
halfway down the seaside wall. It consisted of a pair of ten-inch
columbiads and a 150-pound British Armstrong rifle, reputed to have
been a gift to Jefferson Davis from the British arms maker Sir William
Armstrong. The weapon, one of the more powerful in the world at
the time, came with brass fittings and a hand-crafted mahogany carriage. It was an imposing cannon, and well cared for, but it lacked
one crucial element: ammunition. Lamb only had thirteen rounds
for the gun. Farther south was a pair of batteries and the telegraph
station, before the line terminated in a sixty-foot-tall earthwork
known as the Mound. A pair of cannons were mounted here to supplement the ricochet fire of the wall batteries with plunging fire. The
position also acted as an observation post and, at night, burned a beacon that blockade runners used to fix their positions before making
a morning dash into the New Inlet.

For nearly a mile south farther along the beach was low-lying ter-rain that was only a few feet above water at high tide, and often un-derwater during strong storm surges. At the end of this, and at the southern extremity of Federal Point was Battery Buchanan. The earthwork was really a small fort unto itself and mounted a pair of eleven-inch and a pair of ten-inch guns, which, manned by Confed-erate sailors, completely dominated the New Inlet and a large portion of the Cape Fear River as well.[3]

In all it was an impressive array of fortifications built over the course of several years by Lamb's men and a large number of slaves. Armed with twenty heavy guns on the landside, twenty-four more along the seaside, and a powerful garrison not only to man the guns and repair damage to the fort but to repel an infantry attack on the works as well, it would seem a location more likely to be taken by a drawn-out siege than a quick strike. There were two problems, how-ever. First a shortage of ammunition haunted Lamb and his men. In December 1864 Lamb had a little under 3,600 shot and shell in his magazines, and for some guns only a handful of rounds. While this diminished the strength of the works, the lack of manpower is what ultimately made the defensive complex vulnerable. With his own reg-iment, a few companies of artillery, and a detachment of naval gun-ners the colonel had perhaps seven hundred men at his disposal. This would be fine under normal circumstances given that a relief force could come by water via the landing at Battery Buchanan and that the brigade at the entrenched camp and field works a few miles up the peninsula would be quick to respond, pinning any Union landing between the two forces. The problem, however, was that there was a chronic shortage of infantry at Wilmington. For long periods of time during Whiting's Cape Fear command he had at least an infantry brigade stationed in the area, as Wilmington was used as a reserve lo-cation for North Carolina troops and was a frequent first stop for new regiments. As the war dragged on, however, more urgent demands slowly stripped Wilmington of its troops much to the displeasure of Whiting, who complained to the War Department that, "The fortifi-cations that have been erected against that are of the best character, but they depend on security by land, and there can be no security, no system of defense in this peculiar locality without the presence of a large body of troops."[4]

Union plans to strike at Cape Fear were first discussed in 1862, but the army, after witnessing the shortcomings of previous amphibious operations and reluctant to commit badly needed troops to a risky venture against an established position, expressed no interest. By the fall of 1864 much had changed. The Confederacy was being stretched thin. The port of Mobile had been captured, and beyond Galveston there was no major Confederate port open on the Gulf Coast. Along the Atlantic Coast Charleston and Wilmington remained, and of the two, Wilmington was a particularly good target as it was the primary supply line for Lee's army in Virginia. In September 1864 Secretary of the Navy Welles approached the new commander of the Union Army about troops to attack Cape Fear. In General Ulysses S. Grant Welles found a receptive audience. Knowing this, Welles applied to the secretary of war for troops to conduct operations against Fort Fisher, and with Grant's support, the request was granted.

Rear Admiral David Farragut was selected to command the naval portion of the expedition, but after years of campaigning he declined because of his failing health. Upon hearing the news Welles wrote to his second choice, Rear Admiral David Porter, in command of the Mississippi Squadron. Porter was ordered to turn his command over to a senior captain and report to Beaufort, NC, where he would relieve Rear Admiral Lee and take command of the North Atlantic Squadron. Although the move certainly surprised Porter the reasons became clearer when he met with Assistant Secretary of the Navy Fox and General Grant in Virginia where they discussed the operation against Fort Fisher, the troops to be allotted, and the choice of army commander.

While Grant had suggested General Weitzel to command the army element of the expedition, Weitzel's superior, Major General Benjamin Butler, caught wind of the idea and pointed out the operation was on such a scale that command should rightly fall upon him. The involved parties did not argue and the hope was that the entire venture could be launched in October while the weather was still good.

This was not to be the case. Porter reported to Hampton Roads and gathered together his fleet, which by October 15, 1864, numbered close to one hundred. "There was a great variety of vessels," he later wrote of the experience, "as every class in the Navy was represented, from the lofty frigate down to the fragile steamer taken from the mer-

The first three landside traverses as viewed from the interior of Fort Fisher. The picket fence on the Confederate left and the gun platforms between the traverses can be seen in the photo. (*Library of Congress*)

chant service, but all mounted good guns." To stiffen the assortment of gunboats, steam frigates, and converted merchantmen a squadron of ironclads was attached to the fleet led by the newly built eighteen-gun armored frigate *New Ironsides*. While all of these armored vessels drew too much water to force their way through the New Inlet and attack the fort from behind, Porter planned to use them to bombard the fortifications at close range with their heavy guns. As he waited for the army contingent to organize, the admiral occupied his time drilling his new fleet in signals, maneuvering, and endless firing drills, which he believed would pay off when it came time for the attack.[5]

By mid-November there was still no news of Butler's command, but good news had arrived with reports that Union forces had recaptured Plymouth, North Carolina, on October 31. The venture was led by Commander W.H. Macomb who was looking to strike a blow against Plymouth after the loss of the *Albemarle*. Macomb took his gunboat flotilla up the Roanoke River to attack the Confederate batteries guarding the town but turned back when he encountered a barricade across the waterway near where the *Southfield* was sunk. The next day the commander sailed his six warships through the Middle Channel which merged with the Roanoke River above Plymouth. Along the way his gun crews shelled the town from over a mile and a half away.

On the morning of October 31, Macomb lashed his vessels together, "so as to keep the vessels in motion should their engines be
damaged," and dropped downriver to engage the Confederate batteries. The firing on both sides was heavy at the start of the engagement,
but when one of the Confederate magazines exploded showering the
Union vessels with debris, the firing slackened, and after an hour of
bombardment, the garrison abandoned their guns and retreated toward Washington. Macomb organized a landing party and took the
town along with twenty-two guns, thirty-seven prisoners, and a large
amount of ordnance stores including several hundred rifles.[6]

Porter commended Macomb for the effort, but as far as the Wilmington expedition was concerned, it did not appear that there would
be an opportunity to attack. Although Secretary Welles appealed directly to Lincoln to speed up Butler's portion of the campaign it
would not be until late November that the general and several of his
staff met with Porter at Hampton Roads. The general agreed to march
his division to Beaufort and, after boarding the assembled transports
there, proceed to Wilmington where he would rendezvous with
Porter's fleet.

In the meantime, Butler introduced an idea that he believed might
aid in the taking of the Confederate stronghold. The general had become interested in large explosions, mostly in regard to accidents at
munitions factories. He had become convinced after reading the reports and surveys of the collateral damage from such events that the
shock wave from such explosions was a powerful weapon. In Butler's
opinion, all that was required to harness this effect was to replicate
the same magnitude explosion by filling a vessel full of powder and
setting it all off at once. The plan then would be to run the vessel up
on shore a few hundred yards from Fort Fisher and set it off. The
shock wave from the blast should be large enough to level the nearby
walls and stun most of the garrison into submission.

Porter and the War Department were skeptical, with the head of
the Army Corps of Engineers giving his opinion that "I can find no
reason to believe that these solid masses of sand hills and massive
walls, distant more than 450 yards from the site of the powder explosion, are to be removed or destroyed or in any way injuriously acted
upon by the air or atmosphere as a projectile, propelled by the explosion of any quantity of powder." Many agreed, but at this stage any-

thing that moved the project forward was considered a success, and
so it was agreed to make the attempt. The 150-foot iron gunboat
Louisiana, which only drew eight
and a half feet of water, was selected
for the task and outfitted at Beaufort by a team of explosive experts.
Two hundred and fifteen tons of
powder was loaded into the holds
and strapped to the deck of the ship
in barrels. The real issue became
how to detonate all of the powder at
once. "Electricity was proposed as
offering the most probable means
of securing this result," a pair of

Colonel William Lamb, the architect of
Fort Fisher. (*Library of Congress*)

Ordnance Department inspectors wrote in their report. "But as this
agent is known to be very unreliable in action, it was determined to
use several clockwork arrangements, a slow match, and finally to set
the vessel on fire before the crew abandoned it.[7]

On December 13 after being pressed by Grant to proceed, Butler
loaded his division of veteran New York, Indiana, Pennsylvania, and
New Hampshire troops onto the transports, along with a division of
black troops commanded by Brigadier General Charles J. Paine.
Porter's fleet arrived at Beaufort on the afternoon of December 15.
Since Porter needed a day to take on supplies and provisions, it was
agreed that Butler's transports and a few escorts would proceed to
Cape Fear. The admiral's warships would follow the next day.

Porter was delayed longer than expected and it was not until the
evening of the seventeenth that he spoke with Butler again. The
troops were ready, and the warships under his command had been
given their orders and assigned positions for the bombardment of
the fort. It also seemed time to send the *Louisiana* forward and test
Butler's theory. The North Atlantic, however, had other ideas, and before the orders could be sent the wind and surf began to pick up. It
was enough to call off the powder boat attack, and as the weather
seemed to be worsening, Butler elected to return to Beaufort to resupply.

By December 21 the weather had become a tempest with gale-force winds and tall waves crashing upon the shore. Butler's force, still on its way back to Beaufort, was pummeled by the wind and waves. Filled to the brim with seasick soldiers, the transported rolled back and forth before the onslaught. "Everything movable was dashed and slammed round in the most confused manner," one soldier recalled. Porter's vessels had a similar experience riding out the cold fury off of Cape Fear. The crews were battered and tossed about by the swells with the low-lying monitors causing the admiral a great deal of concern as the waves crashed over their decks briefly obscuring them in a cascade of blue-green water.[8]

The storm broke early on the morning of the twenty-second leaving behind manageable gusts and whitecaps. To Porter's delight all vessels, including the monitors, were accounted for. Butler was happy as well at the change of weather and finally arrived at Beaufort that day. The following morning the backside of the storm left cold clear skies in its wake. It also created a problem for Porter as Butler had yet to return. In the end, Porter decided that taking advantage of the good weather was more important, given that the general and his troops could not be more than a day away. He passed orders for the *Louisiana* to attack at nightfall and for the fleet to be prepared to commence bombardment the next morning so "that the rebels may have as little time to rebuild as possible."[9]

At 10:30 p.m. the gunboat USS *Wilderness* slowly towed the *Louisiana* past the outer picket vessel and toward Fort Fisher. An hour later the Union gunboat cast off the line and took a position not far away. From here Commander A.C. Rhind and his crew of volunteers gently inched the *Louisiana* forward until they ran out of water some three hundred yards from the seaside wall of the fortress. After dropping a pair of anchors, the crew took to their boats as Rhind and his executive officer Lt. S.W. Preston lit the fuses and started several fires. With this done the entire force rowed out to the *Wilderness* without a shot being fired at them.

With Rhind and his men aboard, the *Wilderness* steamed off, taking a position a dozen miles away to observe the upcoming explosion. Rhind and Preston had set the fuses for an hour and a half, but when both of their watches read 1:18 a.m. nothing happened. By now the flames had spread on the vessel making it visible to all. The Confederate sentries likely thought it was a blockade runner which had met a bad end, while the Union officers onboard the *Wilderness* forwarded theories as to what had happened. With the aft part of the vessel engulfed in flames, at 1:40 a.m. a series of explosions erupted on the vessel, "the shock being hardly felt and four distinct reports heard," Rhind reported.[10]

The result was nothing but a burning fractured vessel along the shore and a few startled enemy sentries, who still thought that a blockade runner had met a bad end and never suspected that it was an intentional act. "My opinion is that owing to the want of confinement and insufficient fuzing of the mass, much of the powder was blown away before ignition and its effect lost," Rhind wrote of the incident. Ordnance inspectors agreed, pointing to the fire being responsible for the series of detonations. Porter, who had questioned the logic to begin with, shook his head at the incident and later wrote, "this futile attempt to destroy such a powerful work as Fort Fisher at the risk of so many valuable lives, in order that the pet scheme of a Major-General of Volunteers should be carried out, we may wonder that any one should countenance such an absurdity."[11]

NINETEEN

The Sands of
Fort Fisher

T HE NEXT MORNING, CHRISTMAS EVE, was clear with a westerly breeze that rippled the ocean's surface and tugged at the flotilla's flags. The fleet of fifty-one warships raised steam and prepared for action. When it became clear that Butler was still nowhere to be found, Porter ordered the signal flags raised aboard the flagship *Malvern* setting the flotilla in motion toward Fort Fisher. The admiral had assigned stations to the warships, and unlike the earlier attack on Fort Hatteras where the Union fleet had used its maneuverability to reduce the fort, Porter had elected to follow a more traditional path and anchor the fleet in a crescent-shaped line from three-quarters of a mile to a mile from the structure.

At 11:30 a.m. Porter raised the signal to engage. He had nothing but compliments on how the ships' captains and their crews took their stations as if each vessel was trying to outdo the other in a display of seamanship. On the right of his line Porter stationed the ironclads and a few wooden vessels close to the shore, within three-quarters of a mile of the fort. Under the leadership of Commodore William Radford of the USS *New Ironsides* the monitors *Canonicus* and *Mahopac*, along with the odd-looking double turret monitor *Monadnock*, wheeled to port and slid into position dropping anchors both fore and aft. The last vessel had yet to finish when the *New Ironsides* greeted the fort with a broadside of seven eleven-inch guns and a pair of 150-pound Parrott guns. The monitors soon followed with the thump of their fifteen-inch guns echoing across the water.

The larger vessels in the center of the line, like the forty-four-gun steam frigates *Minnesota* and *Colorado*, as well as the twenty-one-gun *Brooklyn* and the forty-nine-gun *Wabash* glided into position, firing ranging shots at the fort as they dropped their anchors and set their maneuvering springs. Once set, these vessels began a rapid fire on the stronghold sending shifting columns of earth into the air and slowly obscuring the northeast corner of the structure in a haze of dust and falling debris. The remaining fourteen vessels assigned to this part of the line soon joined in with another hundred guns of various calibers.

The next portion of the line consisted of half a dozen warships targeting batteries along the sea wall, and a few hundred yards beyond this, the line ended with a pair of vessels, the *Monticello* and the *Rhode Island*, whose task was to engage the Mound Battery a little over a mile away. To support this bombardment and act as couriers, Porter stationed a second line of nineteen smaller vessels which he planned to hold in reserve.

"A grander sight than the approach of Porter's formidable Armada towards the fort was never witnessed on our coast," Lamb watching from the pulpit later wrote of the Union fleet's deployment. By the time the *Monticello* and *Rhode Island* reached their stations on the far left some two miles away, the sound of cannon and explosive rounds rippled down the length of Federal Point. Thus far the defenders had only fired sporadically at the Union warships. The initial barrage had damaged the main barracks and set them ablaze and in several other places the woodwork in the fort was on fire as well. After an hour and fifteen minutes of this bombardment, during which the admiral calculated that shells were striking the fort at the rate of over a hundred per minute, Porter was convinced that he had driven all the Confederate gun crews into their bombproof shelters. "Such a torrent of missiles were falling into and bursting over the works," he later wrote, "that it was impossible for anything human to withstand it." Unable to get a reply from the Confederate batteries he ordered the fleet to slow their rate of fire to conserve ammunition in hopes that Butler might arrive that afternoon.[1]

The rest of the day proceeded along a similar line, but Porter was mistaken in believing that the Confederate guns had been silenced. In fact, their slow response to the Union bombardment was not because they had been put out of action, but because Lamb had ordered that the guns be fired no more than once every half hour in order to conserve ammunition that might be needed to repel an infantry landing. While the Union bombardment shook the ground and rattled the wooden ceilings of the bombproof shelters, it was having very little effect on the fort. A number of guns were hit, but in most cases, it was the gun carriage that had been damaged and not the gun. Even casualties were low, partly because the bulk of the garrison was huddled in their shelters, and partly because the large traverses were providing adequate shelter to the gun crews. With the fort's guns being fired at long intervals, after discharging a round or two, the gunners who remained at their stations had ample opportunity to observe the bombardment. One of these was Midshipman Clarence Cary of the *Chickamauga*, who was serving with a naval gun detachment in the fort. "So, between the discharges, and while crouching in comparative safety under the sand mounds, ample opportunity was found to watch the antics of the hostile missiles showered into the fort," he later wrote of the barrage. The midshipman quietly studied the variety of whizzing and whistling sounds the rounds made, and noting the variations in the resulting concussions he finally concluded that, "with the continuous roar of the firing, and the scarcely frequent reports of bursting shells, the aggregate noise was not unlike that of a rolling, volleying, long-sustained thunder storm."[2]

By mid-afternoon the fires from the barracks had mixed with the dust and smoke from the guns to create a sprawling grey shroud that clung to the fortifications. Twice bright orange flashes backlit this pall as a pair of small magazines in the parade ground exploded, disgorging their fiery contents into the atmosphere. To make matters worse, several smaller warehouses near the barracks containing ample amounts of tar and pitch soon added their fuel to the inferno. The fort's stable had also been hit early on and set ablaze. This released the garrison's horses into the maelstrom. When there was a lull in the

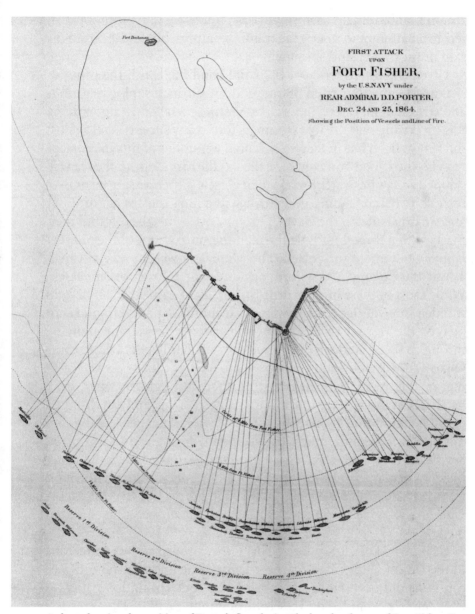

A chart showing the position of Porter's fleet during the bombardment of Fort Fisher, December 24th and 25th. (*Library of Congress*)

Union bombardment men would dash out of their bombproof shelters in an attempt to rescue the frantic creatures, but few survived the
rain of shot, shell, and shrapnel.

Given the infrequency of their fire combined with the ground-
shaking detonations from 350-pound fifteen-inch explosive rounds
and strings of air bursts that rained searing metal down upon them,
it is surprising that the fort's gunners found any success at all against
the Union fleet, but in fact, they scored a number of hits on Porter's
vessels. The Union gun crews watched as the rounds from the sea wall
skipped across the water toward their vessels, either passing by or over
their ship, before ending their voyage in a long rooster tail of water
and sinking beneath the waves. On a few occasions these found their
mark, with a three-foot hole through the smokestack of the *Susquehanna* a testament to the fact. The *Minnesota* was hit several times,
as was the *Colorado*, *New Ironsides*, and half a dozen other vessels.
While most of these hits did little in the way of damage the nine-gun
wooden sidewheeler *Osceola* was an exception. A ten-inch solid shot
pierced the vessel two feet below the waterline and, after plowing
through a set of sandbags, ruptured the starboard boiler before coming to a stop. A billowing cloud of steam filled the lower decks, scalding anyone in its path before it escaped through the open deck
hatches. On fire and rapidly filling with water the gunboat dropped
out of position, and at one point, there was a real danger that the ship
might sink before the flooding was finally brought under control.
Several other vessels received minor damage, but perhaps the worst
incident occurred around 3 p.m. when a ten-inch columbiad round
from the Mound Battery plunged through the deck of the USS *Mackinaw* and exploded in the boiler room, killing or wounding a dozen
men.[3]

As it turned out, the guns of Fort Fisher proved far less dangerous
to the Union sailors than their own guns. The hundred-pound Parrott guns did nothing to alter their dangerous reputation when no
less than five exploded on vessels throughout the fleet. The first incident occurred at 3 p.m. when the hundred-pound Parrott gun on the
aft deck of the *Yantic* exploded on its twentieth time being fired. The
blast killed two of the crew and wounded three others as well as
caused enough damage that the captain hauled out of the line to effect repairs. Fifteen minutes later a thunderous fireball erupted on

the USS *Ticonderoga* as the hundred-pound Parrott gun burst upon firing. The shrapnel and concussion leveled the gun crew, killing eight of their number and wounding another eleven. The *Juniata* was next when its Parrott gun detonated, killing or wounding over a dozen, and not long after the *Quaker City* suffered the same fate but fortunately escaped with only a few wounded.

By late afternoon the fire from Fort Fisher had slackened to a few shots every hour. With the firestorm unleashed upon the fort, and the lack of a Confederate response, Porter and many of his officers believed that if troops were on hand to land at this point that the fort would be in Union hands by nightfall. Butler, however, was nowhere to be seen. "There being no troops here to take possession, I am merely firing at it now to keep up practice," the admiral penned. "The forts are nearly demolished, and as soon as troops come we can take possession."[4]

Butler would not arrive with the transports until after sunset, long after Porter had ordered a cease-fire and directed his ships to fall back for the evening. With the infantry now on hand and the fort battered from the day's bombardment it was agreed to resume the bombardment at daylight while the army landed above the fort. General Weitzel, formerly of Foster's Newbern command and now Butler's chief of staff, would take command of the landing forces.

At 7 a.m. on Christmas Day the signal flags were raised sending the detachments into motion. This time Porter moved the entire fleet a few hundred yards closer to the fort. The *New Ironsides* once again led the procession of monitors, now reinforced by the recently arrived *Saugus*, and commenced fire on the northeast bastion while it came to anchor. It was a repeat down the line, with the exception that the fleet's fire was slower and more methodical than the day before, as Porter wished to conserve ammunition to deliver a barrage on the fort in support of Butler's infantry attack. The fort returned fire in the same sluggish fashion as the day before, looking to conserve ammunition as well. It almost appeared that both sides were waiting for the inevitable—a Union landing above the fort.

The Union fleet and the defenders of Fort Fisher would soon realize that they had a mutual enemy: faulty cannons. The fleet was reminded of this when another hundred-pound Parrott gun exploded on the *Wabash* and the already damaged *Mackinaw* had its hundred-

pound Parrott gun detonate not long after. Along the seawall Midshipman Cary and his detachment were assigned to a pair of Brooke
rifles from the *Chickamauga*. The order to fire was given once the
Union fleet had come to anchor. There was an explosion as a shell
burst over the battery and then a blinding flash as the Brooke cannon
blew itself apart upon firing. The fifteen-thousand-pound gun was
nearly split in two. A large piece of the breech was hurled backward,
whizzing over the heads of a group of officers on the platform, and a
portion was driven downward destroying the carriage before burying
itself in the ground. Most on the gun platform were knocked down
by the blast, although Cary pointed out that "whether they were
knocked down by concussion or astonishment they never knew." A
pair of men lay dead, killed from the shrapnel, while another half
dozen or so were wounded. "One man was leaping about the battery
like a lunatic," the midshipman recalled, "crying out that he was on
fire. He could scarcely be comforted, even when on stripping off his
shirt he was found only to be tattooed by grains of powder and sand
blown into his back and shoulders."[5]

Around 10 a.m. Captain Oliver Glisson of the sidewheeler USS
Santiago de Cuba and a flotilla of seventeen gunboats closed in on
the proposed landing zone five miles above Fort Fisher. A pair of Confederate gun positions, Battery Gatlin (Flag Pond Battery) to the
north and Battery Anderson (Half-Moon Battery) to the south posed
a threat to the landing operations, and as such, Glisson was tasked
with neutralizing these positions before landing operations commenced. Glisson's flotilla began to shell the two Confederate locations, which were manned primarily by old men and volunteers.
Battery Gatlin managed a few shots, but it was quickly silenced, and
its demoralized garrison proved happy to surrender. Battery Anderson was also pummeled and its shaken garrison, having never experienced an artillery barrage before, surrendered as well.

Around noon Glisson informed Butler that the Confederate gun
positions had been captured and that the landing could commence.
Two hours later the army transports arrived and found nothing to
oppose a landing but the sea, which also proved cooperative as the
small boats provided by the navy shuttled troops and supplies onto
the beach. General Weitzel and Brigadier General Newton M. Curtis
landed first with five hundred New York troops from the latter's

The USS *Santiago de Cuba*. (*NHHC*)

brigade. After sending a detachment north to look for enemy activity, Weitzel ordered Curtis to form a skirmish line and push forward toward Fort Fisher.[6]

Lamb watched the Union fleet from the pulpit as Porter's ships stepped up their fire to cover the landing operations to the north. As intense as the barrage had been the day before it had done little in the way of damage to the fort. Even the garrison's casualties, some twenty-three wounded, a few severely, did not reflect the ferocity of the bombardment. The damage was quickly dealt with; the earth was filled in, the fires put out, and six broken gun carriages repaired. "I cannot speak too highly of the services of these men," Major William Saunders, chief of artillery, wrote in his report. "As evidenced in the remounting of guns and filling and distribution of ordnance stores and general repair of damages to the carriages during the night of the 24th." Along the landside wall a pair of guns had been disabled, but otherwise there was no significant damage and nineteen guns still remained operational along this length. Even the firing lines to the torpedoes in front of the palisade line appeared intact and operational.

Lamb's garrison had also been reinforced the previous night with 133 regulars and 300 North Carolina Junior Reserves. While the latter were questionable, it put his numbers at around 1,350 men. To the north, farther up the peninsula and across the Cape Fear River from Fort Anderson, was Sugerloaf, an oblong hill that acted as a Confederate post. Reports were that eight hundred men of Major General Hoke's division, which had been dispatched when news arrived that Fort Fisher was under attack, were encamped at this location. The remainder, along with the general, would arrive at any time.[7]

Around the same time that Butler's men were going ashore, the ten-gun USS *Iosco* under Commander John Guest and a number of double-end gunboats gathered near the New Inlet and began lowering their launches. When discussing the attack on the fort with Weitzel and Butler earlier, the former suggested that the admiral explore the idea of sending some gunboats into the New Inlet and, after running the guns of Fort Buchanan, bombard the walls of Fort Fisher from behind. Porter had little faith in the idea, which he viewed as a suicide mission, but agreed. If a channel could be found, he would send six double-enders past the guns into the river.

To lead this survey and sounding mission, which would be conducted under fire from batteries a few hundred yards away and might involve navigating a torpedo field erected by the enemy, Porter logically turned to Lt. William Cushing of *Albemarle* fame. Cushing agreed and, dressed in his parade uniform, he led nine longboats in a vain attempt to find a way through the channel. The shrieking rounds from the Confederate batteries and the columns of water that erupted nearby nearly swamped several vessels, some to the point that the crews had to stop and bail out their crafts. After a few fruitless hours Cushing ordered the boats back to the fleet and arrived a short time later having lost one of his craft in the withdrawal.

The flotilla of half a dozen Union double-enders waiting for Cushing proved an inviting target, and Lamb ordered the 150-pound Armstrong gun to fire at the Union flagship, the *Iosco*. There is little doubt that the sound of the big gun raised the spirits of the garrison, but the first few shots splashed around their target, until the gun crew claimed that the fourth shot, a steel bolt, pierced the side of the Union vessel and drove it off.[8]

The winds picked up and the skies turned threatening as three thousand Union troops came ashore over the span of the next few hours. Led by Curtis and his men, the skirmish line had come within seventy-five yards of the fort's landside palisades before they were forced to seek cover after being fired on by grapeshot and shell. General Weitzel had accompanied this detachment with specific orders from Butler to ascertain the true strength of the fort before making a decision on whether or not to storm the structure. As the New York troops exchanged shots with the wall's defenders, one of Curtis' staff, Lt. William H. Walling, darted forward and, after passing through a hole in the palisades, retrieved the fort's flag which had been knocked down during the naval bombardment. The Union ironclads and a number of nearby gunboats were still shelling the fort's landside wall sending towers of sand and earth high into the air near Walling, and black bursts overhead rippled the nearby ground with shrapnel. While a serious threat to the young lieutenant it also kept the fire from the fort's defenders down, as many were still in the bombproof shelters. With the huge Confederate battle ensign still attached to twelve feet of the original pole in his hands, Walling retraced his steps, working his way through the ragged opening in the wooden fence line as musket balls and grapeshot sought to stop him. Once clear of this obstacle, he made a mad dash for his own lines amidst the cheers and bursts of gunfire from both sides. Curtis, who along with a number of others watched the entire spectacle unfold, referred to it in his official report as "one of the most gallant exploits of the war." His troops were inspired by Walling's actions, and seeing a possible opportunity to storm the works as the musket fire from the fort had slowed down, Curtis sent a messenger back for the two hundred men he had kept in reserve.[9]

General Weitzel was with Curtis' reserves some eight hundred yards from the fort's outer lines. As Weitzel and his staff gazed upon the wall with their field glasses, they at first became suspicious and then alarmed at what they saw. The general counted seventeen guns along the wall separated by large traverses which he was sure sheltered the garrison. A wooden palisade ran from the counterscarp of the fort's ditch past the northeast bastion down to the water's edge, and to his surprise it was still intact after the naval bombardment. Although the scars from the pounding could be seen on the structure's sloped walls, Weitzel could not detect any material damage to the structure. There were signs that a few of the guns might have been disabled, but the bulk appeared operational. The lack of activity along the wall was not surprising to the veteran of several assaults on large earth fortifications. He knew that enough men were stationed on the parapets to warn the garrison, who would surge out of their nearby shelters and up on the ramparts in the event of an infantry attack. The general was about to report to Butler, who was on the army gunboat *Chamberlain*, when Curtis' message arrived. Having made up his mind, Weitzel sent the runner back with orders for Curtis to fall back.

Weitzel spoke with Butler aboard the *Chamberlain* anchored nearby and informed him that "it would be butchery to order an assault on that work under the circumstances." After listening to Weitzel's reasons and examining the work through naval binoculars Butler agreed and issued an order for the troops to reembark.[10]

When the runner returned to Curtis, the burly brigadier pushed his hat back and had the runner tell him again. He then shrugged and ordered his troops to fall back to where the reserves were positioned. Here Curtis encountered General Ames who had moved forward with a few of the regiments in his brigade. Ames had yet to receive an order to withdraw, so he reinforced Curtis with detachments from the 3rd and 117th New York. This force, along with the two hundred men Curtis had originally requested, moved forward. The general ordered the detachment from the 117th New York to cut the Wilmington Road, while he pushed on to the fort's outer works.[11]

Lamb and Whiting watched the advance of Curtis' troops in the twilight, which when combined with the naval fire against the landside wall and the disruption of the telegraph lines out of the fort, had every appearance of an infantry assault on the position. It was a crucial moment for Colonel Lamb and General Whiting, the latter of whom had arrived in an advisory role on the twenty-fourth. With every appearance of a Union infantry assault massing against the landside wall Lamb called out the garrison to man the defenses. With exploding rounds going off within the parade ground and along the sloped earth walls, and the flashes from air-bursts raining high-speed pieces of jagged metal that now littered the fort, it proved difficult to get some of the garrison to grab their arms and leave their shelters.

Major General Benjamin Butler, left, commander of the 6,500 Union troops detailed for the capture of Fort Fisher. Rear Admiral David Porter, right, commander of the Union fleet. What would start as a friendly professional relationship between the two officers would soon devolve into accusations and counter-accusations regarding their conduct before Fort Fisher. (*Library of Congress*)

"It was difficult at first under the furious fire to get the Junior Reserves out of the galleries," Whiting wrote of the moment, but the general quickly noted, "They soon recovered." Midshipman Cary saw the matter slightly differently, writing that the Junior Reserves,

> composed of decrepit old men and young boys, without experience of service, and wholly unfit for the field, it was somewhat of a task to dislodge them from the rat-hole where they had sheltered in security while the two days' cannonade had thundered overhead. But by dint of scolding and swearing on the part of the officers of the staff, and an occasional use of the flat of the sabre, the unhappy creatures were finally marshalled out on the parapet where they made a show of numbers, and so helped out the gallant soldiers of the regular garrison.[12]

As Lamb raced over from the Armstrong battery, Major James Reilly with his battalion of the 10th North Carolina Artillery, who had been manning their cannon along the wall throughout the day, surged forward with the reserves in a wave of cheers and shouts "over the parapet and through the sally-port and man the line of palisades." A pair of field guns were dragged out onto the redoubt in the center of the line, and as much of the wooden wall had been unharmed by the bombardment, the defenders had secured a strong position against any Union advance.

At nightfall the naval guns fell silent and Curtis noticed an increase in grapeshot and musketry as he established his new position a few hundred yards from the palisades. Here he and his troops would stay until recalled a few hours later. The detachment of the 117th New York proved far more successful when they surprised a battalion of North Carolina Junior Reserves. Made up of young boys and a handful of old men, the unit's commander and Colonel Rufus Daggett of the 117th New York quickly came to terms and fortunately no shots were fired. The Junior Reserves were allowed to keep their arms in a gesture of good will and were peacefully marched away as prisoners.[13]

Most of Weitzel's troops were extracted from the beachhead that evening as rumors of the arrival of General Hoke's division at Wilmington circulated throughout the army. Unmolested by the Confederates, the remaining troops spent a rainy evening at the landing zone under the watchful eye of Captain Glisson's gunboats. Poor weather hampered the operation and it was not until the afternoon of December 27 that the last of the Union troops had been evacuated.

It turned out that the rumors were true and confirmed by several Confederate prisoners who belonged to Hoke's division. This only cemented Butler's opinion that the fort could only be taken via a regular siege, something his army was not equipped to do. As such, he informed Porter that he was calling off the operation and returning with his troops to Hampton Roads.

Porter, and many senior officers within the expedition, were stunned by the decision. The admiral pleaded with Butler to reconsider, pointing out that he could conduct rapid-fire operations on the fort, keeping the garrison under cover until the attacking columns were a few dozen yards from the walls, but it did nothing to alter Butler's opinion. The transports departed the next day as did much of Porter's fleet. The admiral departed as well, anxious to return to Hampton Roads. He had already forwarded a message to General Grant and wished to speak in person with him about a second attack on Fort Fisher.[14]

For Lamb, Whiting, and the defenders of Fort Fisher it was an impressive victory. Colonel Lamb's fort had been tested and the great

sandcastle had held. After one of the most intense naval bombard-
ments seen during the war, Fort Fisher was serviceable and still quite
capable of defending itself. The earthworks aside, it had come down
to the men who mounted the parapets of the landside wall under
shellfire, and to the army and naval artillery detachments as well as
acts of heroism from all corners. "I cannot speak too highly of the
coolness and gallantry of my command," Lamb wrote in his official
report.

> In the fierce bombardment of twelve hours by the heaviest armed
> fleet that ever floated on the seas not one-gun detachment was driven
> from their piece. The last gun on both days was fired by Fort Fisher.
> The battalion of the Thirty-sixth North Carolina Regiment that had
> helped to erect the works fought with a determination never to allow
> the enemy to take them, and the gallant officers and men representing
> the other artillery organizations of the Old North State Tenth North
> Carolina Regiment, First, Third, and Thirteenth Battalions North
> Carolina Artillery equaled in bravery and heroism their comrades of
> the Thirty-sixth.[15]

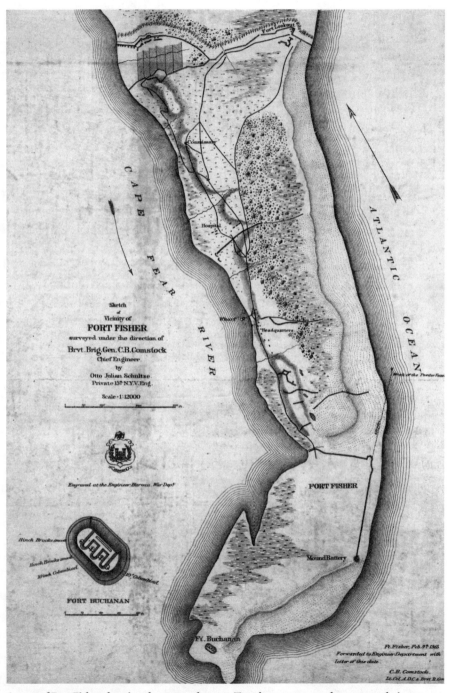

A map of Fort Fisher showing the entrenchments Terry's troops erected to protect their rear during the assault on the fortress and the terrain before the landside wall of the fort. (*Library of Congress*)

TWENTY

The Armada Returns

PORTER WOULD INDEED HAVE HIS MEETING with Grant, where he quickly leveled a series of accusations at Butler and Weitzel. There was a good deal of truth in Porter's argument that, had the two commanders acted with the courage of Lt. Walling, who had seized Fort Fisher's fallen flag, the Union would now be in possession of the defenses of Wilmington, and Lee would have lost his last lifeline. Grant agreed with Porter's assessment. In the end the issue was not whether the attack on the fort was called off. If General Weitzel was correct and the naval bombardment had not achieved its objectives, why was the problem not corrected and a second effort made? In fact, while Weitzel supported Butler's decision to call off the attack, he was surprised when Butler followed this by abandoning the entire expedition.

Grant also understood Admiral Porter's point that the fleet could not be kept together indefinitely, and while it was together another attack should be made. Grant, who approved of Porter's aggressive approach toward the matter, had already made up his mind that Butler was not the man for the task. The general had already decided to dismiss Butler from service and appoint General Edward Ord in his place as commander of the Army of the James. As for Fort Fisher,

Grant turned to Major General Alfred Terry to command the expedition. Terry was currently a division commander in the Army of the James. He was a seasoned Connecticut officer who had been involved in operations around Charleston and whose troops were involved in the capture of Fort Wagner in 1863. When Grant wrote Terry informing him of his appointment, he urged Terry to consult freely with Porter saying that, "I have served with Admiral Porter, and know that you can rely on his judgment and his nerve to undertake what he proposes." He then made clear to Terry that, once a foothold had been established on the peninsula, "the siege of Fort Fisher will not be abandoned until its reduction is accomplished or another plan of campaign is ordered from these headquarters." To ensure the success of the expedition a division of troops under General Sheridan had been ordered to Baltimore and placed upon transports. These troops would sail to Fort Monroe and wait there to be called upon by Terry if he required their service.[1]

The troops employed in the previous effort were refit and resupplied. They were also augmented by an infantry brigade and a siege train consisting of four hundred-pound Parrott rifles, twenty Coehorn mortars, twenty thirty-pound Parrott rifles, five hundred artillerymen, and a company of engineers complete with tools and transportation. In all, it gave Terry close to nine thousand men at his disposal not counting the division sent by Sheridan waiting on Terry's orders.

Terry's force departed Fort Monroe and rendezvoused with Porter's fleet near Beaufort on January 8, 1865. The initial meeting between the general and Admiral Porter did not go as well as might have been expected. Terry, a long-time division commander under Butler, came across as cold and stiff. Porter suggested that, with a storm coming, he should take his transports into Beaufort to ride out the weather, but the general declined and elected to ride out the winter tempest with the fleet.

The next meeting went far better and soon the two professional soldiers began to see eye-to-eye on the expedition. The general soon found an admirer in Porter. Unlike Butler, who required a large staff and seemed to insist on every pomp and formality that came with his position, "Terry had no staff, wore no spurs, and we do not think he owned a sword," the admiral would later say of him. "He had a well-formed head, full of sense, which served him in lieu of feathers, sword, boots, spurs and staff—of which a General can have too many."[2]

It was agreed to first land the troops at the previous location. Once the troops were ashore the navy would start the bombardment of the fort. Weather delayed the expedition's departure from Beaufort, but by 4 a.m. on January 13 a line of Union gunboats was arrayed before the landing area. Two hundred yards behind this arched line sat Terry's transports. At 7:30, while scouts were reporting back that the beach and inland areas were deserted, Porter's ironclads, the *New Ironsides*, the monitors *Saugus*, *Canonicus*, *Monadnock*, and *Mahopac* steamed into their familiar

General Alfred Terry. Appointed by Grant to replace Butler in a second effort against Fort Fisher, the initial meeting between Terry and Admiral Porter showed signs of concern, but the two men quickly aligned their views and orchestrated the downfall of the Confederate stronghold. (*Library of Congress*)

positions about a thousand yards from the landside wall of the fort. Fort Fisher's guns greeted the armored vessels, which returned fire in a methodical fashion.

Terry's men went ashore around 8 a.m. without incident. Two hundred naval boats shuttled the men and supplies ashore while Porter's ironclads lobbed eleven-inch and fifteen-inch rounds at the landside wall of the fort. Later in the day the large wooden frigates *Minnesota*, *Wabash*, and *Colorado* joined in on the bombardment firing their broadsides in rapid volleys until sunset. One Confederate naval officer watched the bombardment from Fort Buchanan. The smell of sulfur clung to everything and the shells were exploding so fast, he wrote his cousin, "that it would seem to be but one roaring sound and the sand and water rising in great clouds so that you could not see in ten feet in any direction."[3]

By that evening eight thousand Union troops were ashore along with supplies for a week, and the next day the expedition's guns were to be landed. Terry's original plan was to build a line of earth entrenchments across the peninsula to protect his troops from being attacked from behind. The matter now seemed even more important when prisoners reported that Hoke's division was still in the area. The first idea for the earthworks stretched from the head of Myrtle Bay, which would cover part of the line, to the Cape Fear River, but upon examination it proved that the shallow waters of the bay were no obstacle to attacking troops. The line was then moved farther south to take advantage of a small pond that would cover a portion of the line, but Terry soon dismissed both positions and the army marched to within two miles of the fort and built their entrenchments there, where the peninsula was about a mile across and where the naval gunships could dominate the terrain before the works.[4]

It had proven to be a particularly bad Friday the thirteenth for Colonel Lamb and his men. The colonel had been pleased with the fort and his garrison's performance during the Union attack on Christmas Eve and Christmas Day. The stronghold, later to be called the "Malakoff of the South," in reference to the Russian earth fort which had withstood a combined Franco-British naval bombardment in the Crimean War, had proven to be robust, and although he had lost seven guns in the attack, half of these were returned to service almost immediately. Even his casualties were low, given the intensity of the attack, with eleven killed in the assault and another fifty-six wounded.

Both he and General Whiting had asked for more men and materials, suspecting that the Union armada might return. Their superior, General Braxton Bragg, who had a reputation for poor decisions and indecisiveness, was too delighted by the Union repulse to be interested in the fort's requests. Richmond proved to be of a similar mind, pointing out that even if they had wanted to, there were no units to send to Cape Fear. Even the ammunition expended in defending the fort during the last attack could not be replaced. It was clear that the last lifeline to the Army of Northern Virginia would have to stand on its own resources.

Lamb's lookouts notified him of the Union armada's return on the night of January 12. The alarm was sounded and Lamb's 36th North Carolina, some seven hundred strong, dashed to their stations. "Sunrise the next morning revealed to us the most formidable armada the world has ever known, supplemented by transports carrying about

8,500 troops," the colonel would later write. The Union began landing troops right away as Porter's ironclads moved toward the fort and "suddenly that long line of floating fortresses rained shot and shell, upon fort and beach and wooded hills, causing the very earth and sea to tremble." Major William Saunders, in charge of the artillery in the fort, saw the Union fire as more deliberate in pace, and as it only targeted the landside wall of the fortress, he was soon convinced that their aim was to disable the Confederate guns along this wall and destroy the wooden palisade on the counterscarp of the ditch as a prelude to an infantry attack. His gunners responded slowly through the day and claimed to have hit the Union ironclads several times but with no effect.[5]

In fact, the guns of Fort Fisher had struck the monitor *Canonicus* thirty-six times that afternoon, including a ten-inch shell that burst on the turret knocking down most of the gun crew inside. Although their fire did very little damage to the Union warship, the ironclad's captain, Lt. Commander George Belknap, was impressed with the enemy gunners and noted on one occasion that two of the three shots fired simultaneously at the monitor struck the vessel's side armor below the turret. The *Monadnock* reported being hit several times with nothing in the way of damage being done, and the *Saugus* was struck several times, once in the pilot house, but remained fully operational. Onboard the monitor *Mahopac* near disaster took hold when the second fifteen-inch gun in the two-gun turret exploded a few feet from the muzzle. While the gun was destroyed, fortunately the blast occurred outside the turret, limiting the damage and preventing any serious injuries. If the gun had come apart near the breech it would have killed everyone in the turret and taken the monitor out of action. Instead, the *Mahopac* spent the rest of the day firing at the fort with its remaining gun.

As air bursts created shifting patterns above the fort and explosive rounds hurled earth and sand skyward, Lamb who was positioned on the Pulpit was suddenly surprised by a group of visitors. Standing before him was General Whiting and his staff, all of whom had walked to the fort from Fort Buchanan in the midst of the shelling. Lamb was stunned by their appearance, but Whiting dismissed the odd circumstances of his arrival with a wave of the hand and, placing a hand on Lamb's shoulder, told him,

"Lamb, my boy, I have come to share your fate. You and your garrison are to be sacrificed." I replied: "Don't say so, General; we shall certainly whip the enemy again." He then told me that when he left Wilmington, General Bragg was hastily removing his stores and ammunition, and was looking for a place to fall back upon. I offered him the command, although he came unarmed and without orders; but he refused, saying he would counsel with me, but would leave me to conduct the defense.[6]

When the Union gunfire fell silent after sunset, a portion of the garrison moved forward and manned the palisade lines. Saunders dragged half a dozen light guns forward and from the central redoubt and other locations along the line, he spent the evening occasionally firing a load of grapeshot into the dark to discourage any Union advance. Thus far the fort had withstood the pounding, but as noted by Whiting, Saunders, and Lamb among others, this time the concentrated naval bombardment had already led to mounting casualties.

Lamb's men returned to the fort before sunrise and were happy to see that seven hundred reinforcements had arrived. Most were from the 14th and 10th North Carolina with the rest being small detachments from the nearby garrisons as well as a detachment of Confederate marines and sailors to man some of the fort's heavy guns. Whatever greetings and reunions that occurred from this event were cut short as Porter's ships reformed before the stronghold not long after and, at first light, continued the bombardment focusing on the landside wall once again. Soon strings of explosions appeared along the length of the wall and smoke from clusters of air bursts mixed with the rising dust to create a haze over the fort. Subjected to this galling fire the fort's guns responded as best they could, but the majority of the wooden vessels were just out of range, and although the nearby monitors were much easier targets, repeated hits on the armored craft accomplished little.

To the north, Terry spent the fourteenth bringing his guns and additional supplies ashore. Paine's division supported by Abbott's brigade continued the northern entrenchments and by 8 a.m. they had erected a defensible line from the river to the sea. Not long after, Terry ordered General Curtis' brigade forward, and led by a wave of skirmishers, they slowly made their way toward the fort which was

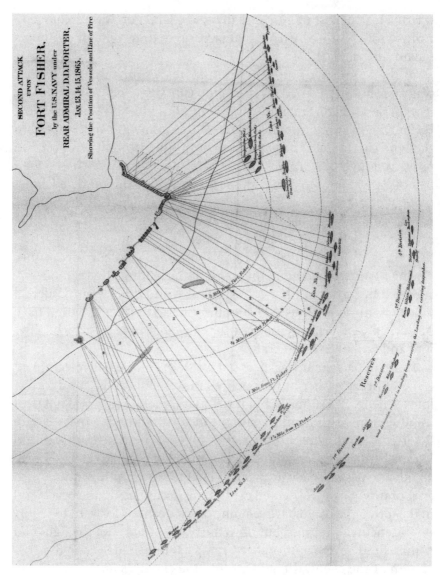

The second bombardment of Fort Fisher, January 13-15, 1865. (*Library of Congress*)

being battered by Porter's fleet. A hillock on the western side of the fort, alongside the road from Wilmington, partially obscured the troops from the Confederates, but nonetheless, a handful of shells were fired at Curtis's men. These shots, however, came at a price. "It was at a fearful cost of limb and life that a land gun was discharged," Lamb wrote, "for to fire from that face was to draw upon the gunners the fury of the fleet."[7]

At the moment, of more concern to Terry's men was the former commerce raider turned gunboat, the *Chickamauga*. With much of its experienced crew manning the naval guns at Fort Fisher and Fort Buchanan, the undermanned Confederate gunboat had managed to shell the Union lines throughout the morning from the river. It had proven enough of a problem that a battery was hurriedly raised for a pair of Parrott guns to deal with the threat. Before this occurred, however, an odd event took both sides by surprise. The Union columns had already moved past the wharf at Craig's landing, which was the routine water landing for the fort, when around one o'clock participants on both sides watched as a flat-bottomed Confederate steamer towing a barge glided up to the wharf at the landing. It was soon surrounded by scores of blue-coated soldiers and quickly surrendered. Loaded with munitions and supplies for Fort Fisher it would have proven an easy prize were it not for the *Chickamauga*, which "fired into and sank the stupid craft."[8]

Lamb in particular was incensed by the event. He had telegraphed General Bragg earlier of the enemy's movements and a need for reinforcements and supplies, but it was as if General Bragg was not paying attention. "This incident gave me the first intimation that we were deserted," Lamb later wrote on the subject. There is some merit to Lamb's frustrations, and the event is certainly puzzling. General Bragg could have passed safely from Sugar Loaf toward Smithfield and, with a set of field glasses, observed everything occurring on the beach and in the fort, or he could have sent one of his steamers forward to report on the enemy's progress; but now, thirty-six hours after the fight had commenced, several hours after Craig's Landing had been in the possession of the enemy, Bragg sent into the enemy 's lines a vessel full of sorely needed stores, which at night could have gone to Battery Buchanan in safety.[9]

With the bulk of his brigade moving along the riverside of the peninsula Curtis seized a partially completed redoubt on the north edge of a rise eight hundred yards from where the Wilmington road entered the fort. From here he arranged a skirmish line across the peninsula, and then with Terry and Chief Engineer lt. colonel Cyrus

Comstock, he conducted a reconnaissance of the fort. Advancing to within six hundred yards of the structure, the scouting party was not fired upon as the steady rain of shot and shell from the fleet occupied the defenders. The effect of the gunfire could be seen along the length of the wall. Covered in sod and marsh grass to help protect the earthwork from the elements, much of this overcoating was gone and replaced by huge pockmarks. In some places even the slope of the traverses was being altered through explosive erosion. Even so, Comstock was impressed with the strength of the works, noting that even after the beating "all damage done to the earth-work can be readily repaired." The engineer counted nine guns along the length of the battered wall. More importantly, the wooden palisade fifty feet in front of the works was badly damaged by the barrage, being completely obliterated in several places.

Comstock questioned whether or not there was enough ammunition with the siege train to actually form a breech in the wall, which effectively ruled out a traditional siege. Instead Terry, Curtis, and Comstock agreed that an infantry assault was in order. That is, they would attempt to take the strongest fortification in North America by storm. With the naval bombardment on the wall in place, the three believed that an attacking force could get within two hundred yards of the wall before encountering any serious resistance. Thus, the charge would be from here once the barrage was lifted. In addition, the attack would be aimed at the western end of the wall where the road entered the fortress. By capturing the traverse and gun positions at the western edge the attacking forces could move along the length of the wall while taking the gun positions from behind at the same time.

While Comstock had been correct about the earthworks being easily repaired, that assumed that the naval gunfire would end at sunset. It did not. Terry and Porter had met and agreed to launch an attack at 2 p.m. the next day. The army forces would attack the western edge of the land wall while a naval and marine brigade would make an attempt to seize the northeast bastion by attacking along the shoreline. This time the naval barrage would not stop when the attack went forward but instead would shift to targets on the seaside wall, which might attempt to reinforce the rest of the fort.[10]

With the nonstop bombardment, Lamb and his garrison could not repair the earthworks, nor was the situation any better regarding the guns. Only five cannons remained operational on the landside wall. Just as importantly, his casualties were mounting, coming close to two hundred after the two days of shelling. He had Whiting cable Bragg, pleading with him to attack from the north that evening with Hoke's men while the garrison sallied out in support. Although Bragg had not responded to the telegraph, it seemed clear to both Lamb and Whiting that, from his elevated position at Sugar Loaf, he had to be aware of the situation, and as such, "could not fail to respond." At nightfall the two officers gathered together ten companies and advanced out of the fort and over the shattered palisades. Skirmishers traded shots with Union pickets, but with no sign of Bragg's attack, Lamb and his men slipped back into the fort a few hours later, occasionally shaken and covered with dirt from the nearby exploding rounds.

A little after nine o'clock on the morning of January 15 Porter's wooden warships moved into position and added their weight of metal to the frenzy. The pace of fire was quicker than the previous day. At times the hills and earth seemed to boil from the repeated salvos, shaking the garrison with an odd tempo of concussions from the impacts and occasionally startling the denizens of the bombproofs when several concussions arrived at the same time. It was now only a question of when for Lamb and the garrison. The Union ironclads in particular were purposely aiming for the Confederate guns and, given that they had been anchored in place for two days, they were able "to obtain and keep a very perfect range." The results were telling and by noon only a single gun remained operational along the landside wall. A handful of pieces still fired along the seawall, but it was to little effect, and more often than not it brought a rapid and concentrated firestorm in response.[11]

Terry met with Curtis around noon to discuss the brigadier's plan to attack the fort. Curtis and his men had been busy throughout the night digging rows of rifle pits a few hundred yards from the enemy works. His plan was to advance in line, moving from one set of rifle pits to another, until finally making a dash from the last line toward the western edge of the wall with all four of the New York regiments in his brigade. Colonel Galusha Pennypacker's second brigade would follow shortly thereafter to either support or exploit the effort, and behind them would be Colonel Louis Bell's brigade.

Along the shoreline six hundred yards from the northeast bastion several hundred sailors and marines toiled away with shovels and picks throughout the early afternoon. They were the advanced guard of Lt. Commander Kidder Breese's naval task force which consisted of 1,600 sailors and 400 US Marines drawn from the fleet. Like Curtis, Breese's advance guard erected a main breastwork and then constructed a line of rifle pits to within three hundred yards of the fort. Breese had decided that the marines would hold the rifle pits and provide covering fire, in part because they had carbines and a few rifles, while the majority of the naval troops were armed with only pistols and swords. The 1,600 or so sailors in his command had been divided up into three detachments and would advance through the Marine Corps line, before dashing forward to mount the fort's walls.

A few hours before the attack was to commence Curtis spoke with a naval lieutenant about his plans for the upcoming engagement. "I told him of the plans for a gradual approach, and that the final rush would be made when the garrison remained on the parapet, at which time the column on the beach should also start," the brigadier later wrote. He then thanked the naval officer for the zeal his service was showing toward the task at hand but warned him "That I did not approve of the formation the Navy seemed inclined to make, and feared the result would not be satisfactory." The lieutenant appeared to take an affront to the comment, so Curtis clarified his remarks. "Your men are too compactly formed—your front is too narrow for the depth of your column. To go into action as your men are now formed," he pointed out, "places you under a great disadvantage. You should hold back your main body until your advanced line gets a foothold on the fort." While he admired the effort, and even pointed out that it would split the garrison, which would be of great help, the brigadier hesitated "to commend it when I think of the heavy loss they must sustain in making it in the formation you have adopted." The officer left unconvinced, promising the brigadier that the navy would do its part in the upcoming engagement with or without the approval of the army.[12]

Covered by a detachment of sharpshooters, a company of which was recently armed with repeating rifles, around 2 p.m. Curtis ordered his men forward in small waves to limit the troops' exposure to fire from the fort. After three small advances through the lines of rifle pits the brigade was ready, having suffered almost no casualties. The same could not be said for the garrison which during each advance came to the parapet in the midst of the naval bombardment prepared to repel an infantry attack, only to dash back to the bombproofs when Curtis' men halted in their rifle pits. When the Union forces had arrived close enough that the garrison stayed on the parapets, Curtis signaled he was ready to commence the attack. The message was relayed to the fleet and a little after three o'clock the vessels' fire was shifted toward the seaward wall.

Curtis stood at the center of the final line of rifle pits and, with a sword in one hand and a revolver in the other, began advancing on the fort and motioning his men forward. The naval bombardment had devastated large portions of the wooden palisade, but damaged sections on the western end or river side of the fort still posed an obstacle. As such, a hundred axes had been issued to the brigade, which, used in a furious fashion, hacked holes through the fence for the advancing New Yorkers. The Confederate troops on the gun platform between the first and second traverse fired furiously at the wave of blue-coated soldiers running toward them with fixed bayonets. The cannons had been previously disabled, and the defenders could only manage to get off a few shots before the attackers were leaping over the parapets. The call went out to explode the torpedo field, but it failed, the wires having been destroyed by the naval bombardment.

Numbers quickly told and suddenly there was a US flag flying over the second traverse compliments of the 117th New York. With more troops arriving Curtis and his men quickly enveloped the first traverse and captured the Confederate detachment and gun crew guarding the gate barring the road. This opened the road by which some of Pennypacker's second brigade, which was now advancing, entered the fort. The rest of the brigade, like Curtis's men, were moving through the openings in the palisades. Soon a US Flag could be seen flying over the first and second traverses, as now reinforced by the Pennsylvania and New York troops in Colonel Pennypacker's brigade, Curtis led a charge on the third traverse.[13]

At 2:30 p.m. Lamb was returning to the pulpit from another battery when one of the lookouts called out that the enemy was advancing. The colonel raced to the landside wall and ordered the entire

Three of General Adelbert Ames' 2nd Division brigade commanders. Left to right, Brigadier General Newton M. Curtis, 1st Brigade, Colonel Galusha Pennypacker, 2nd Brigade, and Colonel Louis Bell, 3rd Brigade. Both Curtis and Pennypacker would be wounded in the attack on the wall while Bell was killed on the causeway leading into the fort on the river side. In addition, Curtis and Pennypacker were both later awarded the Congressional Medal of Honor. (*Library of Congress*)

garrison to the parapets as artillery rounds from the Union Navy still burst around them. He gave Major Reilly an additional 250 men and placed him in charge on the left of the wall, while he kept the bulk, another five hundred, to deal with an emerging threat to the northeast bastion. Lamb asked Whiting to send one last request to Bragg for him to attack, before ordering a pair of South Carolina regiments that had been landed earlier at Fort Buchanan, and had just arrived after dashing through the barrage, to march to Reilly's aid. Suddenly the naval guns fell silent and were replaced by steam whistles from the fleet. "It was a soul stirring signal both to besiegers and besieged," Lamb noted, as it was clear to all that the moment had come.

The Union naval brigade was lying prone a few hundred yards behind the advanced rifle pits held by a detachment of marines when the signal to attack came. Breese ordered the first detachment to advance along the edge of the beach past the shattered palisade and then turn for an assault on the bastion. The second and third detachments would follow close behind while the marines fired on the parapets and then joined the assault once the naval units cleared their skirmish line. The matter went badly from the start. The first detachment marched into position under the fire of a few light field guns, a few small mortars, and the last working cannon on the landside wall, an eight-inch columbiad. As this force reached the wooden palisade it stopped and began to move along the north side of this barrier until open gaps from the naval bombardment could be found. As the men pushed through these ragged openings to form up for an assault against the bastion, the second and third detachments arrived. The result was what General Curtis had feared, as the now-compact columns of men emerged before the fort's walls which were lined with five hundred Confederate troops.

At fifty yards Lamb gave the order to fire and a murderous volley poured down upon the mass of sailors. The blast of a small field gun carved a hole out of the formation with a cloud of grapeshot. The column filled in and surged forward, but another volley, and a second wave of grapeshot, collapsed the formation sending it reeling backward. "The men fell like ten-pins along our line," one witness recalled. Lt. Colonel Nathan Johnson of the 115th New York, which was to advance against the landside wall, watched the disaster unfold. "We were about to charge when we saw the Marines advancing on the fort with pistols and cutlasses from the east," Johnson wrote a friend. "Great Caesar's ghost! Didn't we look with some amazement at such a performance. Pistols and cutlasses to storm the strongest work in America with!"[14]

After a headlong flight for cover, some of the naval troops were rallied and led back to the palisades, but the attack soon broke down into futile charges by small clusters of men as the bulk of the force found itself pinned down along the palisade and dunes in front of the fort. Here the shattered detachment, having suffered almost four hundred casualties in the span of half an hour, would lay until finally withdrawing after dark.[15]

The Confederate garrison was understandably too occupied to notice the faint sounds of gunshots coming from the north, or the puffs of smoke on the northern side of the Union breastwork occupied by General Paine's division of black troops. Bragg had finally committed to following Whiting's advice and ordered Hoke to move forward against the Union lines around four o'clock. Hoke's skirmish line moved forward and overran a few of Paine's outposts, but the attack never translated into anything more than being just a diversion. It seems that this was due in part to Bragg believing that the Union fleet resuming fire after the infantry assault had been launched meant that the attack had been repulsed.

The advance of the Naval Brigade at Fort Fisher, January 15, 1865. (*NHHC*)

A thunderous cheer went up from Lamb's men when the Union naval column broke and sought cover. It was certainly loud enough to be heard over the gunfire, but it also proved a premature celebration as Lamb and a number of officers about him quickly caught sight of the pair of U.S. flags flying from the western end of the line. General Whiting, who had been stationed in the center of the wall, had been the first to notice the Union foothold, and after gathering up what men he could lay his hands on, he launched a counterattack that left him gravely wounded and an ongoing melee swirling around the third traverse.

Muskets and pistols flashed on the battlements, and around the traverse the contest had devolved into one of sabers and bayonets. Both sides rushed what men they could to the scene as hand grenades flashed, briefly illuminating the heights. Lamb was informed that the South Carolina troops had refused to march when he ordered them to support Major Reilly and that the latter had already committed his reserves to the action. There was also news that more Union troops were arriving and that General Whiting had been carried off the field gravely wounded.[16]

Lamb sent all the men he could to recapture the traverse as Colonel Pennypacker's arriving brigade charged up the incline. What ensued next according to one officer in the 97th Pennsylvania was "a hand-to-hand conflict, which, for desperation and determination, has not been surpassed since this war began." The fighting swayed back and forth as darkness set in. The Confederates threw hand grenades down the slopes against the attackers who seemed to appear endlessly out of the darkness. The Union troops responded in kind and burst over the parapets only to be pushed back with cold steel before returning again moments later. Colonel Pennypacker, bearing one of the regimental standards, fell badly wounded in one of the early charges on this traverse, and Colonel John Moore of the 203rd Pennsylvania was mortally wounded not long after leading his men forward against the position.

The strength of numbers eventually overwhelmed the defenders who, upon retreating to the fourth traverse, encountered Lamb and a number of his men rushing forward. The influx of men allowed the colonel to push the Union troops back from the fourth traverse and to recapture the gun platform just before sundown, but it was a temporary victory. The third Union brigade led by Colonel Louis Bell had appeared, and another under Colonel Joseph Abbott was arriving on the scene. The naval gunfire had also resumed, scattering death and chaos among friend and foe alike as both sides pushed at each other for possession of the wall.

Lamb raced to the seawall and ordered what guns that could be brought to bear to fire on the Union columns that were now entering the interior of the fort via the Wilmington Road. A few guns responded and with one hundred men the colonel had gathered from the gun crews along the seaside wall he returned to the landside wall and found that his men had been pushed off the parapets. Viewing the massed Union columns in the interior of the fort as the primary threat, Lamb ordered a bayonet charge, but he had no more than lifted his sword and yelled "Forward!" when a musket ball struck him in the hip bringing him to his knees.

After days of bombardment and several hours of a bitter close-range infantry engagement, it was too much to ask of the defenders. The volley that wounded Lamb was not particularly well aimed, but it was of sufficient size to break the last major cluster of Confederate resistance in the fort. Reilly took command and, having convinced the South Carolinian troops to follow him, he managed to stem the Union tide for a time, but by eight o'clock it was coming to an end.

The ammunition was exhausted and a fourth Union brigade had arrived expelling what was left of the defenders from the landside wall. Reilly ordered Whiting and Lamb, who both insisted that they would not surrender the fort, removed to Fort Buchanan where he had ordered the remaining garrison to make a last stand.

When he arrived at Fort Buchanan, Lamb still held out hope that what was left of the garrison along with the guns of the fort could keep the attackers at bay long enough for Bragg to dispatch vessels and evacuate the cornered troops, but instead he found the guns spiked and the stronghold deserted with no vessels in sight. When the Union troops arrived a little before 10 p.m. and began encircling the beleaguered Confederates, it became clear that further resistance was senseless and General Whiting's chief of staff, Major James Hill, officially surrendered the fort and its garrison.[17]

The Second Battle of Fort Fisher was a devastating blow to the Confederacy. With Union possession of Fort Fisher and naval access to the New Inlet, the Confederate defenses of Cape Fear were doomed. Moreover, once the Union Army occupied Cape Fear and the Union Navy blockaded the Cape Fear River the principal port supplying Lee's army would be closed. With only a few months of supplies at their disposal the Army of Northern Virginia's days were numbered.

It is difficult to be critical of Lamb's defense of the fortification given his material and manpower limitations. Certainly, if he had possessed an ample supply of ammunition the Union Navy might have paid a higher price to conduct their bombardment on the first day, but even this would not have mattered much. With the more vulnerable portions of the Union fleet anchored out of range for much of the engagement, there was little for the gunners of Fort Fisher to do but occasionally launch a round at the nearby ironclads more out of frustration than any chance of success. In the end, however, it was not guns but the lack of manpower that was responsible for the loss of the fort. There had been ample opportunity to throw a large force into the fort on the night of January 13 or, as Whiting and Lamb suggested, launch a coordinated attack against the Union landing that evening which might have produced even better results. Yet neither occurred, leaving one to seriously ponder Bragg's motivations behind these decisions.

A picture of Fort Fisher after its capture showing a number of damaged cannons and gun platforms. The photograph was taken from the landside wall looking east toward the Great Redoubt and the seaside wall. (*Library of Congress*)

For Porter and Terry, the victory was a triumph of combined arms. Porter had been correct in his assessment of Butler's will to fight, but he also seems to have acted on the former general's complaints about the naval bombardment during the December attack on the fortification. All the ranking Confederate officers who witnessed the first bombardment of the fort in December immediately noticed the different approach taken in the second bombardment a few weeks later. The goal was to silence the fort's guns and a focus was put on this task, particularly on the landside works. The fleet was methodical, often selecting a particular battery for concentrated rapid fire for half an hour leaving the gun platforms and gun mounts devastated. The difference was immediately seen in the number of Confederate guns put out of action: a necessary condition for a massed infantry attack on the earthworks. The coordination between the navy and the army in managing the bombardment went much differently than the first attack, and even the use of a naval landing party, while perhaps poorly arranged, still accomplished the task of dividing Lamb's resources at a critical time.

The battle ultimately came down to Terry and the Union army. Both performed at a high level during the brief campaign. The plan was executed as designed. The western edge of the wall was captured, and just as importantly, the stockade gate barring the Wilmington Road was seized early on, which allowed Union troops to flood into the fort. The attack on the traverses and gun platforms was conducted and led with a spirit that is perhaps best characterized by the large number of casualties among the field officers and men of the four brigades involved in the attack. One officer who witnessed the attack noted that the Union brigades had struck "with the force and rush of a cyclone." A blue one that even the walls of Fort Fisher could not weather.[18]

For the Union the seizure of Fort Fisher and the closing of Cape Fear was the sign of something much greater, the South's demise. Even if little was done to press the point, at this stage their opponents would starve and run out of the means to wage war in a few months, while in that time the North would raise another two divisions of troops and launch a dozen more warships.

It had taken four years, but the long struggle was coming to a close.

A destroyed gun emplacement looking over the sandy approach from where the Union soldiers and sailors charged Fort Fisher. (*Library of Congress*)

TWENTY-ONE

The Last Days

WHILE ITS GARRISON HAD EITHER GIVEN UP or surrendered, it appeared Fort Fisher was not finished resisting. Dawn rose on January 16, 1865, with the tents and wagons of several Union regiments scattered about the fort's parade ground, interspersed with the wreckage and carnage of the previous evening's action. Campfires were lit, arms were stacked, and breakfast had been served to the haggard conquerors of Fort Fisher. The wounded had been tended to and rest was sought by most. A pair of curious Union soldiers, however, thought otherwise and looking for booty entered one of the large earthen mounds a little over a hundred yards behind the northwest bastion. Using their lamps and candles in the darkness they began rummaging around for items of interest and, at some point, carelessly detonated the fort's main magazine around eight o'-clock.

The immense explosion tore through the encampment leaving a black mushroom cloud in its wake that rained debris down upon the vicinity for almost a minute. The blast buried the three new garrison regiments in "one to ten feet of debris," and in some places more. The stunned survivors and a host of volunteers dug through earth and shattered timber in search of the fallen or, in a rare case, a buried survivor. The damage was so extensive that this effort was carried into the evening before the search was considered complete. The event resulted in over 150 men killed and several times that number wounded, with the Union army's morale included on the casualty list.[1]

Fortunately, the sight across the river for the next few days lifted their spirits. With the capture of Fort Fisher Smith Island was evacuated, as was Fort Campbell and Fort Caswell, which now no longer served a purpose. Fort Johnston was soon abandoned as well, as Bragg withdrew all Confederate troops along the west bank of the river back to Fort Anderson. The occasional explosion as the enemy detonated the forts' magazines and the drifting columns of smoke punctuated the northern flight. The long lines of wagons and men along the west shore were shadowed by the gunboat *Chickamauga* and a host of smaller vessels seeking refuge in the waters above Wilmington. A huge amount of supplies had been destroyed or abandoned, and with no means to transport them, most of the army's heavy guns had to be abandoned as well. It was a loss that the defenders could ill afford. "Thus in twenty-four hours after the fall of Fisher and its outworks," Porter informed the secretary of the navy, "all the formidable chain of forts in this river (at the entrance), built to keep out anything we had, have fallen into our hands." As the Stars and Stripes appeared over these abandoned locations it soon became clear to all involved that Wilmington's days were numbered.[2]

So too were the days of blockade running into the Cape Fear River. A number of blockade runners were initially captured, unaware that Union forces now held the cape, but most soon heard the news and, with Charleston's closure, either returned to the Bahamas or Bermuda or set sail for another neutral port. Remarkably, a few even managed to slip through and reach Wilmington, but it was a one-way trip. Union gunboats, led by Lt. Commander Cushing, soon found their way into the Cape Fear River, and after some difficulties with the "rip," Porter reinforced this detachment with several additional vessels, all but sealing Wilmington off from the sea.

With the Cape Fear Inlets lost, General Bragg had consolidated his defenses at Fort Anderson on the west bank of the river and on a line extending across Federal Point from Sugar Loaf on the east bank. Hoke's division of five thousand troops had held this latter line of entrenchments since the fall of Fort Fisher. This had given them time to perfect their rifle pits and gun emplacements, all the while "living amidst sand and dust and on un-sifted corn meal and spoiled Nassau bacon until life became almost unendurable." Across the river Brigadier General Louis Herbert commanded a garrison of about half Hoke's numbers at Fort Anderson. Many were refugees from the abandoned fortifications at Cape Fear, and almost all were short on rations and ammunition. The local militia was called out and the works around Wilmington improved with pick, shovel, and saw. A set of piles were driven into the main channel before the town, and several vessels were sunk to close the gaps in the barrier. Torpedoes were liberally placed among these works and at other points in the channel. A few were even set adrift in hopes of striking a Union block-ader downriver. These defenses aside, although approximately equal to Terry's forces in manpower, the ability of the Union gunboats, once they passed Fort Anderson, to silence every gun he had mounted along his makeshift lines on Federal Point led Bragg to express little hope that his forces could hold on to Wilmington. While perhaps true, the projection of this mood did little to help the situation even though almost all involved realized that the general was correct.[3]

While Porter's warships shelled the Confederate lines and busied themselves with clearing the river of torpedoes, "which were very thick," little else was done. Terry wished to push forward against Hoke's position, but Porter was reluctant, envisioning huge casualties from storming defensive works that the enemy had been continually improving for several months. After some debate Terry finally agreed to hold their current position and request reinforcements.

The two men would not have to wait long. In late January Grant arrived at Fort Fisher to personally speak with Porter and Terry. Here he informed the two officers that it was imperative that Wilmington be taken. In order to break the deadlock in Virginia, Grant had or-dered Sherman and his corps to proceed north through the Carolinas and rendezvous with his army in Virginia. Together they would out-flank Lee and break the stalemate. To accomplish this task, he needed a rail line from the seacoast to Goldsboro, where Sherman could be supplied along his march. Newbern was a possibility, but the railway from this location to Goldsboro had been completely destroyed while the lines from Wilmington to Goldsboro were still intact.

Grant informed Porter and Terry that to aid in this venture he had ordered Major General John M. Schofield's 23rd Corps to the area. The third division of this corps under Major General Jacob D. Cox would be sent to support Terry at Cape Fear, while the other two divisions would disembark at Newbern and join with Palmer's troops already on station. The force from Newbern would then move forward toward Goldsboro while the other, after securing Wilmington, would march north to rendezvous with it. "The object is to open communication between the sea-coast and Goldsborough by rail, so as to meet Sherman with supplies for his army and to put at his disposal an available force," Grant wrote Schofield who, because of his rank, would assume command of all operations in North Carolina.[4]

With the arrival of Schofield and the 4,500 men of Cox's division during the second week of February, plans were quickly formulated for an operation designed to outflank Hoke's position. On February 10 Terry's troops would advance and establish a new line of entrenchments closer to Hoke's men. While Terry's men were busy skirmishing with the enemy and raising their new lines Cox's division would occupy the old lines. At nightfall Cox's troops would then march along the eastern shoreline to the swampy waters of Myrtle Sound, well behind the Confederate lines. Here the navy would provide them with pontoons to build a bridge and small boats to navigate the hazard.

While risky, Schofield approved the plan, as it avoided a direct assault on either Hoke's entrenchments or Fort Anderson. Porter was surprised when Schofield informed him of the attack. The admiral was skeptical as to its possible success but pledged his fleet would do everything in its power to support the operation. Porter would prove to have reason for his doubts. For the next several days Schofield attempted to turn Hoke's flank. On the night of February 12 the operation was halted by bad weather. "We move just after sundown, the wind blowing a gale from the northeast, as searching and cold a blast as I ever felt," Cox recalled. The column pressed forward against the blowing sand, the heavy surf drowning out all sounds of their trek. While the inclement weather helped obscure the Union columns' march, it also made delivery of the pontoons impossible, forcing the troops to return to their starting positions. On the fourteenth the plan was undertaken again, but this time the wagons carrying the

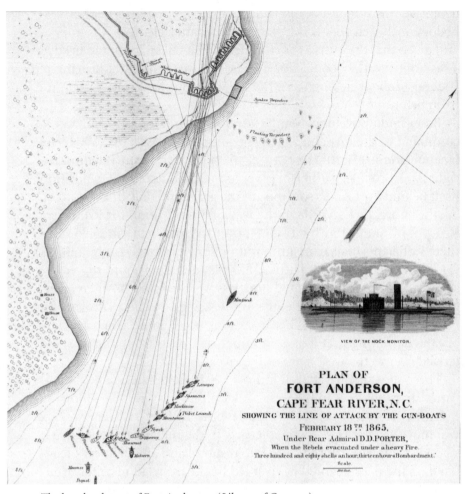

The bombardment of Fort Anderson. (*Library of Congress*)

pontoons bogged down in the sand and could not reach Myrtle
Sound in time, leading to another aborted effort.[5]

After the second failure Schofield shifted his focus to Fort Anderson. The earth fort was built along the same lines as Fort Fisher albeit
on a much smaller scale. The L-shaped structure boasted thirty-foot
tall traverses and mounted nine thirty-two-pound guns, most of
which were located on the water side. While the river was actually
several miles wide at this point the narrow main channel came to
within six hundred yards of the fort making it a particularly strong

defensive position, especially when supplemented by a field of torpedoes anchored across the passage. The latter element was important given that the guns of Fort Anderson had been mounted in such
a fashion that they could not fire upriver, meaning that if just one
Federal gunboat steamed past the stronghold it could take every gun
from behind.

Bragg had put veteran South Carolina general Johnson Hagood in
command of the fort and its badly equipped garrison of 2,300 or so.
Hagood soon realized the peril of his position. Orton Pond on his
right flank provided sufficient cover for an enemy column to position
itself behind Fort Anderson and cut the garrison's only line of retreat.
Furthermore, he had little in the way of ammunition for his thirty-
two-pound guns and his twelve-pound Whitworth rifle. Nor was
there sufficient small arms ammunition for a prolonged fight, rations
for a long siege, or even sufficient tools to improve and repair the
stronghold. While it appeared hopeless, Hagood and his men occupied their time digging rifle pits and bracing the gun platforms on
the fort with sandbags. This work was accelerated when rumors
began circulating that a large number of Union troops were being
ferried over to the west bank of the river.

These rumors proved well founded. Schofield had sent Cox's and
Ames' divisions over to the west bank on February 16. The following
morning Schofield penned a simple letter to Porter: "General Cox
will move against Fort Anderson early in the morning. Please give it
a good shelling." Porter was eager to respond and after a flurry of signal flags the fleet steamed upriver led by the ironclad monitor *Montauk*. A little after noon the flotilla dropped anchor before the fort,
just out of range of the garrison's thirty-two-pound guns. While the
fleet of fourteen wooden warships were busy positioning themselves
and setting their anchor springs the *Montauk* continued on, finally
coming to a stop and dropping anchor a thousand yards from the
fort. A few minutes later Porter raised the flag "commence firing."[6]

The action continued throughout the day at a steady but brisk pace
as the warships found their range and focused on the enemy gun emplacements. Lt. Commander Edward Stone of the *Montauk* was certain that his vessel and the gunboats behind him had disabled several
of the fort's riverside guns, but Hagood claimed that little in the way
of damage was done in the bombardment. The fort's commander also

claimed that his thirty-two-pound guns fired forty-seven solid shot at the ironclad, and while several had found their mark it had no apparent effect on the monitor. The garrison's twelve-pound Whitworth, which could reach Porter's wooden warships, fired away in sole opposition to this line, striking several vessels, until it fell silent for want of ammunition.

At dusk the fleet's fire slowed and the vessels moved off for the night. After resupplying that evening, the next morning the flotilla returned in force. By early morning the fort had become engulfed in a billowing cloud of dust and raining debris. The wooden platforms and buildings inside the parade ground disappeared in a cloud of splinters whenever a round found its mark, and the response from the fort's guns was sporadic at best, "more in defiance than in the hopes of injuring the enemy." Anchored a mere eight hundred yards from the structure the *Montauk* spent the day lobbing 350-pound explosive rounds at the stronghold, acting almost as a bass for the chorus of nine-inch and eleven-inch shells guns and the rhythm of rifled cannons from 30 to 150 pounds in size. It was a one-sided affair. Over 2,700 shells were thrown at the fort "Nearly all of which," Hagood noted, "struck the work or exploded within it." At sunset Porter's fleet stayed in position, spending the night harassing the fort and its defenders with the occasional outburst.[7]

The fort itself was badly damaged but nothing that work crews couldn't repair over the course of the evening. The guns, although of little use, were still functional, and the casualties had been light particularly given that "not a man of the garrison took shelter in the bombproof." While Hagood was satisfied with how his fort had stood before the Union bombardment, more pressing issues were coming to the forefront. The Union troops had split into two large groups at White Spring Branch. The first group pressed on Hagood's skirmishers along the waterside road to the fort and eventually drove them back to the shelter of the rifle pits in front of the fort. On the Confederate right, along the west side of Orton Pond, matters were quickly deteriorating. The second Union force had launched an attack on the Confederate line here and pushed it back to within a few miles of the Wilmington Road at the head of Orton Pond. Hagood rushed the handful of reinforcements at his disposal to the area, but it was a fluid situation and by the early hours of February 19 it appeared that

Fort Anderson was on the verge of being enveloped. "The enemy are on my right and rear," he telegraphed General Hoke who had taken command with Bragg's departure for Richmond, and "I have a very much larger force than my own 600 yards in my front, in full view by daylight, and with the fleet to co-operate. Therefore, when the force on my right rear moves, I must abandon this position, or sacrifice my command."[8]

After a few questions, Hoke gave Hagood permission to evacuate the fort, and a little before 3 a.m. the fort's commander gave the order. Given the circumstances it would not be possible to demolish the structure. The field batteries, ordnance wagons, and ambulances were all sent across Orton Canal with the infantry following close behind. The last of these movements were just underway when a little before dawn the Union infantry in front of the fort advanced, scattering and capturing a number of the Confederate pickets and climbing over the walls of the fort. These blue-clad troops arrived just in time for the first round of the morning to come whistling into the fort from Porter's fleet. The explosion was quickly followed by a white flag and then an American flag, which halted any further shelling. The retreating Confederate column was able to make good its escape by destroying the bridges behind them, but it made little difference; Fort Anderson was in Union hands and the road to Wilmington open.

At this point there was little for Hoke or the returning Bragg to do but abandon their position on the peninsula. To make matters worse there was not even the possibility of making a stand at Wilmington, as news had arrived that a division of Union troops under General Palmer had departed Newbern, which, if he came to Schofield's aid, threatened to envelope the Confederate forces. Once again, the order was given to retreat, and what was left of Bragg's command shuffled off toward Goldsboro. Union troops entered Wilmington on February 22, thereby occupying the last major position along the North Carolina coast.[9]

As for the war in North Carolina, it had but a few weeks left. Lee had ordered General Joseph Johnston, who had been operating in Tennessee, to mobilize the military resources of North Carolina and delay Sherman's advance. As part of this directive Bragg, who had retreated to Kinston, was directed to intercept an approaching Union column from Newbern that was rebuilding the railroad line. Bragg

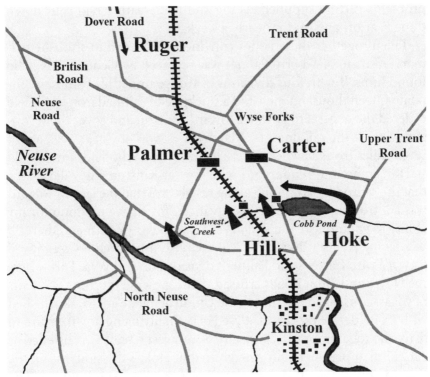

A sketch of the Battle of Southwest Creek. The limited number of crossings over the fast-flowing creek made it an ideal location for Confederate forces to contest Union efforts to reconstruct the rail line between Newbern and Kinston. (*Author*)

moved his command to a position about eight miles away on the northern side of Southwest Creek. Here he dug in and awaited General D.H. Hill, who he was informed was on the way with two thousand reinforcements.

For Schofield the capture of Wilmington did not give him the immediate supply route to Goldsboro that Grant had hoped for. Terry advanced to the Northeast Cape Fear River to find the Wilmington-Weldon railroad bridge in ruins, as was the smaller span over Smith's Creek. This, however, was not the primary headache Schofield faced. The general contacted the nearby Wilmington and Manchester Railroad Company and confiscated their equipment, but there were very few cars and engines available. While these could be shipped in, it would take time and at the moment the general himself was having problems getting supplied, as fog and bad weather had shut down Cape Fear off and on for nearly a week.

Taken together these issues convinced Schofield to shift the primary effort to Newbern. Palmer was replaced by General Cox, who found himself with four divisions of troops under his command totaling fifteen thousand men and a stockpile of railroad iron. Schofield ordered the general to advance toward Kinston and cover the reconstruction of the rail lines. By March 4 Cox was at Core Creek about seven miles from Newbern. Here he informed Schofield, who would start his march to rendezvous with Cox at Kinston a few days later, that the railroad was coming along slowly and that the lack of wagons was controlling the pace of his advance, "for I have no doubt of my ability to go into Kinston whenever I can feed my command there."[10]

Leaving Ruger's division at Core Creek, on March 6 Cox moved forward with Carter's and Palmer's divisions toward Wyse Fork where the Dover and Trent Roads crossed. The following morning elements of Claassen's brigade, acting as the Union advance guard, skirmished with Confederate pickets at Wyse Fork, finally using howitzer fire to drive the rebel troops back toward Southwest Creek. Cox listened as a handful of prisoners informed him that Hoke's division was on the north bank of the creek and that it was soon to be reinforced. The information was enough to convince Cox to bring up Palmer's division along the railroad line and Carter's division via the Dover Road. A brigade from each of these divisions supported by cavalry was pushed forward to monitor the crossings over Southwest Creek, "an unfordable stream." The resulting movements created a small amount of skirmishing and a few sporadic artillery exchanges until dark, but neither side seemed anxious to escalate the matter.

For Cox the situation seemed secure. He had a pair of brigades covering the crossings along the south bank of Southwest Creek, supported by their respective divisions encamped a mile to the rear. In addition, the general had another division in reserve a few hours' march away at Core Creek. The path before him seemed clear. He would first secure the south side of the creek crossings, select one, concentrate his forces, and capture it before continuing on with his march. At the moment, however, the slow progress of the railroad and the arrival of General Schofield the next morning seemed the most pressing issues. For General Bragg standing on the north bank of the creek the matter was even simpler. He was awaiting the arrival of D.H. Hill and the two thousand troops of his command. Without them he had no intentions of doing anything more than skirmishing.[11]

Hill's command arrived early the next morning at which point Bragg showed a different side of his character than had appeared at the siege of Fort Fisher. Shifting to the offensive, he ordered Hoke to take his division and march southwest along the length of Cobb's Mill Pond and cross at the creek at the Upper Trent Road. Hill would push on to the second crossing guarded by one of Palmer's brigades to help cover the flanking movement.

Cox was riding to Palmer's headquarters with the recently arrived Schofield when a little past midmorning the sound of gunfire to the west attracted both senior officers' attention. A messenger reached Cox not long after with a report that a large column of Confederate troops had crossed upstream above the Union left and were on the march toward the Upper Trent Road. The information was initially regarded as exaggerated and dismissed, but not long after, urgent news arrived from Carter that spoke to its authenticity. Hoke's division had crossed two miles above the Union left at the Upper Trent Road and fallen upon Colonel Charles Upham's second brigade, which was guarding the Dover Road crossing. Upham's troops had been put to flight, and the Confederates were advancing on Carter's left in large numbers.

Cox was quick to react. He sent word to Palmer for him to shift one of his brigades to the left to make contact with Carter's troops and help cover any retreat. He then ordered Ruger at Core Creek to move two brigades to Wyse Fork. Cox soon countermanded this order and directed Ruger to immediately bring his entire division up save one regiment. With this done both Cox and Schofield rode off for Carter's position with a small cavalry escort.

When the two officers arrived at Carter's headquarters, they not only found the Confederates advancing in large numbers but dispatches from Palmer saying that his brigade covering the lower creek crossing had been pushed back. With reports arriving that Hood's division and elements of Lee's army were pressing on the Union right, and Hoke's division after having severed Carter's division was advancing, Cox ordered both Carter and Palmer to fall back and "strengthen their position as rapidly as possible, on the favorable line from Wise's Forks to the railroad." A message was sent to Ruger as well directing him "to form in the space between the two other divisions," as soon as he arrived.[12]

Hoke's attack on the Union left was a complete success. Caught by surprise the 27th Massachusetts and the 15th Connecticut Regiments near the Dover Road crossing were overrun when Hoke's men suddenly burst out of the woods and dashed upon them with a yell. It was over quickly, leaving most of the shattered brigade in Hoke's hands. On Hoke's left, Hill launched his men across the creek as soon as he heard the gunfire from Hoke's column. While not a rout, the Confederate force pushed back Palmer's lead brigade. "I had nothing to do now but to press forward rapidly to the firing and intercept the foe fleeing from Hoke," Hill noted of his success, but orders soon arrived for his troops to press forward toward the intersection of the Neuse and British Roads in hopes of cutting off the enemy's retreat. There was little to find and the maneuver, for all practical purposes, removed Hill from the day's fight.

Thus far the Confederate advance had proven remarkably successful. It had netted almost nine hundred prisoners, "fresh troops from New Bern, well dressed, well fed, well armed and well liquored," one Confederate soldier noted. There were also piles of weapons and supplies, as well as a few small howitzers. The Yankees appeared to be on the run, so Hoke's men pushed forward. What they found disappointed them. The Union troops, the bulk of both Palmer's and Carter's divisions, were forming a blue line along the south side of the British Road, and their cannons were now coming into action. Hoke's troops probed the hastily erected Union position, but as the day progressed, they found the enemy both more numerous and more stubborn than they had originally thought. Disorganized from their attack, Hoke halted his men to rearrange their ranks, but by this time it was already late afternoon and orders had arrived from Bragg for both Hill and Hoke to fall back and unite their forces for another effort the next morning.

It would prove to be a missed opportunity as General Ruger marched his division into the gap between Carter and Palmer's divisions as night fell over the battlefield. While the occasional musket shot rang out it was not gunfire but the rhythm of shovel and saw that disturbed the night, or in many cases, where "no shovels and picks being on hand, knives, bayonets, tin-cups, and bare hands were used." Both sides entrenched on opposite sides of the British Road and by daylight a fortified stalemate had emerged. Bragg would continue sparring with the Union forces, and on the morning of March 10 he made one last effort to secure victory by sending Hill against the Union lines while Hoke circled around the enemy fortifications and struck the Union forces in the left flank. By now Cox was prepared for such a move, and he quickly shifted forces to diffuse the threat. "An order was given too soon to charge the enemy's line," an officer in the 66th North Carolina recalled, "and when the charge was made we found that the enemy had prepared for us with his breastworks facing both ways, and the same protected by small pines, which had been cut down, lapped over each other and their limbs trimmed and pointing in our direction." Although Hoke's men pushed their attacks with abandon, it was clear the enemy was too well entrenched, and the effort was called off.[13]

Facing superior numbers and an entrenched foe, Bragg sounded the recall and later that evening ordered a withdrawal to Kinston. It had been a costly affair with 269 killed and wounded and another 938 captured on the Union side, with Confederate casualties coming in about half the Union totals. While it could be viewed as a minor Confederate victory, in the end, Bragg had failed to stop Schofield's advance and disrupt the railroad building effort. From Kinston Bragg's forces would proceed to Goldsboro, where they would join with General Johnston's command and participate in a last-ditch attempt to halt Sherman's advance at the Battle of Bentonville. Union letters and journals speak to the desperate tenacity of the Confederate troops at the battle, but it made little difference at this point. At one time a draw or a marginal victory might have sufficed, but now even an outright victory was no longer enough. The enemy would just grow stronger, reform, and attack again a week later. After several days of fighting against superior numbers, Johnston withdrew, ending the last major engagement of the war in North Carolina.[14]

At this point nothing could stop the junction of Sherman's army with Schofield's command at Goldsboro. With a force of over a hundred thousand Union troops arrayed before the capital, Raleigh surrendered on April 12 and a few weeks later on April 26 Johnston

General William T. Sherman, left, and General Joseph E. Johnston, right. (*Library of Congress*)

surrendered his haggard command to Sherman at Bennett Place, North Carolina, officially ending the conflict in the state. Sherman had granted Johnston the same liberal terms that Grant had granted Lee; go home. Keep your arms, horses, and whatever else would be of help. It was planting season and the year had been difficult enough. It would be far worse without a crop to harvest. Go home and tend to your farms. It was over.

Johnston thanked Sherman and presented him his sword, but Sherman stopped him with a raised hand; he was to keep that too. The defeated general departed with a salute, and with the formalities over he issued one last order to his men before dismissing them. "I earnestly exhort you," he asked each of them, his pen shaking from the emotions welling inside him,

> to observe faithfully the terms agreed on and to discharge the obligations of good and peaceful citizens as well as you have performed the duties of thorough soldiers in the field. By such a course you will best secure the comfort of your families and kindred, and restore tranquility to the whole of your country.[15]

Epilogue

ONE HISTORIAN OF THE US NAVY'S ROLE in the Civil War remarked that "The conflict was so novel in its character, that
there were no precedents to consult, and no old landmarks to
guide." These words ring especially true along the coast of North Carolina. While perhaps a forgotten theater in the American Civil War,
the campaigns along the coast and interior waterways of this state offered a number of unique characteristics and challenges that would
quickly test both sides' ability to adapt to the emerging lessons of littoral warfare in the industrial age.[1]

With a naval capability in hand, the Union made the first move in
this region with the seizure of the Cape Hatteras forts early in the
conflict. It would prove to be one of the most decisive decisions made
in the theater, and a strategic blow from which the Confederate command never recovered. With the capture of Hatteras, General Burnside and Commodore Rowan seized the initiative and conducted a
systematic campaign in 1862 to secure the interior waterways of Albemarle and Pamlico Sounds. This not only helped lead to the Confederate evacuation of Norfolk but restricted Confederate movement,
dealt a severe blow to the regional economy, and placed the interior

transportation lines throughout the state in jeopardy. Working well together, the two Union commanders directed several successful large-scale landing operations and in the process demonstrated to an overstretched and ill-prepared opponent how quickly power could be concentrated and deployed through the use of combined arms and the establishment of naval superiority.

In fact, once the forts at Cape Hatteras fell and the patchwork Mosquito Fleet was eliminated, the loss of naval control over the interior waterways all but guaranteed that the Confederate hold over Pamlico and Albemarle Sounds would be fleeting. While the Confederacy repeatedly attempted to retake several of the important posts along the sounds such as Newbern, and even found success at Plymouth, the failure of the South to enact its ironclad plans for the interior waterways of North Carolina and challenge for naval control of the region, meant that no success along these lines could be permanent. The CSS *Albemarle* showed the potential of the approach, but the inability of the Confederacy to support the *Albemarle* with another ironclad froze the plan at this point and dashed any hopes of ever recovering the region.

While the South would never really develop a satisfactory solution to the threat posed by the Union beachhead along Pamlico and Albemarle Sounds, this was at least partially mitigated by the Union's failure to exploit their success in the area. This region was perhaps one of the most overlooked opportunities of the conflict. Foster's raid on Goldsboro in 1862 demonstrated the possibilities of local Union superiority, and it is surprising that such a successful raid was not repeated, particularly when one considers that, beyond marginal victories at South Mills, the first attack on Fort Fisher, South Creek, and the successful capture of Plymouth in 1864 the South lost every major engagement in the region. This includes an impressive string of six major battles in 1861 to 1862 starting with Cape Hatteras and ending with Goldsboro Bridge. It seemed clear to all involved that North Carolina and the vital railroad links that traced the state were vulnerable, but Union efforts in the area settled in on occupation and raiding as troops were slowly withdrawn to other theaters. These actions not only proved a relief to the outnumbered and beleaguered Confederate forces in the region but even allowed the South to shift over to the offensive in the spring of 1864.

Another component working in the Union's favor early in the conflict was leadership. While Burnside would later be known for his loss at Fredericksburg, there is little to criticize when it came to his actions in North Carolina and at Fort Macon, although much of this rightly belongs to General Foster who managed the battles and engagements, as well as his brigade commanders. Coupled with Commodore Rowan and his naval resources, which made quick work of its nautical opposition at Roanoke Island and Elizabeth City, the Union made few mistakes in the North Carolina sounds early on, with the sole Confederate victory at this time coming at South Mills where Colonel Rush Hawkins foolishly ordered a charge against fortified enemy lines.

The same level of leadership was not present in the Confederate forces stationed in North Carolina during this period. Generals Huger, Branch, and Wise, with the last two being political appointees, did little to improve the Confederates early chances. Huger, in particular, proved totally unsuited for the task before him, while Wise and Branch were more inexperienced than incompetent. When combined with a command and logistical system created from scratch, it proved a disastrous combination for the Southern cause in North Carolina. As the war progressed more capable Confederate commanders like Whiting, D.H. Hill, and Hoke appeared on the scene and rectified many of the leadership issues but not all, as seen with the case of General Braxton Bragg. Union leadership in the region after Burnside's and Foster's departures remained solid if unspectacular, although much of this latter element was likely the product of shifting to a defensive mindset, and the general inactivity that came with the approach.

A few dozen miles south at Cape Fear, it was the Union that made the early mistake and not the Confederacy. It took no stretch of the imagination to see that Wilmington would become a major port for the South. The natural approaches to Cape Fear, consisting of two entrances miles apart and a chain of islands and peninsulas upon which forts and defensive batteries could be erected to guard these passages, made the location exceptionally strong. Yet the same planners that seized Fort Hatteras passed on Cape Fear and settled for a resource-starved blockade to halt the vital supply of military and industrial goods into the South. While it could fairly be said that the

Union had resource issues of its own at this point, it was clear to many that the moment to attack was now, before the enemy fortified Federal Point and the various islands at the outlet of the river. Fortunately for the Confederates, such plans never materialized, and although constantly fighting for troops and supplies, both Whiting and Lamb soon erected a series of fortifications that placed any such thoughts out of mind of Union planners until the last months of the war. Thus, Wilmington remained a major Southern supply port for most of the conflict.

The coastal waters of North Carolina also offered a set of lessons in terms of executing and running a blockade at the dawn of modern naval warfare. The speed and maneuverability of the steam-powered warship was quickly demonstrated in blockade operations by the near annihilation of sailing vessels involved in the trade. On the other hand, sleek and stealthy steamships were developed to penetrate the blockade and proved successful in doing so for several years, pressing the blockaders and their limited numbers. One of the major problems on the blockader's side, however, stemmed from the advancement of cannon. In the past the limited range of guns meant that a blockading fleet could maintain a station closer to the port, increasing its chance of an encounter, and thus its efficiency. Long-range rifled guns like the British Whitworth suddenly pushed the daytime stations of the blockaders farther out to sea, essentially making the area to be patrolled larger and decreasing their chances of an encounter. These guns also meant that the morning hours, which was the favorite time for runners to enter the river, were perilous times for the blockaders and that any chase was limited by the range of the Confederate shore batteries.

This is not to say that the blockade was ineffective, in fact it did work, and like any long-term proposition, improvements were made based on the accumulated experience of the participants. While patrolling farther out to sea was of limited success, patrolling the shores north and south of Cape Fear, where the runners would typically first make landfall, did result in an increased number of captures, as did shifting to the source by patrolling near Bermuda or the Bahamas, although this last approach chanced a confrontation with the Royal Navy if not conducted with tact.

In the end, however, the effectiveness of the Cape Fear blockade was a first order function of the number of blockaders on station. It was here that the Union stumbled. For much of the early conflict only a score of vessels patrolled the Carolina coast, and often, given the difficult weather conditions and the continual battering the vessels were subject to, the numbers on station were actually far smaller. However, as the war progressed and Union industrial power began to ramp up the numbers of blockaders steadily increased, and a slow erosion of Confederate trade began to take hold. Just as importantly, the quality of Union blockaders was steadily improving as well. Learning their lessons, faster and more powerful warships were being turned out of the Northern naval yards, and when coupled with the Union Navy's policy of turning captured blockade runners into warships, it created a slow death spiral for Confederate maritime commerce.

While the logistical mechanisms, operations, and outcomes behind the various joint expeditions were providing their own set of feedback and corrections for future planners, perhaps the more recognized lessons were those that occurred at the technological level. The unique challenges posed by the North Carolina coast led to it being a testing ground for a number of emerging technologies, new weapon platforms, and even the enablement of old ideas once thought abandoned. Foremost, it was clear that this transformation of littoral warfare was primarily due to the introduction of more compact and more powerful cannon and, in particular, the employment of the steam engine. The effects of the former could be seen in a new age of rifled guns that could strike objects miles away or hurl hundreds of pounds of explosives at a target. Such guns were not only far more powerful than their predecessors that had dominated the sailing engagements of the Napoleonic Age but were lighter and faster to reload. These products of the machine age gave a simple gunboat the striking power of a field battery, and when employed in conjunction with the second technological development, the steam engine, it gave such a craft not only mastery over the interior and coastal waterways but the ability to carry large numbers of troops and deploy them quickly at selected locations.

These basic ideas in turn fostered several new weapons systems and platforms such as the ironclad, the torpedo, and the ram. The first of these is perhaps the most enduring legacy of the conflict. The introduction of armor, made possible by the advent of the steam engine, which could still propel and maneuver a vessel burdened by the weight of this protection, would revolutionize naval warfare. In the waters of coastal North Carolina this was aptly demonstrated by the CSS *Albemarle* and, to some extent, by the CSS *Raleigh*. While the South was never able to capitalize on this invention, the North did, and one aspect of this that soon emerged was the effectiveness of Union ironclad monitors in terms of naval bombardment duty. At both Fort Fisher and Fort Anderson Union monitors were able to engage the fortifications at short range with little fear of retaliation. Indeed, most of the Union ironclads engaged in this duty were struck dozens of times with no significant impact on their fighting abilities. This would change as firearms developed, but for the moment it called into question the current nature of shoreline fortifications.

In the North Carolina theater the torpedo, or mine in this case, demonstrated more of a psychological rather than actual threat on the battlefield. Very few of these crude devices proved successful, but they did serve a purpose as a force multiplier and in delaying the full potential of the Union Navy's capabilities to influence an engagement. Even so, the potential for this technology was clearly understood, and when the defenders of Wilmington launched dozens of these torpedoes downstream at once making the blockading vessels dance and weave about in response, the first indications of the power of a self-propelled torpedo must have become obvious even to the layman of the day. At Fort Fisher these torpedoes were used in what today would be considered a conventional minefield. While a logical use of the technology, the fact that the devices were not autonomous and activated by contact led to the failure of the system when the delicate wires that were used to fire the torpedoes were destroyed during the naval bombardment.

The second type of torpedo, the spar torpedo, gained far more acclaim in North Carolina waters with Cushing's daring destruction of the ironclad *Albemarle*. A number of motor torpedo boats were constructed after this and the device soon became a common fitting to wooden warships as protection against ironclads in much the same vein as magnetic mines were used as a defense against tanks; it will work, but one has to be uncomfortably close to make it happen. More than any other new technology employed in the conflict, the

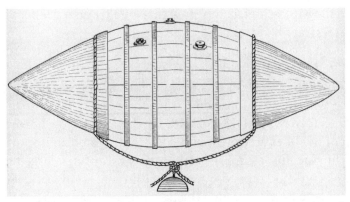

One type of torpedo employed was known as a barrel mine. The diagram shows how these mines were anchored and the plunging type detonators used to fire the device upon contact. (*NHHC*)

spar torpedo would haunt naval planners around the world for decades. This even led at one point to questioning why one would build a capitol ship when a fleet of torpedo boats could be built instead. Little did anyone know it was just the preliminary stages of the "torpedo terror."

Perhaps the oddest lesson of all was the return of the ram. It is interesting to note that the introduction of the steam engine reenabled one of the earliest naval tactics: ramming. Ramming under sail was nearly impossible, so galleys employing large amounts of manpower were used to ensure maneuverability. As cannons improved these vessels proved particularly vulnerable and soon became relegated to coastal or inland waters. Even in this role they were of questionable use given the massive casualties that would result from just a few hits from a medium-sized cannon. As a result, the idea was eventually abandoned. The steam engine, however, solved these problems. Only a handful of crewmen were required and the vessel could be navigated to the target without regard for wind or wave. Moreover, the steam engine also meant that the ramming vessel could strike the target at a high rate of speed creating catastrophic damage in one blow. When coupled with an ironclad vessel, the approach showed great promise, especially when the *Albemarle* sank the *Southfield* and then chased away the rest of the Union fleet. Combined with other results from ramming, especially in the west during the struggle for naval superiority on the Mississippi, it appeared that an old and quite deadly form of naval warfare had returned.

Mention should also be made of two other technological advances that altered the battlefield in coastal North Carolina: railroads and telegraphs. The first was not a new invention, nor was it new to military use, with some troops being transported by rail during the Mexican-American War of 1846-1848. By the late 1850s, however, the growth of rail lines across the east coast had created an important logistical lifeline. Just as importantly, it now meant that large numbers of troops could be moved quickly, within a few days or even a few hours in some cases, changing the traditional dynamic. The telegraph was also making its mark on the battlefield, allowing commanders a better understanding of the enemy and the status of their own forces. General Palmer, who defended Newbern in February 1864 from a Confederate attack, noted that moments after the attack had begun the telegraph chattered to life and "informed me of all that was going on in front."[2]

In the end the short war the South was looking for did not materialize. Nor did their hoped for French and British alliance. Instead the Confederacy found itself in an untenable situation, too weak to win but too strong to yield. It was at this point that the long-term planning and investments into the military's infrastructure came to fruition for the Union. More vessels, more material, and more men became available, further pressing the Confederacy, and more and more blockaders now traced the waters off Cape Fear and other locations along the eastern seaboard strangling the South's lifeline. The Confederate ports were isolated and shut down one by one, until the last, Wilmington, guarded by the huge earthworks of Fort Fisher, was captured on February 22, 1865, after a five-week campaign.

Admiral Porter, who was present, would later write of the moment:

> The capture of the defences of Wilmington closed the last door through which the Southern Confederacy received their supplies of clothing, arms and ammunition; therefore, when Fort Fisher fell, it was only a matter of a short time when the rebellion would collapse. No matter how brave an enemy may be, or how well commanded, he must have provisions and military stores; and at this time General Lee had not enough material of war to last him three months.[3]

The Union army at Newbern pushed inland to rendezvous with Sherman's army approaching from the south to hasten this demise, and the final desperate battles seen in all lost causes played themselves out. They simply delayed the inevitable, and within a few weeks Lee, North Carolina, and most of the Confederacy had surrendered. The long grim struggle was over.

The first major conflict of the industrial age would stun the world with a new set of horrors brought about by man's improved efficiency to destroy one another, both on land and at sea. "War at the best, is terrible," President Lincoln would remark, "and this war of ours, in its magnitude and in its duration, is one of the most terrible." A quick comparison speaks to this point. To put the conflict in a purely American scope, the number of soldiers killed in the Civil War, some 620,000, would not be surpassed by all the other American conflicts combined until the Vietnam War. And when one considers that the total number of wounded was several times the number killed, and then factors in the civilian casualties and the economic disruption that would claim yet more victims, a better appreciation emerges not only for the scale of the American Civil War but for the nature of warfare in the machine age as well.[4]

Lincoln touched on these points in his second inaugural address on March 4, 1865. With the war winding down and victory in sight, the president turned toward the future. Regardless of the struggle, regardless of the cost, the Union would be preserved. And while the future seemed uncertain and chaos and destruction lay across large portions of the nation, Lincoln spoke to this matter by beckoning one of the most powerful beliefs possessed by men—hope. "With malice toward none," he concluded his short address,

> with charity for all; with firmness in the right, as God gives us to see the right, let us strive on to finish the work we are in; to bind up the nation's wounds; to care for him who shall have borne the battle, and for his widow, and his orphan to do all which may achieve and cherish a just, and a lasting peace, among ourselves, and with all nations.[5]

Still sound advice today.

Glossary and Terms

ARMSTRONG RIFLED CANNON: In the 1850s Sir William Armstrong designed a new breech-loading rifled cannon, where the barrel was reinforced by several successive iron sleeves applied one after another on the outside of the main barrel. This laminated or banded design made the Armstrong very durable and, coupled with their breech-loading action, capable of high rates of fire. Produced in the late 1850s and early 1860s, and made in sizes ranging from 2.75-inch (six pounds) up to eight-inch (150 pounds), these guns were used primarily by the Royal Navy and a number of British colonies.

BROOKE RIFLED CANNON: Developed by Confederate engineer John Mercer Brooke, this muzzle-loading rifle was similar to the "soda bottle" shaped Dahlgren guns of the time, albeit not so pronounced in form as the latter. The breech of the piece was reinforced much like a Parrott gun with several iron bands and proved to be one gun's distinguishing features. Built in Richmond, it would not be until 1863 that the cannon, which came in bore sizes from eight to eleven inches and was also cast in smoothbore, became widely employed with Confederate naval and coastal defense units.

CAISSON: A two-wheeled ammunition cart that is typically attached to the gun carriage for transport.

CANNON: At the time of the Civil War the vast majority of cannon were still muzzle loaders, meaning that the charge and projectile had to be loaded through the front bore of the gun. These cannons also came in two types: smoothbore and rifled. Smoothbore guns, like those from the days of Napoleon, were still popular in both armies, and were sized in the traditional fashion by the weight of the shot they used. These guns could fire solid shot, grapeshot, and explosive rounds known as shells, which employed a pre-cut fuse. These guns came in a number of sizes with twelve-, twenty-four-, and thirty-two-pounders being the types most commonly encountered in naval or coastal duty. Larger smoothbore pieces such as the Dahlgren pieces on Union monitors were measured not by projectile weight but by bore size, which would soon become the standard practice

The second type of cannon employed in large numbers were rifled guns. By cutting grooves in the barrel a spin could be imparted to the cylindrical projectile which stabilized its flight. This made for not only a more accurate long-range gun but one capable of firing a high-velocity round as well. Like their smoothbore cousins, rifled guns fire solid shot and explosive rounds, but as grapeshot would ruin the rifling, cannister rounds were used in this role. As with smoothbores, rifled guns also came in a wide variety of projectile sizes, with the gun either characterized by projectile weight or by the bore size (in inches). Field artillery typically used ten- to twenty-pound rounds and naval vessels frequently employed eighty- to hundred-pound projectiles.

The last type of artillery piece encountered is a mortar. Although the technology behind these guns and the basic principle of a high-trajectory explosive round that could be used to fire over walls or obstructions had not changed in the last few centuries, what had changed was the explosive power and range of these rounds. Smaller mortars were employed in field batteries, while coastal or siege mortars frequently fired a ten or thirteen-inch diameter 150-pound explosive round half a mile or more.

CANNON AMMUNITION: Ammunition came in four basic types. Round shot or solid shot was typically used against vessels or fortifications. As the name implies these solid projectiles used greater powder loads which in turn would create higher exit velocities and more kinetic damage to the target. The second type of cannon ammunitions are explosive rounds, referred to as shells. Fuses were cut in seconds of flight time, which, knowing the exit velocity of the round with a specific powder load, can quickly be translated into range. These rounds were designed to create shrapnel and concussive damage. The third ammunition type is grapeshot or cannister. Both were designed to fire dozens of musket balls in a close-range anti-personnel manner. Cannister, which was used in rifled guns to prevent damaging the rifling, was basically musket balls packed in a case. The case would travel down the barrel and the musket balls would soon separate from it once it had left the barrel. The last ammunition type is associated with mortars. This spherical cased, fused explosive round had traditionally been known as a bomb, which is a good description of its function.

CANNON MOUNTS: While field artillery was fired from wheeled carriages, larger coastal or naval guns were mounted in two fashions: via a carriage or a pivot mount. The former of these were the older and more commonly recognized gun carriages of the Napoleonic age. These were moved via block and tackle to either run the gun forward into the battery for firing through a gun port or run back for reloading. Only small lateral and elevation adjustments could be made in this configuration. The pivot mount on the other hand eliminated the limiting firing arc of the former arrangement. An American invention first employed in the War of 1812, it quickly caught on with militaries around the world. Rollers and a block and tackle arrangement was used to swing the gun through a wide arc, and the gun could still be run back to provide room for loading. In the case of the Union monitors the two methods were combined by fixing the guns in standard naval carriages and providing the required firing arc by mounting them in a rotating turret.

CASEMATED: A casemated gun is one that is fired out of a defensive structure that is designed to protect the gun crew from overhead and off-angle fire. A casemated gun will usually fire *en barbette*, through a slit-like opening in the casemate, although an embrasure method would also work.

DAHLGREN CANNON: In response to the catastrophic failure of several large muzzle-loading cannon in the late 1840s, Lt. John Dahlgren designed a muzzle-loading cannon that was purposely reinforced at the breech where the pressure for firing was at the greatest. This effort yielded a smoother more curved design that gave the gun a unique "soda bottle" look. It was a nickname that would stick with the cannon. Dahlgrens could fire shot or shell but are perhaps better known for the latter. Sizes ranged from the standard thirty-two pounds to the fifteen-inch guns of the Union monitors, which fired either 350-pound shells or 440-pound solid shot.

EMBRASURE: A cutout or notch in the parapet through which a cannon can be fired. While firing from such an arrangement can restrict the angles at which the gun can be deployed it offers good protective cover for the gun and crew from direct fire.

EN BARBETTE or BARBETTE: A cannon mounted such that it can fire over the parapet. While such an arrangement does not offer as much protection for the gun or its crew it does allow the gun to be trained over a much greater field of fire.

GUN CREWS: Gun crews of the day ranged in size from four men to approaching two dozen for some of the larger naval or coastal guns. Even this manpower requirement does not tell the entire story as, without a supply of ammunition, the guns would not mean much. Beyond the crew, an additional dozen men could easily be involved in moving ammunition forward or, in the case of avessel, from the magazine to the gun crews. In many cases these men operated from exposed gun positions, making them vulnerable to shrapnel and cannister.

CANNON TABLES: The following tables, taken out of the 1866 *Ordnance Instructions for the United States Navy*, summarize and compare a number of common cannon types encountered in this text.

CLASS	PROJECTILE	WEIGHT OF PROJECTILE (LBS)	APPROXIMATE RANGE (YARDS)
SHELL GUNS			
XV-inch	Shell	350	2,100
XI-inch	Shell	136	3,400
	Shell	186	2,140
	Shrapnel	141	1,710
X-inch	Shell	103	2,840
	Shrapnel	101	2,841
IX-Inch	Shell	72.5	3,357
	Shrapnel	75	1,690
XIII-inch	Shell	51.5	1,770
	Shrapnel	52	1,775

Smoothbores and Howitzers

32-pounder)	Shot	32	2,730
(5,700 lb.	Shell	26	1,850
	Shrapnel	32	1,930
32-pounder	Shot	32	1,750
(4,500 lb.)	Shell	26	1,710
	Shrapnel	32	1,750
32-pounder	Shot	32	1,690
(2,700 lb.)	Shell	26	1,610
	Shrapnel	32	1,690
24-pound	Shell	20	1,270
Howitzer	Shrapnel	26	1,300
12-pound	Shell	10	1,085
Howitzer	Shrapnel	13	1,150

Rifled Guns

Parrott	Solid shot	100	6,900
100-pound	Hollow shot	80	8,450
Parrott	Shot	30	6,000
30-pound	Shell	29	6,700
	Shrapnel	29	1,000
Parrott	Shot	20	3,800
20-pound	Shell	19	4,400
	Shrapnel	20	950

MASKING (UNMASKING): To cover or obstruct a gun's line of fire. Unmasking a gun is to show its position, typically accomplished by drawing fire from the gun.

PALISADE: A wooden fence of vertical or angled wooden poles, often erected on the opposite side of a fort's ditch to break up an infantry attack against one of the structure's walls. These were usually cut with firing ports or loopholes to allow the fort's garrison to defend the position.

PARAPET: The extended vertical portion at the front-top portion of a curtain wall or bastion designed to offer cover to the defenders. Embrasures may be cut out of this portion of the wall to create firing ports.

SCARP and COUNTERSCARP: The scarp is the slope of the ditch adjacent to the fort while the counterscarp is the slope on the ditch opposite the fort.

SHELL GUN: While a shell gun such as a Dahlgren is capable of firing other types of ammunition the name speaks more to the weapon's primary function than its capabilities.

STEAM ENGINE: In its most basic form, a wood or coal-fueled fire is used to boil water and create steam in a high-pressure container. This steam is then used, via piping and valving, to move a piston and generate a rotational motion. This rotational motion can then be coupled to a propeller or to a paddlewheel to provide the desired propulsion. How the heat was transferred in this process as well as the size of the steam engine, and how the mechanical energy was coupled and controlled, varied among the competing designs of the day. There was, however, one thing that all steam engines agreed upon; the better the fuel, the more power available.

While the steam engine revolutionized littoral warfare, early efforts to employ steam power came at a frightening cost. The high-pressure boilers were vulnerable and likely to detonate when pierced. Paddlewheels were vulnerable as well, as was the network of high-pressure steam lines that threaded portions of the ship. Oddly one of the most vulnerable elements was the smokestack. The stack was designed to vent the smoke from the boiler fires in such a fashion so as to create a draft that stoked the fire and caused it to burn hotter. Thus, damaging the smokestack meant interfering with this draft, and, if damaged enough, it would restrict the amount of steam that could be generated reducing the vessel's performance.

TORPEDO: The torpedo was essentially a mine, typically used for naval purposes. These crude devices, which initially consisted of a sealed barrel of gunpowder triggered remotely by a lanyard, were credited to the work of Virginia Captain Matthew Maury in 1861. Maury would go on to employ and design several variations of these naval mines, progressively more powerful, and most fired electronically once a supply of insulated wire could be obtained from England. Detonation by contact was later added to these devices, which created a peril for friend and foe alike as pointed to by the CSS *Shultz*. The *Shultz* struck one of these mines and sank in the James River upon returning from delivering several hundred Union prisoners of war to City Point. These contact mines were also set adrift downriver in the hopes of striking a blockading Union vessel. There is little doubt that torpedoes altered naval warfare and provided the defender with a powerful force multiplier. Estimates range from forty to fifty Union vessels damaged or destroyed by these devices, making the torpedo one of the greatest threats faced by Union warships. A variation of the lanyard-fired torpedo was the spar torpedo. In this case the device was mounted on a long spar at the bow of a small torpedo boat. The idea was to lower this spar under an enemy ship and, after backing away, pull the lanyard to detonate the charge, preferably without blowing up the torpedo boat at the same time.

WHITWORTH RIFLED GUN: This unusual artillery piece was invented by British arms dealer and entrepreneur Sir Joseph Whitworth. To circumvent an 1854 rifled barrel patent Whitworth developed an octagonal barrel, the shape of which imparted a spin on the similarly shaped projectile as it traveled down the length of the barrel. Made in a variety of calibers (or pounds), the Whitworth was used primarily by Confederate troops who purchased a number of these guns and ran them through the blockade. The odd ammunition used and problems with the breech-loading mechanism that left many muzzle-loaders were drawbacks to the design. On the other hand, the Whitworth was known for its long range and extreme accuracy. While the maximum range of the gun was over five miles it was the latter trait that amazed people. In one instance, ten shots were fired at a target just under a mile away. When the target was checked it was found that all ten shots were within a ten-inch diameter circle.

Notes

ABBREVIATIONS

CMH	Confederate Military History
WOR	War of the Rebellion (series 1 unless noted)
ORN	Official Naval Records
SHSP	*Southern Historical Society Papers*
CV	*Confederate Veteran*
HNCR	Histories North Carolina Regiments

CHAPTER 1: PLANS AND PRIVATEERS

1. ORN, I, xv-xvi; VI, xvii; *Report of the Secretary of the Navy*, 1861, 9-11. These vessels carried 555 guns and 7,600 men.
2. Of the 1,200 commissioned officers, the secretary of the navy reported that after March 4, 1861, 250 officers resigned their commissions or were dismissed from the service. (Ammen, 4.)
3. Boynton, I, 102.
4. Ibid., 89-90, 101.
5. *Report of the Secretary of the Navy*, 1861, 11-16. The Union Navy had purchased 136 vessels by the end of 1861, 79 of which were steamers. A number of vessels were recommissioned and when added to the existing fleet, expanded the Union naval forces to 212 ships manned by 22,000 men. In addition, plans were laid down to construct for 52 warships, 14 screw sloops, 23 gunboats, 12 side-wheel steamers, and 3 ironclad steamers. During this same period the Marine Corps was almost doubled in size to 2,964 men. (Ibid., 19-20.)
6. Soley, 21-25; Scharf, 17-25.
7. ORN, V, 766-767; VI, 158-159, 172-175; Parker, 211-212; Soley, 163-165.
8. WOR, IV, I, 587-588; ORN, I, 60-61, V, 744-745; "The North Carolina Navy," 299-301; Scharf, 83-85.

9. ORN, VI, 72-73.

10. Ibid., V, 688-689.

11. Merrill, "The Hatteras Expedition," NCHR, XXIX, No 2. (April 1952), 208-211; Boynton, I, 331-335.

12. ORN, VI, 82.

CHAPTER 2: THE GREAT SOUTHERN EXPEDITION

1. CMH, IV, 25-26; WOR, IV, 574-575, LI/2., 83-86, 116, 120-121, 136.

2. WOR, LI/2, 136-137.

3. ORN, VI, 713-714; WOR, IV, 584, 590-592; LI/2, 136-138.

4. WOR, LI/2, 193-194. On July 22, 1861, Gwynn reported five companies of the 7th N.C. at Ocracoke Inlet, three at Hatteras Inlet, three at Oregon Inlet. For a view on North Carolina's efforts to arm its troops see "North Carolina Troops: How They Were Armed in the War Between the States," SHSP, XXIX, 144-151.

5. WOR, LI/2, 193-194; ORN, V, 791-792; CMH, IV, 12-15, 25-26.

6. WOR, IV, 581-582; ORN, VI, 120-121.

7. WOR, IV, 581-582, 589; ORN VI, 121-131; Ammen,163-167.

8. ORN, VI, 121-122, 134-136.

9. Ibid., 140-141. "The Hatteras Expedition, August 1861," 204-219.

10. "The Fall of Hatteras," 36-37.

11. ORN, 121, 125-127, 134-135. "The fort fired slow as we came out, and did not return our last three shots," Gillis wrote in his report. "Owning, no doubt, to the promptness with which the flag-officer and the other vessels opened upon them for our relief."

12. WOR, IV, 582-583, 589.

13. Parker, 212-214; ORN, VI, 138-144; WOR, IV, 592-594; Graham, 78-83.

14. Scharf, 374-376; "The Fall of Hatteras," 38-54; ORN, VI, 160.

CHAPTER 3: THE GATHERING STORM

1. Graham, 84-90; ORN, VI, 221-224.

2. WOR, IV, 607-610; 618. ORN, VI, 161-164, 172-176.

3. WOR, IV, 619-620, 624-625.

4. ORN, VI, 277-278, Scharf, 380-381.

5. *Virginia Biography*, III, 137; *Naval War Records, Officers Confederate States Navy*, 83.

6. "North Carolina Navy," 299-314; Scharf, 377-379, "The Confederate States Navy," 125-134.

7. ORN, VI, 20-23.

8. ORN, VI, 712; "North Carolina Navy," 299-314; "The Confederate States Navy," 125-134.

9. "The 3rd Georgia Regiment, No. 7; ORN, VI, 275-277; WOR, IV, 595-596; Scharf, 377-379.

10. ORN, VI, 278; Scharf, 380-381.

11. "Chicamacomico," 55; Scharf, 381; "The 3rd Georgia Regiment," No. 7.

12. Graham, 93-94; "The 3rd Georgia Regiment," No. 7; "Chicamacomico," 55.

13. Scharf, 381; "Chicamacomico," 56; WOR, IV, 623-625.

14. "Chicamacomico," 56; ORN, VI, 289-293.

CHAPTER 4: BURNSIDE'S EXPEDITION

1. *Burnside Expedition*, 5-10; Sprague, 427-430; ORN, VI, 469, 472-473, 507-508, 526.

2. Allen, 51.

3. Sprague, 431-432; *Burnside Expedition*, 15-20; *Burnside and the 9th Army Corps*, 20-28; *Harper's Weekly*, Jan. 18, 1862, 36; Feb 15, 1862, 111; Allen, 52-53; Day, *Diary*, 21-23. "Everything on the deck that was not lashed was swept overboard, and the men, furniture and crockery below decks were thrown about in a most promiscuous manner." (*Burnside Expedition*, 16.)

4. ORN, VI, 527-528, 536-539, 551.

5. Ibid., VI, 552-553; WOR, IX, 75-76; *The Burnside Expedition*, 24-26.

6. WOR, IV, 573-575, 663, 689, 693-694.

7. "The 3rd Georgia Regiment," No. 6; WOR, IV, 642-643, 647, 655.

8. WOR, IV, 682.

9. WOR, IV, 575, 693, 705, 715, LI/2, 425, IX, 111-114. Huger admitted to Jefferson Davis that he had informed Wise that it was supplies and hard work that the island's commander needed, not men, but he also noted that after this he stated that, "If men can help you, you shall have them, if we have boats here to take them." (Ibid., 114.)

10. WOR, IX, 122-140, 151-153, 156, 184; Trotter, 75-78.

11. "North Carolina Navy," 299-314; "The Confederate States Navy," 125-134; Scharf, 389.

12. ORN, VI, 550-552, 789; WOR, IX, 170-171.

13. ORN, VI, 761.

14. WOR, IX, 124-128, 170-171.

CHAPTER 5: THE BATTLE FOR ROANOKE ISLAND

1. ORN, VI, 552, 561, 588; "A Minor Naval Engagement," CV, XXIII, 165.

2. ORN, IV, 552-553, 559, 565-566.

3. WOR, IX, 181; ORN, VI, 561, 566-567, 588, 598-599; "Battle at Roanoke Island," CV, XVII, 605.

4. ORN, VI, 557-559, 561, 564-565, 568-569; Allen, 67-70.

5. ORN, VI, 559-561, 575.

6. Parker, 225-226; WOR, 183-185; ORN, VI, 594-599.

7. Parker, 227-229. "Neither of us believed that we would be successful," Parker recounted. "Nor was there a naval officer in the squadron who thought we would. The force opposed to us both naval and military was too over whelming. Ten thousand men to our two thousand on land, and nineteen vessels and 54 guns to our eight vessels with 9 guns." (Ibid., 228.)

8. ORN, VI, 588, 561-562.

9. Parker, 229-230; "A Minor Naval Engagement," CV, XXIII, 165; WOR, IX, 81;

ORN, VI, 594-595. The USS *Morse* claimed to have been responsible for sinking the *Curlew*. (Ibid., 571.)

10. "A Minor Naval Engagement," CV, XXIII, 165; ORN, VI, 594-595, 597.

11. WOR, IX, 75-76, 85-86; ORN, 588-589.

12. ORN, VI, 588-589, 598-599; CV, XVII, 605; "Fall of Roanoke Island," 64-65; WOR, IX, 76,175-177. "Having no horses for our artillery," Jordan later informed Shaw, and "fearing that we might be cut off, or at least that the shells from the enemy's guns in the sound might confuse and disconcert the men under my command and cause the eventual loss of the field pieces, which you enjoined upon me at all hazards to save, I considered it judicious to order a retreat." (WOR, IX, 175.)

13. WOR, IX, 170-172, 175-177.

14. ORN, VI, 578-579; Day, *Diary*, 34-35.

15. WOR, IX, 86-87, 93-96; Day, *Diary*, 34-35; Putnam, 72-75.

16. WOR, IX, 87, 93-98.

17. Trotter, 85.

18. WOR, IX, 94, 98,100-104, 174-175, 180; Derby, 61-64; Walcott, 31-35.

19. Graham, 138-142; Walcott, 31-35; WOR, IX, 87,106.

20. "Fall of Roanoke Island." 65-67; WOR, IX, 87-88, 93-102, 106, 172-173, 185-186.

21. Ibid., 87-88, 172-173.

22. WOR, IX, 79, 85, 172-173.

23. *The Carolina Watchman*, Mar. 10, 1862; *The North Carolina Standard*, Mar 5, 1862. An investigative panel looking into the loss of Roanoke Island exonerated both Shaw and Wise and disagreed with Davis' comments. (WOR, IX, 183-190.)

CHAPTER 6: THE DESTRUCTION OF THE MOSQUITO FLEET

1. ORN, 594-595.

2. Ibid.

3. Parker, 234-236; ORN, VI, 595-596; WOR, IX,191-192. When he viewed it, Parker was unimpressed with Fort Cobb. "The magazine of this fort resembled an African ant-hill more than anything else, and had its door fronting the river, and was of course entirely exposed." (Parker, 234.)

4. Parker, 235-236.

5. ORN, VI, 554, 562-563, 566-567, 573.

6. Ibid., 562-563.

7. Ibid., 590, 604-607. The Union vessels were the *Louisiana, Hetzel, Underwriter, Delaware, Commodore Perry, Valley City, Morse, Seymour, Whitehead, Lockwood, Ceres, Shawsheen, Brinker*, and *Putnam*. (Ibid., 606.)

8. Parker, 236-237; ORN, VI, 595-596.

9. "A Minor Naval Engagement," CV, XXIII, 165-166; ORN, VI, 595-597, 607-608, 614-616; Parker, 238-239. In his official report to Goldsborough Rowan noted Gunner John Davis' actions in saving the *Valley City* and recommended him for a Congressional Medal. (ORN, VI, 609.)

10. ORN, VI, 607-608, 617-618; WOR, IX,191-192. "The naval officers were of the opinion that the enemy would not attempt to pass [the] battery until silenced," Colonel Henningsen wrote in his report.

11. Allen, 77-80; CV, XXIII, 165-166.

12. ORN, VI, 607, 613-614, 596-597; CV, XXIII, 165-166.

13. ORN, VI, 597, 607.

14. "A Minor Naval Engagement," CV, XXIII, 165-166; ORN, VI, 618-619.

15. Scharf, 390-392; ORN, VI. 611.

16. Parker, 239-240; ORN, VI, 596-597.

17. Parker, 240; ORN, VI, 596, 621. The casualties on both sides were low with Lynch reporting four killed and seven wounded, and Rowan, two killed and seven wounded. (Ibid. 596, 621.)

18. ORN, VI, 596-597.

CHAPTER 7: THE SIEGE OF NEWBERN

1. ORN, VI, 608-609, 611. It seems that Lynch's order to burn the CSS *Forrest* was not carried through, as Rowan found this vessel, a gunboat still on the stocks, and a smaller vessel at the Elizabeth City shipyard and burnt all three. (Ibid., 608.)

2. Trotter, 93-99; Graham, 160-164; ORN, 654-655.

3. Burnside, 26-27; WOR, IX, 201-202; ORN, VII, 117.

4. WOR, IX, 197, 201-202; ORN, VII, 108. The brigades were as at Roanoke Island being led by Foster, Parke, and Reno.

5. WOR, IV, 682-683, 694; IX, 241-242, 248

6. Estvan, II, 137-139; ORN, VII, 109.

7. WOR, IX, 241-243, 248, LI/2, 464, 469, 492.

8. ORN, VII, 108, 110-111; WOR, IX, 242.

9. Roe, 24th Mass., 78-81; Oliver Case Letter, Mar. 16, 1862; Burnside, 27; Walcott, 61-63; WOR, IX, 208-209; Dollard, 54; Day, *Diary*, 42.

10. ORN, VII, 110-11; WOR, IX, 201-202.

11. Burlingame, *5th Rhode Island*, 31-32.

12. WOR, IX, 242-245, 248.

13. Oliver Case Letter, Mar. 16, 1862; ORN, VII, 133-134; WOR, IX, 202-203, 212-213; Trumbull, 70-71. Emmerton, 64-65.

14. ORN, VII, 111-112, 115-118.

15. Walcott, 63-65; WOR, IX, 220-221, 224-225; Day, *Diary*, 44.

16. WOR, IX, 225-226, 244-245, 250-251, 262-263, 267-268. Branch was not alone in this observation. Colonel Reuben Campbell, the commander of the 7th North Carolina stated that "About one hour after the firing commenced Colonel Sinclair came to me, and in much excitement said that the enemy had flanked him and was coming up the trenches which had been vacated by the Militia. I ordered him to leave the trenches for the purpose of charging bayonets upon the advancing columns; but he failed to form his men and left the field in confusion." (Ibid., 250.)

17. Walcott, 64-67; WOR, IX, 220-228, 234, 237-238, 244-251, 259-261; Lewis, 7-9; Allen, 93-95.

18. WOR, IX, 234-240; Burlingame, *5th Rhode Island*, 35-37.

19. ORN, VII, 113-114; Lewis, 7-9; WOR, IX, 212-214, 243-244; Putnam, 107-108.

20. ORN, VII, 108-118.

21. WOR, IX, 265; ORN, VII, 112, 117-118.

22. Ibid.,111, 116; Estvan, II, 148-149; WOR, IX, 204, 245, 268-269; Derby, 85-86.

CHAPTER 8: FORT MACON

1. WOR, IX, 199, 371-373.

2. ORN, VII, 150-153; WOR, IX, 198-200, 206, 211, 246-247, 269-270; Roe, 105-107.

3. WOR, IX, 199-201.

4. Barry, "Fort Macon,"163-169; WOR, LI/2, 11; CMH, IV, 43-44; Pool, "The Tenth Regiment," 489.

5. WOR, IX, 276-277, XLIX/2, 116-117; Barry, "Fort Macon," 171-172.

6. WOR, IX, 276-278, 293; Pool, "The Tenth Regiment," 489-490.

7. Burlingame, *5th Rhode Island*, 54-56; WOR, IX, 278-283, 286; Oliver Case Letter, Apr. 6, 1862.

8. WOR, IX, 283, 286, 289; Burlingame, *5th Rhode Island*, 59-61.

9. WOR, IX, 283.

10. Ibid., 293-294.

11. "The Tenth Regiment," 507-508; WOR, IX, 293.

12. Ibid., 273-275, 293-294.

13. Hall, 123-124; WOR, IX, 284-289. Oliver Case of the 8th Connecticut spoke to the fire from Fort Macon in a letter to his sister. "The bombardment commenced early the next morning and continued without intermission until four in the P.M., our regiment meanwhile lying behind the breastworks while a perfect rain of shot and shell came upon all sides of them, many times caving the banks upon them so it was necessary to dig one another out with shovels." (Oliver Case Letter, Apr. 28, 1862.)

14. ORN, VII, 278-281.

15. Ibid.

16. Hall, 125-126; WOR, IX, 290-292; Allen, 112-115.

17. WOR, IX, 273-275, 293-294; Hall, 125; "The Tenth Regiment," 508-510; Burlingame, *5th Rhode Island*, 63-65.

CHAPTER 9: THE MARCH TO SOUTH MILLS

1. WOR, IX, 270-272.

2. WOR, IX, 273.

3. ORN, VII, 250-251; Parker, *51st Penn.*, 137-139; WOR, IX, 305, 309-310; Graham, 170-172.

4. Parker, *51st Penn.*, 139-140; WOR, IX, 305-309, 317-320; Avery, *Marine Artillery*, 20-21.

5. WOR, IX, 326-327.

6. Ibid., 327-328.

7. WOR, IX, 305-306, 309-310, 317-321.

8. WOR, IX, 310.

9. Graham, 175-177; Parker, *51st Penn.*, 142-143; WOR, IX, 310-313. Reno was critical of Hawkins' report and his actions at South Mills, informing General Burnside that, "As to the statement that a charge through an open field directly in front of the enemy's position was thought to be the only way in which they could be dislodged. I have to state that if the intention be to convey the idea that I, the commanding officer, thought so, it is untrue, as it was directly contrary to my opinion. If the intention be to convey the idea that he or other officers thought so and that he acted upon that conclusion, it was an act of insubordination, as it was contrary to my orders." (Ibid., 313.)

10. WOR, IX, 321-329; CMH, IV, 41-42; Jackman, 43-45; Avery, *Marine Artillery*, 20-24.

11. WOR, IX, 307, 317; Jackman, 46-47. The 6th New Hampshire advanced as Wright's men were retreating and delivered a near perfect volley on the retreating Confederates. A wounded prisoner from the 3rd Georgia remarked that "their men didn't care much for those red-legged Zouaves; but when the regulars poured in that volley they thought it best to get out of that place." (Ibid., 46.)

12. "Hist. 3rd Georgia"; WOR, IX, 327-329; ORN, VII, 250-251.

CHAPTER 10: WILMINGTON

1. Sprunt, *Lower Cape Fear*, 15-16; Ibid., *Chronicles Cape Fear*, 38-40, 45-46.

2. *Hist. Wilmington Harbor*, 23-26.

3. WOR, IV, 573-579, 633, 637.

4. Ibid., 639, 705, 715, LI/II, 304-305; *Hist. Wilmington Harbor*, 12-20; Price, "Blockade Running as a Business...," 53.

5. Marchman, *Hist. Fort Caswell*, 1-5; WOR, IV, 656-657; Sprunt, *Chronicles Cape Fear*, 281, 295-298; "A Capture before the War," HNCR, V, 23-28.

6. WOR, LI, 326-327, 329, 355-356, 405, 481.

7. French, *Two Wars*, 140-146; WOR, IX, 423-424, 431-432, 447-449, 460, 463, 469.

8. Ibid., XVIII, 773-776. Whiting was no stranger to Cape Fear having written a dismal report on the defenses of the area in May 1861 while he was acting as an inspector general for the state of North Carolina. (WOR, LI/II, 83-86.)

9. Lamb, SHSP, XXI, 259-261; WOR, IX, 354, XVIII, 414-415, 783-784. By Dec. 1862 Whiting had been reinforced and now had six thousand troops manning the defenses of Cape Fear and Wilmington. (WOR, XVIII, 809.)

10. ORN, VIII, 263-264. The secretary of the navy had suggested attacking Fort Caswell in May 1862, and even offered Admiral Goldsborough a pair of ironclads to assist in the operation, but Goldsborough never carried through with the idea. (ORN, VII, 341-342.)

CHAPTER 11: THE BLOCKADE OF CAPE FEAR

1. ORN, VI, 440, 493-494, VIII, 127, 152. The Whitworth guns were salvaged from the wreck of the blockade runner *Modern Greece*.

2. WOR, XVIII, 34; ORN, VIII, 230-233.

3. Taylor, 24-25, 44-47; Wilkinson, 130-131.

4. Price, "Ships that Tested the Blockade," 196-200; *Report Sec. Navy* (1862), 25-29; Lamb, *Fort Fisher*, 1.

5. Price, "Ships that Tested the Blockade," 199-200, 215-237.

6. Taylor, 124; Sprunt, *Chronicles Cape Fear*, 420.

7. Arthur Wardle, "Some Blockade Runners of the Civil War," 131-140; Price, "Blockade Running," 31-62; Sprunt, *Chronicles Cape Fear*, 415-416. When the highly successful blockade runner *Banshee* was captured in late 1863, Taylor noted that after eight successful rounds trips the vessel had paid "her shareholders 700 per cent on their investment." (Taylor, 82.)

8. Taylor, 73-75; Sprunt, *Chronicles Cape Fear*, 407-408, 419-421; Almy, "Incidents of the Blockade," 4. The Captain of the USS *Shenandoah* noted a trend toward an even lighter color in an attempt to mask the interlopers. "The blockade runners are now all painted white, and run so close to the beach that it is impossible to see them 100 yards off at night." (ORN, IX, 295.)

9. Sprunt, *Chronicles Cape Fear*, 421.

10. ORN, VI, 691-692.

11. Bright, *Modern Greece*, 1-7; ORN, VII, 514-515.

12. Ibid., VII, 514-518; Bright, *Modern Greece*, 1-12; WOR, LI/II, 584-585.

13. Bright, *Modern Greece*, 12-19; Lamb, "Fight with Blockaders," 351-352.

14. ORN, VII, 695-698, VIII, 5.

15. Ibid., 80-82.

16. ORN, IX, 141, 149-150.

17. Taylor, 84-85; ORN, IX, 162, 187-189, 287-291, 318-324; Wilkinson, 174-176.

18. ORN, IX, 249-251, 295-297. Several other vessels on the *Venus'* list, such as the *R.E. Lee*, would be captured by years' end.

19. Porter, 683-685; ORN, X, 287, 473-474.

20. Wood, "Blockade Running," 1-2; Price, "Ships that Tested the Blockade," 236-237. Surprisingly, several vessels still penetrated the blockade and reached Wilmington up until the city fell.

21. Dullum, "Unremitting Vigilance," 126.

22. Price, "Blockade Running," 53; Ibid., "Ships that Tested the Blockade," 215-237.

23. Ibid., 215-237.

CHAPTER 12: THE CAPE FEAR FLOTILLA

1. WOR, IV, 681.

2. Scharf, 43; ORN, VIII, 89, Ser. 2, I, 259, 270, 370-371; Bisbee, 100-101; WOR, IV, 686, IX, 354, XVIII, 829-830. The ironclad dimensions were specified at 150 x 23 x 12 feet.

3. Bisbee, 100-104; Peebles, 35-39, 59; Melton, 199; ORN, X, 509, 751, Ser. 2, I, 262, 270.

4. Scharf, 414-415; ORN, IX, 561, 798, 809-810; Bisbee, 105-106. Peebles, 35-37, 39-42.

5. ORN, X, 21-22; Melton, 199-201.

6. Scharf, 414-415; Peebles, 45-49; ORN, X, 20-24.

7. Peebles, 45-49, ORN, X, 18-24.

8. ORN, X, 24-25; Peebles, 49-52; Bisbee, 106-107.

9. Peebles, 66-69; WOR, 42/2, 1294, 1297.

10. Bisbee, 179-181.

11. ORN, X, 751-752, 774-775, 793-794; Scharf, 806-807.

12. ORN, X, 340-341.

13. Ibid., III, 137-151, 701-710.

14. Scharf, 806-808; ORN, III, 151-187, 701-710; Sprunt, 423, 468, 478-479.

15. ORN, III, 324-330, 836; Scharf, 807-808; Soley, 227-229.

16. Scharf, 808-809; ORN, III, 315-340, 710-714; Soley, 227.

CHAPTER 13: THE ROAD TO GOLDSBORO

1. Pool, "10th N.C.," 492-493.

2. ORN, VIII, 6-8; WOR, XVIII, 4-8. General Foster attributed the loss of the gunboat *Picket* to "carelessness or accident." (ORN, VIII, 8.)

3. Sanders, "Sketch 10th Reg.," 511-514; WOR, XVIII, 5-9; Pool, "10th N.C.," 492-493.

4. WOR, XVIII, 13-15, 20-23.

5. Ibid., 53-55; Howe, 9-14; "R. Hall to Mother, Dec., 22, 1862," UNC Coll.

6. WOR, XVIII, 105-106; ORN, VIII, 284-288; Sanders, "Sketch 10th Reg.," 515.

7. WOR, XVIII, 112-115; Sanders, "Sketch 10th Reg.," 515-517; Edwards, *Hist. 17th S.C.V.*, 21-23; Pool, "The Battle of White Hall," 84-85.

8. WOR, XVIII, 75-76, 54-56, 63-67, 91-92, 94-96; Howe, 14-17.

9. Mann, *Hist. 45th Mass.*, 110; WOR, XVIII, 82-83.

10. Ibid., 63-68, 83-84, 96-100; Mann, *Hist. 45th Mass.*, 105-109.

11. Fall, *Hist. 17th S.C.V.*, 24-25; Sanders, "Sketch 10th Reg.," 517-518; WOR, XVIII, 114-116.

12. Howe, 17-22; Sanders, "Sketch 10th Reg.," 517-518, WOR, XVIII, 55-56, 60-61, 63-68, 91-97, 109-116; Edwards, *Hist. 17th S.C.V.*, 26; Pool, "10th N.C.," 493-494.

13. WOR, XVIII, 64-65, 67, 69, 72; Howe, 24-27; Pool, "The Battle of White Hall," 83-88.

14. WOR, XVIII, 56-57, 69-72, 121-122; Pool, "The Battle of White Hall," 87-91; Everts, *Hist. 9th N.J.*, 88; Birdsong, *Sketches N.C. State Troops*, 128-129.

15. WOR, XVIII, 106-108.

16. Ibid., 109-110, 113-114, 117-118; Burgwyn, "Clingman's Brigade," 481-483.

17. Sanders, "Sketch 10th Reg.," 519-521; WOR, XVIII, 77-78, 93-95, 117-118.

18. Howe, 35-38; WOR, XVIII, 64-69, 84-86, 93-95; Everts, *Hist. 9th N.J.*, 88-89.

19. WOR, XVIII, 120-121.

20. "R. Hall to Mother, Dec. 22, 1862," UNC Coll.; WOR, XVIII, 109-114, 117-121; Robinson, "52nd Regiment," 229-231.

21. WOR, XVIII, 57-59, 65-66, 84-88, 109-114, 117-121; Howe, 38-40; Robinson, "52nd Regiment," 229-231.

CHAPTER 14: GUNS AND BREAD

1. WOR, XVIII, 890-891.

2. Ibid.

3. CMH, IV, 150-153; WOR, XVIII, 898, 901-903. "If there is a chance of doing anything we should not be idle," Longstreet replied to Hill. "We are much more likely to succeed by operating ourselves than by lying still." (Ibid.)

4. WOR, XVIII, 188-192, 905-914, 918, 920-921.

5. Ibid., 190-192, 195-196.

6. Putnam, 165-167; WOR, XVIII, 183-184, 188, 196-197.

7. CMH, IV, 152-153; WOR, XVIII, 192.

8. Hist. 26th N.C., 6-7; WOR, XVIII, 183-198; ORN, VIII, 603-608; Hall, 158-160; Burlingame, 132-138. One witness in the 5th Rhode Island summed up the Confederate effort by saying, "The rebel attack on New Berne, on the first anniversary of its capture by our forces, had ended in an ignominious failure." (Ibid., 138.)

9. WOR, XVIII, 183-184, 188-189.

10. Ibid., 936-938, 941-942.

11. Hall, 160-165; ORN, 649-698; WOR, XVIII, 210-255; CMH, IV, 150-155; Day, *Diary*, 85-89.

12. WOR, XVIII, 998-999, 1007.

CHAPTER 15: THE LAST BATTLE OF NEWBERN

1. WOR, XXVII/2, 659-867.

2. Ibid., 963-976.

3. Ibid., 979-981.

4. CMH, IV, 218-219; WOR, XXVII/2, 975-976; Trotter, 208-213.

5. WOR, XXVII/3, 948, 1003; XXIX/3, 746, XXIX/3, 773-774.

6. Ibid., XXXIII, 1064-1065, 1073-1074.

7. "Major General Robert Hoke," CV, XX, 437-439; WOR, XXXIII, 1061.

8. Ibid., 55-58, 92-93, 1099-1103.

9. "Eight N.C.," HNCR, I, 396-398; WOR, XXXIII, 62-76, 95-96. One of the casualties in this skirmish was Col. Shaw of the 8th North Carolina, who moving to the front alongside General Clingman to observe the action, was struck by a musket ball and killed early in the engagement.

10. *Civil War Papers*, II, 501.

11. WOR, XXXIII, 92-96, 101-102; Lewis, "Life of W.G. Lewis," 15-17; *Hist. N.C. Reg.*, III, 132-133, 273-274, 333-334; Burlingame, 187-190. Colonel W.G. Lewis who led the attack with the 43rd North Carolina recalled that "General Hoke told me if he had got the train, he intended putting the Forty-third North Carolina and the Twenty-first Georgia on it and running it into New Berne and surprise and capture the forts." (Lewis, "Life of W.G. Lewis," 17.)

12. WOR, XXXIII, 93, 97-99; CMH, IV, 220-221; *19th N.Y. Vol.*, 193-195.

13. Scharf, 395-396.

14. Ibid., 397.

15. "Capture of the Underwriter," 136-140; Scharf, 397-398.

16. ORN, IX, 439-454; "Capture of the Underwriter," 140-144; Scharf, 398-401. Admiral Lee would write in late March that "the hull of the *Underwriter* was ascertained to be so much injured that it was not worth raising." (ORN, IX, 449.)

17. Lewis, "Life of W.G. Lewis," 17; WOR, XXXIII, 49-59, 93-94, 97-102; "Clingman's Brigade," *Hist. N.C. Reg.*, IV, 486-488.

18. WOR, XXXIII, 77-89; "Third Batt. N.C.," HNCR, IV, 265-266.

19. WOR, XXXIII, 57-59; Burlingame, 187-195; *19th N.Y. Vol.*, 195-197.

20. WOR, XXXIII, 92-97, 1145, 1187.

CHAPTER 16: THE SIEGE OF PLYMOUTH AND THE CSS *ALBEMARLE*

1. "The Capture of Plymouth," HNCR, V, 175-176; WOR, XXXIII, 1201-1202, 1244-1245, 1265-1266.

2. ORN, IX, 633-635; WOR, XXXIII, 296-297; Dickey, *103rd Penn.*, 257-258; "The Capture of Plymouth," HNCR, V, 175-177; "56th N.C.," HNCR, III, 337-338.

3. ORN, IX, 635; WOR, XXXIII, 295-296; "56th N.C.," HNCR, III, 337-338.

4. ORN, IX, 636-637, 641-645; WOR, IX, 297-298; "The Capture of Plymouth," HNCR, V, 177-178.

5. "The Capture of Plymouth," HNCR, V, 178-180.

6. "Eight N.C.," HNCR, I, 399.

7. WOR, XXXIII, 301-303; Dickey, *103rd Penn.*, 261-264; "24th, N.C.," HNCR, II, 282-283; Lewis, "Life of W.G. Lewis," 17-18; "The Capture of Plymouth," HNCR, V, 180-181; "56th N.C.," HNCR, III, 338-339.

8. Dickey, *103rd Penn.*, 260.

9. Scharf, 47, 402-405. Edward's Ferry was chosen because a set of shoals in the river at this location acted as an obstacle to any Union gunboat attack.

10. Bisbee, 149-153; Scharf, 405; "Ram Albemarle," HNCR, V, 315-318; Melton, 183-187; Smith, "The Confederate Ram Albemarle," 1-5; Elliott, "Career of the Albemarle," 420-422.

11. ORN, IX, 656-57; "Ram Albemarle," HNCR, V, 318-319.

12. ORN, IX, 643-644.

13. Ibid., 636, 638, 644-646.

14. "Ram Albemarle," HNCR, V, 319-320; ORN, IX, 57-58, 640; Boynton, II, 500-502.

15. ORN, IX, 639-645; "The Capture of Plymouth," HNCR, V, 181-182; Ammen, 200-203; "The Confederate Ram Albemarle," SHSP, XXX, 207-211.

16. ORN, IX, 641-642, 657-658; "Ram Albemarle," HNCR, V, 320-321; "Career of the Albemarle," 423-425. One officer aboard the *Miami* wrote that, "The opinion of all the officers who saw the ram and the effect of solid shot upon her agree that another attack would result only in the sinking of the *Miami*." (ORN, IX, 639.)

17. ORN, IX, 640-641.

18. "The Capture of Plymouth," HNCR, V, 181-183; ORN, IX, 657; "Eight N.C.," HNCR, I, 399-402; Reed, *101st Penn.*, 36-38.

19. "56th N.C.," 339-348; Lewis, "Life of W.G. Lewis," 18-21; "The Capture of Plymouth," HNCR, V, 183-189; WOR, XXXIII, 298-299; "24th N.C.," 283-284; Dickey, *103rd Penn.*, 59-61, 261-270.
20. ORN, IX, 657-658.
21. "The Capture of Plymouth," HNCR, V, 190-195; WOR, XXXIII, 301-304.

CHAPTER 17: THE BATTLE OF ALBEMARLE SOUND

1. Ammen, 203; ORN, IX, 658, 682-685, 770; "Ram Albemarle," HNCR, V, 320.
2. ORN, IX, 669, 683-685, 699-700, 718-719; Ammen, 205.
3. "Ram Albemarle," HNCR, V, 320-322; ORN, IX, 734, 753; Scharf, 409-410.
4. ORN, IX, 734, 738, 744, 747-751; Scharf, 410-411.
5. "Ram Albemarle," HNCR, V, 320-322; ORN, IX, 734-744, 749-750, 763-764, 768-770.
6. ORN, IX, 760-771; "Ram Albemarle," HNCR, V, 321-322.
7. "Albermarle and Sassacus," 426-432; ORN, IX, 734-747, 753-754, 769-771; Melton, 191-194.
8. "Ram Albemarle," HNCR, V, 322-323; ORN, IX, 747-754, 769-771.
9. "Career of the Albemarle," 425-426; ORN, IX, 734-735, 747-754, 769-771, X, 31-32; "Ram Albemarle," HNCR, V, 323. Elliott, who helped build the ship, counted 114 holes in the smokestack made by shot and shell. ("Career of the Albemarle, 426.)
10. ORN, X, 32.
11. Ibid., 86-87, 95-96.
12. "The Destruction of the Albemarle," 432-433; ORN, X, 248. Cushing's first plan called for the use of "India-rubber boats, to be inflated, and carried on men's backs." In lieu of this, "two low-pressure and very small steamers, each armed with a torpedo and howitzer" would be used. ("The Destruction of the Albemarle," 432-433.) Cushing had previously volunteered to attempt and board the *Raleigh* (really *North Carolina*) in the Cape Fear River on a moonless night.
13. Porter, 687; ORN, X, 539-541.
14. Porter, 687-689; ORN, X, 610-615, 618-624; Boynton, II, 506-509; "Destruction of the Albemarle," 432-439; Warley, "Note of the Destruction of the Albemarle," 439-440.
15. ORN, X, 618-620.
16. Warley, "Note of the Destruction of the Albemarle," 439-440.

CHAPTER 18: THE DESCENT OF THE ARMADA

1. Marchman, *History of Ft. Caswell*, 1-6; ORN, IX, 21-22, 300-301, 329-331, X, 440-444, 508-510; WOR, XXIX/2, 691, 704-705, 770-771, 829-830, 862, 1022.
2. Lockwood, 622-623; Curtis, 300-302; "Fort Fisher," SHSP, XXI, 259-262; Lamb, *Battle of Ft. Fisher*, 1-2.
3. Ibid.; Fort Fisher," SHSP, XXI, 262-268.
4. WOR, XXIX/2, 770-771; Lamb, *Battle of Ft. Fisher*, 3.
5. ORN, X, 430-432, 441-444, 450, 461; Porter, 683-686; "Porter Letters," 464-465.

6. Porter, 689-691; ORN, XI, 11-25.

7. ORN, XI, 3, 207-219, 233-237; Porter, 691-693.

8. WOR, XLII/1, 964-967, 985: ORN, XI, 243, 268; Lockwood, 623-626; Sands, 13-14.

9. Porter, 695-696; ORN, XI, 222-226.

10. "Fort Fisher," SHSP, XXI, 268-269; ORN, XI, 226-227; Lockwood, 626-628. Lamb later said of the explosion that "I thought so little of it that the only entry I made in my diary was a blockader got aground near the fort, set fire to herself, and blew up." ("Fort Fisher," SHSP, XXI, 269.)

11. ORN, XI, 226-227, 230-241; Scharf, 422-423; Porter, 696.

CHAPTER 19: THE SANDS OF FORT FISHER

1. ORN, XI, 245-248, 254-256; "Fort Fisher," SHSP, XXI, 269; Porter, 696.

2. "Fort Fisher," SHSP, XXI, 269-270; Scharf, 423-424.

3. Scharf, 418-419, 424-425; ORN, XI, 256, 300-302, 319-320, 336-337; "Fort Fisher," SHSP, XXI, 270-271.

4. ORN, XI, 253, 256, 312-313, 321-322, 327-329, 359-360.

5. Porter, 697-698; ORN, XI, 256-258; Scharf, 424-425.

6. ORN, XI, 257-258, 260-261,266, 333-334, 343; WOR, XLII/1, 981-982.

7. "Fort Fisher," SHSP, XXI, 271-274; WOR, XLII/1, 1001-1005, 1019.

8. ORN, XI, 286-287, 330-331; "Fort Fisher," SHSP, XXI, 272-273; WOR, XLII/1, 1004-1005. The *Iosco* reported no damage and did leave but under orders to assist with the landing.

9. WOR, XLII/1, 975-984. Walling would be awarded the Medal of Honor for this exploit.

10. WOR, XLII/1, 985-987. In his official report Weitzel wrote: "I saw plainly that the work had not been materially injured by the heavy and very accurate shell fire of the navy, and having a distinct and vivid recollection of the bombardment of Fort Jackson, of Vicksburg, of Charleston, and of Fort Wagner, in all of which instances an enormous and well-directed shell fire had done but little damage, and having a distinct and vivid recollection of the two unsuccessful assaults on Fort Wagner, both of which were made under four times more favorable circumstances than those under which we were placed." (Ibid.)

11. WOR, XLII/1, 980-985.

12. Scharf, 425-426; WOR, XLII/1, 993-995, 1002-1005; "Fort Fisher," SHSP, XXI, 273-275.

13. "10th N.C. Artillery," HNCR, V, 497, 528-529; WOR, XLII/1, 968, 980-984, 993-1007.

14. Porter, 700-709; WOR, XLII/1, 965-971, 977-980.

15. WOR, XLII/1, 1005.

CHAPTER 20: THE ARMADA RETURNS

1. Porter, 710-712; ORN, XI, 388-396; WOR, XLVI/1, 423. When Porter heard that Grant was prepared to make a second effort against Fort Fisher Porter wrote him,

"Thank you for so promptly trying to rectify the blunder so lately committed. I knew you would do it." ORN, XI, 401.

2. Porter, 711.

3. ORN, XI, 432-433; "R.P.G. to Cousin," Jan. 24, 1865, UNC Collections.

4. WOR, XLVI/1, 395-397, 423-424.

5. Lamb, "Defense of Ft. Fisher," HNCR, V, 222-224; WOR, XLVI/1, 437; ORN, XI, 462-463; "Fort Fisher," SHSP, XXI, 275-277. Lamb reports his numbers as 1,550 officers and men on the morning of Jan. 15. He would be reinforced by the 21st South Carolina later in the day to bring his final numbers to 1,900. (Lamb, "Defense of Ft. Fisher," HNCR, V, 239-241.)

6. ORN, XI, 461-468; "Fort Fisher," SHSP, XXI, 277.

7. WOR, XLVI/1, 396-397, 437-438; Lamb, "Defense of Ft. Fisher," HNCR, V, 223-225, 239-241.

8. "Fort Fisher," SHSP, XXI, 278; Lamb, *Battle of Ft. Fisher*, 4; WOR, XLVI/1, 406-407.

9. Lamb, "Defense of Ft. Fisher," HNCR, V, 225.

10. Curtis, 308-309; WOR, XLVI/1, 397-398, 406-408; Ames, 10-11.

11. "Fort Fisher," SHSP, XXI, 278-279; ORN, XI, 462-463; Lamb, "Defense of Ft. Fisher," HNCR, V, 225-226; *Report Sec. Navy, 1865*, 92-108, 113-117, 143-145, 159-160, 170-171.

12. Curtis, 310-312; ORN, XI, 440.

13. Harkness, 167-169; WOR, XI, 398-399, 418-422; Ames, 12-14; Curtis, 313-315; Palmer, *48th N.Y.*, 179-182.

14. "Col. Nathan Johnson to Col. John Crocker," Jan. 30, 1865, N.Y. State Library, Albany.

15. "Fort Fisher," SHSP, XXI, 279-281; Harkness, 171-173; ORN, XI, 429-430, 446-449, 481, 485, 495-500; "36th N.C.," HNCR, II, 641-642.

16. WOR, XLVI/1, 423-424, 432-434, 435-441; "Fort Fisher," SHSP, XXI, 280-281; Tanner, 11-12; Palmer, *48th N.Y.*, 179-182.

17. WOR, XLVI/1, 398-402, 415-417, 431-447; "Fort Fisher," SHSP, XXI, 279-290; Ames, 14-16; Harkness, 171-173; Price, *97th Penn. Vol.*, 351-356; Eldredge, *3rd N.H.*, 612-613; "R.P.G. to Cousin," Jan. 24, 1865, UNC Collections; "Col. Nathan Johnson to Col. John Crocker," Jan. 30, 1865, N.Y. State Library, Albany.

18. WOR, XLVI/1, 401, 405; Eldredge, *3rd N.H.*, 612-613. Union casualties were 659, while the Confederates had close to 400 killed, wounded, and missing and over 1,200 men taken prisoner including Colonel Lamb and General Whiting, the latter of whom would die of his wounds in captivity.

CHAPTER 21: THE LAST DAYS

1. WOR, XLVI/1, 425-431; Clark, *Iron Hearted Brigade*, 164-167.

2. ORN, XI, 618-621; WOR, XLVI/1, 44, 399-401, 434-435.

3. Porter, 717; Hagood, *Memoirs*, 331-334; "66th N.C.," HNCR, III, 694-695. In the last days of the defense of Wilmington large numbers of torpedoes were released into the Cape Fear River. Porter wrote the secretary of the navy about one such

large-scale attack. "That night (the 20th) the rebels sent down 200 floating torpedoes, but I had a strong force of picket boats out, and the torpedoes were sunk with musketry. One got in the wheel of the *Osceola* and blew her wheelhouse to pieces, and knocked down her bulkheads inboard, but there was no damage to the hull. Some of the vessels picked up the torpedoes with their torpedo nets. The next morning, I spread two fishing nets across the river." (ORN, XII, 45.)

4. WOR, XLVII/2, 101-102, 131, 175-179, 189-190, 492; Porter, 717, 727, 749; Shiver, *Fort Fisher Campaign*, 89-91; "Zaccheus Ellis to Sister, 12 Feb., 1865," Wilson Library, UNC.

5. WOR, XLVII/1, 910-912, 922-929, 958-959, XVLII/2, 403, 425-426; ORN, XII, 23-30.

6. Hagood, 333-335; ORN, XII, 31-33, 37; WOR, XLVII/1, 910-912, XLVII/2, 437, 470.

7. ORN, XII, 32-33, 35-38; Hagood, *Memoirs*, 335-336.

8. WOR, XLVII/1, 928-929, 959-961, XVII/2, 470; Hagood, *Memoirs*, 338-339.

9. WOR, XLVII/1, 961-964, 1077-1078, XLVII/2, 492-493; Hagood, *Memoirs*, 340-349; ORN, XII, 33-36. "14th N.C.," HNCR, II, 761-763. Hagood's brigade would fight a rear-guard action at Town Creek after the retreat to contest the crossings over this waterway. After putting up a stiff resistance the defenders were outflanked and forced to retreat with 461 killed, wounded, or missing; with at least 330 of the latter now being Union prisoners. Cox states that "the fire of the enemy was so uncertain that it produced little damage, our loss in that charge being but thirty in killed and wounded." (WOR, XVII/2, 509, 964; Hagood, *Memiors*, 346-347.)

10. WOR, XLVII/1, 1077-1078, 1086, XLVII/2, 558-559, 594-595, 619-620, 683-684, XLVII/2, 1339-1340; Hagood, *Memoirs*, 349-351; Emmerton, 244-246.

11. WOR, XLVII/1, 931-932, 973-976, XLVII/2, 706.

12. Thorpe, *15th Conn. Vol.*, 86-96; WOR, XLVII/1, 932, 939-940, 976-986, 993-1000; Derby, *27th Mass. Vol.*, 458-465.

13. WOR, XLVII/1, 978-980, 1078, 1086-1089, XLVII/2, 1349-1350; "17th N.C.," HNCR, II, 10-13; Hagood, *Memoirs*, 352-355; "66th N.C.," HNCR, III, 696-698; "72nd N.C.," HNCR, IV, 53-55; "Kirkland Brig.," HNCR, IV, 543-547; Everts, 162-163.

14. WOR, XLVII/1, 979, 1088-1089, XLVII/2, 1361, 1372-1373; "66th N.C.," HNCR, III, 696-698.

15. "Last Days of the Confederacy in North Carolina," CV, XXXIX, 24.

EPILOGUE

1. Boynton, I, 89.

2. WOR, XXXIII, 57-59; Burlingame, 187-195; *19th N.Y. Vol.*, 195-197.

3. Porter, 748.

4. Lincoln, June 16, 1864, Speech at Philadelphia.

5. Lincoln, Second Inaugural Address, Mar. 4, 1865.

Bibliography

Adams, James. "History of the. 26th N.C.," UNC Collections.

Allen, George. *Forty-Six Months with the 4th R.I. Volunteers*. Providence: J.A. & R.A. Reid, 1887.

Almy, John. "Incidents of the Blockade." *Military Order of the Loyal Legion*, No. 9, 1892.

Ames, Adelbert. *Capture of Fort Fisher, North Carolina, Jan. 15, 1865*. Boston: Military Order of the Loyal Legion, 1900.

Ammen, Daniel. *The Navy in the Civil War: The Atlantic Coast*. New York: Charles Scribner & Sons, 1883.

Ammen, Daniel. "Our Second Bombardment of Fort Fisher." *Military Order of the Loyal Legion*, No. 4, 1887.

Anderson, John. "Last Days of the Confederacy in North Carolina," CV, XXXIX, 20-24.

Andrews, Charles H. "Condensed History of the 3rd Georgia Volunteer Infantry," Transcript (1885) Georgia Archives.

Anon. "Major General Robert Hoke," CV, XX, 437-439.

Anon. *Ordnance Instructions for the United States Navy*. Washington, D.C.: Government Printing Office, 1866.

Anon. *Naval War Records: Officers Confederate States Navy*. Washington, D.C.: Government Printing Office, 1898.

Anon. "A Minor Naval Engagement," CV, XXIII, 165-166.

Anon. "Battle at Roanoke Island," CV, XVII, 605.

Anon. *Wilmington, N.C. History of its Harbor.* Wilmington: J.A. Englehard, 1872.

Avery, William. "The Marine Artillery with the Burnside Expedition," *Personal Narratives of Events in the War of the Rebellion*, R.I. Soldiers and Sailors Historical Society No. 4, 2nd Ser., 1880.

Barry, Richard S. "Fort Macon: Its History," *North Carolina Review*, XXVII, (April 1950), 163-177.

Birdsong, James. *Brief Sketches of the North Carolina State Troops.* Raleigh: State Printer, 1894.

Bisbee, Saxon. *Engines of Rebellion.* Tuscaloosa: University of Alabama Press, 2018.

Boynton, Charles. *The History of the Navy during the Rebellion.* 2 vols. New York: D. Appleton, 1867.

Bright, Leslie. *The Blockade Runner Modern Greece and Her Cargo.* Raleigh: State Printer, 1977.

Brown, Wesley. *An Analysis of the Relationship between Technology and Strategy and how they shaped the Confederate States Navy.* Thesis, U.S. Army Staff College, Leavenworth, Kansas, 1999.

Burgwyn, A.A.G. "Clingman's Brigade," HNCR, IV, 481-500.

Burlingame, John. *The History of the Fifth Rhode Island Heavy Artillery.* Providence: Snow & Farnham, 1892.

Burnside, Ambrose. *The Burnside Expedition.* Providence: N. Bangs Williams & Co., 1882.

Cantwell, John. "A Capture before the War," HNCR, V, 23-28.

The Carolina Watchman.

Clark, James. *The Iron Hearted Regiment, An Account of the Battles, Marches, and Gallant Deeds Performed by the 115th New York Volunteers.* Albany: J. Munsell, 1865.

Clark, Walter. *Histories of the Several Regiments and Battalions from North Carolina in the Great War, 1861-1865.* 5 vols. Goldsboro, N.C.: Nash Brothers, 1901.

Cushing, W. B. "The Destruction of the Albemarle," *Century Magazine*, XXXVI (1888), 432-440.

Curtis, Martin. *The Capture of Fort Fisher.* Boston: Military Order of the Loyal Legion, 1900.

Davis, George, Perry, Leslie, & Kirkley, Joseph (eds.). *The War of the Rebellion: Official Records of the Union and Confederate Armies.* Series I, 52 vols., Series II, 8 vols., Series III, 5 vols. Washington, D.C.: Government Printing Office, 1880-1901.

Day, D.L. *My Diary.* Milford, MA: Private Printing, 1884.

Derby, W.P. *Bearing Arms in the Twenty-Seventh Massachusetts Regiment,* Boston: Wright and Potter, 1883.

Dickey, Luther. *History of the 103rd Pennsylvania Volunteers.* Chicago: L.S. Dickey, 1910.

Dillard, Richard. The Civil War in Chowan County. Raleigh: North Carolina Historical Commission, 1916.

Dinkins, James. "The Confederate Ram Albemarle," SHSP, XXX, 205-214.

Dollard, Robert. *Recollections of the Civil War and Going West to Grow Up with the Country.* Scotland, S.D.: By Author, 1906.

Dullum, John. *Unremitting Vigilance: Naval Intelligence and the Union Blockade during the Civil War.* Thesis, U.S. Army Staff College, Leavenworth, Kansas, 1986.

Edwards, W.H. *A Condensed History of the Seventeenth Regiment S.C.V.* Columbia, S.C.: R.L. Bayan Co., 1908.

Eldredge, D. *The Third New Hampshire.* Boston: E.B. Stillings & Co., 1893.

Elliot, C.G. "Kirkland Brig.," HNCR, IV, 527-550.

Elliott, Gilbert. "The Career of the Confederate Ram Albemarle," *Century Magazine,* XXXVI, (1888), 420-427.

Elliott, Gilbert. "The Ram Albemarle," HNCR, V, 315-323.

Emilio, Luis. *Roanoke Island, its Occupation, Defense, and Fall.* New York: Roanoke Associates, 1891.

Emmerton, James. *Record of the 23rd Regiment Mass. Vol. Infantry.* Boston: William Ware & Co., 1886.

Estvan, B. War *Pictures from the South.* 2 vols. London: Routledge, Warne, & Routledge, 1863.

Evans, Clement. *Confederate Military History.* 12 vols. Atlanta: Confederate Publishing Co., 1899.

Everts, Hermann. *History of the 9th Regiment New Jersey Volunteers.* Newark: Stephen Holbrook, 1865.

French, Samuel. *Two Wars*. Nashville: Confederate Veteran, 1901.

Gardner, Donald. *The Confederate Corps of Marines*. Thesis, Memphis State, 1973.

Graham, John. "The Capture of Plymouth," HNCR, V, 175-196.

Graham, Matthew. *The Ninth Regiment New York Volunteers (Hawkin's Zouaves)*. New York: E.P. Coby & Co., 1900.

Graham, Robert. "56th N.C.," HNCR, III, 313-404.

Hagood, Butler. *Memoirs of the War of Succession from the Original Manuscripts of Johnson Hagood, Brigadier General, C.S.A.* Columbia, S.C.: The State Co., 1910.

Hall, Henry and James. *A Record of the 19th New York Volunteers*. Auburn, N.Y.: Truair, Smith & Co., 1873.

Hall, Rowland to Mother, Dec., 22, 1862, Transcript, UNC Collections.

Hallock, Charles. "Bermuda in the Blockade," *New England Magazine*, May 1892, 337-343.

Harkness, Edson. *The Expeditions against Fort Fisher and Wilmington*. Chicago: Military Order of the Loyal Legion, 1890

Harper's Weekly

Harris, J.S. *Historical Sketches of the Seventh Regiment North Carolina Troops*. Mooresville, N.C.: Mooresville Printing, 1893.

Holden, Edgar. "The Albemarle and the Sassacus," *Century Mag.* XXXVI (1888), 426-432.

Holloman, Quinn. *Union Joint Operations in North Carolina during the Civil War*. Thesis, Air War College, Maxwell AFB, Alabama, 1999.

Howe, W.W. *Kinston, Whitehall and Goldsboro Expedition, December 1862*. New York: Private Printing, 1890.

Lamb, William. "Fight with Blockaders," HNCR V, 351-352.

Lamb, William. "Battles of Ft. Fisher," SHSP, XXI, 257-290.

Lamb, William. "The Defense of Ft. Fisher," HNCR, V, 218-246.

Lamb, William. *The Battle of Fort Fisher, North Carolina*. Wilmington: Harriss Printing, 1895.

Lamb, William. "36th N.C.," HNCR, II, 629-657.

Lamb, Wilson. "17th N.C.," HNCR, II, 1-14.

Lewis, W.G. *A Sketch of the Life of W.G. Lewis, Brigadier General Confederate State's Army.* Transcript. North Carolina State Library, Raleigh.

Liles, E.R. "The Fall of Roanoke Island," HNCR, V, 63-70.

Lockwood, H.C. The Capture of Fort Fisher. *Atlantic Magazine,* May, 1871, 622-636; June, 1871, 684-690.

Loyall, B.P., "Capture of the Underwriter," SHSP, XXVII, 136-144.

Ludwig, H.T.J. "Eight N.C.," HNCR, I, 387-416.

Lyman, Jackman. *History of the Sixth New Hampshire Regiment.* Concord: Republican Press, 1891.

Mann, Albert. *History of the 45th Regiment of Massachusetts Volunteers.* Jamaica Plains, N.Y.: Brookside Printers, 1908.

Marchman, James. *History of Ft. Caswell.* Chapel Hill: University of North Carolina Press, 1967.

Melton, Maurice. *The Confederate Ironclads.* New York: South Brunswick, 1968.

Merrill, James. "The Hatteras Expedition, August 1861," *North Carolina Hist. Review,* XXIX, No. 2 (April, 1952), 204-219.

Moore, John "Third Battalion N.C. (Light Artillery)," HNCR, IV, 261-269.

Murphy, David. *Naval Strategy during the Civil War.* Thesis, Air War College, Maxwell AFB, Alabama, 1999.

The North Carolina Standard.

Ohls, Gary. "Fort Fisher – Amphibious Victory in the American Civil War," *Naval War College Review,* Vol. 59, No. 4 (Autumn), 2006.

Olds, Fredrick. "North Carolina Troops: How They Were Armed in the War Between the States," SHSP, XXIX, 144-151.

Oliver Case Letters. The Letters of Oliver Cromwell Case, Simsbury Historical Society, Simsbury, CT, 1861-1862.

Osborne, Arthur. *The Capture of Fort Fisher.* New Haven: Tuttle, Morehouse, & Taylor Press, 1911.

Palmer, Abraham J. *The History of the Forty-Eight New York State Volunteers.* Brooklyn: Charles Dillingham, 1885.

Parker, Thomas. *History of the 51st Regiment Pennsylvania Volunteers.* Philadelphia: King & Baird, 1869.

Parker, William. *Recollections of a Naval Officer, 1841-1865.* New York: Charles Scribner's Sons, 1883.

Peebles, Martin. *CSS Raleigh: The History and Archaeology of a Civil War Ironclad in the Cape Fear River.* Kure Beach, N.C.: State Printers, 1996.

Pool, Stephen. "The Tenth Regiment," HNCR, I, 489-498.

Pool, Stephen. "The Battle of White Hall," HNCR, I, 83-91.

Porter, David. "Letters," NCHR, Oct. 1958, 461-475.

Porter, David. *The Naval History of the Civil War.* New York: Sherman Publishing, 1886.

Porter, John W.H. "The Confederate States Navy," SHSP, XXVIII, 125-134.

Price, Isiah. *History of the Ninety Seventh Regiment of Pennsylvania Volunteers.* Philadelphia: Published by Author, 1875.

Price, Marcus. "Ships that Tested the Blockade of the Carolina Ports, 1861-1865." *American Neptune,* July 1948, 196-241.

Price, Marcus. "Blockade Running as a Business in South Carolina during the War between the States," *American Neptune,* Jan.1949, 31-62.

Putnam, Samuel H. *The Story of Company A, Twenty-Fifth Regiment, Mass. Vols. In the War of the Rebellion.* Worcester, Mass.: Putnam, Davis & Co., 1886.

Reed, John. *History of the 101st Pennsylvania Volunteers.* Chicago: L.S. Dickey, 1910.

Report of the Secretary of the Navy (for the years 1861- 1865). Washington, D.C.: Government Printing Office, 1862-1866.

Roberts, A. *Never Caught.* New York: William Abbatt, 1908.

Robinson, John. "52nd Regiment," HNCR, III, 223-253.

Roe, Alfred. *The Twenty-Four Regiment Massachusetts Volunteers, 1861-1865.* Worcester, Mass.: Blanchard Press, 1907.

Rose, George. "66th N.C.," HNCR, III, 685-702.

Rose, W.N. "24th N.C.," HNCR, II, 269-290.

Rush, Richard & Woods, Robert (eds.). *Official Records of the Union and Confederate Navies in the War of the Rebellion.* Series I, 27 vols., Series II, 3 vols. Washington D.C.: Government Printing Office, 1894-1922.

Sands, Francis. "The Last of the Blockade and the Fall of Fort Fisher." *Military Order of the Loyal Legion*, No. 40, 1902.

Sanders, John W., "Additional Sketch 10th Reg.," HNCR, I, 499-536.

Scharf, J. Thomas. *History of the Confederate States Navy*. New York: Rogers & Sherwood, 1887.

Shiver, Joshua. *The Politics of Command in the Fort Fisher Campaign.* Thesis, University of North Carolina, 2011.

Smith, Burton H. "The Confederate Ram Albemarle," UNC Collections.

Soley, James Russell. *The Navy in the Civil War: The Blockade and the Cruisers*. New York: Charles Scribner's Sons, 1885.

Sparrow, Thomas. "The Fall of Hatteras," HNCR, V, 35-54.

Sprague, A.B. R. "The Burnside Expedition," *Civil War Papers, II*, Boston: F.H. Gilson, 1900, 427-444.

Sprunt, James. *Tales and Traditions of the Lower Cape Fear*. Wilmington, N.C.: Legwin Brothers, 1896.

Sprunt, James. *Chronicles of the Cape Fear*, 1660-1916. Raleigh: Edwards & Broughton, 1916.

Tanner, Zera. "The Capture of Fort Fisher." *Military Order of the Loyal Legion*, No. 25, 1897.

Taylor, Thomas. *Running the Blockade*. London: John Murray, 1897.

Thorpe, Sheldon. *The History of the Fifteenth Connecticut Volunteers*. New Haven: Price, Lee & Atkins, 1893.

Tredwell, Adam. "The North Carolina Navy," HNCR V, 299-314.

Trumbull, Clay. The Knightly Soldier: A Biography of Major Henry Ward Camp, 10th Conn. Vols. Boston: Noyes, Holmes & Co., 1871.

Trotter, William. *Ironclads and Columbiads*. Winston-Salem, N.C.; John Blair, 1989.

Turner, William. "The First Twelve Months of the 3rd Georgia Regiment," *The Countryman*, 1864. Copies University of Georgia, Athens, GA.

Tyler, Lyon. *Encyclopedia of Virginia Biography*, Volume III. New York: Lewis Historical Publishing, 1915

Walcott, Charles. *History of the Twenty-First Regiment Massachusetts Volunteers*. Boston: Houghton, Mifflin, & Co., 1882.

Wardle, Arthur. "Some Blockade Runners of the Civil War," *American Neptune*, April 1943, 131-140.

Warley, A.F. "Note on the Destruction of the Albemarle," *Century Magazine*, XXXVI, (1888), 439-440.

Wilkinson, J. *The Narrative of a Blockade-Runner*. New York: Sheldon & Co., 1877.

Wood, —. "Blockade Running in North Carolina during the Civil War," UNC Collections.

Woodbury, Augustus. *Major General Ambrose Burnside and the 9th Army Corps*. Providence: Sidney Rider & Brother, 1867.

Yellowly, E.C. "Chicamacomico," HNCR, V, 55-56.

Acknowledgments

P ART OF THIS BOOK coincided with a move to a new home. After having been in the same place for sixteen years and four kids, this was not a trivial matter. Order was supplanted by speed as the Arizona summer came a bit too early, if for no other reason than to complete the experience. A whirlwind week of trucks, cars, and contractors mercifully ended, leaving me writing on a table in a forest of boxes that obscured the actual confines of the room. As the book progressed the forest began to recede, and somehow these two events will forever be tied together in my mind when I think of this text. Thus, for my wife who chopped down the forest, and my sons Ryan, Andrew, and Nathanael, and my daughter Brittany who helped bring order to this self-imposed chaos, my many thanks. To my old friend Ernie Botos, as always, my heartfelt thanks for your help. To my colleagues and friends and those who encourage my efforts, my thanks as well. And lastly, I would like to put another shout-out to Folgers. You guys are the best.

Index